ONE SIGNAL
PUBLISHERS

ATRIA

There She Was

THE SECRET HISTORY OF MISS AMERICA

Amy Argetsinger

ONE SIGNAL
PUBLISHERS

ATRIA

New York • London • Toronto • Sydney • New Delhi

ONE SIGNAL
PUBLISHERS

ATRIA

An Imprint of Simon & Schuster, Inc.
1230 Avenue of the Americas
New York, NY 10020

First One Signal Publishers/Atria Books hardcover edition September 2021

ONE SIGNAL PUBLISHERS / ATRIA BOOKS and colophon are trademarks of Simon & Schuster, Inc.

For information about special discounts for bulk purchases, please contact Simon & Schuster Special Sales at 1-866-506-1949 or business@simonandschuster.com.

The Simon & Schuster Speakers Bureau can bring authors to your live event. For more information or to book an event, contact the Simon & Schuster Speakers Bureau at 1-866-248-3049 or visit our website at www.simonspeakers.com.

Interior design by Joy O'Meara @ Creative Joy Designs

Manufactured in the United States of America

1   3   5   7   9   10   8   6   4   2

Library of Congress Cataloging-in-Publication Data has been applied for.

ISBN 978-1-9821-2339-0
ISBN 978-1-9821-2341-3 (ebook)

To Jean Sause Argetsinger, who also had an amazing century.
And who would be so delighted that I had written
a book and that it was not about her.

And to Bill and Eliza, for absolutely everything.

CONTENTS

CONTENTS

Chapter 8

"Do you think I'm the first woman to have an interest?"

1991

157

Chapter 9

"I wanted to be a little out of the box"

Becoming Miss America: November 2019

188

Chapter 10

"Everyone wanted something from me that I couldn't give them."

2007

201

Chapter 11

"You don't leverage the Godfather"

2017

227

Chapter 12

"That title isn't going to win everything"

2018

262

Chapter 13

"There she is . . ."

Becoming Miss America: December 2019

———

276

AUTHOR'S NOTE

Miss America is an institution forever grappling with its own legend. That's why this story interweaves narratives from its past and present rather than following a straight chronology. Meanwhile, some of the customs and vernacular of the pageant world embedded in this narrative may require a little explanation.

Before 1950, a Miss America received a title matching the calendar year of her crowning. After 1950, the title was postdated to reflect the upcoming year. So, Phyllis George, crowned in September 1970, was Miss America 1971. From 2006 to 2013, the pageant was held in January, and those winners received a title marking the new year.

The words "pageant" and "contestant" have been officially discouraged by the Miss America Organization since 2018, but they remain in common parlance and are frequently used in this book—along with the occasional colloquial use of the word "girls," echoing conversational style within pageant circles and by pageant women themselves.

For consistency, this book mostly uses the names women were known by when they competed. And all characters are referred to on second reference by their first names. The historic Atlantic City Convention Hall became Boardwalk Hall in 1997 after the city built a modern new convention center; this book sticks with its original name.

With my focus on Miss America's most recent half century of existential struggle, I could not do justice to all the personalities and intrigue of its earlier decades. Readers will find them more fully evoked in Frank Deford's groundbreaking 1971 history, *There She Is: The Life and Times of Miss America*.

PROLOGUE

The Miss Americas started arriving at the house around noon on Friday, and most never left until Sunday. They had everything they needed in the rambling vacation rental in Kissimmee, Florida, for this January weekend in 2018—food, wine, spa treatments, swimming, each other.

It was only the fourth time they had gotten together like this, but already the multigenerational gathering was starting to feel like a tradition—a secret society of women bonded by an ineffable honor and a brief dance with fame. BeBe Shopp, the vibraphone-playing farmgirl crowned in 1948, was there, and so was Kira Kazantsev, the golf-prodigy daughter of Russian immigrants who was Miss America 2015. So was Nina Davuluri, from 2014, the first Indian-American Miss America, and Heather Whitestone, '95, the first hearing-impaired winner; Jacquelyn Mayer, '63, who charmed pageant fans in her day by trilling "My Favorite Things," and Leanza Cornett, '93, who shocked them with her ahead-of-the-curve AIDS advocacy, among a dozen other former winners.

They always set aside some time for serious talk—and this year, they needed it.

It was one of the group's younger members, Laura Kaeppeler, '12, who had started the tradition when she invited them all to the Malibu home she shared with her husband, reality-TV magnate Mike Fleiss. Now photos of their annual reunion filled scrapbooks and Facebook feeds: the time Ericka flirted with the handsome chef at Tawny's party in Santa Ynez; the time Maria analyzed everyone's astrological sign; the year Elizabeth returned to the fold after three decades of distance. And the time Vonda reenacted her winning 1964 ventriloquist act, but with Lee—their beloved Lee Meriwether, '55, whose glorious 1970s TV career they were so proud of—playing her dummy. Things get lively when you have that many Miss Americas in one place. And sometimes rather loud.

"It's hard to win an argument in a room like that," Caressa Cameron, Miss America 2010, said later, "when everyone is equally articulate and equally passionate."

Gretchen Carlson was attending for the first time that year. Even in a house full of semi-famous women, Miss America 1989 was something of a visiting celebrity. She had just come off the highest-profile period of her career, the decade-plus she had spent as a Fox News host until she accused the network's powerful cofounder, Roger Ailes, of sexual harassment; he stepped down after other women were emboldened to share their horror stories. Now Gretchen was an in-demand public speaker and magazine cover star considered a godmother of the roiling MeToo movement. Just weeks earlier, she had been named the new chair of the Miss America Organization—the first former Miss America to hold the job.

Gretchen could not stay through the weekend. But she made a point of flying in for a couple hours: She had business to discuss with her Miss America sisters.

And so they all gathered in an airy upstairs den, snuggling into the sectional sofa and pillows on the floor. Gretchen had stepped into the job after a wildfire scandal took out the entire Miss America leadership just before Christmas—a leak of emails showing the previous chair, a man, mocking, gossiping, and griping about former Miss Americas, even laughing ("bahahaha") at a colleague's particularly vulgar slur.

The Miss Americas had banded together in protest; they had pushed for his resignation and Gretchen's takeover. The crown had left its mark on them. Now they were eager to claim ownership—and redefine what this crazy, lofty, dusty title was supposed to mean in a changing world.

But their new leader had a blunt warning. Miss America was in financial peril, the organization's very survival was in question. At the heart of the problem, Gretchen said, was the swimsuit competition.

Pretty girls in bathing suits: That was what had put the pageant on the map from the time Atlantic City launched it as a Roaring Twenties tourist attraction. But Gretchen warned that everything had changed in the MeToo era. Would society still tolerate a show that asked young women to compete for scholarships in bikinis?

In fact, the pageant's problems ran deeper than even Gretchen seemed to realize. Within months, the world of people who still cherished Miss America would be at war. Many of the women in this room, who had traveled so far to be together, would no longer be speaking.

But who in that moment could have imagined? Of *course* Miss America was in crisis: That was the story of its past fifty years, if not one hundred. And yet it had always endured. And now the Miss Americas themselves were ready to take charge. They uncapped their pens and started brainstorming.

Introduction

"SOMEWHERE OUT THERE IS WHAT YOU WANT TO DO"

The 1969 Miss America pageant kicked off on the evening of September 7, 1968, as if everything were normal—fifty women aged eighteen to twenty-four swanning across the stage in tailored suits, jaunty hats, and white gloves, the television lights sparking their expressions of wide-eyed delight.

"Tonight, each of our fifty girls feels as if she were living a character in one of the happiest and most exciting of all storybooks!" intoned our glamorous hostess for the night, Bess Myerson, the Bronx-born Miss America 1945, in her Upper East Side accent. Veteran emcee Bert Parks emerged from a puff of stage smoke, in white tie and tails, to serenade them.

"Somewhere out there is what you want to do!" he crooned amid a swelling chorus of strings. "Somewhere out there is a 'someday you'!"

They had come from all fifty states, as usual, to compete for a $10,000 scholarship and a rhinestone crown on live TV. But the real action on this night was just outside the doors of Atlantic City's Convention Hall, where another hundred or so women had mustered on the Boardwalk in granny glasses, miniskirts, jeans. They, too, had traveled from across the country—for the express purpose of demonstrating to the world their scorn for what was happening inside.

"Miss America represents what women are supposed to be: inoffensive, bland, apolitical," declared the manifesto from the group called

New York Radical Women. They compared the pageant to the livestock contest at a county fair—but also to the workaday oppression of all women living in a patriarchal culture, "forced daily to compete for male approval, enslaved by ludicrous 'beauty' standards we ourselves are conditioned to take seriously."

These were women who had marched for civil rights and against the Vietnam War—who, in fact, had done much of the vital behind-the-scenes planning of those movements, only to confront the sexism of the supposedly progressive men who fronted them. These women had bigger goals, of course, a more complex set of complaints to register with society than just the annual spectacle on NBC.

But in 1968, they needed a way to crash through a news cycle freighted with street turmoil and assassinations. And even in 1968, everyone *still* followed Miss America.

"You could spend six months leafleting on the corner of St. Mark's Place," organizer Robin Morgan explained later, "but it was more important to have six seconds on the 6 o'clock news."

They rolled into town with puppets and posters ("Up Against the Wall, Bert Parks") and a sheep in a beauty queen sash. Yet none of it thrilled the press as much as their sensational work of street theater: a "Freedom Trash Can" heaped with girdles, curlers, old issues of *Cosmo*, and other "instruments of female torture"—most spectacularly, a pile of brassieres.

Bras in the *trash can*! This was the moment that launched the "bra-burning" image that clung to second-wave feminism for decades to come. But nothing was actually set on fire that day—it wasn't permitted on the wooden Boardwalk—except, of course, this new movement, dubbed "women's liberation."

The feminists who got inside Convention Hall didn't manage to disrupt the broadcast. One of them sprayed a bottle of noxious Toni hair-perm solution on the floor but was quickly arrested. And when they unfurled a "Women's Liberation" banner from the balcony, television viewers couldn't see it or make out their chants of "no more Miss America!" Yet the brilliant stunt stole the headlines from that night's Miss America, Judi Ford, the eighteen-year-old trampolinist with a cornsilk-yellow bouffant that never budged as she hurtled through the air to "The

Blue Danube Waltz." And then the feminists, victorious, moved on to bigger targets—pay equity, discrimination, abortion rights.

But they left the Miss America pageant reeling.

It was the first time in its forty-seven-year history that anyone had so brazenly challenged the very idea of the pageant—what it meant to celebrate young women in this way, what it meant to judge them and put them on a pedestal.

Was the pageant still "relevant"? Was it truly doing right by its young ladies? The pageant's leaders were nagged by these questions, prompting years of rationalizing, second-guessing, and changes large and small.

The debate would linger, in one form or another, for the next fifty years, until 2018, when Gretchen Carlson, taking over Miss America at a tenuous moment, would gamble the pageant's future by pulling the plug on the swimsuit contest—the cheesy, uncomfortable, increasingly hard-to-defend ritual that was also Miss America's most potent link to its far more glorious past.

I started reporting this book that summer, after Gretchen's management had triggered something of a civil war in the pageant world, raising questions about what Miss America would look like in its second century, should it even make it that far.

Yet as I traced the roots of the conflicts tearing at the pageant, a parallel history emerged—one that almost seemed to tell a success story.

How had this pop-culture relic of the 1920s survived so far past its natural shelf life? The answer seemed to lie with the women who competed for its crown, and the unexpected new energy that emerged in their ranks circa 1970.

Coincidence? Hardly. The women's movement had set out to vanquish Miss America—and ended up accidentally resuscitating it instead.

The pageant evolved because young women in America had evolved. Even the young women who could still be convinced to enter a beauty pageant. Even those who did not consider themselves feminists.

Among the Miss Americas who gathered that weekend in Kissimmee were not just a former cable-news host but also the president of the Actors' Equity union, an assistant state attorney general, and a soon-to-be contender for statewide office. There were scientists, entrepreneurs, motivational speakers, and moms. Far from "bland and apolitical," they were ambitious and highly opinionated, from a wide range of the political spectrum. And yet not only did they remain devoted to a beauty pageant, they were ready to run it themselves.

✦   ✦   ✦

This is where I tell you that I love the Miss America pageant. And I'm not going to apologize for it.

I was born the same day the 1968 protest sent a hairline fracture shooting through the culture on the question of Miss America. By the time I was a teenager, it had grown into a rift.

A lot of people still watched the pageant on television in those three-channel days; the winners still made the cover of *TV Guide* or *Parade*. But the feminist criticisms of Miss America had stuck—and they had begun to sink in with the public. No longer did the media elevate the winners as exemplars of American girlhood; the reporting now was much more wry. Late-night comedians mocked them as airheads or bimbos; cultural critics fretted that they were trapped in a cult of unattainable beauty standards, or at least way too scary-thin. As many as eighty thousand young women still competed every year in the sprawling national network of local pageants that led to Miss America. But growing up in the suburbs of Washington, D.C., my friends and I were raised on the side of the culture that would consider the event a guilty pleasure at best—gaudy, big-haired, kitsch. We had a knee-jerk sense of superiority to it, even as we knew, intuitively, we could never be good enough to play this game. When I heard that a college acquaintance was competing in local pageants, my reaction was confusingly split between "why is she doing *that*?" and "well, *she* must think highly of herself."

Then, at twenty-two, I moved to Iowa. My first two years there, women from my new community placed in Miss America's Top 5. I spotted one of them later in a Burger King on her lunch break, looking like any recent college grad—looking kind of like me. Local pageant queens roamed the county fairs, riding the Giant Slide in tiaras and sashes. One of my friends even entered a local pageant within the Miss America system—strictly, she said, for the scholarship money. Shayla was a short, quirky, small-haired indie-rock connoisseur who would later become a college professor. Not the pageant type, I thought, but what did I know? Shayla didn't win, but two years later, when we were both living on the East Coast, we learned that the girl who beat her for Miss Clinton County had gone on to win Miss Iowa. We suddenly realized that we could simply drive to Atlantic City and buy a ticket to see her compete in person. And so we did.

Somehow, it just became a *thing*. One friend would hear about our trip, and then another, and suddenly there was a group that wanted to go, and a second trip, and a third, and a fourth and a seventh.

What no one ever tells you about Miss America: It's *fun*. The road trip to the Jersey Shore, the hike down the Boardwalk in cocktail garb. The crowd was amazing: sequined women flaunting jumbo-sized buttons of their contestant's face, tuxedoed men hoisting banners with her name, adorable preteen princesses with titles like Miss Teen Scholastic Connecticut or Junior Miss Indiana Ambassador fluttering around—and one year, an elderly woman wearing a crown and sash of "Miss Ozone Park 1948." ("Oh, not really. My daughters just dressed me up like this.") We would scour the program books to make our Top 10 predictions and cackle at the chipper self-intros from each Miss State parading across the stage ("My favorite quote is one by Gandhi: 'Be the change that you wish to see in the world'!" "My childhood dream is to do a voice-over for a Disney character!"). We would cheer for the good talents, laugh through tears at the bad ones, and basically shrug at the swimsuit competition—come on, they were all under twenty-five, of course they all looked great.

And we would somehow find ourselves rooting for a contestant in whom we had become inexplicably invested—and then sulk over her loss.

The horse race was irresistible. I would later learn that these same delicious dramas were playing out on a small scale all across the country, at the local and state pageants that formed a pipeline to Miss America.

Why did I find this contest so engrossing? Probably because the rules of the game were so richly confounding. Trying to crack the code of who wins Miss America turned out to be a variation on a game I had been playing in my head all my life: Why did everyone have a crush on the boy who wasn't even all that good-looking? Why did every sorority want my roommate to pledge? What made everyone laugh when my uncle told a story that wasn't all that funny? How did that inexperienced candidate break out of the pack? Why her, why him, what was it *about* them?

During my eight years as the *Washington Post*'s gossip columnist—really, the beat reporter covering money, power, and celebrity—I got to indulge this thought experiment on a higher level. At political conventions, movie premieres, inauguration galas, and the Oscars, I moved in the same rooms and frequently in conversation with people who had drawn the world's attention. As you'd expect, their magnetism was often linked to their exquisite physical appeal—radiant skin, piercing eyes, everything proportioned just so. But frequently, their charm lay somewhere in their composure; a quality of being both intensely alert and admirably serene at the same time. There were celebrities who had struck me in photos as being so blandly attractive I couldn't understand why they were a big deal. Yet in person, in motion, their faces were mesmerizing, filled with life. This was also when I first met some reigning Miss Americas, who frequently made the rounds in Washington in those days. Each was a winner I had not picked while following the show—*Wait, why her?* Yet in the room, it was viscerally clear.

This was in the first dozen years of the new century, when It Girls were everywhere in popular culture, and for once the "Girls" half of the cliché wasn't so far off: Some of the hottest young actresses and singers had roared to international fame before they could legally drink. A few wilted in the spotlight, which somehow turned their personal emotional health into fodder for public debate, while others marched unscathed toward total global domination. By now their fame far outstripped Miss America's. But Miss America had once occupied that place in public life. Did she have anything to teach them?

Miss America still generated a lot of hand-wringing: Was the pageant bad for women? Was it fair? Was it representative of a diverse population? But she was no longer the queen of a monoculture like she had been in 1968; it made little sense anymore to fret that the pageant was imposing oppressive expectations on a nation of girls, when they mostly weren't watching it. As a niche sporting event, the pageant suddenly seemed quaint. And arguably healthier than the new competitions our culture had designed for young women—where, instead of just objectifying themselves in swimsuits and heels, they were now fighting one another on television for the romantic attention of men, or being fought over as if they were trophies.

◆   ◆   ◆

Why tell the story of Miss America and not, say, Miss USA?

The two always got confused in the public eye. In fact they went way back—to 1951, when longtime pageant sponsor Catalina asked the new Miss America to go on a publicity tour for its line of swimsuits, and she said no.

A bright and forceful Alabama beauty who would later march for civil rights and nuclear disarmament, Yolande Betbeze was simply *done* with posing in swimsuits. She preferred to focus on her singing career.

"The leg shows were all right back in the early 1920s," she told the press. "But the public now has a better sense of values. There's a growth in culture and a greater appreciation for the girl who has talent along with physical beauty."

Catalina, though, promptly pulled its sponsorship—and launched its own pageants. Miss USA and Miss Universe were the ones that would later have Donald Trump as a part-owner, the ones that were a lot sexier, and far less conflicted about it. Bigger hair, bigger boobs, sultrier styles, no talent required. Miss USA also endured crises over the years—not least Donald Trump himself, who bragged about ogling half-dressed contestants and ultimately sold the franchise after his network partners cut ties with him. But it came of age during the sexual revolution, a for-profit enterprise at peace with the entertainment value of parading gorgeous young women in bikinis.

That would never be the case for Miss America, a small-town nonprofit with Prohibition-era roots. The pageant was forever chasing after respectability to prove it was more than just a "leg show"—with scholarships, talent prizes, morality clauses, good works. That's what made it the kind of pageant that would attract even more Yolande types: young women who wanted a title that could mean more than just a sash and a crown.

This dynamic could be positive, such as in the 1970s when a wave of assertive baby-boomer contestants—trailblazing sportscaster Phyllis George just the most prominent example—began to see the pageant as a platform for self-expression and the new aspirations suddenly open to young women.

It could curdle as well, especially in the 1980s: Vanessa Williams, the first African-American winner and perhaps the most blazingly talented of all, had hoped for a career boost from the pageant. Instead she found herself turned uncomfortably into a symbol of racial progress, and then abandoned and humiliated when a secret from her teenage past threatened the pageant's hard-fought image.

But it also helped the pageant recover in the 1990s, when it recast its winners as women of accomplishment and socially conscious advocates—a new strain of alpha queens who would one day try to save it again. And that same dynamic—the hunger for meaning, respect, and relevance—fueled the debate erupting under Gretchen Carlson's leadership over what, exactly, Miss America should stand for.

✦   ✦   ✦

I had seen group portraits of the former Miss Americas from when they would return to Atlantic City for the pageant, fancy-dressed, like the crowned heads of Europe convening for a royal wedding. But those photos almost had a *Sgt. Pepper's* quality, hazily familiar faces patched together from disparate eras.

And yet it turned out that they were real women, sharing a real-world timeline; that they were friends, hanging out together in Kissimmee or Malibu, without the TV cameras and with so much in common.

Miss America wasn't just a year of their lives: It was everything that happened before, and everything that happened after. It was this connection that empowered them to force a rapid overhaul of the pageant when it mattered—and that would frustrate them when their differences on how to complete it became apparent.

My reporting also took me on a journey into the lesser-known ecosystems of the Miss America pageant, past and present. The former was a lost world of small-town parades and community newspapers, department-store fashion shows and dinner theaters, Lions Clubs and the Jaycees: The kinds of institutions that once fueled the mission of a Miss America hopeful were the cornerstones of a larger civic life that increasingly seemed unable to compete with our screens.

Yet even though the world that once nourished it had shrunk, I found that pageant culture raged on, not just in Atlantic City but in towns across America at the beginning of the pipeline—a passionate core of volunteers, coaches, and fans who still raised the scholarship money, cheered the contestants, and filled the seats, maybe even in a high school auditorium somewhere near you.

Here was a chance to meet the young women who still wanted to be Miss America—and see what it would take to accomplish it.

1

"IT'S LIKE A PERFORMANCE OF FEMININITY"

Becoming Miss America: October 2018

Only three young women showed up to rehearsal the night before the Miss Arlington pageant. But their presence was enough to put Chip Brown's mind at ease.

"Okay, I see Monica and Caroline and Taylor here," he said, peering out at the scant crowd in the dim of the Wakefield High School auditorium on a Friday night in October.

Three other Miss Arlington hopefuls couldn't make it, which meant they would be coming in cold to the competition the following day. In all, they added up to a field of six, not exactly a bumper crop for a local pageant of this stature. In Chip's seventeen years running the pageant with his partner Scott Freda, seven of his Miss Arlingtons had gone on to win the Miss Virginia prize. And one of *them* had gone all the way, to win the ultimate title—Miss America.

Caressa Cameron's coronation on live national television in 2010 was a victory for Chip as well, establishing him as a director who knew how to train and coach a girl to victory. In a typical year—a less tumultuous one for the Miss America system—he might have had ten or more young women vying for his crown.

Yet Chip, a rumpled travel agent in his late fifties with a gentle drawl, was not dismayed by the turnout, even if he fretted over the reasons for it. He knew these three girls, and he knew the other three who said they would show up Saturday. They were all good. They would all hit their marks. They were more than enough for a pageant, and a pretty good one at that: This was nobody's first time trying to become Miss America.

And so his underpopulated rehearsal carried on in a casual style, feeling more like a family talent show than a contest with a couple thousand dollars at stake and the first step to a national title. "I know all three of you young ladies are very talented and will make us very proud," Chip told the girls who'd shown up. He would leave it up to them how he should craft their onstage questions, where judges would size up their poise and intelligence: Did they want to go with current events, or topics gleaned from their personal bios?

"I'm going to let y'all decide," he said.

One bright spot of glamour lit the auditorium: None other than Miss Virginia Emili McPhail was in the house. A year earlier, she had won Chip's title before going on to claim the state crown; now she had returned to crown a new woman as Miss Arlington.

Competing at the Miss America pageant, Emili had caused a brief sensation when she fielded a question about Colin Kaepernick's national anthem protests with a directness and political edge rarely seen on the Atlantic City stage. "It is not about kneeling," Emili had declared. "It is absolutely about police brutality." Despite Miss America's historic tendencies for gentle conservatism and playing it safe, the judges selected Emili as the interview winner, and this made national news for a couple hours.

Miss America, they say, is won or lost in the interview room—the closed-door, deeper-dive sessions with judges not seen on TV. And yet for all the rhetorical confidence she displayed on stage, Emili didn't go on to make the Top 15. Some anonymous cranks on the online fan forums blamed her talent presentation—an error-free but rather basic piano recital of a *Phantom of the Opera* tune, her keyboard skills upstaged by her Liberace-caliber black velvet cape.

"I'll be the first to admit I'm not a classically trained pianist," she told me.

But others wondered if Emili had been *too* outspoken—not on stage, but in an Instagram video she posted before Atlantic City. In it, she had delicately addressed the controversy roiling the pageant world at that moment: outgoing Miss America Cara Mund's complaints about how she'd been treated by the new pageant leaders during a chaotic transition. Emili spoke positively of the pageant's "new mission" and, without echoing Cara's grievances, simply praised her for "being so brave as to share your story." Still, there was a sense that Emili had *gone there*, that she had touched a third rail of pageant politics by ever-so-indirectly expressing discontent with the status quo. And these days, the national anthem culture wars were a cakewalk in comparison.

Emili cut a sharp figure at the Miss Arlington rehearsal, in a black sleeveless palazzo-pant jumpsuit and long, shiny high ponytail, roaming the auditorium to greet her pageant-world friends—contestants, moms, volunteers. Despite some grumbling that a border-hopper like Emili—a North Carolina native eligible for Miss Virginia by dint of attending Roanoke's Hollins University—had seized the state crown on her first try, everyone seemed delighted to see her. At twenty-two, with laser-beam eyes and bright-penny alertness, she was a zeitgeisty cross between Kate Middleton and Anna Kendrick, carrying herself with the unwrinkled maturity that had made it impossible for me to fully comprehend that any Miss America contender was younger than me until I was nearly forty.

What was she up to these days? I asked.

"Well," she said patiently, "I am still Miss Virginia."

This was a full-time job, it turned out, to which she was committed for the full year. It came with a free apartment in Roanoke, a loaner car, a sponsored wardrobe, a laundry service, and a stipend healthy enough to build up her savings. "It is a *sick gig*," she told me later, with a grateful laugh. She was visiting schools to talk to kids about healthy choices, as well as community festivals and do-gooder events for more decorative pageant-queen duties. "Anything you might imagine that a, quote, local celebrity or, quote, special guest might do I probably have done," she said. She was having a blast.

I followed her backstage, where the three contestants were taking turns rehearsing their talent. Emili knew them all. They had each won different local titles last year and had all competed with her at the 2018 Miss Virginia pageant in Lynchburg just four months earlier. And now already the 2019 season was getting underway.

Taylor Reynolds was stretching in the wings to prepare for her dance routine. Glasses, ponytail, bare face, a drab cardigan over leggings—she looked like the weary grad student she was, and she laughed about how she had ended a long week of studies by driving a hundred miles to enter a pageant.

Taylor was nearly twenty-four and starting her seventh year on the Miss Virginia circuit. It would almost certainly be her last. Though Miss America was now allowing women as old as twenty-five to compete, the following year would be Taylor's third in pharmacy school, when she would be buried with work-study requirements. She sometimes wondered why she was still doing pageants—the extra hours, the travel, the suiting-up in elaborate gowns and a game face. But she found it therapeutic. Competing for a sparkly crown activated a different part of her brain, enabling her not to think about pharmacy for a while.

"I don't think you should let school or your job take over your life," she told me later. "You need to have something else extra, something entirely different."

It was my first glimpse into the grassroots of Miss America—the sprawling network of hundreds of small-time local pageants that sent their winners to state pageants, which in turn selected the women whom TV viewers would see in competition for a national crown.

Volunteer local organizers like Chip had always been the backbone of the entire Miss America infrastructure. And now, at a time when the national pageant no longer had the TV ratings to demand multimillion-dollar contracts from networks or sponsors, the Chips of this world were the no-cost content providers who made the numbers work—the unpaid casting agents, essentially, whose little pageants recruited and auditioned the legions of young women necessary for the big show to make sense.

This was a world both more sincere and less earnest than I'd expected. These collegial young women hauling their own sequin-stuffed roller bags and doing their own contour makeup were the first to make a joke about Pageant Girl types; they seemed more like weekend warriors than wannabe stars, driven less to crush the competition than to keep their game sharp. It was like half-marathoning or Masters Swimming, but with mink eyelashes.

As I spoke with Taylor, a loud, staticky crackle erupted to my right.

There, under the stage lights, a dark-haired woman was wielding a Fender Jaguar, propelling familiar power chords into the empty seats.

"He got joo joo eyeballs," she crooned in a quirky, girlish alto. "He's one holy roller."

An electric guitar! This was unusual for Miss America. It felt jarringly modern, in a good way. And in all my years of following the pageant, I couldn't remember ever seeing anything that qualified as quite this *cool*.

Was this what they were looking for? Could this be the future of Miss America?

◆   ◆   ◆

What Miss America was looking for—what Miss America *should* be looking for—was certainly the hot question that fall in rooms like this, especially since the pageant, under Gretchen Carlson's new leadership, had eliminated the swimsuit competition.

But that question had always lurked beneath the mystique of a contest whose theme song heralded its winner as "your ideal." And in 1979, George L. Miller decided to quantify it.

He was a statistician, a business professor at Northern Illinois University whose previous research project had modeled potential cash-flow needs in the energy sector. A man of data, George knew full well that the process of selecting Miss America was more art than science, a judged and highly subjective competition.

"I've watched the pageant on and off all these years," he once said, "and I could never pick them just sitting there watching."

Yet, despite its subjective nature, Miss America still offered a tantalizing wealth of data to work with. Ages. Weights. Bust-waist-hips measurements. Education levels, college majors, geographic origins. Hair color and eye color. And with that data—more than fifty years' worth, covering some twenty-five hundred candidates that could be charted against their placement in Atlantic City—George went in search of patterns and probabilities, the approximate contours of the Miss America ideal.

He and a fellow NIU statistician, Dr. Chipei Tseng, compiled seventy-five hundred punch cards of Miss America data and plugged them into the university's bulky IBM mainframe computers. At the annual meeting of the American Statistical Association in Washington, D.C., that August, George presented the results to an uncharacteristically crowded room.

Their findings: The average Miss America was five-foot-six, 119 pounds, and twenty-one years old, with brown hair, brown eyes, and an hourglass silhouette of roughly 36-24-36. She was from a small town—but not one in Delaware, Maryland, Missouri, Montana, Nebraska, Nevada, New Mexico, North Dakota, or Vermont, states that had then never come close to fielding a winner—and she was almost certainly of Northern or Western European extraction. She had a name that was not too common but not too challenging, either. She was an undergraduate, perhaps a junior or senior. And she most likely played the piano or sang—no talent more exotic than that.*

Miller and Tseng's paper, "The Anatomy of Miss America," was the buzz of the conference. And George was so confident in his algorithm that he raised the stakes by making a daring prediction to a handful of journalists: According to his models, only one woman among the fifty competitors at the upcoming national pageant had odds of winning as high as 9–2. She was Miss Mississippi.

Cheryl Prewitt of Ackerman, Mississippi, didn't precisely match

---

* Pageant trivia buffs love the stories of the more exotic talents, like the Miss Montana who rode her horse on stage, or the figure-skating Miss Cincinnati whose pop-up ice rink melted. Most Miss Americas, though, won with conventional performances—except for Nancy Fleming, '61, whose talent was demonstrating different ways to accessorize a little black dress.

George's algorithmic ideal. But she resided comfortably within what he saw as the narrow range of dimensions and qualities that could feasibly launch a woman to victory. She was twenty-two (George saw little hope for anyone younger than nineteen or older than twenty-four). She was five-foot-seven and 110 pounds. She had just completed her senior year at Mississippi State. She played the piano *and* sang. And on September 8, Cheryl was crowned Miss America 1980.

George accepted the accolades modestly: It was just math.

"Miss Mississippi had a 25 percent chance with everybody in the field of 50 contestants," he explained. "She was just way ahead of the field to start with."

George's astonishing prescience landed his name in the Rolodex of every journalist assigned to the pageant through the next decade. And every year, he took their phone calls. He looked pretty much like what you'd expect for a business professor who'd made tenure in the mid-century Midwest: square, dark-rim glasses, a conservative comb-over. He didn't seem to have been an especially devoted Miss America connoisseur.

But in 1979, you didn't have to be a superfan to have Miss America on the brain. The pageant was viewed by more than 60 million people—a happening on par with the Academy Awards or the Super Bowl. Its winners were interviewed on the *Today* show and made the front page when they came to your town; they got to meet the president, tour with Bob Hope, ride in the Macy's Thanksgiving Day Parade, adorn national ads for Kellogg's and Oldsmobile, and appear on all the top-rated talk and variety shows of the day.

With Miss America, George had found a topic that drew national attention to his obscure academic discipline. A year later, he doubled down by declaring that Miss Kansas was the next mathematical favorite to win. This brought an uncomfortable spotlight to Wichita's Leann Folsom—especially when she failed to make the Top 10. But George had already recalculated his picks in the days leading up to the broadcast, after he learned which women had won talent or swimsuit preliminary contests—and Leann wasn't one of them. This wasn't exactly the stuff of algorithmic galaxy brain: Any serious pageant fan knew that preliminary scores factored into the judges' Top 10 calculations. But with these additional data points, his computer told him Miss Oklahoma, Susan Powell, a coloratura soprano who had won the talent prize, would take the crown—and she did.

In 1981, he gave 6–1 odds to Miss Texas, Sheri Ryman. When the perky gymnast maxed out as fourth runner-up, George began to second-guess the judging. "There's quite a bit of prejudice against weightlifters," he protested, referring to her athletic physique.

In 1982, his algorithms deemed Miss North Carolina, Elizabeth Williams, the new Can't Miss. When she fell short of the Top 10, her father blamed George for souring the judges on her.

In many ways, George Miller was just attempting a higher-tech version of what Miss America watchers have always done. As we wandered out of Convention Hall in September 1999, my friends and I met a veteran press photographer who explained how he had known Heather French of Kentucky would win that night. That firm jaw and pointy chin? The winners all have that same profile, he said. But I had also picked her days earlier on a slightly different operating theory: that the winner is the one who looks most like Phyllis George, a Miss America so legendary she could have been the logo.

Following the Miss America pageant is like a cross between betting on the Kentucky Derby, assessing the rookies at spring training, and filling out your office Oscar-pool ballot. The fun isn't just in rooting for a personal favorite; it's also in trying to game out the serious contenders, which means anticipating what the judges will like—and how the cultural moment might influence their preferences.

George's data analysis was revealing when it came to the past tastes of Miss America judges. But his crystal-ball track record was hardly better than that of the average pageant groupie. George predicted Vanessa Williams's victory in 1983, but only after the woman destined to become the first black Miss America had conquered both the swimsuit and talent contests. In 1987, George didn't see Kaye Lani Rae Rafko coming at all; a four-named nursing student who did Tahitian dance seemed a mathematical impossibility. And yet in two consecutive years, he foretold victories for Susan Akin and Kellye Cash before they ever set foot on stage. The two Southern blonde singers were a validation of his computer model, and of the notion of a Miss America "type."

"No one in all my eight years of forecasting Miss America has ever come so close as to the composite Miss America," George said of Susan, a twenty-one-year-old senior majoring in public relations who stood five-foot-nine and measured 35-22-35. "She deviated the least."

So George was probably feeling reasonably confident in September 1988 when he unfurled his 7–1 pick for Miss America 1989: Patti Thorn of Arkansas. And then the crown went to a woman who hadn't even made his statistical Top 10: Miss Minnesota Gretchen Carlson. The Stanford University senior was unusually petite for Miss America, only five-foot-three and 108 pounds. She was also unusually serious—a valedictorian with a wonky major (organizational behavior) and high-powered career goals (corporate law). Her talent? Classical violin, a Convention Hall first.

A year later, George retired from the Miss America game. The data was drying up, his computer model was shot. Pageant officials had stopped publicizing contestants' measurements and kept recalibrating how to score their various virtues.

"The interview counts for 30 percent this year, and I can't get any information related to the interview," he complained. "They've downgraded swimsuits so much that it took care of poor old George."

And suddenly, the pageant was throwing a wrench into his calculations with an entirely new requirement—asking contestants to pick an advocacy cause, of all things. On moral grounds, he approved; this was all *good* for women! But personally, he was ready to move on to a more quant-friendly sport, like baseball. (Just as well: Miss America 1990, Debbye Turner—a marimba-playing veterinary student from Missouri—might have short-circuited his mainframe.)

George's model betrayed him because he made the mistake of assuming an ideal that was rooted purely in measurable qualities. Had no one taught this statistician about the X factor?

And it betrayed him because he failed to consider the most quietly volatile variable in the contest: the women trying to become Miss America.

As early as 1970, pageant CEO Albert Marks had warned that it wasn't just the "women's libbers" who bristled at the swimsuit contest—the new generation of contestants wasn't so keen on it, either. So in the 1980s, as a statistics professor tried to turn these women into datasets, the pageant was at least trying to make them feel less like meat—limiting the amount of ogling time the cameras would spend on their bodies, for example. It wasn't to spite poor old George after all that they dropped bust-waist-height data from the press kits.

But those were baby steps. It was when a Miss America from the 1980s unexpectedly took over the pageant in 2018 that everything changed at once.

"We are no longer a pageant," Gretchen Carlson declared that summer as she announced the end, at last, of the swimsuit competition. "We will no longer judge our candidates on their outward physical appearance." The tiny, brainy Miss America who broke George Miller's algorithm was now the chair of the board. The new competition, she said, would "represent a new generation of female leaders focused on scholarship, social impact, talent and empowerment." And it would be "open, transparent, and inclusive"—particularly to women who may not have felt comfortable participating in a contest of looks. She called it "Miss America 2.0."

But that fall, as Chip Brown and several hundred volunteers like him were launching the annual cycle of local pageants, the Miss America community was in chaos.

The abrupt change had exposed doubts about Gretchen's management skills and the organization's financial future. Board members were resigning, state pageant directors were sent packing, and longtime friends were feuding on Facebook—including some former Miss Americas. Key contracts that had sustained the pageant were set to expire, and it was unclear exactly when and where and even *whether* the next Miss America pageant would take place.

And now the old question burned more urgently: What was Miss America looking for anyway? Was Gretchen's vision—with emphasis on academic achievement and high-end talent—poised to exclude a certain kind of young woman who once found a leg up in the world through pageants? Which aspects of a pageant were "empowering," and which were "objectifying," and could you always separate the two? What were the new rules of this game—and who gets to decide what Miss America should be anyway?

✦   ✦   ✦

Emili wasn't startled to see a rock musician at a local pageant. She had seen all kinds of exotic talents, she told me: At the national pageant that fall, Miss Delaware had done a speed-painting routine.

But I figured the judges would swoon for the freshness of this act. Gretchen's pageant rebrand had tapped into the aesthetic of *you go girl* feminism, a clean, aspirational sensibility reminiscent of yogurt commercials and Taylor Swift videos. The TV ads were earnest and sequin-free, contestants chatting in close-ups that highlighted their youth, spontaneity, and clean pores. In Atlantic City, the stage back-drop had been emblazoned with words like "FEARLESS," "ROLE MODEL," "INTELLIGENT," "STRONG." On the Miss America web-site, a waist-down image of a woman caught her in mid-jeté, the gauzy layers of her pale peach skirt lofting to expose a pair of sassy high-tops. A girl with an electric guitar felt like the perfect avatar for this Miss America moment.

Her name was Caroline Weinroth. She was an actual singer and guitar player in an actual indie rock band and an MFA candidate in po-etry. She had read the history books and the feminist criticism on Miss America, and she had a refreshingly meta take on pageantry.

"It's like a performance of femininity," she said enthusiastically.

Caroline's polish and confident gleam were typical of the pageant women I had met, even if the overall package seemed like something new: a vaguely retro style of dressing that, with her high cheekbones and saucy overbite, evoked a nervy young Barbara Stanwyck. While her ethnic mix—Taiwanese-American mother, an American father of Jewish heritage—promised an intriguing narrative for a pageant world eager to celebrate "firsts," I was struck by a vision of something else entirely: the first hipster Miss America?

Time to place my bet for Miss Arlington.

Caroline Weinroth was going to win.

✦   ✦   ✦

The parking lot at Wakefield High School was packed the next day, a perfect Virginia early-fall Saturday, the grounds bustling with young people—runners on the track, football players in the field.

But there was no obvious sign that the Miss Arlington pageant—a competition that would take a young woman to within one step of the national contest—was happening on these premises. You had to know what you were looking for.

Caroline was hauling her gear through the hallway outside the auditorium that led backstage. Her interview with the five judges that morning had gone well, she thought. One had asked her about gun violence, and she was able to connect personally with the topic—she had worked at the Washington pizzeria Comet Ping Pong at the time of the frightening 2016 incident when a gunman addled by a far-right conspiracy theory invaded the restaurant in search of a nonexistent child trafficking ring.

As we spoke, a woman in a short gold dress walked past and said hi. It took me a second to recognize her. Sleek pageboy, striking cheekbones, sparkling eyes. It was Taylor Reynolds, the weary pharmacy student, cleaning up very nicely.

As the contestants disappeared backstage, a small crowd started to line up for tickets. Parents, friends, two small girls in princess gowns, and a smattering of young women in cocktail dresses, sashes, and crowns. Miss Central Virginia was there. So was Miss Virginia Beach and Miss Shenandoah Valley. Technically they were rivals of the future Miss Arlington, but they carried themselves more as ambassadors of friendly realms, here to salute her with their presence.

Miss Chautauqua MacKenzie Adamson and Miss Greater Charlottesville Dorothy Cosner were chatting amiably in line. They had both nailed down the titles that would be their ticket to Miss Virginia 2019 the previous weekend and seemed untroubled by the fact they would compete against each other in June. After all, they had faced off at Miss Virginia the previous June, when MacKenzie was Miss Capitol Region and Dorothy was Miss Southwestern Virginia, and before that on Virginia's borderless circuit of local pageants. So now they stood together and tapped each other's arms as they tried to remember where they had first met. Roanoke Valley? Or Miss Apple Blossom?

"I saw you compete in Roanoke," Dorothy reminded MacKenzie, "because I didn't get my paperwork in on time."

Most Virginia pageants were "open" competitions, meaning any woman who lived within the state could compete. If she lost at one local pageant, she could head down the road to sign up for the next. None of the contestants for Miss Arlington lived in Arlington, and that was fine. They were members of the same tribe: Their coworkers or sorority sisters might not relate to their post-adolescent piano lessons or relentless charity fundraising, but their fellow competitors did, and the camaraderie was sincere. Dorothy's father recalled a pageant where one woman arrived at rehearsal to find a ceiling too low for her flag-twirling routine. When she fled the room in tears, "half the girls went off the stage to go get her," he said.

The pageant was scheduled to kick off at 4:30 p.m., but Chip had put out the word that 4:40 p.m. might be more realistic, and still the sunlight was turning golden in the windows before they bothered to close the doors. Finally: showtime. There were maybe thirty-five or forty people in the seats, and a couple half-hearted decorations on stage—a cluster of seasonal hay bales and pumpkins, two limp scarecrow dolls. But the lights were bright, the music was loud, and the six contestants cheerfully marched across the stage in cocktail dresses to introduce themselves.

It took about two minutes for me to start second-guessing my original bet.

"A twenty-one-year-old senior dance major at Shenandoah Conservatory hoping someday to get her doctorate in dance, I'm Dot Kelly— Contestant Number Four!"

It was the first I had seen or heard of Dot, a Korean-American woman with a widow's peak and a dancer's posture; all I knew of her at that point was contained in that unremarkable sentence. But it was the way she said it—a naturally energetic voice, warm and musical, not too high and not too low. Caroline and the other contestants had trouble projecting over the loud music. But Dot's voice cut through the roaring soundtrack. It drew you in.

I thought back to 2013, when I'd put my money on a Miss District of Columbia who checked the curious combination of boxes that had come to define a classic Miss America résumé. Allyn Rose was a high-cheekboned blonde; her talent was a crowd-pleasing dance on roller skates to a Michael Jackson song. But it was her personal history that stopped you in your tracks: At twenty-four, she was preparing to get a preventative double mastectomy, having learned she was a carrier for the rare disease that doctors believed was linked to her mother's fatal breast cancer. Serious and well-spoken, she had been devoted to cancer education for years. The Miss America Organization was eager to present itself as serious about women's issues; here was a woman who offered traditional Miss America charms as well as a new-era sense of mission and the credibility to sell it. I advised all my pageant-watching friends to put Miss D.C. on their lists.

But during the traditional "parade of states" that kicked off the 2013 Miss America pageant, Allyn stepped forward to introduce herself—and her words were somehow swallowed by the atmosphere. It wasn't her fault. Her voice just didn't project. She was vanishing from the radar. Minutes later, a woman who had made zero impression during our scan of the program booklet passed briefly across the screen: "I'm Miss New York, Mallory Hagan!" *That* was the voice: warm, upbeat, slightly husky, effortlessly resonant. A voice that punched a hole in the air. Two hours later, she was Miss America.

Dot Kelly was going to win.

Within thirty seconds, though, I was jolted again, when a short woman with curly hair and a baby-face smile stepped up.

"A twenty-year-old third-class midshipman at the United States Naval Academy, I'm Elena de la Rosa!"

Wait, what?

Ask any Miss America hopeful why she got into pageants, and she will inevitably tout her scholarship winnings; ask any booster or volunteer why they have stuck with the pageant through controversies and doubts, and they will deploy the S-word, too. It's the Miss America profession of faith: *the nation's largest scholarship provider for women.*

ture naval officer, and three college women strutting across the stage
bathing suits. A month earlier, the national pageant had seemed a lit-
sleepy without the bikini parade—a mid-show jolt of flashing lights,
nce music, tossed hair, and pony kicks. But here at Miss Arlington, it
ddenly felt a little embarrassing. Maybe it was the unflattering high
hool theater lights. Maybe it was just a new era in America. There
re great bodies and there were ordinary bodies, and it seemed impos-
le to draw any conclusions other than that Taylor Reynolds's lime-
en bikini popped beautifully against her mahogany complexion.

Finally, though, the safe space of the talent competition. Jazz dance,
dern dance, song, modern dance—Caroline Weinroth would have
trouble standing out from this field. "Come Together," the Beatles'
ampiest tune, as performed by a lady in an evening gown, can't help
t have a David Lynch vibe, and Caroline *worked* it. As her Fender
iled through a minor-key guitar solo of her own creation, she saun-
ed up to the front of the stage, arcing one long leg out of the sexy
ck hot pants—and-streamers ensemble that passed for a skirt.

But then wouldn't you know it? There was Dot Kelly again, the one
th the voice, and it turned out she wasn't just any old dancer, but a tap
ncer, with an explosive, contemporary style. Her a cappella routine—
nctuated with shouts of "No music! No music!" and "Hey, Arlington,
eck this out!"—seemed like a crowd-pleaser, or could have been if a
l crowd had been there.

I sympathized with the judges: How could you assess performers
such different fields? How could you not end up gravitating to the
man you simply liked best?

It was the same for the onstage interview. Was the winning answer
the substance or the delivery? Taylor opened with an engaging an-
dote ("my best friend actually has a bad habit of texting and driving,
l when I'm in the car with her . . .") but then talked in circles about
at to do about the problem. Would it hurt Caroline's chances that she
ne out in support of gun control?

And what about the evening gown? Were we judging the walk? The
ice of a dress? The figure inside it? Everyone looked their loveliest.
t, while pausing at the front to let the judges assess her, gazed up and

So eagerly has the pageant wrapped itself in this fina
that it has sometimes stretched it too far. In 2014, the
Oliver raised an eyebrow at the figures touted on the broa
lion a year, *really?*—and checked the math. It turned out
contrived that number by counting all *available* scholars
the total sum of stipends that multiple pageant-friendly
be willing to offer to a single state contestant, who of
possibly use more than one. Miss America later acknow
actual number was closer to $6 million. Yet scholarships
a cherished part of the talking points. Even pageant
absorbed the scholarship argument to flip it around: *Wh*
have to wear a swimsuit for a scholarship?

As if that's what it was entirely about—or even m
woman seeking a crown. Elena de la Rosa had a full
lis, paid for by the Pentagon. She didn't need a scholar
was simply a born competitor—swim-team captain, de
hockey, cheerleading, festival queen. What did her Nav
periors think of her weekend pageant habit? I asked h
face broke into a dimpled smile.

"Well, they don't necessarily *know* . . . ," she said.

This résumé of Elena's was *such* an intriguing wild
generation of female leaders . . . ," Gretchen Carlson ha
what she meant? But there was no time to process it. It
Miss Arlington swimsuit competition.

Oh. *That?*

Miss America had killed off swimsuits four months
first national pageant without them had come and gone.
ies still rocked the stages that fall at hundreds of local p
the country. It was a quirk of the sprawling pageant
women on the yearlong path to become Miss America 2
punched their ticket at a local contest even before Gretc
announcement of a swimsuit ban. These last-hurrah sw
were carrying on not as a gesture of resistance, organiz
a playing-field leveler: If some of the women angling t
2019 had competed in swimsuit, then all of them shoul

So there they were: a rock guitarist–poet, a pharmaci

out to the empty balcony with a charming little shiver of joy, as if she were already in Convention Hall.

And then came Taylor.

The weary pharmacy grad student walked out in a dark red gown with a very deep V, and the room caught its breath. The narrow bodice of this gown traced Taylor's slender torso and healthy cleavage, swooping out into a spectacular mermaid train. The dress wasn't just bolder than everyone else's, it was literally bigger, spilling out over a swath of stage. She was marking her turf with that gown.

Taylor held her frame high in a slow but confident stroll, somehow making eye contact with everyone in the room. This was a woman who could hold her own in Atlantic City. A woman who clearly knew what she was doing. A woman who, if it came to it, you just might follow into battle. This time, I knew it:

Taylor Reynolds was going to win.

✦   ✦   ✦

I had gone behind the scenes at a pageant, learned a bit about the background of the contestants, talked to them one-on-one. Had it given me enough intel to make the correct call? Finally, the prizes.

Elena got something called the "spirit award."

Taylor got the award for best interview.

Dot won the award for talent.

All the scholarships on the local level were modest relative to the cost of higher education these days—$100 here, a $50 savings bond there, topping out at $1,000 for Miss Arlington. Yet ticket sales, at $20 each, would have barely covered the cost of renting the auditorium. Chip had to hustle for the prizes, turning to the benevolence of former winners and parents and longtime supporters, as well as his own wallet.

Second runner-up and recipient of a $100 scholarship: Monica Osborne, a jazz-dancing Hollins undergrad.

First runner-up and recipient of a $200 scholarship: Dot Kelly.

Was Caroline going to win after all? I couldn't imagine her walking away completely empty-handed. Did those early awards serve as consolation prizes or a hint of where the judges' hearts lay?

When her name was called as Miss Arlington, Taylor Reynolds bent nearly in half, like the wind had been knocked out of her—eyes wide, one hand to her mouth and the other to her chest—a look of pure astonishment and joy. As Emili affixed the crown to Taylor's head, the emcee tipped off the audience to the drama of this victory.

"Taylor has competed how many times at state?" she asked. The new Miss Arlington, still speechless, held up seven fingers. This would be her seventh time at Miss Virginia.

Of course Taylor Reynolds was going to win Miss Arlington. She knew what she was doing. But even after her fourth-, third-, and second-place finishes at Miss Virginia, there was nothing contrived about her joy over this little local crown. The Arlington competition might have been small, but it was tough—and now her ticket to the state pageant was secure. She could rest easy for several months before suiting up again.

As Miss Arlington 2019 greeted her public, Caroline watched from the edge of the stage, disappointed but chipper.

"At least my next pageant isn't until the end of the month," she said: Miss Apple Blossom, at the famous Shenandoah Apple Blossom Festival in Winchester. It was still early in the cycle. She would find her way to Miss Virginia eventually.

2

"SOMETHING ELECTRIC IN THE ROOM"

1980

Things had been tense between Phyllis George and Jimmy the Greek for months, or maybe forever. Yet it was Phyllis's practice to keep up a good front, to maintain the veneer of civility. So on the Sunday before Thanksgiving 1980, when the two of them took their regular places on the CBS set of their hit show *The NFL Today*, she naturally tried to initiate some small talk with her gruff fellow sports pundit in the minutes before the show began.

It was important to stay positive. And Phyllis could talk to *anyone*.

But Jimmy ignored her.

"Oh, you don't love me anymore," she teased.

And that's when Jimmy spoke up.

"I love you, I just hate your fucking husband," he snarled.

Phyllis burst into tears. With minutes to go before the show went live, she fled from the set.

It's not like she hadn't heard cruel words before in her young, charmed life. At thirty-one, Phyllis was America's sportscasting sweetheart, a cream-puff beauty who exuded effortless Southern charm, but she had been in some tough rooms. There was the Texas pageant boss who dismissed her as "a bouncy-assed piano player who'll never be Miss America." There were the sportswriters who called her an "airhead." To be honest, she had even heard worse before this from Jimmy "the Greek" Snyder himself, a raffish, gold chain–wearing Vegas oddsmaker twice her age whose spiky personality and insider knowledge of sports had catapulted him late in life to a TV stardom just as unlikely as hers.

This time was different. Jimmy's swipe at her husband—an out-of-the-blue reference to some old, unhappy business dealings—seemed bitterly intended to wound. And even as she reached enviable new heights of fame and success, Phyllis could still be discombobulated by the idea that anyone would want to hurt her.

But it was also different because she knew she no longer had to put up with it.

Just a decade removed from her crowning as Miss America 1971, Phyllis had begun to realize her power. And she decided to flex it.

If you have ever seen a movie or sitcom featuring a TV anchor with a pageant past, you can trace the inspiration straight back to the amazing life and times of Phyllis George. Same with any story of a beauty queen–turned–political wife or fabulous lifestyle guru with a Miss State sash hanging in her closet: Phyllis lived those lives, too. Precious few Miss Americas ever became household names, but Phyllis did—a vivacious free-form celebrity who held her own against movie stars on the magazine covers and talk shows of the jet-set seventies and high-gloss eighties.

It was her roller-coaster ride in television—starting with her triumph as a sportscasting glass-ceiling smasher—that embodied the ambitions, and frustrations, of a generation of young women trying all the doors that were just then creaking open. Phyllis was the one who navigated an evolving medium to find a use for the exotic skill set that came from being Miss America—a way to channel all that leftover charisma into a lasting career.

But in doing so, she would face the problem that had always lurked on the far side of the Miss America promise: What happens when all your wildest dreams come true too fast?

✦   ✦   ✦

In the summer of 1969, a twenty-year-old Phyllis spoke to a luncheon gathering of the Denton Hi-Noon Lions Club about her first attempt at the Miss Texas pageant a few weeks earlier. She had come in third, and that was okay: "The best girl won," she said, "or she wouldn't have been named Miss Texas."

Phyllis was simply stunned that her fellow contestants had voted her Miss Congeniality. Because she had feared that they would resent her instead.

"I'd won the swimsuit competition, which I didn't expect to win, and then won the talent competition, too," she explained.

Everything Phyllis would become was already there in that moment: The glib post-game analyst. The budding politician. The alert student of interpersonal dynamics. The adorable raconteur. The girl you just find yourself immediately liking—and who secretly cares very much that you do.

Phyllis Ann George grew up happy and secure in the kind of town where they never locked their doors, an only child until she begged for a baby brother and got one. She had a new Madame Alexander doll every Christmas, and a Princess phone, and slumber parties where her friends sang Beatles songs. Her engineer dad and homemaker mom did volunteer work and raised money for charity; they took her to church and put her in Methodist youth fellowship and vacation Bible school. Wonderful, loving parents: Her dad didn't even get mad when she smashed up her new yellow Ford Falcon the first day she drove it to school. And they put her through years of piano lessons with a renowned teacher who pushed her to try harder and sent her to competitions. Piano could have been her career, but then came the distractions of cheerleading and high school plays. She was junior class president and a nominee for homecoming queen. Her general understanding was that she was cute; she never thought of it as beautiful.

In other words, she was utterly special in a way that was common to thousands of other girls across a prosperous nation in 1970. So why did Phyllis become the one?

Probably no one has spent more time mulling what qualities make a Miss America than the Miss Americas themselves.

"Any Miss America could walk into a room of one hundred people, and you would notice she is Miss America," says Rebecca King, the 1974 titleholder.

"It's not a strut," says Deborah Bryant, Miss America 1966. "That can be artificial. But that *quiet* confidence." As a judge in 2016, Debbie felt it the moment she met Miss Arkansas, Savvy Shields—"just so positive, this great big smile, this happy person," and soon thereafter the winner.

Which is not to say the Miss America aura is entirely inborn. The other Miss Americas have seen it take hold after a young woman is crowned. Perhaps it's like social psychologist Amy Cuddy's much-debated theory of "power posing," but instead of the Wonder Woman arms-akimbo stance, it's the erect posture and lifted chin required to balance a crown that instills a regal confidence. Or maybe just knowing that she's Miss America, and being treated like Miss America, is all the boost she needs.

"She sort of takes on that mantle," Rebecca says, "and begins to shine even more than she did."

But Phyllis seemed to have it from day one—or at least from the time she arrived in Atlantic City as Miss Texas in 1970.

"Instantly, there's something electric in the room," Norton Mockridge, one of the judges, recalled of the moment Phyllis walked in for her interview. When she smiled, "that electric something flashes, and quivers, and irradiates the room . . . It's a moment none of us will ever forget!"

She was tall, which helps a woman stand out, but hardly the tallest. She had an hourglass figure, with the .7 waist-to-hip ratio that science tells us the eye favors—though probably most Miss America contestants boasted roughly the same.

Connoisseurs will tell you that Miss Americas have a very specific kind of beauty—not too voluptuous, not too chiseled. Some researchers argue that the features we are hardwired to recognize as beautiful fall within a mathematical average—noses that are not too big or small, eyes that are not too wide- or narrow-set—and Miss Americas may well exemplify this. "Beauty pageant winners often appear generic-looking—extremely attractive but not distinctive," wrote the psychologist Nancy Etcoff. "The face seems familiar, a better-looking, less irregular version of other faces we have seen."

Beauty can futz with our radar. Studies suggest we are more likely to help pretty people than homely people; that they are more likely to win arguments and win our confidence; and that we not only expect them to be smarter, but we also often perceive them to be more clever and accomplished than they actually are.

Why did the judges think it was so hilarious when Phyllis explained she didn't like beer? ("Ah jus' like to drink Dr Pepper, on the rocks!") Did the pageant press corps chortle a little too hard over Phyllis's stories about her pet hermit crab, Moon Child, which she brought to Atlantic City for good luck? ("The day he finally crawled out of his box here, I won!") Or maybe she truly told the joke well. If so, was that because her beauty gave her the confidence to sell the story? Or was it her communication skills that added an extra point to how they assessed her looks?

She's our most beautiful, the other Miss Americas would say about Phyllis. Long, glossy brown hair back then, eyes forever smiling. If you had to single out a physical feature that distinguished her from all the other bright-eyed and symmetrical faces, it would be the unexpected dimples above her strong jaw. Dimples "so deep a scoop of rocky road ice cream could fit in each one," rhapsodized her first husband, the Hollywood producer Robert Evans. Was that the "electric something" that sparked through the judges' room? Dimples do have the effect of making a smile seem merrier. Then again, Phyllis was a true-blue extrovert. She was probably genuinely happy in that moment to meet a big room of new people.

But to try to situate the locus of Phyllis's native charisma—the kind of thing some politicians and executives hire expensive coaches to help them master—is an unfair exercise. Because it might imply that everything that came after Miss America came easily.

✦   ✦   ✦

Phyllis didn't hurt for work in those early years following her reign. She did commercials for Jergens, for Pan Am, for Playtex bras and Woolite. There was a guest spot on a game show, a promotional gig with Gillette, and so many jobs hosting state and local pageants. But nothing that clicked as a career.

The challenge was that Phyllis's undeniable star quality didn't manifest as any clearly marketable skill. She could sing well enough to fake her way through a pop tune during the variety-show filler in her frequent return trips to the pageant—but she was no singer. She was a skilled pianist, though half the delight of her winning performance of "Raindrops Keep Fallin' on My Head" was the way she swayed and smiled through the whole thing. And by the 1970s, that wouldn't get you any further than a piano bar.

Three years after giving up her crown, she was in New York, still taking meetings and trying to break into acting, when her agent sent her out to meet another television executive. But Bob Wussler was something different: He was the new head of CBS Sports.

Bob's challenge in November 1974 was to catch ABC in the ratings. It had been a decade since a young ABC producer named Roone Arledge had cracked the code for TV sports with a bag of tricks swiped from Hollywood—enlivening games with dynamic camera angles, quick edits, and slow-motion replays; gleaning human-interest stories from the Olympics; dignifying oddball sports like rodeo or badminton with a narrative about "the thrill of victory and the agony of defeat" on *Wide World of Sports*.

Bob saw no reason why CBS, which boasted the top-rated entertainment shows—*All in the Family*, *The Waltons*, *M*A*S*H*—couldn't tap into that same energy for sports. But he knew he couldn't chase after the same pool of die-hard fans. "There just aren't enough of them to make it pay," he said that fall.

The key to expanding the audience, he decided, was women. He telecast women's tennis tournaments, wagering that men and women alike would enjoy the longer rallies and higher drama. He invested in ladies' golf, arguing that the average male golfer could learn more from watching female pros anyway. And he reassessed CBS's corps of sportscasters, which until recently had been entirely male, same as the other networks. With the brassy, cantankerous Howard Cosell, ABC had an iconic personality in the announcer's booth, and Bob hoped to create a team of superstars for CBS, too.

"At least one of them will be a woman," he vowed in November. "I don't know who yet."

When Phyllis's agent had a chance to bend Bob's ear, he knew exactly what code words to use. You should meet this Texas girl, he said: She was the "living embodiment of 'Semi-Tough.'"

Any sports bro in 1974 would get the reference. Dan Jenkins's best-selling novel was a locker-room satire about two pro-ballers and their roommate, Barbara Jane Bookman, a brown-eyed bikini model from Fort Worth who was down-to-earth, funny, and "so damned pretty it makes your eyes blur." The ultimate 1970s Cool Girl, in other words: a low-maintenance knockout who loved naughty jokes, football, and hanging with the guys.

Bob and Phyllis met for cocktails at the Hotel Dorset in midtown Manhattan, and after some chitchat, he asked if she knew anything about sports.

"Well, yeah," Phyllis told him. "I've dated athletes." She had also played golf and powder-puff football back home in Denton, her dad was a high school referee, and she *loved* the Dallas Cowboys.

Bob offered her a job on the spot.

Figuring out what to do with her was another question. Her first assignment was as a sideline correspondent for the Fiesta Bowl. Her producers' directions: Just talk! You know—about the crowd, the balloons, all the festivities . . .

It was a fiasco.

"I was out on the field looking very snappy in my boots, long skirt, and blazer. But I didn't know what I was doing," Phyllis fumed later. "I felt like the icing on the cake. And that bothered me."

She went back to her producers and demanded clarity about her role.

It was a wise move: She was not the first woman Bob Wussler had tried in sports. Earlier that fall, he had hired Jane Chastain for a plum seat in the NFL announcers' booth, the first female sportscaster on national TV. But despite her decade of covering sports in local markets, Jane encountered an ugly backlash. "Tell that babe to take up cooking," said one of the nasty callers to the CBS switchboard. "She sure can't announce football."

Bob resolved to introduce Phyllis to viewers slowly, on a wide variety of sports, with soft features on lady golfers, a "roving reporter" gig at the Preakness. Critics—which is to say male sportswriters—called her a "bundle of giggles" and out of her depth. She did tend to riff a little freely in her early months. At the Belmont Stakes, she suggested that the horses seemed calm "because they know this is the last leg of the Triple Crown."

But she found her groove when she interviewed Dave Cowens, a famously taciturn young Boston Celtics star. Hitching a ride with him from practice to his house, she turned on the Texas charm, loosening him up with small talk. And then when they sat down, camera rolling, she started asking questions not about basketball—but his life.

What would he do when basketball was all over? Where would he want to live? Did he want to get married and have kids?

It was the equivalent of first-date chatter, nothing all that probing or startling. But it was revelatory for fans, who had known so little about his off-court life. This was "softer" stuff, yes, but it added texture to sports TV—a welcome break from three guys in blazers litigating a game to death. Bigger interviews followed with NBA star Elvin Hayes (they talked religion) and tennis champ Jimmy Connors (she asked why people hated him).

"A surprisingly competent broadcaster," the *Baltimore Sun* decided. "Articulate and bright and clever enough to realize what she was hired for."

Six months after her debut, CBS promoted her to *The NFL Today* on Sundays with veteran sportscaster Brent Musburger and former player Irv Cross. They were a cool, appealingly diverse trio, by 1975 television standards—a white guy, a black guy, and a dazzling young woman—in a pre-cable era when winning your time block amounted to gold-plated fame. At twenty-six, she was no longer a "former Miss America." She was simply *Phyllis George*. And her interviews got bigger and buzzier.

"You have an all-American image," she teased Cowboys quarterback Roger Staubach. "You're kind of a straight guy. Do you enjoy it, or is it a burden?"

She had clearly put the uptight, long-married navy veteran at ease because he laughed as he replied: "You know, I enjoy sex as much as Joe Namath. Only I do it with one girl!"

The quote went the 1975 equivalent of viral. As for Joe Namath, she cajoled the hard-partying quarterback into confessing that he felt responsible for the Jets' losing streak. Then his mood shifted and he abruptly ended the interview—*walked out*, on Phyllis George!—but it made for great television. And when she interviewed Muhammad Ali, they bonded over a favorite face cream.

The commentary on her performance, negative or positive, almost always circled back to her looks, and CBS played into this, planting banners in the stands during one game reading, "Phyllis is prettier than Frank Gifford," the rival ABC sportscaster. Phyllis was shrewd enough to laugh it off. When the Miss America thing came up, she would self-deprecate, retell the story about the time the crown fell off her head. In interview after interview, for stories whose headlines were all too often a variation on a theme of "Not Just a Pretty Face," she made a point of praising her cohosts or looping them into the conversation. ("Don't you think, Brent?") So new to this, she had already figured out something about fame, how it could destabilize your alliances and blow back on you if you weren't careful.

✦　✦　✦

In 1976, Phyllis became the first woman to cohost a Super Bowl broadcast—an uncomfortable and largely unheralded victory for the women's movement.

Feminists didn't know what to make of a woman who got a history-making job through a pageant rather than years in the trenches; who said things like "I'm not a feminist in any way"; who sat out the battles other women were waging. ("Why would any woman want to go in there while the men are dressing?" Phyllis wondered about the female sportswriters seeking the right to conduct interviews in the locker rooms alongside their male colleagues. "Just not my style. Not my technique.")

But it was a breakthrough nonetheless, and a significant one. Phyllis was normalizing the idea of a woman talking as a peer with men in the very male bastion of sports, at a time when women were only beginning to make inroads in television news. It had just been a year since Barbara Walters became the first female cohost of a U.S. news program, NBC's *Today*. Local television had only recently started to recruit women—opening the door for future network stars like Jessica Savitch and Lesley Stahl—largely because the National Organization for Women was threatening to sue stations that didn't live up to new FCC affirmative-action guidelines.

In Oklahoma City, a former Miss America named Jane Jayroe was surprised to get a call one day at her low-paid state government job from a local news director: KOCO-TV was looking to add a female anchor to its all-male news team. Would she like to audition? A decade after handing off her 1967 crown, Jane had a young child, a fresh divorce, and a very sparse résumé.

"I got that opportunity because there weren't very many women that had the credentials," she says now. "So the field was kind of open to anyone who had this skill set to be live on television."

The anchorman quit rather than work with a beauty queen, and the local TV critic scoffed that they should have hired "the station scrubwoman" instead: "She would have had more news experience than Miss Jayroe by simply pushing her mop around the assignment desks." A few months in, the same critic semi-apologized. The beauty queen, it turned out, "is one of the few bright spots of that program, showing an aptitude for news coverage and anchoring." Two decades later, after a long career in broadcasting, Jane was named to the governor's cabinet, as the state secretary of tourism and recreation.

The smash success of Phyllis George had given the Miss America title new credibility and market value. Broadcasting was looking for telegenic women with speaking skills at the same time the pageant, with a new cohort of ambitious, outspoken young boomers, had become a reliable pipeline of them. You didn't even have to *win* Miss America to get caught up in the gold rush. In 1978, when Phyllis signed a new $250,000-a-year contract that moved her to CBS's entertainment division, Bob Wussler, by then the head of the network, scouted the pageant to search for replacements and ended up signing Barbara Mougin, a dancer from small-town Indiana who was the 1978 first runner-up, for a tryout. Phyllis's seat on *The NFL Today* ultimately went to Jayne Kennedy, a twenty-six-year-old former Miss Ohio USA, and by then, CBS brass was ready with the response to critics on her lack of sports credentials: "This is a role for a personality."

Tawny Godin was eighteen and a rising sophomore with straight A's at Skidmore when she was crowned Miss America in 1975, just as Phyllis's career was taking off. She had planned to become a linguistics professor. But by the end of her reign, she was swamped with TV offers. At twenty, with no college degree, she landed a job as a reporter and anchor in Los Angeles, the nation's number two broadcast market.

Forget about the scholarship—the real Miss America prize was these coveted job opportunities in an exciting field that now fell in their laps.

"I had always been a news junkie," says Marjorie Vincent. "But I had never thought about being able to pursue that as a career"—until she was crowned Miss America 1991. She detoured from her nearly completed Duke law degree to take a job in local TV. "I thought, 'I'm still young, law's not going anywhere.'"

The rapid expansion of cable television in the 1980s and 1990s created even more openings for attractive young women who knew how to read teleprompters and keep a line of banter going. Many of these jobs were not in news, exactly, but softer-side infotainment—Susan Powell, '81, on the Discovery Channel, Debra Maffett, '83, on the Nashville Network, Kira Kazantsev, '15, on the Golf Channel.

But most of the Miss Americas' on-camera roles would not last long into middle age. Marjorie felt worn down by the demands of raising a young child while climbing the ladder of midsize markets; she went back to law school and became an assistant attorney general for the state of Florida.

For Tawny, the job with KABC News during its controversial but wildly popular "happy talk" era—celebrity gossip, car chases, and lively anchor chatter—threw her at a young age into a glamorous and dizzying social scene. She dated Burt Reynolds and Kevin Costner and got married, for a while, to John Schneider at his *Dukes of Hazzard* peak. She also found herself working late hours or pigeonholed into frivolous magazine shows with names like *Hollywood Close Up* that seemed unlikely to lead to a network job.

Two decades and a few divorces later, when Tawny was in her final years as an L.A. anchor, she expressed some regrets about the academic life she never pursued. But what other choice could a former Miss America have made at twenty?

"I knew these people wouldn't be knocking on my door in five years," she said.

◆   ◆   ◆

Her children say that there were two Phyllises: Phyllis Ann and Phyllis George. And they were frequently in conflict.

Phyllis Ann was the girl from Denton. Phyllis George was the superstar from CBS Sports. Phyllis Ann was devoted to her church, her family, and feared that marrying the Jewish boyfriend she loved would be too much of a culture clash to work. Phyllis George sought out the parties, the magazine covers, and hastily wed a notorious showbiz lothario.

Phyllis Ann knew who her real friends were. Phyllis George fretted over what strangers thought of her.

Phyllis Ann wanted more than anything to be a wife and mother. Phyllis George wanted *everything*.

Restless in sports, she was dismayed when her general-interest magazine show, *People*, flopped quickly in 1978, and she started exploring movie roles. (Not such a crazy idea, when affable sports personalities like Don Meredith and O. J. Simpson were finding crossover success in Hollywood.) Though often seen in the company of Manhattan's most eligible bachelors, Phyllis had somehow resisted the snare of early marriage that would muffle the ambitions of fellow Miss Americas of the era. Even that short-lived mismatch of a marriage to Robert Evans, the much older, thrice-divorced playboy producer of *Chinatown* and *The Godfather*, in 1977 did nothing to slow her broadcast career.

"Ego was what motivated my perversity in wanting to make Miss America Mrs. Evans," he later wrote. "I couldn't understand what she saw in me. I was everything she was not."

Hollywood life "was not what I thought it was," she concurred delicately. "I like to go to church on Sundays."

But she had always yearned for a family. In late 1978, a few months after her divorce, she ran into John Y. Brown at a party. John Y., as everyone called him, was a Kentucky political scion who had made a fortune by turning Colonel Sanders's homey fried-chicken joints into a nationwide fast-food icon. On St. Patrick's Day 1979, they were married in a star-studded, flashbulb-popping ceremony in Manhattan.

During their St. Martin honeymoon, they decided he should enter the race for governor, just two months ahead of the Democratic primary. (Phyllis credited a chance encounter with Jackie Kennedy on the island for giving them the nudge. "You remind me sooo much of Jack!" Phyllis recalled Jackie whispering as she gazed at John Y.'s hooded eyes and bushy forelock.) The newlyweds, perpetually kissing or holding hands, electrified the campaign trail.

"Y'all look like you're on a damn honeymoon," a Paducah voter sniped.

"We are," Phyllis said, beaming.

John Y. won handily, and suddenly Kentucky had a powerhouse first lady, just thirty years old and in possession of her own mega-fame. And Phyllis had to figure out for herself how to make this gig work—just as she had five years earlier as a first-of-her-kind in TV sports.

"I certainly didn't have a role model to pattern my life after," she said later. Granted, there had been previous governors' wives. But none like her. "I was not just a tea-and-coffee person," she said. She had had a taste of politics and wanted to stay in it. She wanted to have a voice.

The Browns' flamboyant style raised eyebrows in the Bluegrass State—his frequent travel outside Kentucky, miles racked up on a state-owned helicopter, and fondness for high-stakes gambling; her designer wardrobe, frenetic schedule, and occasionally self-involved speeches. But he got kudos for balancing the budget, and she channeled her star power into good works, raising private funds to renovate the decrepit governor's mansion and promoting the work of Kentucky artisans in high-end department stores nationwide. Whispers of a potential White House run followed them throughout their term-limited four years in Frankfort.

She also managed to go back to work for CBS Sports in October 1980, less than four months after the birth of their first child, a son named Lincoln, while still juggling the duties of first lady. And that's when Phyllis confronted a slow-burning workplace conflict of the kind that no one was yet calling sexual harassment.

✦   ✦   ✦

Jimmy the Greek had been hired on to *The NFL Today* as a commentator in 1976, a year after Phyllis, Irv, and Brent made it a hit. It was *her* show, in other words—but Jimmy saw her as an interloper in his world. And Jimmy didn't hold back when sharing his impressions with a local sports columnist during a 1977 visit to Michigan.

"You look at her on the screen, this gorgeous girl, and you know a lot of guys are having bad thoughts," the Greek told George Puscas of the *Detroit Free Press*. "We all considered her like a kid sister, a good kid, which she is, so sweet, a great gal . . . Actually, she's the dumbest broad. They had to prime her and tell her everything to say and write it all out on cards."

Today, a comment like that would instantly go national. In 1977, it basically went unnoticed until *People* magazine recycled it for page filler, where Phyllis read it a month later. She was furious—but Jimmy denied making the comments, and their CBS bosses underreacted. Yet it fit in with his pattern of behavior toward her, she said—derisive comments with sexual overtones muttered under his breath just seconds before they would go on air.

When CBS Sports begged Phyllis to come back after a two-year absence, she was eager to make up for lost time. She was also a little insecure about the very public weight gain that had drawn taunts from the tabloid press at a time when few other famous women let themselves be photographed while pregnant. Her much-hyped return pushed Jimmy out of his seat, to a standing spot at the end of the desk, and undeniably cost him some airtime. But it was a stressful environment for everyone—four big personalities on a top-rated show that had made them all stars, but with barely twenty-two minutes to split among them.

One night after the show, about a month into Phyllis's return, Jimmy punched Brent in the jaw at a Manhattan bar, during a blustery spat over Jimmy's diminished status. Phyllis wasn't even there. But it was her oversized glamour shot the *New York Post* put on the front page, with the headline: "Face that Launched a Barroom Brawl."

The *NFL Today* team tried to laugh it off on the next episode— Phyllis ringing a bell and shouting "Round Two!" to introduce Jimmy's game-day predictions, Brent wearing boxing gloves. But tensions still seethed.

And a month later came the day when he made her cry on set.

Years later, Phyllis would express sympathy for Jimmy, a son of hard-scrabble Steubenville, Ohio, who lost his mother at age nine to an angry man with a gun, who lost three children to cystic fibrosis, and who would eventually lose the CBS job over his bunglingly offensive commentary about slavery producing superior athletes.

She would remain extremely proud, though, of how she dealt with their clash. How she had stood up for herself, told her bosses she would not be treated this way.

That wasn't all she did.

Her contract was up for renewal, and her CBS bosses had made it publicly clear that, yes, yes, of course they wanted Phyllis back on *NFL Today* next season.

But Phyllis didn't give them an answer.

She gave interviews letting it be known that she was terribly busy as Kentucky's first lady. She pointedly took a substitute-host gig over at ABC's *Good Morning America*. She kept everyone guessing for months, all through the summer, until about two weeks before the start of the next football season.

And only then did she sign a new deal, with one key condition—that she never have to appear on set with Jimmy the Greek again.

It was a deal that radically altered the dynamic of a hit show: The Greek was relegated to pre-taped spots and cut out of the live banter. But Phyllis had drawn her line in the sand. She said she simply couldn't maintain her enthusiasm, her energy, her buoyant on-air magic, with Jimmy in the room.

And CBS agreed. CBS chose her.

Jimmy had his fan base, but Phyllis was the star. She had the glossy gravitas of women like Barbara Walters and Jessica Savitch, who had been ushered into network anchor chairs a few years earlier. From the time her career at CBS took off, it was whispered that sooner or later, she might be groomed for one of these roles, too—but now she had firmly established her value to the network.

And when she finally got the call, in October 1984, to move to the news division as a morning-show host, it looked like the obvious next step in a ten-year climb, with many more levels yet to come.

◆   ◆   ◆

A funny thing about her move to *CBS Morning News*. After a full decade as simply *Phyllis George*, she was once again getting written up as a "former Miss America."

Morning TV had been built on the backs of "personalities" with credentials as eclectic as Phyllis's, if not more so. The first host of NBC's *Today* in the early 1950s was Dave Garroway, a jazz DJ occasionally paired with a trained chimpanzee. David Hartman, the longtime host of *Good Morning America*, had joined the show as an actor with no journalism credentials. Even the newswomen who cohosted the rival morning shows in the 1980s, Joan Lunden at ABC and Jane Pauley at NBC, had been propelled into those coveted seats after just a couple of years of local-news experience. And Bryant Gumbel, the new anchor of *Today*, had come to that job after working exclusively in sports.

But at CBS, Phyllis was walking into a culture clash that predated her arrival. The news division, infused with the values of Edward R. Murrow and Walter Cronkite, had long been the pride of the network, buffered from petty commercial concerns. That had begun to change in the early 1980s, under a series of leaders slid in from other corporate roles without a news background. Their push for zippier graphics, emotion-packed moments, and magazine-style shows chafed the sensibilities of journalism traditionalists. And the pressure was highest at that moment on *CBS Morning News*, which had trailed *Today* and *Good Morning America* in the ratings for years. Even Diane Sawyer, the future broadcasting legend, had barely averted being fired from the morning job a couple years earlier as network executives agonized over the show's flagging performance. Now, as she prepared to leap to *60 Minutes* in 1984, CBS brass pushed news executives to replace Diane with someone "presold"—a talent "already known to viewers," as one of them put it; perhaps an actress or variety-show host?

In many ways, then, Phyllis was a deft compromise choice—not a traditional hard-news veteran, but at least a seasoned broadcaster with a track record of serious interviews for CBS Sports.

It didn't matter. CBS news staff still openly decried the hiring of Miss America 1971 as the ultimate selling out.

"It's the last straw," former CBS News president Richard Salant told the *New York Times*, "on the question of where the hell are we being made to go these days."

Phyllis was under the impression that they would remake *CBS Morning News* in her image—a bright, casual gabfest like *Good Morning America*. But they didn't quite do that, nor did they make much attempt to retrain her as a serious newswoman.

Critics noted that while she lit up the screen as usual, she looked uncomfortable doing interviews and seemed to cling to her notes. The press ruthlessly chronicled every tiny gaffe. She asked Billy Crystal about his famous impersonation of Fernando Lamas and whether the Argentine movie star had ever called him about it—and when the comedian dryly noted that Fernando had died a couple years earlier, she was roundly scorned. Never mind that Fernando had indeed seen the routine before his death, his son later said, and loved it. She was chided for cutting off slow-talking Nobel laureate Linus Pauling as the show was hurtling toward a commercial break. Never mind that cutting guests short is a daily hazard of live TV. She was mocked when she described Andrew Lloyd Webber as the composer of *"Jesus Christ Superstore."* Never mind that it was an ordinary slip of the tongue.

Phyllis was baffled by the reaction.

"Am I the kind of person people want to go after?" she wondered out loud to a reporter. "I don't think I am. I never have been. I'm the least controversial person I know, to become so controversial."

Her sprawling, restless ambition had brought Phyllis so far, so fast. But wanting *everything* left her vulnerable. It was all too easy to let others dictate what *everything* should entail.

CBS news execs warmed to Phyllis—who didn't? And they noted how confident she was doing the softer-side stuff they had hired her for—interviews with movie stars or health experts. But then her agent would show up and whisper that she should be doing bigger, heavier-hitting interviews like her cohost Bill Kurtis. And her anxiety about this would manifest on air.

And then came The Hug.

It's often described as the time that Phyllis George urged a rape victim and the man she wrongly accused to hug on live TV. But the backstory was darker and sadder and weirder. The "victim" was Cathleen Crowell Webb, who as a troubled teenager had fabricated a rape claim because she feared she was pregnant and would get in trouble for having sex. When she picked out Gary Dotson's face from a mug shot, he was convicted and sentenced to twenty-five to fifty years. Eight years later, she found religion and came forward to recant. When he was released from prison in May 1985, the two were swept up together in a warped media circus, all three networks vying to book them as their consultants attempted to nail down movie or publishing deals.

In Phyllis's telling, CBS had given up on trying to arrange an interview because the duo had already committed to same-day spots on NBC and ABC—but then they showed up unexpectedly at the network's Manhattan studio later that morning. Phyllis was pushed in front of a camera with them, with inadequate briefing on their complex saga. Then again, she *had* been pestering her bosses for bigger interviews. With a panicked sense she had to "go a different route" than other interviewers, Phyllis's softer-side instincts kicked in; she smilingly asked

Gary about his movie offers and whether he felt "like a celebrity." In closing, she suggested: "How about a hug?" And they declined.

The reviews were scathing.

"Perhaps only Phyllis George would see this bizarre rape case as a story about celebrityhood," wrote Tom Shales of the *Washington Post*.

Phyllis fretted over these reviews all summer, and those ratings she knew she was expected to jolt but which refused to budge. She took some unexpected time off. In August 1985, just eight months after she had been hired, CBS News president Ed Joyce called her at her home in Kentucky to tell her she was being replaced.

"I won't pretend I'm not very, very hurt by this," he recalled her saying. "But I'm a big girl and I'll get over it."

As he got off the phone, he realized this was probably the first big rejection of her life.

✦   ✦   ✦

Phyllis had other acts after that. How could she not? She launched a line of pre-marinated cook-at-home chicken breast entrees ("Chicken by George") and promoted the heck out of it, then sold the brand to Hormel. She wrote a self-help book. She even made her acting debut, at age fifty-one, a tiny role in *Meet the Parents* as the immaculate mother of the groom at the wedding weekend ruined by hapless Ben Stiller.

But while she did other TV shows, they were small, lower-profile, short-lived. Her fireball of a broadcast career, fueled by that larking, breathless charisma, hit a brick wall in 1985.

And it devastated her. What happened at CBS ate at her every day for a decade at least, her children say. She never really got over it.

"She had these huge dreams, and then this big failure. And she could never get back to where she was," says her daughter, Pam.

Miss America put Phyllis at the top of her generation at the right place and time—unlocking ambitions a girl from Denton might otherwise never have realized she had, opening the doors that would let her fulfill them. That made everything that came after so much harder—or perhaps left her a little less prepared to cope with it.

Her marriage failed, too, after John Y.'s political career petered out, and the excitement of a shared mission that amplified the rush of new love was gone. She struggled with money, having always had so much from a young age that she never learned how to manage it.

Her obsession with keeping up appearances was why she never spoke publicly about the other life-altering development of 1985. She was so sick that year but assumed it was just the stress of traveling between New York and Kentucky, between children and work, and her growing unhappiness in the CBS job. It wasn't until she threw up in the tulips one morning that her dad insisted she see a doctor. This was not "exhaustion" or "nerves" or any other common malady of the spotlight. It was polycythemia vera, the rare blood disorder she would grapple with for the rest of her life.

Could her diagnosis have bought a measure of understanding from the CBS executives who were losing patience with her? Maybe. But it wasn't Phyllis's style to share her struggles. Nor could she march back to her producers and demand better guidance, as she had after the Fiesta Bowl—not when she was already a star.

Her son, Lincoln, thinks she should have stayed in sports, deploying her uncommon emotional intelligence and affinity for athletes in human-interest stories. But Phyllis had been there, done that. She probably wasn't a natural for news, he says: She didn't love the hours of research needed for a serious interview.

"But if they gave her more time there," he says, "she would have figured it out."

Phyllis George got too big before she could find her lane. And she was hardly the only woman in television to be promoted too far, too soon, and dropped too quickly. But others would learn from her experience.

Twenty-one years after Phyllis left CBS, another gorgeous young woman barreled out of the South to launch a broadcast career in the big city. Pamela Brown also had great hair, strong bone structure, and unexpected dimples, and her arrival in Washington generated the kind of buzz that can open doors—though she had never even entered a single beauty pageant.

But Pam kept her head down. She skipped most of the parties. She worked all the time, gritty assignments that had less to do with interviewing famous people than reporting from the scene of house fires in the middle of the night. Unlike her mother, she was an introvert by nature who didn't find it hard to resist the invitations. But to the extent she was driven by perceptions, it presented in a concern that her bosses and colleagues recognize how hard she worked.

Life as an It Girl, she had come to realize, was not a sustainable career path.

This was something Pam and her brother had talked about a few years earlier, when she first toyed with the idea of an on-camera career, either in acting or as a showbiz correspondent. Ironically, in his dad-like lecture, Lincoln didn't cite their mom's career. He reached for more timely examples—Britney Spears, Jessica Simpson. But they both knew what fame had done to Phyllis.

Phyllis was thrilled by Pam's career. And when Pam moved up to CNN, after several years at a local station, Phyllis watched her segments faithfully, and texted her every time, often with bits of professional advice—fix your hair, boost your energy—mixed in with the praise.

"She was my biggest advocate," says Pam, who was promoted to an anchor job at CNN in 2021. "Her pain was my gain, in a way."

3

"THEY CAN EXPLOIT ME ANY DAY"

1970s

On a Saturday in November 1971, a young professional singer named Terry Meeuwsen left her parents' home in De Pere, Wisconsin, and drove an hour south to catch up with Phyllis George, who was in town to host the Miss Fond du Lac pageant.

At twenty-two, Terry was in the grips of a spiritual awakening—and a major career crisis.

Three years earlier, she had dropped out of college after her freshman year. Not because she was burned out: She was burning with ambition. And the world was moving so fast, she feared she would never catch up if she spent another three years at sleepy St. Norbert College. She had grown up in the crowded classrooms of the boomer generation, keenly aware of the competition. The Rodgers & Hammerstein musicals she once dreamed of starring in were losing ground to harder-edged fare—*Easy Rider, Hair*—and she was anxious to find her foothold as a performer.

That's why she had leapt at a chance to audition in 1969 for the New Christy Minstrels, a folk-music ensemble with a couple pop-chart hits to its name—and at the call that came two weeks later to join the band.

The clean-cut group sang old-timey tunes with a hootenanny vibe; they still filled concert halls, and some alums of the ever-churning lineup, including Kenny Rogers and Barry McGuire, had gone on to bigger things. Terry knew a band member through her aunt and uncle who had helped her jump the line at the cattle call. But she was pretty compelling in her own right, a former Miss Green Bay with brimming eyes and an ear-to-ear smile—an electric mix of Mary Tyler Moore and the Cheshire Cat. She spent the next two years traveling the world with the Minstrels, polishing her act, learning to project her clear, bright soprano over the deeper, older voices on stage.

With their plaid shirts and upbeat harmonies, the Minstrels came off as squares. But they were young adults earning good money in show business at the height of the counterculture. The road was a nonstop party—alcohol, drugs, and diet pills—and Terry indulged like all the rest. One night, the Kingston Trio turned the Minstrels on to a strain of marijuana called Acapulco Gold; she remembered little else of that evening. Within the band there were cliques and rivalries and a pressure to keep up. A once sheltered Lutheran girl, Terry started taking birth control pills, she later wrote, "and entered into a series of liaisons to prove to myself that I, too, could be sophisticated and worldly."

She didn't recognize how unhappy she was until a chance encounter in a Texas diner with a young fan who talked to her about Jesus and shared a pamphlet extolling God's power of love and forgiveness. Soon, Terry was looking for a new way to live, a more wholesome way to pursue a career in show business.

She had met Phyllis when the reigning Miss America performed with the Christy Minstrels in a Bob Hope show in Oklahoma City. And now Terry wanted the advice of this woman who was four months younger than herself, and also still searching yet already a couple steps ahead.

"Well, if you could do anything now, what would you do?" Phyllis asked.

Terry said that she wanted to study acting in New York. But she couldn't afford it.

"Why don't you enter the Miss America pageant," Phyllis said, "and try and win enough scholarship money?"

And with that, Terry had a plan so bold that she laughs out loud now to think of it. She packed her bags, moved to a town called Appleton, and signed up for classes at the community college to qualify as a bona fide student, eligible to compete in the local pageant.

For at some point along the way, Terry had resolved that *this* was the moonshot course she *had* to take in life, that the one and only way she could further her professional ambitions was not just by entering the Miss America pageant but by winning the whole thing.

"What was I thinking that that sounded like a logical idea?" she says nearly fifty years later. "It's beyond crazy!"

Today, it's hard to imagine Terry Meeuwsen as a culture-disrupter. She is the longtime cohost of the Christian Broadcasting Network's *700 Club*, where she exudes an old-school femininity and conservatism, eyes luminous as ever as she waits out an extended soliloquy from the show's ninety-year-old founder, Pat Robertson. Even in 1971, you might have mistaken her at first for a traditional pageant girl—sweet, earnest, and knockout gorgeous.

Yet she would become one of a series of Miss Americas who jolted the pageant of the 1970s, as they hauled its prim traditions into a bell-bottom decade.

More worldly and opinionated from the outset than earlier winners of the pageant—and notably older—their paradoxes would fascinate a public still trying to make sense of the sixties youthquake and women's liberation. And they would try to put the pageant in its place—treating it less as a crowning glory of girlhood than as a stepping stone to the new kinds of grown-up ambitions suddenly opening to all young women.

✦   ✦   ✦

"Do blondes really have more fun?" a reporter asked Judi Ford, shortly after her crowning in 1968.

"I've never been a brunette to compare it with," she responded.

This was the kind of inquiry that greeted a new Miss America in the mid-1960s. After the dreamlike victory lap—a crown pinned teeteringly to her hair, the tearful walk down the runway—she would meet the press, and the contours of her sudden new fame would snap into focus.

The questions were puffy, polite, and apolitical. When Debbie Bryant greeted reporters in three news conferences during her first thirty-six hours as Miss America, she divulged her hopes for becoming a pediatrician—a rare goal for a young woman in 1965. But the press focused on other things.

> *When Deborah Bryant was 12 years old, she was chubby and had freckles. The Kansas beauty still has the freckles but today she reigns as Miss America in slim loveliness.*
>
> *"I work quite hard at keeping my figure," said Debbie, 19, a resident of Overland Park, a Kansas City suburb. "I just love hamburgers. Eat them all the time."*

This Associated Press story generated giddy nonsense headlines across the nation: "Ex-Chubby, Miss America Still Fond of Hamburgers," "Hamburger-Eating Beauty Wins Miss America Title," "Non-Chubby Debbie Still Has Freckles."

But in her third meeting with the press, at New York's Hotel Barclay, Debbie did get thrown a curveball. One reporter asked about a criticism filtering up through civil rights circles: Why didn't Miss America have any Negro contestants?

"I don't know about it," Debbie replied, as Lenora Slaughter, the pageant's executive director, brought the press conference to a hasty end.

"She shouldn't have to answer a question about a national problem," Lenora chided the journalists as she hustled Debbie out of the room. "She's not the president."

The questions were about to get harder. For more than forty years, the purpose and meaning of Miss America—the reasons for the pageant's very existence—had gone largely unquestioned. But now it was an institution, and a wildly successful one, with an identity tied grandly to a notion of ideal young American womanhood, at a time when all institutions were being challenged, and young people were leading the way. If someone was going to go around calling herself "Miss America," the press reasoned, it was of public interest what she thought about the women's movement, about civil rights and the fiery protests on campuses and in the streets.

And yet, Miss America was an institution beholden to corporate sponsors and heartland volunteers. It would have to step carefully through these culture wars. And the newly crowned Miss Americas swiftly internalized the institution's strategy, most of them well before Miss Slaughter would ever have to body-block a bunch of reporters.

"I'm a firm believer in authority," Pamela Eldred said after her 1969 crowning, to explain why she hadn't developed any political opinions worth mentioning. "The people who were voted into office must have the intelligence to know what to do."

Even Phyllis George—whose later broadcast career was fueled by her innate good-ol'-girl spontaneity—edged cautiously around controversy in 1970.

What did she think about the women's movement? one reporter asked.

"I'm interested in finding out more about it," Phyllis said. "Down in Texas we don't hear much about it at all."

It was "no comment," translated into the language of *bless-her-heart*.

And then came Laurie Lea Schaefer.

Miss America 1972 was hardly a revolutionary. She was an aspiring musical-comedy star and Nixon fan from Bexley, Ohio, devoutly religious, with thick brown hair and a pert chin. She had never owned a pair of blue jeans. The most radical thing the press could perceive about her on her first night as Miss America was that she had competed an astonishing three times at Miss Ohio before finally making it to Atlantic City. Yet in any inherently conservative organization, change, when it happens, will have been pushed by conservatives. And Laurie was no debutante. She was twenty-two years old—the oldest Miss America in two decades.

Yes, she had made three attempts at Miss Ohio. The first time because her sorority at Ohio University asked her to represent it at Miss Southern Ohio. And even though she was so clueless that she had to wear her mom's oversized tent dress to the interview because she neglected to bring a proper suit and gloves—she won. Over-coached and over-groomed for the state pageant, she failed to place, but the next year, as a sophomore who'd figured it all out, she returned to the state pageant as Miss Central Ohio and made the Top 10. The third time—well, there almost wasn't a third time. She was a little cocky going through the Miss Ohio University pageant with all that experience . . . and was mortified to come in second. The next morning, the frat brothers who organized the pageant buzzed in on her sorority house intercom. There was a mix-up, they told her. The emcee read the names wrong: Laurie *did* win! Calls were made to the state pageant, but there was nothing to be done, they couldn't take that crown from the other girl. Still, would Laurie come to the pageant anyway to perform with the professional entertainers?

So she did. And she was so much more relaxed than she had been in competition. People noticed. And a few months later, in her senior year, when the man from Miss Central Ohio called and said: "Laurie, will you give it one more shot, just to be able to tell yourself you did all you could do?"—she said yes.

This was the new kind of girl entering the Miss America pageant. She may have looked a lot like the past winners and shared most of their values—but she was a product of the baby boom, someone who had had to wait her turn amid the crushing competition and fight a little harder for it. And realized along the way that she *liked* the fight. This was the case with jobs and admissions to elite schools, of course, but also at Miss America, whose local contests in 1970 drew an estimated seventy thousand women. Some in those days, like Judi, had won it all on their very first try. Laurie had not, so she kept going, in search of a personal best.

"The goal was not to be Miss America," she says. "It was to see how far I could go."

It was that outlook, common to a generation, that may have explained a sharp increase in the average age of Miss America—from just over nineteen in the 1960s to well past twenty-one in the 1970s. Half the women crowned in the sixties were teenagers; since then, only four have been under twenty. Laurie was a more confident Miss America than the pageant was used to, the first in twenty years crowned with a bachelor's degree completed.

And when the journalists asked about her politics, she shared them. "I am a conservative," she told the press. "I'm very proud of that."

The night after her crowning, Laurie and her mother dined with pageant officials at the Rainbow Room atop New York's Rockefeller Center, discussing the logistics of her upcoming year. Their cautions were subtle, but she could catch their drift—that it would be best if she were not to offer her opinions on controversial subjects.

Why, she could just respond with "no comment," they suggested, or "I don't feel comfortable answering that."

But Laurie suggested to her new bosses that they let her at least *try* to field controversial questions. Because at that first press conference, she had found herself intrigued by these questions—and by the unexpected interest these journalists had in what she, twenty-two-year-old Laurie Lea Schaefer of Bexley, Ohio, thought about the state of the world.

And Laurie—a member of the women's auxiliary for the Ohio University Air Force ROTC—certainly had opinions. In May 1970, the outrage over the National Guard shootings of unarmed student antiwar protesters at nearby Kent State University had spilled over onto her own campus; the building that housed the ROTC supply closet was firebombed. Wearing her uniform, she had been jeered at by protesters. She was dismayed to realize that actual combat veterans were getting similar treatment. So she suggested that the Miss America leadership let her focus on some talking points. That instead of letting her press interviews drift into talk of boyfriends or hair care, she could emphasize her concern for supporting the troops.

Laurie was a little ahead of her time: It would be twenty years before the Miss America Organization would require its titleholders to take up an advocacy cause. And a review of Laurie's press coverage suggests her issue rarely broke through with journalists.

But they were undeniably beguiled by this outspoken beauty queen. Laurie Lea Schaefer felt that drugs were a serious problem on campus. She didn't believe in sex before marriage. Yes, she supported President Nixon on Vietnam, she told a reporter, but while "America's intentions were originally honorable and just, the situation has turned sour. Certainly the war should end, but I'd hate to think the thousands of dead and wounded have suffered in vain."

She chafed at being pigeonholed as conservative. On the once-taboo subject of abortion, she insisted on nuance. "Every woman should have the right to decide whether she wants to bring a child into the world," Laurie told another newspaper. "But the sanctity of life must be preserved. And if easily obtained abortions leads to promiscuity, then I'm against that."

"The first Miss America to give her views on controversial issues," a UPI correspondent marveled. In truth, she sounded like a very young woman still trying to figure them out. But she was doing it out loud and in public.

◆   ◆   ◆

In September 1972, Bert Parks was hosting the Miss America pageant for the eighteenth time, and his smarmy grin and booming delivery, honed during the early days of radio, were beginning to feel like camp.

Lord knows, he wasn't doing much anymore to help earn cred with young viewers. One of the longest-running shows on television was an anthology with an ever-changing cast, thanks to the rule that let no woman compete at the national level more than once. And so Miss America's default face was a middle-aged man—a human manifestation of the patriarchal vibe that so chafed the feminists about the pageant. And sometimes Bert just couldn't help himself.

"Debra, you are *tall!*" he greeted Miss Kansas Debra Barnes on the pageant broadcast in 1967, shortly before she was crowned Miss America. "But *pretty*. Tall and pretty!"

But his defenders—and there are still many—recall Bert's warmth and professionalism. "You look beautiful," he whispered on stage to Debbie Bryant in 1965, noticing her jitters, and it was the confidence-booster she needed in that moment. Plus, the cornball humor and vaudevillian gestures that left TV audiences cringing constituted exactly the kind of energy an emcee needed to command the cavernous Convention Hall.

On one occasion, though, Bert delivered a moment of divine made-for-TV subtlety. It came just after Terry Meeuwsen—that road-weary

veteran of the New Christy Minstrels who was now Miss Wisconsin—
performed in the talent round.

Reader, she crushed it. All those years on the road paid off as she
eased with exquisite control into "He Touched Me"—a yearning ballad
that had been a minor Barbra Streisand hit. Lilting and sighing through
the sweet opening lines (*He put his hand near mine and then he touched
me . . .*), Terry built to a soaring head-thrown-back Broadway finish with
a from-the-gut growl (*Suddenly . . . nothing, nothing is the same!*). Just
like a professional.

As she skipped off stage, Bert beamed warmly in her direction. Then
he turned and shot the camera a knowing look—shaking his head as if
dazed, eyes wide with amused wonder. It was a look that simultaneously
said *Hoo, boy!* and *We all know how this is going to end tonight.*

So of course Terry Meeuwsen was going to win. As soon as everyone
stopped talking about Miss Vermont.

Miss Vermont was never going to win. But during pageant week,
while Terry was collecting all the preliminary trophies for swimsuit and
talent, she was completely upstaged in the eyes of the press by twenty-
one-year-old Kathy Hebert of Burlington.

On Labor Day, Ewart Rouse, a young reporter in the Associated
Press's Atlantic City bureau, showed up at the reception hall where the
press had a first opportunity to mingle with the arriving contestants,
most of them decked out incongruously for a beach resort in wool suits
and high-heeled pumps. He ran into a journalist friend, an older woman
who wrote for the local society page.

"Ewart," Ellie said, "you aren't going to believe this."

Ellie told him she had just interviewed the most offbeat contestant
she had encountered in her years of covering the pageant. She pointed
her out: the young woman with the flowing halter maxi-dress and big
head of curls, sitting at a table with her chaperone, all but ignored by
the other reporters, who were busy swarming the glossier state queens.

Ewart beelined. In Kathy's recollection, the reporter got to the point
quickly: What did she think about the Vietnam War?

Well, Kathy deplored the war; she had marched against the war,
and she told him so. His eyes lit up. He asked about her views on

premarital sex. She was decidedly in favor. And the interview was off and running.

"I can't believe I'm here," she told him. "This is not the real me."

Kathy tended to laugh every time she said something controversial— as if she knew darn well it would be controversial—and Ewart took it all in. Kathy Hebert was a *great* story. But he knew Ellie wouldn't write it. She was a lifelong resident of Atlantic City, invested in helping Miss America uphold its old-fashioned ideals—and perhaps reluctant to embarrass a young woman she took to be naïve about the ways of the pageant. But Ewart was younger and hungrier; for him, the pageant was no sacred cow but a curious slice of anthropology. On Tuesday, hundreds of newspapers across the country carried his story:

> ATLANTIC CITY, N.J.—"My dad calls me a kooky freak. . . . I believe in astrology and my sign says I'm schizophrenic. I sit here and I watch the other girls and it's like watching television in color. I can't believe I'm here."
>
> Miss Vermont, 21-year-old Kathy Hebert, one of the 50 contestants in the Miss America 1973 pageant, sounded lost during registration at the Chalfonte-Haddon Hall yesterday.
>
> "I can't believe it," the contestant, who was dressed in a floral print long gown, kept saying, half to herself. "This is not the real me. If I were to be my real self, I'd be here in hot socks, jeans, T-shirt, no bra and with my hair hanging loose and natural.
>
> "Were I to become Miss America, I'd change the whole concept of Miss America."
>
> Miss Hebert, a hazel-eyed ash blonde, said she was aware she wasn't exactly the "typical" Miss America contestant. "I'm anti-Nixon, I've demonstrated against the war, I support Jane Fonda, and believe in premarital sex," she said without pause or prompting.

That morning, every reporter at the pageant put in a request to talk to Kathy. "Miss Vermont's Views Shake Up Status Quo," declared the *Camden Courier-Post.*

"I think it's a shame they let her in," a scandalized pageant volunteer told the paper. Miss Vermont was "getting all the publicity" at the expense of the "nice" girls.

The curious thing about the stories on the Miss Vermont controversy is that Kathy hadn't *done* anything. She had simply given an interview stating opinions shared by a significant portion of the population under thirty. And that was okay! The Laurie Lea Schaefer experiment had worked out just fine, as far as longtime Miss America board chairman Albert Marks was concerned; he ruled that contestants were now free to talk to reporters about any controversial topics they pleased—part of his attempt to melt Miss America's "plastic image."

But the Miss Vermont controversy quickly became a real-life thing. It was a distillation of everything that had always been fraught about the pageant—this game of putting young women under a spotlight to judge their abstract appeal—but intensified by 1972's anxieties about what women wanted and what the kids were really up to these days. At the Miss America parade on the Boardwalk, Kathy's float got a rude silence as it passed the reviewing stands; some spectators made faces at her. Al Marks defended her outspokenness to reporters but sidled up to her later with a warning, she recalls: "If I find out this is a publicity stunt . . ." Every meal was interrupted by a request for another press interview. The world wanted to know: Who was this radical chick out to disrupt the Miss America pageant?

Yes, she was the bona fide bohemian she appeared to be—a Pratt Institute design student who sewed her own pageant wardrobe, a guitar-playing folkie with the very 1972 talent of singing "I Don't Know How to Love Him" from *Jesus Christ Superstar* in a muslin gown. With her head of tumbling natural curls, she was "one of the few contestants who looks more like Barbra Streisand than Grace Kelly," marveled the *Philadelphia Inquirer*. But she was also a naïve and searching small-town kid, her mind still blown by her move to Brooklyn for college. "I believed in my church, I believed in my government, I believed in people I trusted who would not steer me wrong," she says now. Kathy may have been a free spirit, but she did not yet feel free and easy in her own skin.

What on Earth was she doing in a beauty pageant? "My mother signed me up," she says. She knew she was overweight. But "at that point, I didn't know how to say no to people." She won Miss Vermont on her second try after pageant organizers urged her to drop thirty pounds and try again; only six other women competed, and the struggling state pageant had to mount a special fundraiser to send her to Atlantic City— outwardly optimistic that the national judges might see her as the perfect "new generation" ambassador.

Kathy knew she wasn't going to win. But she was beginning, in small ways, to find her voice. She was done with people telling her what to say or how to say it. She resolved that whatever anyone asked her, she would tell them—truthfully. "The best thing to happen to Atlantic City since salt-water taffy," the *Inquirer* declared. "A delightful contrast to the all-too-familiar Miss America contestants who dutifully say precisely the right things and never come off their pedestal."

By her third day of national fame, though, Kathy was a mess. She never wanted the attention, but there she was—the counterculture's unofficial representative to the Olympics of American femininity.

"I'm not really in it for myself anymore," she told a reporter. "I'm in it for the youth of America. And not just the freaks. Anyone who wants to be themselves." Stressed out, she sobbed before taking the stage for the talent competition, her strongest area. She did not win a prize.

Al Marks pulled her aside again. "Are you okay?" he asked. It was a nice gesture—albeit one he promptly described to the journalists eager for the latest Miss Vermont news.

The high point came, unexpectedly, courtesy of Walter Cronkite. The CBS anchorman sent a camera crew to interview her. But instead of demanding her views on sex or marijuana like everyone else, they took her down to the beach, in her homemade red-velvet pantsuit and platform shoes. "Just talk," they told her—whatever she wanted to say, for as long as she wanted. It was the calmest she felt all week.

At their final breakfast, the morning after Terry Meeuwsen was crowned Miss America and the world finally looked away from Miss Vermont, Kathy had a chance to talk with some of her fellow contestants— the women she had never quite gotten to know because the press had pulled her away from every meal. Some wanted her to know that they agreed with her on these so-called controversial issues. But they weren't ready to say so in public. Not yet.

✦   ✦   ✦

The press cast a suspicious eye upon Terry Meeuwsen at first. It had less to do with the new Miss America's advanced age—at twenty-three, Terry was more than a year older than even Laurie at her crowning— than her unusually robust résumé.

The *New York Daily News* tsk-tsked that her journey to Miss America "began with a calculated decision to enter a local beauty contest to further her professional singing career." She "used the stage presence and experience gained through two years of singing with the New Christy Minstrels," the story continued, as if exposing an Olympic hopeful as a slick veteran of the Ice Capades.

Of course, Terry's maturity and performing panache were almost certainly the reason she won—the qualities that set her apart from a field of sorority pledges and music majors. And the truth was, as Miss America, she was an immediate hit.

"The most heavily booked winner I can recall," Al Marks boasted. "Terry seems to have more personality and charisma than our former winners . . . She has the verve, the personality, the femininity, and the talent that convention managers find desirable."

Today, you can sense her discomfort as Terry recalls this kind of talk. Miss Americas value humility; they are loath to present themselves in competition with their Miss America sisters. "Al Marks liked to stir up the pot," she sighs.

But her crowning truly was a shot in the arm for a rattled institution. Even while television ratings remained stratospheric, the blistering criticism sparked by the women's liberation protest had begun to go mainstream. Pepsi-Cola suspended its longtime sponsorship in 1969, deciding that its primary market was cool young urbanites, and Miss America just didn't "represent the changing values of our society." The University of North Carolina student newspaper called in 1972 for the banning of all beauty pageants, "an outright insult to women, who are individuals not mere objects of ogling on the part of males and wishful thinking on the part of females." Dissidents began to make their voices heard: "I was named Miss Congeniality, but I'm not so congenial anymore," declared Miss Michigan 1942 Patricia Hill Burnett, campaigning in 1973 to join the board of the new National Organization of Women. "We were badly used, virtual slaves to the organization."

Terry was as conservative as other Miss Americas of the era, a Nixon fan who spoke passionately about her faith. But she also came out swinging in defense of the pageant at a time it needed it most.

"If this is exploitation," she told the press, citing the scholarship and appearance fees she would collect as Miss America, "then they can exploit me any day."

Four years after the watershed 1968 protest, here was Miss America's retort to the women's movement—an accomplished young professional who had happily accepted the Miss America crown. She was at ease with the press: "What qualifies Terry Meeuwsen to tell girls how to behave?" she parried when asked her opinion on premarital sex. She was a stylish dresser: When she met President Nixon at the White House, she eschewed a ladies-who-lunch frock for a modish dark velvet suit with an ankle-skimming skirt and a groovy spread collar. She carried herself like the new breed of sporty young single women with office jobs and apartments and VW Beetles, or at least their sitcom embodiments, like Marlo Thomas or Mary Tyler Moore.

Here, finally, was a new archetype for Miss America. No longer the debutante but the career girl—a bold but safe step forward. The world was changing for young Americans of all political stripes, after all. And you didn't have to agree with the feminists about the Equal Rights Amendment or leg-shaving to endorse the idea of women entering the workforce and earning a living for themselves. Al started talking about Miss America as a job, and a damned good one. He bragged that Terry was on track to earn a record $125,000 from all her bookings that year. She actually maxed out at about $83,000, according to later accounts— nearly half a million in today's dollars.

And by the time she was ready to give up her crown in September 1973, the Miss America pageant was ready to *own* this spirit of now.

"Movin' on! We got to be moo-oovin' on!" sang a chorus of show-biz pros as the Miss America hopefuls circled in a rococo parade of multicolored bell sleeves, empire waists, halter necks, and ruffled collars.

Sure, it was still your mother's pageant in most ways. The contestants minced in the shoes dyed to match their pointy-boobed, hip-covering swimsuits. They all seemed to be music majors, trained to deliver a highbrow repertoire of piano sonatas and operatic arias. Bert Parks at one point slipped up and referred to them fondly as "little girls." But the pageant was trying its darndest to signal solidarity with this new era. Miss America 1965, Vonda Kay Van Dyke, sang "Aquarius" with a cadre of groovy dancers. Bert broke out a heavy rap: "Is personal achievement relevant? Is scholarship relevant? . . . That's what Miss America is all about, that's what the youth of America is all about! Ever learning and expanding to meet the needs of tomorrow!" And there was the women's lib anthem written just for the pageant, sung by a shoulder-shimmying Phyllis George and two former state winners in swingy halter dresses.

Why won't you keep a woman in mind
when you're trying to find a plumber?
I want you to call me! I said, call me!
But when you call me—
Call me 'Ms.'!

And yet a shock went through the pageant world when they crowned Miss America 1974. In the gaggle of bouffants and Opry-caliber curls, Rebecca King looked like a flower child by comparison, in her long, straight Jan Brady hair and simple white spaghetti-strap gown.

Rebecca was undeniably attractive, a preppy-looking blonde who could have been a cousin to the new school of low-maintenance cover girls, like Patti Hansen and Lauren Hutton. She barely wore any makeup—a little mascara and lip gloss—but it was the seventies, almost none of them did. And she was hardly a flower child: While the press heralded her liberal stances on marijuana, abortion, and the ERA, she was also a Republican who yearned to see Barry Goldwater as president and did not dig protest marches. "I was more of a women's libber," she says now, "than a liberal."

Yet in a couple key ways she broke the Miss America mold. If you could call Terry's pursuit of the crown "calculated," then Rebecca was unusually candid about her calculations.

"She's in It for the Money," gasped one headline.

Indeed, Rebecca said that she had entered the competition solely to pay for law school. She wanted to be a lawyer—a first for Miss America—and eventually, a judge. And when Bert Parks called her name at the end, she smiled and waved—but unlike virtually every Miss America in history, she did not cry. Not a tear. "I'm very surprised," was all she said, in her low and serene anchorwoman voice, sounding not very.

"I've never been a particularly emotional person," she explained later when asked about her unnerving non-hysteria. "I don't feel like crying."

And for these reasons, Rebecca King was a "controversial" Miss America. She was invited to emcee the Rose Bowl parade, toasted in the pages of *Vogue*, and beloved by the corporate sponsors, some of whom kept her on contract for years after her reign. Yet in the weeks after her crowning, more than two hundred pageant watchers wrote to the Miss America organization to complain—criticizing the judging process, her looks, her support of marijuana legalization ("give the crown to the first runner-up before she disgraces us with her pot opinion"), and calling upon Senator Sam Ervin, the leader of the Watergate probe, to turn his investigatory powers to the pageant.

Of course, we only know about this backlash because the chairman of the Miss America pageant chose to share these incredibly mean letters with the press.

This was typical of Al Marks, an Atlantic City stockbroker in his early sixties, whose mythmaking impulses matched his contract-negotiating skills. A longtime volunteer, he was brimming with pageant stories, such as the time at the 1952 Miss America parade when he had to push grand marshal Marilyn Monroe up onto her float because her dress, which plunged to the navel in front, was too snug in the back for her to make the step.

And while he showed a grandfatherly fondness toward his contestants, Al couldn't resist creating media-friendly narratives about them, either, especially this outspoken new generation of beauty queens whom he often cast as vivid archetypes—the liberal one, the conservative one, the religious one, the wild one—and even foils to one another.

It was reality TV before reality TV. And the stage was set for especially high drama as the candidates for Miss America 1975 arrived in Atlantic City in September 1974, a month after President Nixon stunned the nation by resigning over the Watergate scandal.

The National Organization for Women had slyly decided to host its regional meetings at the shore the same weekend, with a grand parade of delegates costumed as icons of feminist history—from suffragettes in white blouses to girls in coed Little League uniforms—and Feminist Party founder Florynce Kennedy delivering a pointed speech about the "undue pressure" put on young women by a cultural obsession with beautiful bodies. Security guards escorted the state queens everywhere to keep interlopers at a distance, and tensions were rising behind the scenes. Miss Wyoming, that year's only African-American contestant, found a racist taunt in her mail: "Two coon tickets to Africa, we don't want you here." Miss Washington was at odds with state pageant officials keeping a too-close eye on her weight; even after she finished in the Top 10, they nagged her to lose ten pounds, prompting her to resign before her year was up.

Miss Missouri, Michelle Marshall, a dancer from the St. Louis suburbs, quickly realized that she wasn't going to win—she was one of only a few girls there with short hair or the willingness to get in the water at the poolside photo op. Pageant week felt like a political convention, with so many state delegates angling for advantage and the air crackling with intrigue. Early on, she heard a lurid rumor about the polarizing Rebecca King—that the outgoing Miss America had supposedly shocked a parade crowd by revealing unshaven pits when she waved to them, and that this had prompted Gillette to cancel their sponsorship. "No one could confirm this," says Michelle, later a political blogger and novelist who goes by Taylor Marsh, and of course they could not confirm this, because it was utterly untrue—the kind of urban legend that probably said more about the people whispering it to her.

Still, the crowning of Miss Texas Shirley Cothran as Miss America 1975 felt like a course correction. A twenty-one-year-old graduate student in education, Shirley had won the swimsuit preliminary and carried herself with the mature and ladylike demeanor of mid-century Miss Americas. She had never touched alcohol, let alone marijuana, and she told the press she would never consider living with her boyfriend before marriage. "My body is the temple of God," she said. She had a 1960s-ish bouffant, and she wept when Bert Parks called her name.

"Shirley was pretty damn perfect," recalls Delta Burke, then the eighteen-year-old Miss Florida and later the Emmy-nominated star of *Designing Women* and other sitcoms. "She could walk beautifully and talk beautifully. And she could play that flute like nobody's business."

But was Shirley *too* perfect? A new era of scrutiny—and no small measure of backbiting—had come to Miss America. One of her Miss Texas rivals alleged that state pageant officials had paid for Shirley to get braces and deliberately styled her hair in a way to appeal to national judges. Both criticisms, silly as they seem now, still sting. Yes, she got fitted for a retainer in the run-up to the Miss Texas pageant, thanks to a pageant-friendly dentist, but it hardly constituted a major overhaul, considering she still had to do orthodontia after her Miss America reign. As for her much-discussed "old-fashioned hairdo," as the press called it then . . .

"Well, I'm from Texas," Shirley says now. "And we have big hair in Texas. It didn't seem odd to me. Even today, I go through hair spray like none other. I have very thin hair—I have to have a hairdo! Rebecca King can do that long style. I can't."

Whether or not the pageant was looking for a specific kind of Miss America that year, Shirley says she was never trying to fit anyone's mold. "I can only respond with my truth. When I had my interview, I came out thinking, 'That went very well.' I was exactly who I was. They let you be exactly who you are."

The pendulum swung again the following year with Miss America

1976—Tawny Godin of Yonkers, New York, a live-wire, liberal-leaning eighteen-year-old who was the first coastal Miss America after twenty years of Southern or heartland queens.

What church did she belong to? one reporter asked.

"I believe in my own God," Tawny replied coolly.

And then the pendulum swung again, to Miss America 1977, Dorothy Benham, a cautious conservative from Edina, Minnesota, who refused to wade into controversial topics such as what football team she rooted for or what her New Year's resolutions would be.

Miss America was a *job*, as everyone in this new era kept emphasizing. But which of these women did the job best? This, too, became part of the spectator sport of Miss America, and Al Marks had just the sabermetrics for it. He started publicizing how much each of the Miss Americas earned through paid appearances over the course of their year: How Rebecca earned less than Terry—and was it because heartland hosts were turned off by her liberated ways? (Rebecca notes that the pageant's corporate sponsors kept her far too busy to take many outside bookings.) And how Dorothy earned more than Tawny—clearly the churches wanted to book the pious Midwesterner but not the irreverent New Yorker, he said.

Meanwhile, the media eyed each new winner with analytic anticipation: What sort is *she* going to be? By the time Susan Perkins, a twenty-three-year-old staffer in the Ohio state legislature, took the 1978 crown, she bristled a little at the rush to categorize.

"I don't mind speaking out," she said, "but I think it's ridiculous and irrelevant to ask my views on the Panama Canal treaties."

✦ ✦ ✦

Two mornings after Kylene Barker, a petite, fine-boned blonde from the Blue Ridge Mountains of Virginia, was crowned Miss America 1979, she appeared on the *Today* show. As she waited in the NBC green room, Jane Pauley popped in to let her know that Gene Shalit would be interviewing her.

"I would be much tougher on you!" teased the anchorwoman, just five years her senior.

Kylene was twenty-two, a small-town butcher's daughter who had taken an unusually businesslike route to the crown—researching the local pageant scene, beelining for the Miss Pulaski contest after assessing that the competition might be too tough at Miss Virginia Tech, and settling on a talent she knew few others would try. It was a choice that took her all the way to Atlantic City and straight to the top, because if there was anyone America was bound to fall for in the summer of 1978, it was an Olivia Newton-John look-alike with a Southern drawl and an electrifying gymnastics routine to the theme from *Rocky*. And now here she was.

Gene, *Today*'s Brillo-haired culture critic, immediately had Kylene laughing and feeling at ease. So when he asked about her post–Miss America plans, she just let it spill, this idea she'd been trying out in her head.

Well, she said, since she had a degree in fashion, "I might open my own store on Worth Avenue in Palm Beach." Prior to that weekend, Kylene's big goal had been to maybe open a boutique in Roanoke someday.

Things started happening very fast, as things could in those days for a Miss America. A Palm Beach real-estate mogul who saw the show invited her to officiate at the opening of his new Worth Avenue valet parking lot, where Kylene busted through the ribbon in a special-model Cadillac Seville tricked out by Gucci. She met the mayor and some business leaders, and one of the local grandes dames put an arm around Kylene and said, "I hear you want to open a place." She pointed out a storefront. It would be available for rent in July.

By March, Kylene had a Palm Beach attorney and a Palm Beach bank. She signed a lease and had the place remodeled while she was touring military bases in Europe with the USO. Two mornings after she crowned her successor, Kylene was on New York's Seventh Avenue, a twenty-three-year-old armed with the six-figure seed money, earned through her year of appearances, to buy merchandise for her new boutique, which she dubbed D. Kylene. So there she was, a decade after the feminists marched on Atlantic City, the first Miss America with an actionable business plan, ready to capitalize on the fame and opportunities that still came with the title.

The rest of Miss America's first generation of career-minded winners had more fitful progressions toward their goals—and in many ways, this made them a lot like the young women of the 1970s and '80s who never chased a rhinestone crown.

"You're never going to have success in this business unless you do some nudity," a showbiz manager told Laurie Schaefer.

"Then I'm going to be content with the career I have," she replied.

Despite years of dinner theater and television small parts, Miss America ended up being the peak of her fame. No regrets: "Someone said, 'She was Miss America, but then what did she do?' Well, what I did was have a wonderful life in the arts. I may not be a household name, but I supported myself."

Rebecca King and Shirley Cothran earned advanced degrees, but the business of being former Miss Americas nudged them off their original trajectories. Shirley was swept up onto the lucrative motivational speaking circuit and never ended up using her PhD in education, which was fine, because she got to spend more time with her kids. Rebecca kept getting lured back into PR jobs by the corporate folks so smitten by her during her reign, eventually settling happily into a family law practice. She never became a judge—but how many lawyers do?

And then there were the marriages. Even as many of their peers began postponing wedlock, the 1970s generation of Miss Americas continued an unofficial pageant tradition of tying the knot almost as soon as they stepped down. Boyfriends were all too eager to make a quick commitment, for fear of losing these prized girls, who in turn were eager to settle down with someone who might see them as real women, not a title—and avoid the sheer weirdness of trying to date as a former Miss America. ("You would think men would be asking you out," one of them muses, "but they're intimidated.") Careers complicated marriages, and marriages complicated careers, and almost all of these early marriages ended early.

Terry Meeuwsen, who sketched out the contours of what a beauty queen–turned–career woman could look like, struggled to identify what that career would be.

"In some ways you're still running," she says of her post-pageant years.

"Running here, running there, taking advantage of opportunities—and maybe still on a soul search for who you are."

Her search would take her to Hollywood, where she finally burned out on the hustle and schmooze that had brought her thus far; back home to Wisconsin and a job in local broadcasting, until working-mom struggles prompted her to quit; and finally, to the Christian Broadcasting Network, which called at the right time, when her family was still growing (seven children eventually) and money was tight. And so it was then, in her forties, that she would find her path.

Not the "calculated" plan, but progress in a way, belated proof of what the 1970s generation of Miss Americas had dared to hope—that this crown could mark the beginning of a quest and not merely the end.

4

"UNTIL THERE IS NOTHING MORE TO WIN"

Becoming Miss America: January 2019

Caroline had never met the hula-hooper, but already she was a fan.
Lily was the hooper's name, new to the circuit this year, putting on quite a show with the giant glowing rings she tossed in the air and snaked around her body. Was Lily a good hooper? Caroline had no idea. She was just delighted to see this act on a pageant stage, a respite from all the tap dance routines (sorry, Macy!) and classical flute (with all due respect, Alexis)—a talent as fresh, unexpected, and quirky as her own act on electric guitar.

Granted, Caroline might have chosen to do this routine a little differently, if it were her up there. Chrome hoops instead of light-up ones, maybe a baton twirler costume instead of Lily's simple leotard. Something retro but classic. A little less Electric Daisy Carnival. A little more Miss America.

Yes, this was how Caroline Weinroth, a twenty-four-year-old grad student with a boyfriend and a band, was spending a Saturday night in January 2019—taking mental notes in the two-thirds-empty seats of a middle school auditorium, not even competing in the joint Miss Greater Prince William County and Miss Commonwealth pageant, just watching. This was her world now, too. No one had known what to make of her when she first emerged on the Virginia pageant scene two years earlier, old for a newcomer, with that electric guitar and vaguely ironic air. Even this week, the girl at the pageant-and-prom shop had given her such a *look* when she walked through the door in her Doc Martens and black jeans.

"Oh, I'm just here to look at dresses," Caroline told her breezily. "I compete in Miss Virginia." And let it be known she knew what she was doing.

A local pageant forty-five minutes from home was a good chance to check out the competition and catch up with friends. There in the seats with her was Jacob Manthey, director of Miss Mountain Laurel, the very first title Caroline had ever won. At twenty-eight, he had already been a pageant volunteer for half his life. And up on stage was Hallie Hovey-Murray, a fellow repeat competitor. Hallie was a law student at William & Mary, a broad-shouldered blonde with the very new-era Miss America practice of tying her advocacy platform to a personal struggle against adversity—in her case, Asperger's syndrome.

But Hallie also had a classic throwback Miss America talent of ventriloquism—a cheerfully kitschy act with two dummies singing Johnny Cash's "I've Been Everywhere," customized with shout-outs to towns across Virginia. Caroline had helped nudge Hallie away from her original plan to deliver a monologue—a popular fallback for women who never mastered music or dance, but a genre that Caroline, with the exacting standards of a former high school theater nerd, found cloying.

"Don't do a monologue unless it's one you *haven't* written," she advised.

I had followed Caroline to this small-time pageant expecting to see some of her fellow Miss Arlington also-rans making another bid for a local crown that would qualify them to compete at Miss Virginia. But they were all off the market by then: Olivia had won Miss River City; Dot was now Miss Lynchburg; and Elena had taken advantage of her Annapolis address to compete in Maryland, where she was now Miss Frostburg. Monica, meanwhile, had cinched a dream internship in New York and dropped her Miss Virginia chase for the year. Only Caroline was still searching for a local title. At Miss Apple Blossom in October, she had finished first runner-up. But there was a reason she had decided against competing tonight. A Miss Local title comes with more than a crown: It comes with the pageant director as well, who serves as the winner's manager and mentor as she continues her pageant journey. And while Caroline liked Dale—the sandy-haired pageant director, resembling Chuck Norris's better-groomed younger brother, who presided over the festivities in a be-glittered tuxedo jacket—she was not sure they could collaborate amicably on the quest for Miss Virginia.

"He likes things a certain way," she told me, "and I like things a certain way."

Caroline knew she could afford to be picky about pageants this year. For months, local organizers had been putting out dire signals. "CONTESTANT NUMBERS ARE LOW!" declared the Miss Cardinal Facebook page just four days before the pageant in Richmond, trying to encourage hopefuls to seize the day. The competition seemed anemic everywhere: Only six contestants vied for the two titles offered in Lynchburg; five years earlier, it had been thirteen. Facing a shortage, Jacob rescheduled his Miss Mountain Laurel pageant to join forces with the similarly struggling Miss Roanoke Valley. ("A great opportunity at two titles for you!" they promised on Facebook.)

Dale had mustered six contestants this night—the minimum required to award two crowns. But he had padded out the stage with Miss Outstanding Teen contestants, whose competition he was running concurrently, so his show was just big enough for a respectable opening dance number—fourteen young women in red cocktail dresses—and the show carried on with raggedy charm. One of the reigning teen queens was so overcome while delivering her farewell speech she had to let the emcee read it, while she clung weeping to Dale's sparkly torso. The outgoing Miss Greater Prince William County told the sparse audience that her studies abroad would keep her out of competition this season, but she vowed to return.

"Pageantry for me is a way of life," she said. "I plan to continue until there is nothing more to win!"

It felt like a testament to the enduring power of Miss America. Perhaps the quest was no longer a mainstream hobby, but here was the spirit that sustained it as a happy subculture, ready to march into its second century. And so at the end, when Hallie was crowned Miss Commonwealth and Nicole Hornaday, a gymnastic-dancing flight attendant, won Miss Greater Prince William County, I smiled to see Jacob leap to his feet. Looked like a prime opportunity for him up there—an impressive group of losers to lure into his own pageant.

Instead, Jacob groaned. "Well, now we're in *terrible* shape."

Only four women had signed up to compete at Miss Mountain Laurel, just one week away—and two of them were Hallie and Nicole. Suddenly, he was down to two.

✦ ✦ ✦

Where had all the pageant girls gone?

Their numbers had plummeted over a generation—from as many as eighty thousand a year competing in the national pipeline of local pageants in the late 1980s to what the Miss America Organization, coming up on its centennial, acknowledged might be a mere four thousand in 2019. Some close observers suspected it was far fewer.

Gretchen Carlson never led with this detail as she tried to sell the world on a new and improved pageant during the summer of 2018. (Actually, please don't even call it a *pageant* anymore,* she said; it was a *competition*). Still, the waning participation was there in subtext, as she outlined her vision for a post-swimsuit Miss America.

"For the young girl sitting at home who doesn't want to be judged that way, now she can participate," she said as she promoted the new brand at the Cannes Lions advertising-industry convention on the French Riviera, about five months after she became chair of Miss America. "We're going to be so much more inclusive, with so many more young girls who are going to say, 'Wow, this is for me.'"

---

*   The irony is that if "pageant" had taken on unseemly big-hair-and-bikinis connotations, it was largely because of its association with Miss America. The word originally denoted a procession of people in elaborate costumes and only attached firmly to the concept of a beauty contest after the 1921 event took off.

This was as close as anyone associated with Miss America would come to acknowledging a crisis that threatened to undermine both its business model and its entire mystique. What was the Miss America crown even worth anymore if you had to convince young women to seek it?

✦   ✦   ✦

In the spring of 1942, Jo-Carroll Dennison was walking down the street in Tyler, Texas, when the president of Citizens National Bank rushed out to the sidewalk to ask her a question: Would she do him the honor of serving as the bank's contestant at Miss Tyler?

He had to move fast. All the local businesses were eager to sponsor a candidate for the beauty contest at the Tyler Jaycees' Water Carnival, and everyone had their eye on Jo-Carroll, a dark-haired newcomer whose laughing eyes and creamy complexion turned heads all over town.

But at eighteen, she was already weary of the spotlight. She'd spent an itinerant childhood performing with her family in medicine shows—vaudeville-type revues put on by peddlers of dubious elixirs to promote their wares. Finally, she had gotten off the road, graduated from high school, made some friends, and taken a good job as a secretary for a former U.S. senator. So Jo-Carroll told the bank president no.

He persisted: If she'd do it, they would buy her a new swimsuit.

Okay, Jo-Carroll was in. She won, against sixteen other Tyler girls. And she thought that was it—but then the Tyler Jaycees explained that she had to represent them the next day in the Miss East Texas pageant, against another dozen girls from as far as Lufkin, Nacogdoches, and Mineola.

Jo-Carroll said no. Until they promised her a new set of luggage.

But once she won Miss East Texas, she was shocked to learn they wanted still more from her—who knew there was a Miss Texas pageant? She didn't want to do it, but by then the senator's wife had taken her under her wing and moved her into their house and promised that if she went to the state pageant in Austin, they could stay at the governor's mansion. And because she loved the senator's wife, Jo-Carroll agreed.

The Miss Texas pageant was held at a stadium filled with soldiers from the army's sprawling new Camp Swift. When Jo-Carroll was in-

troduced as Miss East Texas, a huge roar went up; her politically connected pals had put out the word to cheer for her. Imagine her shock,
in those pre-television days, to be told after winning Miss Texas that
there was yet *another* step—this time, in a place she'd never heard of
called Atlantic City. *But*, if she went, they would buy her a whole new
wardrobe. . . .

It was nine months into the war effort, and the army had taken over
Convention Hall, so the pageant was held in a smaller theater, where
the servicemen in the balcony stomped and hollered and raised such
a ruckus when Jo-Carroll, twirling a ten-gallon hat in her cowgirl suit,
sang "Deep in the Heart of Texas"—well, did the judges even have a
choice in the matter? And then she won, and it turned out she was expected to go on the road and perform in theaters and nightclubs across
the nation—exactly what she had been trying to get away from. And
again, she tried to tell them no, she wasn't going to do it. Then they
showed her the beautiful Bulova watch that would be part of her prize.

Well, there went her last chance to be a teenager. After her year
as Miss America, Jo-Carroll felt obliged to pursue the movie roles that
got thrown a beauty queen's way. She was glad when the studio finally
dropped her. She never felt worthy of the adulation.

It took a while to appreciate that those hollering servicemen just
needed her to be a symbol of what they were fighting for. Decades later,
working in a California hospice, she was gratified to see how much this
old title meant to others, a nostalgic bit of stardust that, for the dying or
bereaved people she met, seemed to brighten the day. And yet . . .

"I still have that watch and look at it," says Jo-Carroll, who was
ninety-seven and the oldest living Miss America in 2021, "and wonder
if it was worth it."

✦　　✦　　✦

A couple days after Caroline won her first local pageant in 2016, she
paid a visit to the suburban Fairfax, Virginia, movie theater where she
used to work and dropped her new crown on her old boss's desk.

Would he mind, she asked, if she hung out in the lobby and greeted
visitors in her crown and sash?

He shrugged. Sure, he said, go ahead.

So that's what she did, for three hours one weekend, after alerting her social-media followers that the new Miss Mountain Laurel would be making an appearance. It was just a goofy bit of shtick at a place she loved—her job there had inspired the name of her band, Cinema Hearts. But it was also an excuse to introduce herself to strangers and maybe get some attention for her music. It became a habit: Caroline would bring her crown wherever she went, so if everyone was cool with her wearing it, *ta da!*—she could turn any occasion into an "appearance."

In 2016, no one was going to flag you down on the street and beg you to enter a pageant. You had to want to do it. Being a local queen was pretty much only what you made of it. And Caroline was going to make something of it.

She first tried competing when she was eighteen, a college freshman excited about learning guitar but at a loss for where to play. Seedy bars and bro-centric jam sessions offered no comfort zone for a girl who liked to sing sixties pop. Her mother, who had won a local Junior Miss contest as a teen, suggested she try pageants as a way to showcase her musical talent. Caroline was only hazily familiar with Miss America from watching the broadcasts as a kid.

"I understood these were women who had a talent, who were on TV," she told me. "It took me until I was eighteen to realize, 'Oh wait—anyone can do that. Anyone can sign up. It's not like a special kind of person.'"

She found her way to Miss Northern Virginia, at the time a competitive field of about fifteen. She didn't make the finals; in fact, she hated it. But the pageant stuck in her mind as she searched for her place in the D.C. music scene. When she formed a band with her brother and a male friend, she used it to craft her front-woman persona.

"I asked myself, what's the most womanly thing I could think of," she recalled, "and to me, that was Miss America."

Caroline adopted a mid-century take on the icon: high heels, bold lipstick, ladylike dresses with nipped waists—a retro look that paired smartly with her band's languorous melodies and dreamy surf guitars. After graduating from George Mason University, Caroline again found herself searching for her place. On Instagram, she saw pageant queens touting their civic do-gooding and advocacy work. And in studying the artistry of their polished faces, and the YouTube tutorials she consulted for her concert makeup, she had an epiphany.

Beauty was a skill, Caroline decided—a muscle that could be exercised, a talent that could be rehearsed. She never thought she was beautiful; she had grown up with the nervous habit of picking at her eyebrows and lashes. But in learning to hide the damage, drawing on brows, applying false lashes, she was struck by the power of manipulating her appearance, how it gained her respect and attention.

"I get really existential on people," she laughed. "I'm like, 'I'll take off my eyelashes and there's nothing there, you guys. So why do you value my beauty?'"

And that was how a guitar-playing hipster found the courage, and the interest, to join the pageant world. She didn't win Miss Arlington that year—though she made a big impression when she told pageant director Chip Brown his sound system sucked and could she fix it? She didn't win Miss Greater Prince William County, either. She hadn't planned to keep traveling farther from home to compete, but in a couple years she would turn twenty-five and age out of her crazy new hobby. So she drove two hours to Louisa, Virginia, and there, on her third try, playing and singing Patsy Cline's "I Fall to Pieces," she won Miss Mountain Laurel.

She made it her personal brand: "A pageant queen fronts a rock 'n' roll band." She once worried she wouldn't fit into the pageant scene; now she wondered what her friends in the music scene would make of her pageant habit: Did it make her a sellout?

It helped that Caroline had another provocative side gig at the Hirshhorn Museum at the time. *Woman in E*, an installation by artist Ragnar Kjartansson, consisted of a solitary female guitarist in a golden gown on a rotating platform, strumming a melancholy E-minor chord. A haunting mix of showbiz camp and classical sculpture-come-to-life, it conjured complex ideas—woman as object, but also woman as icon, as formidable as a bronze general on a horse; a woman claiming power in her ability to command attention. Caroline was chosen at an audition as one of fourteen guitarists to take shifts on the platform through the show's three-month critically acclaimed run. It seemed to lend her other exotic new hustle a measure of credibility among her friends.

"They saw me in a gown playing guitar," she said, "and then I won a pageant, and they also saw me in a gown playing guitar. So I think they also kind of saw me taking a pageant like an art piece as well. I still kind of approach it that way."

She failed to make the Top 10 at the state pageant that summer. Jacob, her local director, had advised her to stick to singing—judges might get confused by two talents—but everyone seemed to miss her guitar. Caroline was back a year later as Miss Northern Virginia, with the sultry, strutting take on the Beatles' "Come Together" that I later saw her reprise at Miss Arlington. But she still failed to make the Top 10.

When Caroline and I met for lunch in the middle of her seasonal chase for a third and final shot at Miss Virginia, I asked the question that had been bugging me since Miss Arlington:

Was "Come Together" really working for her? Because it wasn't exactly a banger. She had mastered the tricky guitar solos and meticulously recorded her own backing tracks—but would the judges appreciate that? Judges were just like all of us in the audience, eager to be entertained, happy to hear a tune that evoked some old emotion. I remembered the baton-twirling Miss D.C. my friends and I saw compete in September 2001, barely a week after 9/11, and what did we know about baton, but she twirled to "I Will Survive," and we laughed as we cried because it was everything we needed in that moment.

Caroline had been wondering the same thing. Yeah, "Come Together" didn't exactly bring the crowd to its feet. But it was a classic-rock touchstone, cool and unexpected, and weren't they looking for something different these days? She shrugged. "The pageant dads, they love it." Did I have another song in mind for her? I forced myself to change the subject. It was not my place to coach.

She was frustrated that she hadn't yet made the Top 10. At the last state pageant she was so stressed out that she ended up excusing herself from a dinner and sobbing in front of one of the caterers. Somehow, at some point, she had begun to really want this. She had no illusions about becoming Miss America. But she really wanted to be Miss Virginia, and not just to promote her music. She had experienced the strange power that came from walking into a room in a crown and sash. It spoke to people, especially children. Could this be the way she made a difference? A young woman who plays guitar and works as a sound engineer could prove to princess-besotted girls that they, too, could make it in a man's world.

Caroline was glad the swimsuit contest was gone. Though blessed with a statuesque figure, she loathed working out. In fact, all this talk of "inclusivity" didn't go nearly far enough, in her view. And it wasn't just the paucity of Asian-American women like herself. Miss America needed to expand its notion of appropriate talent beyond the clichés of opera, pop ballads, piano, and dance. Why couldn't a woman lip-sync? Or rap? And would they ever truly accept a rock guitarist? This world seemed to aspire to a certain element of *class*. And "their definition of class," Caroline said, "is just, you know, very privileged."

But if she complained about this world, she loved it, too. Loved the backstage camaraderie, the familiar faces on the circuit, the gossip sessions at the after-parties when the pageant directors got a couple drinks in them. It was *fun*—and at the end of the day, it was just a pageant.

"It's based in kitschiness," she told me. "It's based in joy."

✦　　✦　　✦

Where *had* all the pageant girls gone? The pageant grown-ups wondered if their absence was a demographic fluke, or something larger. Had all their participation trophies and self-esteem mantras sapped this new generation of its drive?

"I don't know if we've lost the ability to compete with other people," a local pageant director told me. "I don't know if young women don't have time to commit to a title. I don't know if this generation *gets* the honor it is to even compete at a local. And I don't know what to do about that."

It had been almost a year since Gretchen had appeared on *Good Morning America* in early June 2018 to announce that the swimsuit competition was over, that physical appearance no longer mattered.

"We've heard from a lot of young women who say, 'We'd love to be a part of your program, but we don't want to be out there in high heels and a swimsuit,'" she had said. "So, guess what, you don't have to do that anymore!'"

The announcement was a publicity bonanza for Miss America—a front-page story in the *New York Times*, coverage from CNN, *The View*, *Good Morning America*, and *The Daily Show*, almost all of it positive, as pundits from beyond the pageant world applauded the move as smart, progressive, and overdue.

But the decision had triggered anxieties in pageant circles that would not be easily understood by outsiders. *Hey, you don't have to compete in a swimsuit—what a relief, huh?* Well, not if you'd built your pageant career on a killer swimsuit walk.

"If they didn't have swimsuit, I couldn't have done this," a former Miss Georgia told Mansfield "Snooky" Bias, the longtime head of the state pageant. "You know I had no talent!"

She was joking—but only sort of. What nagged at a lot of pageant people about Gretchen's swimsuit announcement was her vow to shift the standards ever more firmly toward measurable virtues—talent and academics, in particular—that were exalted in so many other quadrants of the culture already. Where would that leave so many of the women who had excelled at . . . *whatever* it was Miss America had come to stand for?

The women who won state and national crowns generally weren't the best students of the field, not even the best performers—but truth be told, they generally weren't built like *Sports Illustrated* swimsuit models, either. A lot of them were just bright, personable women who'd gutted their way to a crown on the strength of charisma more than anything.

"We have *never* considered ourselves a beauty pageant," Colorado's veteran state pageant executive Suzi Doland told me not long after Gretchen's announcement. "There was nothing in our scoring that says Miss America needs to be beautiful."

But if the pageant people understood this, the general public no longer did. Gretchen had correctly intuited that Miss America had a PR problem. The brand that blue-chip sponsors once chased after had gone blurry—confused in the public mind with secondhand notions taken from *Miss Congeniality*, Honey Boo Boo, and the trainwreck YouTubes of Miss Teen USAs stumbling over simple current-events questions.

"We never really messaged correctly," Gretchen said that summer at Cannes Lions, slipping into marketing jargon. Dropping swimsuit, then, was the nuclear-option reboot—an overhaul of Miss America's identity so dramatic it would force it back on the cultural radar.

It worked. For a couple of weeks.

By the time the first new-era Miss America competition rolled around in September 2018, the entire pageant world was at war over the changes—board members resigning, state directors threatening to leave, lawsuits in the works. And swimsuits had been eclipsed by the bigger Miss America story: Cara Mund, the outgoing Miss America, going public with her claims that she had been "bullied" and "marginalized" by Gretchen's team after they took over midway through her year.

"Are you kind of going rogue this morning?" Hoda Kotb, the host of NBC's *Today* show asked when Cara appeared on the show days before the pageant.

"I'm not sure," Cara replied. "I'm going out on a limb to make sure that whoever the next woman is that takes my job, she knows what she's getting into."

Gretchen strongly denied Cara's claims of bullying, but she did so in a Twitter statement that did little to lower the temperature, chiding her for going public and claiming that a new patron had withdrawn a $75,000 scholarship pledge because of Cara's "explosive allegations."

It made for a tense week in Atlantic City. The usual merry crowd of former Miss Americas had thinned, many opting to sit this one out. The patches of empty seats in Convention Hall seemed more conspicuous. Though pageant die-hards still flew in from across the country, fewer locals seemed to care as much. And a shadowy far-right group known for pro-Trump street-art stunts had moved in to capitalize on the rancor, slapping posters around town that mocked the cover of Gretchen's new book: Instead of her title, *Be Fierce*, it read *So Fake*, with a faux markdown sticker jeering "52% OFF No Swimsuits No Ratings."

Gretchen had bristled at the suggestion that a pageant without swimsuits would equal ratings death. "What that says is, if we put in place an in-depth section with the judges where you get to know the candidates, somehow that's not worth watching," she had said earlier that summer. "I find that highly sexist."

But the new Q&A portion of the broadcast, designed to show "the substance of a woman," as she put it, came across as stiff and over-rehearsed, thanks to softball questions reeking of glib positivity. The next day, after the crowning of Nia Franklin—a flawlessly pretty opera singer with long, sleek hair who was the ninth black Miss America, and the fourth Miss New York to triumph in seven years—the numbers were revealed.

Only 4.3 million people had watched the broadcast on ABC—a third fewer than the previous year, and an ominous development as the pageant's three-year network contract came to an end.

Now, almost a year later, the pageant's overhaul had thus far failed to entice a substantial wave of new young women to sign up. And some in the pageant community wondered if it was actually scaring them away.

As Caroline Weinroth made her third and final attempt at Miss Virginia in 2019, it was clear that most state pageants would field fewer contestants than usual. Some weary local pageant organizers had decided to sit out this chaotic season; many others just couldn't attract enough contestants.

Anyway, the world only seemed interested in one emerging beauty queen that season.

Cheslie Kryst cut a confident, modern, edgy figure—already a practicing lawyer and MBA who represented prisoners pro bono and authored a fashion blog on the side. But it was her startling silhouette that truly had everyone talking—the cloud of jet-black natural curls exploding out beyond her shoulders and halfway down her back.

That this magnificent mane now cushioned a crown seemed to strike a blow for a movement of African-American women trying to overturn the rigid old beauty standards that forced generations into the painful conformity of flat-ironing or chemically straightening their hair.

"For black people in particular, fitting into the acceptable range of 'authentic' has meant being forced to be less of who we are," wrote Christine Emba in the *Washington Post*. With the crowning of Cheslie, she hoped, "stereotypes can be corrected and misunderstandings changed. The new black beauty queens are steps in the right direction."

In every way, Cheslie seemed to exemplify the kind of cool, modern Miss America its new leaders had been talking up, a vision out of a marketing firm's wildest dreams.

Except that in the spring of 2019, Cheslie Kryst had just been crowned Miss USA.

Once, she had aspired to become Miss America. But she had never gotten further than first runner-up at Miss North Carolina. So now it was a Miss USA—the sexier rival that Miss America had always looked down upon—who had the trailblazing look and role-model résumé. And she had worn a bikini on her way to the win.

There was another head-spinning irony about Cheslie's victory. The previous September, an old friend from the North Carolina pageant circuit had called her. This friend, Nia, was sitting in Atlantic City, New Jersey, with a daunting stack of legal contracts. And Nia needed Cheslie's guidance on how to navigate it all.

In other words, the new Miss USA was not simply a practicing attorney. She was *the reigning Miss America's* attorney.

✦   ✦   ✦

The musical chairs of local pageants continued into the spring, an ever-dwindling pool of women near-missing out on one title and trekking down the road in search of the next. Nicole, the bubbly flight attendant I saw crowned as Miss Greater Prince William County, stepped down because of the demands of her job. Elena, the navy midshipman, relinquished her Miss Frostburg title as well, unable to juggle it with her academy duties. Oh well: That's what first runners-up were for.

It came to an end in mid-April, with the odd tradition of the "sweeps" pageant—essentially a last-chance scramble for a handful of titles that would pad out the Miss Virginia roster. Once only open to women who had placed somewhere as a runner-up, sweeps now welcomed basically anyone. And while everyone else in Virginia had competed in swimsuit that season one last time to level the playing field, by the time sweeps rolled around, they didn't bother with it. Seven women vied for the three remaining titles, and that's how Jacob finally found his Miss Mountain Laurel, a Liberty undergrad with a strong singing voice. But he spoke highly of another newcomer—Camille, a pharmacy grad student who did a "chemistry demonstration" for her talent to win the title of Miss Dominion.

Jacob thought Camille's talent seemed like the kind of thing Gretchen Carlson would love. Except of course everyone knew the sweeps girls were just state pageant stage filler, doomed to lose at Miss Virginia.

Twenty-four crowned heads were thus ready to take the stage in June, down from thirty the previous year. A woman who competed in a local pageant in Virginia that season ended up having a slightly better than fifty-fifty chance of making it to the pageant in Lynchburg.

Pretty good odds. Maybe too good.

A week after we sat together in the audience for Miss Greater Prince William County, Caroline Weinroth competed at Miss Roanoke Valley, a pageant two hundred miles from her home that was hastily wrapped up ahead of a snowstorm.

She won. Against a total of two other contestants.

But it still felt damn good.

One of her competitors had made it into the Top 10 at Miss Virginia the previous year, when Caroline had not. "It was definitely steep competition," she told me. "I feel like I earned it." Along with her crown, Caroline had won $2,200 in scholarships and a heap of goodies—jewelry, flowers, teeth bleaching, spa treatments, car washes, and gift cards, courtesy of the hometown mom-and-pops that still gladly boosted this show.

Best of all, though, was the gift from a Miss Roanoke Valley board member who knew Caroline's fondness for pageant history: *Dear Vonda Kay*, a squeaky-clean 1967 advice book for teens. Miss America 1965, Vonda Kay Van Dyke, was on the front, a vision in pink and pale blue with a honey-colored bouffant and a demurely soulful gaze, like a vintage girl-group album cover.

It was kitschy, it was joyful, and it was the perfect gift for Caroline. These people got her. This was her world, too, after all.

5

"IT COULDN'T JUST BE A BEAUTY CONTEST"

1921

Seventy-two years after she was beckoned to Atlantic City, when Virginia Lee was a very old woman living out the final seasons of an eventful life, she still had questions about that one strange week at the shore.

"I must have been pretty," she said, "because, my God, the world was handed to me."

One of the most sought-after artist's models in New York, Virginia had decorated the covers of the hottest magazines of the day before she was swept up into the fledgling film industry, a fetching ingenue who played opposite some of the top male stars of silent Westerns. And yet what happened in September 1921 at the inaugural Inter-City Beauty Contest, when she was twenty years old, still gnawed at her.

"Call Atlantic City and ask them who was Miss America in 1921," she told the film historians who spoke with her in 1993 when she was in her early nineties. "They are bound to tell you that I won it—because I did."

To understand anything about Miss America—this title that slipped away from Virginia Lee, that haunted Phyllis George's career, that enraged the women's movement, and that a younger generation would reinvent and attempt to reinvent again—you have to go back to the beginning.

Back before television, before scholarships, before scandals. Before anyone knew what they were doing. Or what they were looking for. Before they even decided to give the name "Miss America" to this vague ideal they were only just beginning to articulate that first year.

Scholars of pageantry have reached back to antiquity and myth to contextualize the events that unfolded on the sands and streets of Atlantic City in the summer of 1921—to biblical Queen Esther, selected from a lineup of beauties to wed the king of Persia; or Paris, the hapless dude who sparked the Trojan War when he volunteered to judge the loveliest of the Olympian goddesses. Fair enough: The notion of judging beauty was hardly invented in 1920s New Jersey, even if it would prove to be a fertile climate for it.

The great circus huckster P. T. Barnum tried to get a beauty contest off the ground in the 1850s, but it was scuttled for the indecency of women flaunting their figures to be admired and assessed. Legend once had it that the first national beauty pageant was organized in 1880 at Rehoboth Beach, Delaware—a "Miss United States" contest supposedly judged by Thomas Edison and won by a Shinglehouse, Pennsylvania, bathing beauty with the all-too-delicious name of Myrtle Meriwether—a yarn repeated in several history books. But the story has been debunked by Delaware journalists who could find no record of the event occurring outside the active imagination of the folklorist who first spun the tale during Miss America's early 1950s peak. Still, by the turn of the century, as the Victorian sort of queasiness triggered by Barnum's scheme dissipated, small-time beauty contests were popping up at carnivals and dime museums across the country.

Miss America's most obvious inspiration came from the old European festival tradition. But for May queens and harvest queens, there was little notion of having to work or compete for a title. She was simply the *best* girl, chosen by acclamation to reign for a day or a week over her tiny corner of the world. The concept was reimagined in the U.S. in the 1870s at Mardi Gras, the New Orleans bacchanal where "krewes" of the town's elite would tap someone's debutante daughter to serve as queen of their annual parade, alongside a masked, middle-aged king.

And that was more or less the original vision for Atlantic City's queen. The "Inter-City Beauty Contest," as they called it that first year, was only supposed to be one of many sideshows at a sprawling, Mardi Gras–style beach festival, dubbed "Fall Frolic."

The sponsors were the hoteliers and other business leaders of Atlantic City. Their town had exploded out of wilderness in the years after the Civil War, thanks to a few shrewd real-estate speculators and a direct rail line from Philadelphia. It quickly became the most popular beach resort on the East Coast, especially for working-class visitors eager to escape the furnace-like summer of their factories and urban homes. The town's goal in 1921 was to extract more dollars from their guests by enticing them to linger past Labor Day. So the Frolic kicked off the first week of September—a two-day romp featuring a light show, a costume contest, a tented dance floor, a roller-chair parade, a vaudeville stage, and a barge flotilla.

The festival organizers' great PR trick was to invite newspapers in cities within easy traveling distance—as close as Camden and as far as Pittsburgh—to send their "most beautiful" girls, each to be selected in a well-promoted regional photo contest.

This part wasn't entirely new: American newspapers had been sponsoring these contests for at least twenty years, feeding on the new craze for photography at a time printing-press advances made it easier to reproduce images. In one previous national in-person contest of this kind, sixty-one young women, each deemed the fairest of her newspaper's circulation area, traveled to Los Angeles in 1915. The winner, Ruth Maria Purcell of Washington, D.C., was awarded a movie contract but quickly soured on it and returned home to her job as a secretary.

So it's entirely possible the pillars of Atlantic City simply stole this concept—and then made it legendary with the addition of bathing suits.

While the week would be remembered for bathing beauties in swimwear, the Fall Frolic put the whole *town* in swimwear, all revelers dressed for the surf—men, women, and children, including firemen in red bathing suits and policemen in blue.

Sartorial advances made it an especially provocative time to host this party. Until recently, men had been going into the water in the equivalent of baggy shirts and long shorts, women essentially in dresses. But a new athletic sensibility had crept into bathing costumes. Annette Kellermann, a celebrated swimming champion and world-class babe, crafted a stream-lined onesie ending at mid-thigh that she started marketing under her name around 1910. Meanwhile, John Zehntbauer and Carl Jantzen, part-ners in an Oregon knitted goods firm, were asked to design a snug-fitting suit for a rowing team and stumbled upon a rib-stitch technique that they began selling to the public in 1915. The result was swimwear that clung to the body, showcasing the wearer's natural silhouette—and suddenly, respectable young women were comfortable going to the beach in looks that would have been considered downright obscene a few years earlier.

And if there was a place to test the limits, it was definitely Atlan-tic City in 1921. Two years into Prohibition, a community built on a mandate to please its tourists, and run by bootlegger-friendly political bosses, had largely agreed not to enforce it. That's how the town gained its vice-tolerant reputation—the place to go for a naughty good time, long before the legalization of casino gambling. Yet limits did exist: The town was still debating exactly how much bare skin should be revealed on the beach, and police arrested at least one woman that season who left the tops of her stockings rolled too low.

"I most certainly will not roll 'em up," Louise Rosine reportedly told the cops. "The city has no right to tell me how to wear my stockings."

All of this combined to create a highly interesting backdrop for a beauty contest.

The nine young women made their grand appearance in Atlantic City by barge, dressed as "sea nymphs" alongside the honorary "King Neptune"—sixty-eight-year-old Hudson Maxim, a local celebrity owing to his invention of smokeless gunpowder. Then the whole entourage traveled via parade float a mile up the Boardwalk to the Garden Pier theater to meet their judges. The winner would be announced the fol-lowing night.

Two front-runners quickly emerged. And that's when things got complicated.

Miss Washington, D.C., Margaret Gorman, was a bureaucrat's daughter, just turned sixteen, and barely 108 pounds. The high school student resembled a young Kirsten Dunst—fair hair, a soft nose, full cheeks, and a dreamy gaze. "A photograph unfortunately gives no idea of her fine coloring, or rare charm," apologized the *Washington Herald*, her sponsor through the late summer of 1921. "She has a wealth of golden hair, the bluest of blue eyes and fair skin . . . and is a bright conversationalist."

Miss New York, Virginia Lee, was also blonde but already twenty, and she greeted the camera with a bolder gaze. She also claimed a fine pedigree—descended from *those* Lees of Virginia, she said—but a more cosmopolitan history, her trilingual childhood spent in both Mexico City and Canada. While Margaret and most other entrants had been selected by their hometown newspapers, Virginia later recalled that she was tapped by a group of the illustrators for whom she frequently modeled, sophisticated denizens of Manhattan's Hotel des Artistes.

"The decision of the judges, to be given to-morrow night, is known to lie between Virginia Lee . . . and Margaret Gorman," whispered the *New York Tribune*.

But at some point, very late in the hours after Wednesday's competition and ahead of Thursday night's crowning, Virginia was disqualified from the Inter-City Beauty Contest.

She had been deemed a "professional," ineligible to compete against Margaret and the other "amateurs."

Why Virginia merited this classification was never precisely explained in the extensive news accounts. Presumably it had something to do with her film career: She already had a dozen credits to her name. But why was that a problem? While later iterations of the pageant would come laden with strict entry requirements, this first competition seems to have thrown open the doors to any woman—no restrictions explicitly laid out about prior employment or anything else.

Perhaps the festival organizers picked up on a rather glaring conflict of interest: Virginia's friendship and close working relationship with the man they had tapped as chief judge of the contest—Howard Chandler

Christy, the famous magazine illustrator who appears to have been a part of Virginia's hype machine even well before the Atlantic City pageant.

"My most marvelous model," he was quoted calling her in a press item earlier that year that gushed over the number of beaux supposedly vying to marry her. "The ideal Christy girl."

Or could it have had something to do with an even murkier aspect of her bio? It appears that Virginia was actually a married lady, her family says now—something that was not technically against the rules in 1921 but perhaps not the ideal that Atlantic City had in mind. She had been wed two years earlier to a navy officer; her mentor Howard was even on hand to give the bride away, according to a gossip column item from the time. In the summer of 1922, they would welcome their first child.

In fairness, the blurry and conflicting press accounts from 1921 suggest a somewhat chaotic first pageant, with a confusing array of overlapping categories and prizes. Virginia was shunted to a "professionals" category where she handily triumphed over some lesser-known model/actresses who had rolled into the festival with the general public. Some news accounts suggested the trophy Virginia took home made her Margaret's runner-up; others claimed they were coequal.

Yet Margaret won the "Golden Mermaid" trophy, the headlines, and the history books. And seventy-two years later, Virginia still claimed she was robbed.

"They came back and said, 'Oh, Virginia, you won but we can't give it to you.' That's all they would ever tell me," she said. "I won it hands down. They said, 'You not only won it but every judge there voted for you.' Now you can't beat that!"

True or not, there are reasons why the kind of middle-class Americans who were boosting Atlantic City in 1921—and apparently making up the rules as they went along—might have shied from a "professional" lady like Virginia. Change was in the air, and it was disrupting social and sexual norms. Young men had returned from the battlefields of Europe with sophisticated new tastes or deep emotional scars. Young ladies were bobbing their hair, binding their chests, baring their limbs, and painting their faces. Hollywood was beaming its sexy antics—dancing, fighting, kissing—into small-town theaters across the country. And women had just received the right to vote a year earlier, opening so many other cans of worms: Must a wife vote the same as her husband? Could a woman get elected to office?

In that atmosphere, little Margaret Gorman was a tonic. Judges, audience, and press all swooned for the youngest lady in the competition, her curls worn long in the Victorian style. She reminded everyone of Mary Pickford, the film superstar known for nostalgic, unbobbed girl-next-door roles. And while most of the Inter-City contestants wore relatively modest bathing costumes, with skirts to cover their hips, Margaret kept her slender figure draped in the most demure suit of tiered chiffon layers. (Which must have been what allowed her to get away with rolling her stockings below the knee.)

And so, from day one, the pageant staked out its "original bias," as the sportswriter and pageant chronicler Frank Deford called it fifty years later: Girls above women. Amateur rather than professional. Traditional virtues over modern flair.

Margaret made a couple of public appearances back home in Washington but otherwise resumed her schoolgirl life. It was only when she returned to Atlantic City to defend her title in 1922 that she gained soon-to-be iconic status: A new girl had been sent to this contest as Miss Washington, D.C., but the pageant had to call Margaret *something*. And so she became . . . "Miss America."

But the seventeen-year-old returning champion lost her crown to Miss Columbus, Mary Katherine Campbell, a dewier contestant of sixteen. The Ohioan then managed to notch a second victory in 1923—once again beating poor Margaret, even as she blatantly tried to rebrand herself in a slinky knit Kellermann suit. But in 1924, Mary Katherine lost to a church-choir girl from Philadelphia four months her junior.

"You have been my choice," Mary Katherine declared, rushing over to kiss Ruth Malcolmson and nailing that deliriously gracious *so-happy-for-you* tone to be practiced by generations of first runners-up to come.

Even as the competition ramped up—showgirls, actresses, artist's models, and all other sorts of glossy professionals who flooded Atlantic City—the judges gravitated again and again to the wholesome-seeming teenagers in the mix.

The press hailed Miss America 1926, eighteen-year-old Norma Smallwood of Oklahoma, as the anti-flapper for her healthy curves and long dark hair, which she rolled into two braided earmuffs, like a proto–Princess Leia. But then, in a brazen show of ambition, she cashed in her new title on the vaudeville circuit for a staggering $1,500 a week, equivalent to $22,000 today. This rankled the burghers of Atlantic City, who were already turning on this contest and some of the more louche hopefuls it had started to attract. There had been the contestant who bragged that she'd had her dimples insured for $100,000; the "Miss Alaska" who had never set foot in the state; the one who turned out to be married, the one who turned out to have a baby—still not yet against the rules, mind you—and the ones with some fellow trying to rig the game for them. "An epidemic . . . of women who seek personal aggrandizement and publicity," groused the president of the Hotel Men's Association.

"Many of the girls who come here turn out bad later," said another member, "and though it may happen in other cities, it reflects on Atlantic City."

The hoteliers yanked their funding for Miss America. From 1928 through 1934, the town hosted only one half-hearted and lightly attended pageant.

But when the town relaunched the pageant in 1935—either to try to work off the debt it had accumulated in the 1920s or to give somebody's pal a job—they made the fateful decision to put a twenty-eight-year-old woman from Florida in charge.

Pageant organizers were looking to neutralize criticism from women's groups that saw Miss America as tawdry—in no small part because of swimsuits, which had only gotten clingier and more revealing. So they hired Lenora Slaughter, the kind of upper-crust Southern lady who might never have taken a job at all if not for the Depression. Her work organizing a festival parade for the St. Petersburg Chamber of Commerce had caught national attention, and Atlantic City rushed to recruit her.

She had her work cut out for her. That first year, she oversaw the start of the talent competition, which kept the show from giving off the whiff of pure cheesecake, if only barely. She raised the bar by disenfranchising fly-by-night local pageants. And Lenora banished from the judging panels a certain cadre of playboy Manhattan artists whose hardwired tendency was to vote for the hottest body.

"I had to get Atlantic City to understand," she explained years later, "that it couldn't just be a beauty contest."

Eventually, she also set a minimum age of eighteen. The judges' obsession with unspoiled girlhood had taken them to such extremes as choosing a mere fifteen-year-old and, in 1937, a just-turned-seventeen-year-old whose charmingly reserved manner should have been a big red flag that she really did *not* want to be Miss America. In the wee hours after her crowning, Bette Cooper panicked and fled into the night with Lou Off, one of the prominent sons of Atlantic City, who had volunteered to chauffeur her. He hid her on a boat just offshore while the Miss America morning-after press conference fell apart in her absence. The tabloids imagined a secret elopement, but in fact Lou was a chivalrous type, who simply drove her home to Hackettstown, New Jersey, back to the quiet high school life she craved, her Miss America duties negotiated down to a bare minimum.

But while Lenora would allow women as old as twenty-eight to compete, the girlish ideal set in those early years still reigned: For the next thirty-five years, only one woman over the age of twenty-one would be crowned Miss America. And Lenora formalized the mandate that contestants must never have been married.

She was a notorious snob, and certainly the kind of garden-variety bigot that was common in that era. It was during Lenora's early years with the pageant that its "Rule Seven" first appeared, requiring contestants "be of good health and of the white race." For a while she demanded her contestants trace their family trees.

Yet it was also Lenora who launched the college scholarships that would become such an essential part of the pageant's brand. It started with an idea her Miss America 1943, Jean Bartel, brought back from a meeting with her Kappa Kappa Gamma sisters. Lenora latched on to it as a recruiting tool.

"We can get the class of girls that we should have," she told her colleagues.

But Lenora's most defining move was to entrust chapters of the Junior Chamber of Commerce—the conservative young pillar-of-the-community men known as the Jaycees—to run most of the state and local pageants that sent women to Atlantic City. By the 1960s, these small-town and suburban guys would put their stamp on Miss America by crowning modest, cheerful, obedient, and essentially conservative young college women—prime time–ready versions of their own wives and sisters and the daughters they hoped to raise.

These were the white-gloved, beehived creatures who continued to march across the nation's TV screens every September even as the revolutions brewing outside of Convention Hall were about to come knocking on its doors.

6

"MISS NEW YORK IS GOING TO WIN"

1983

"I want you to know," B. Don told Dana, "you're probably not going to win."

It was the summer of 1983, and Dana Rogers had only been Miss Texas for a couple of weeks when her pageant director sat her down to give her the unvarnished truth about what was going to happen in Atlantic City in September.

This was a jarringly early verdict for Dana, who, like so many Miss Texases before her, was getting a lot of buzz—a long-legged twenty-two-year-old with a honey-colored cloud of hot-rollered curls, a gleam in her wide-set eyes, and a legitimate set of blow-the-roof-off pipes.

But who could doubt B. Don Magness, the godfather of Texas pageantry? Everyone called him B. Don, the name spelled out in diamonds on his tie clip. His day job was in public relations for the Fort Worth convention center. But his passion was for Miss Texas; he had served as the state pageant's chairman for thirteen years by then, ushering Phyllis George and Shirley Cothran to the national title and eight others to the Miss America Top 10. Never mind that he was a balding, roly-poly fifty-something in polyester trousers: His advice on wardrobe, performance, hair color, and cellulite was highly coveted, and he gladly bestowed it, not just upon the women picked to represent the Lone Star State but to every aspiring Miss Collin County or Miss Humble/Kingwood who sought his counsel. It frequently came down to *more hair spray*: He once groused that a contestant's hairdo was "so flat it looks like a cat's been sucking on it."

Even for the 1980s, B. Don's shtick approached anti-political-correctness performance art. He referred to his contestants as "thoroughbreds"—because "you can't win the Kentucky Derby with a jackass." He gifted one Miss Texas a T-shirt that read, "In case of rape, this side up." And he made a big old leering fuss over whichever poor contestant in his jumbo-sized pageant—there were eighty-two of them that year—got assigned No. 69. In later years, some contestants would complain about B. Don's handsiness, the social kisses that landed on the lips, the swimsuit-modeling sessions arranged in the privacy of his home. The final straw came when *Life* magazine quoted him calling the 1990 contestants "sluts." That's when he was forced out.

But Dana, a young woman hardwired to get along with difficult personalities, enjoyed B. Don and treasured his guidance, which had ventured into unorthodox strategies and highly personal realms. And Dana was clearly a favorite of his. He bragged that he had discovered her in a junior pageant where, at age fifteen, "she had one of the most fantastic bodies I'd ever seen."

B. Don was always looking ahead that way. And now he had done his research to game out the 1983 season. He was part of Miss America's permanent ruling class—the network of state directors who returned year after year to Atlantic City to wage friendly battle against one another, just with a different girl in the fight each time. ("Don't worry," B. Don told a weeping Miss Texas after she came in fifth. "We'll come back again and try next year." Well, *he* would.) Dana knew that these folks compared notes. They could take the temperature of the room, parse the politics, size up a girl's prospects based on a few data points. So B. Don was just trying to break the truth to Dana gently.

"Miss New York is going to win," he said. "She will be the first black Miss America."

✦ ✦ ✦

"For better or worse, Miss America will always be a part of me," Vanessa Williams once wrote. "It doesn't define me, but it will always be a part of my story."

The feeling will always be mutual.

She was just Miss New York when America first noticed her, stepping in front of the microphone in sporty knitwear like the thirty-one women who had crossed the stage before her. Hers was lacy white with a wide neck and muttonchop sleeves that set off her skin and shoulders and her fluffy light brown hair.

"My pageant was held in Watertown!" she chirped. They all introduced themselves that way. And then as quick as that, the twenty-year-old Syracuse junior was off the screen again. But not for long.

In hindsight, the winner always seems inevitable. "As soon as she walked in the room . . . ," the pageant people like to say. Except for the times they moan that the wrong girl won, of course, but that didn't happen much with Miss America 1984: The moment they put the crown on her head, Vanessa's victory felt not only historic but just. With her matte eighties hair and thick eighties brows, she was barely recognizable as the star she would become in a future, more streamlined decade. But if you're old enough to remember, that face takes you back to Reagan's Morning in America and the L.A. Olympics and peak MTV and *The Cosby Show*, a year full of magazine covers with that sunburst of a face—first marking her triumph and then her disgrace.

The women who crossed the stage with Vanessa in September 1983 have had more than three decades to reckon with that night, that week, that year, the most momentous in Miss America history.

"It was a very proud moment also for me to be a part of that," says Miss North Carolina 1983, Deneen Graham.

"The best thing about that year," says Trelynda Kerr, then Miss Oklahoma, "is I can say I was in the year of Vanessa Williams."

"There are a lot of girls who don't ever get over not winning," says Wanda Gayle Geddie, Miss Mississippi 1983. "But perhaps it's hardest for those who actually won Miss America."

Vanessa Williams almost broke the Miss America pageant, and it almost broke her. But she also saved the Miss America pageant—and then turned around and saved it again.

✦   ✦   ✦

By the 1980s, Miss America needed saving. It had survived the women's movement, thanks to the mature, ambitious winners of the 1970s who broke the debutante mold and gave the public something more to ponder about a young woman in the spotlight than boyfriends and hairstyles.

But it was falling out of step with the culture. The ratings alone showed it. A quarter of the nation's homes could still be counted on to watch every year, but never again the estimated 80 million people who tuned in to see Phyllis George crowned in 1970. And just to *look* at the broadcast in 1979, its twenty-fifth anniversary on television—it was a retread of the cringy variety shows that were all getting canceled by then, endless production numbers where former Miss Americas and no-name guest stars warbled pop hits while jumpsuited chorus boys swiveled around them. The contestants were sidelined when not running the narrow gauntlet of evening gown, swimsuit, and talent, barely heard from except in bumper-sticker speeches.

"For me, the most reassuring phrase is simply *be yourself*," recited the accordion-playing Miss Ohio. "After all, being Tana Carli is the *one* thing *I* know *I* can do better than anyone else!"

Miss America needed a makeover. Instead, the overlords in Atlantic City went straight to the heart of the pageant with a dagger—by firing Bert Parks.

Bert was a kitschmaster ahead of his time. No doubt anyone under forty died a little bit inside when he danced the Charleston in 1976 to a rendition of "Let 'Em In,"—*Someone knockin' on the do'oh! Sumbody ringin' the bell*—even hammier than Paul McCartney's. But in hindsight, Bert was clearly in on the joke, winking at the smarm as he doled it out, fully in control of this game. Had he lasted a few more years, you can imagine maestros of eighties comedic irony like David Letterman coming around to champion him. And through sheer longevity, he had come to symbolize Miss America's most bankable essence—a sense of tradition, a nostalgia for its own past.

In 1979, corporate America couldn't see it. Miss America worked closely with the handful of blue-chip brands that underwrote the pageant—Gillette, Campbell's Soup, and Kellogg's, responsible that year for all the commercials that aired with the show. In the fall, some of those sponsors went to Al Marks, the Atlantic City stockbroker who had been running the pageant for more than twenty years, to ask for a younger, hipper host. Which was awkward because the usually PR-savvy chairman had just been dousing water on rumors of his emcee's retirement, publicly vowing that the job was Bert's as long as he wanted it. But Al decided to fire Bert anyway—over the holidays, via letter, instead of a phone call. The letter went to Bert's home in Connecticut, while Bert and his wife were in Florida. So Bert heard about his firing weeks later from the reporter who called to ask him about it. It became a months-long news story, as Bert gave mournful interviews and former Miss Americas expressed their regrets. Johnny Carson led a "We Want Bert" campaign, inspiring thousands of fans to send hate mail to Atlantic City. The *Orlando Sentinel* polled readers on who should host Miss America—Burt Reynolds? O. J. Simpson?—and, surprise, 81 percent wanted the pageant to stick with Bert.

Instead, the pageant settled on Ron Ely, best known for his star turn in a 1960s Tarzan TV series, a lean, blond Texan with a Matthew McConaughey smolder and a Malibu tan.

"I wanted the show to be sexy," Al Marks explained later. And then added: "But not so obviously so."

Indeed, two years later, Ron was replaced by Gary Collins, who would hold down the job for a decade. The veteran talk-show host, married to Miss America 1959 Mary Ann Mobley, had a little less edge, a lot more warmth, and a far better singing voice. Just the right kind of "folksy," as Al described him, to help spackle over the growing tensions and contradictions in a pageant that was asking its young participants to live up to increasingly impossible standards.

✦   ✦   ✦

Miss America 1980, Cheryl Prewitt, the first winner presaged by statistician George Miller's algorithm, may have had all the perfectly standard attributes of a classic Miss America. But she showed the judges a fascinating other side during the swimsuit contest.

"Thank you, Lord, I am walking!" she declared that night as she was announced the winner of the preliminary.

This was how the 1980s would begin for Miss America: the crowning of a gospel singer with a Farrah Fawcett smile and hairdo who embodied a potent new standard for the pageant—a slamming body and a staunch devotion to Christ.

Endowed with long legs and an hourglass figure, she took it to the next level with a custom-tailored white swimsuit by the same Beaumont, Texas, seamstress who crafted her glittery gowns. Cheryl's was the first, but soon it seemed like every girl on the Atlantic City runway had the same $160 Ada Duckett "supersuit," in a girdle-like fabric you wouldn't dare take in the water, a deep V-neck and a band across the back straps working some lift-and-separate magic. It wasn't Ada whom she thanked from the stage, though. Cheryl was hardly the first Miss America to declare her Christian faith. But she was by far the loudest and proudest.

The pageant had not gotten off to a great start with the church. In 1926, the Southern Baptist Convention condemned "bathing revues" as "evil and evil only . . . emphasizing and displaying only purely physical charm above spiritual and intellectual attainments." But when Lenora Slaughter was hired to resuscitate the moribund pageant in 1935, she made a point of reaching out to religious groups—and religious women in particular. She asked the Quaker wife of the Atlantic City mayor to form a hostess committee of upstanding matrons to chaperone the visiting Misses, and she established rules of behavior—no nightclub trips, no alone time with men—that would impress religious conservatives.

Thanks to Miss America's long affiliation with the civic-minded Jaycees organizations, which ran many of the local contests, church communities came to see pageants as an acceptable forum for their young women to spread the good word by showcasing their swimwear-clad temples of the Holy Spirit. Still, contestants were barred from talking politics or religion until 1964, when Bert Parks asked Vonda Kay Van Dyke about the Bible she'd brought to Atlantic City as "a good-luck charm."

"I do not consider my Bible a good-luck charm," said Vonda, "I consider it the most important book I own."

The crowd went nuts—and the pageant dropped the gag order. By the end of the sixties, Miss America had positioned itself as a safe space for conservatives unnerved by the women's movement, a place where they could celebrate new opportunities for young women without questioning gender roles or challenging the patriarchy or any of that Gloria Steinem stuff. It's why future *700 Club* host Terry Meeuwsen looked to Miss America as a spiritually wholesome route into show business. Her victory as a woman of faith further endeared the pageant to church communities.

But Cheryl had a backstory that claimed the Miss America crown for a charismatic strain of Protestantism—part of the rising tide of evangelical Christians who would help propel Ronald Reagan's victory over Jimmy Carter. A devastating car accident had crushed her left leg when she was a child, leaving it shorter than the right, she said—until she went to a faith-healing service and watched the maimed limb grow two inches in a matter of minutes. *Thank you, Lord, I am walking.* Surprisingly, the jaded pageant press corps gave only the barest eyebrow-raise to her story. Then again, Miss Americas tend to be intensely convincing communicators.

"It's the darndest thing," Cheryl overheard a reporter say. "To hear her speak she could almost make a believer out of me!"

To say that Cheryl started a fad would be simplistic. Yet her testimony clearly liberated other devout contestants to open up about their spiritual beliefs—and her victory probably nudged state pageant judges to send their most godly girls to Atlantic City. But these new Christian beauty queens would shoulder extra burdens. Talking about faith—and by extension, morality—exposed a Miss to ever more questions about her own personal practices.

"It's my life—my love for God, for Christ, for what He's given me," Susan Powell, the raven-haired coloratura soprano from Elk City, Oklahoma, told reporters after she was crowned Miss America 1981. So they followed up by asking her about premarital sex. "It's not right for me at this time in my life," she demurred.

Meanwhile, despite all the trappings of godliness and wholesomeness—*and don't forget the scholarships!*—Miss America remained a beauty pageant, a hit TV show with career-launching potential. And for a young woman in the business of being beautiful in public, the late 1970s and early 1980s offered confusing role models. Despite the gains of the women's movement, pop culture was still only just beginning to process the sexual revolution, and for now, it manifested in the rise of the sex symbol—*Charlie's Angels*, *Three's Company*, and all the hot-pants-and-halter-tops programming known as Jiggle TV. True, there were opinionated and liberated characters, like career gal Mary Richards, but Mary Tyler Moore was already forty when her sitcom wrapped in 1977. A few of TV's hottest babes showed strength and wit—Lynda Carter as Wonder Woman or the Angels, on occasion. But most of the girls-next-door on our screens were patterned on the Daisy Duke or Chrissy Snow model: sweet, bra-less, vacant, always up for a good time. And this was far more character development than was ever given to the nubile coeds who scampered through *Porky's*, *Caddyshack*, and the other big-screen comedies of the day.

If this was the template for young women entering show business circa 1980, then pageants were all too effective a training ground—at least in the experience of Elizabeth Ward.

She was still so young and unformed—a "country bumpkin," she says, from Russellville, Arkansas—when a pageant groomer spotted her in a burger joint the summer after high school graduation and offered to lend her a dress if she signed up for Miss Lake Dardanelle. Barely two years later, she was the new Miss Arkansas, bound for Atlantic City.

It all came easily for her. Elizabeth could sing well enough. She had a confident, candid way of speaking. She was *very* attractive—a big-eyed, full-cheeked Marie Osmond type, with a more flirtatious spark. And her figure was sensational: five-foot-nine and 36-24-36, according to the vital stats the pageant released. "An hourglass to make the Steuben people proud," the *Washington Post* slobbered after she was crowned Miss America 1982. Nearly four decades later, Elizabeth scoffs at this description. "More like a slim-hipped boy with boobs," she says. She was just young, and naturally skinny, drinking milkshakes so she'd fill out, working her calf muscles on a stationary bike so they wouldn't look too scrawny. If she hadn't won Miss Arkansas on her second try, she would have checked out of pageants by then. "I don't know that I really liked it that much," she says. But she had figured out that she fit the mold—big hair, big teeth, good talker—and could hit all the marks. She was going through a religious phase—her boyfriend was a born-again Christian, and she became one, too—so she truly meant it when she told reporters that "premarital sex is not for me." Her boyfriend affirmed that neither would consider living together unwed.

But she was just twenty then, she says, and didn't really know who she was yet. In hindsight, "my identity was very much tied up with a projected self—someone who had to be pretty, a combo of girl next door and fuckable, pliable, and charming. Pageants trained me to be all of those things."

Like many Miss Americas, she also tumbled into an early marriage as soon as her reign ended. It didn't last: She had essentially missed her growing-up years; and after twelve months traveling the country, being so *on* and so *good*, her stifled wild streak was bound to come out. "I went through several years," she says, "of trying my best *not* to be Miss America." There was a one-night fling with then-governor Bill Clinton in 1983 that she reluctantly acknowledged and apologized for fifteen years later, when all the president's past affairs were under scrutiny. There was a 1992 *Playboy* spread and the movie roles for which she shed her clothes early in her career.

"Objectification was a norm that I carried with me through many years of some really stupid choices," Elizabeth says now. "I think at the time I thought I was being fierce and independent, but I was just self-objectifying. If I had to do it over again, I would not have made those same choices."

But when she got her foothold in show business—by then known professionally as Elizabeth Gracen—it was not as a giggly sitcom coed but a bad-ass femme fatale in the syndicated nineties series *Highlander*, with an edgy platinum pixie cut that erased any resemblance to a former Miss America. After keeping a distance from the pageant for more than three decades, she attended the second annual retreat of her fellow former Miss Americas in 2016 and felt such a profound connection with them. Two years later, she cheered when Gretchen Carlson announced the end of the swimsuit competition. Hopefully, she thought, things could be different for the next generation of pageant girls. That instead of finding their power in their looks, they would find it within. That they would go into this beauty queen thing with open eyes, knowing from the start what it took her years of therapy to figure out.

"No one really told me that Miss America is a persona," she says. "I actually believed I had to be perfect."

✦ ✦ ✦

Pageant week 1983 was approaching, and Miss Oklahoma was determined to arrive early. Trelynda Kerr had been waiting for this for, oh, only about fifteen years—ever since she got into kiddie pageants at age five. She had finally clinched the state title on her second try with a killer performance of "Stand by Your Man." Miss America, she hoped, could be her springboard to a country music career.

The smart move was to get to Atlantic City on Friday, three days before the start of the competition, so you could soak up all the attention from the journalists who also showed up early. Anything to please the hometown folks and set yourself apart from the crowd. Knowing this was an upside of hailing from a serious pageant state like Oklahoma, winner of the 1967 and 1981 Miss America crowns. Trelynda's state directors had lavished $25,000 on her training and wardrobe and kept after her about staying in shape. And when they noticed the padding in her swimsuit sliding around during the Miss Oklahoma finals, they did not mince words: *We cannot go to Miss America like that*, they said. They paid for her to get the implants. It was just a discreet B-cup, but Trelynda was thrilled: Finally, she had the boobs to match her hips.

"I had always had a very flat chest, and it affected how I felt about myself," she says. "All I wanted was to be in proportion."

The Miss America press corps couldn't resist the University of Oklahoma cheerleader with the one-of-a-kind name. The UPI guy high-lighted her in four days' worth of stories. The *Philadelphia Daily News* guy sounded ready to propose marriage: "She has long, light-brown hair, wondrously deep brown eyes, a syrup-thick Western drawl that is pure music, and the kind of breathtaking beauty that, even in a Miss America Pageant crowd, immediately turns men's hearts to mush." Meanwhile all the Oklahoma people were out there wearing buttons with her face and T-shirts that said "Oklahoma's Tree"—her nickname—and basically had everyone on the Boardwalk convinced this was hers to lose.

But Trelynda did not get to Atlantic City first. That honor was tradi-tionally ceded to Miss Alaska, who always needed the full extra day to adjust to the time difference. This year's Miss Alaska, though, missed her connecting flight. So the small mob of journalists waiting at the Atlantic City airport for her at 9 a.m. Friday was left at loose ends until another young woman, this one traveling from Syracuse, appeared at 9:25 a.m. with five garment bags and two suitcases.

It was Vanessa Williams, accidentally earning her first moment in the national spotlight just by showing up first. The Associated Press story about her arrival didn't mention that she was the first African-American woman to represent the Empire State. Perhaps they didn't know. There was no internet; the buzz going around B. Don–level pageant circles had not yet reached the beat reporters. And it certainly hadn't reached Vanessa.

This was just her third pageant. Months earlier, she had been sing-ing an old Sinatra tune in a show at Syracuse University. A board mem-ber for Miss Greater Syracuse saw her, and soon the pageant organizers were begging her to enter. When her spring musical got canceled, she figured: Why not? Three months later, she was Miss New York.

How clueless was Vanessa about pageants? At her July 16 crowning in Watertown, she still thought she would get to make her off-Broadway debut in August—a dream since childhood—in the limited-run musical she had just been cast in. They quickly set her straight. She dropped out of the show and spent the next two months doing interview prep, getting fitted for sequins, and waving in farm-town parades. She didn't mind. It was a brief, amusing detour from the mapped path she planned to pick up again in the fall: junior year abroad, graduation, Yale drama school, Broadway.

On Sunday, the contestants gathered for their first group dinner. Miss Ohio, Pamela Rigas, a tall, serene law student with long dark hair and a natural Brooke Shields kind of beauty, chatted with Vanessa for a few minutes. "Some people have that something that makes them stand out," Pam says thirty-six years later. "There was something unique about her. And she was very poised." Pam reported back to her Ohio pageant officials that New York was going to win. They immediately corrected her: Nope, they were convinced it would be another black woman, Miss New Jersey, Suzette Charles—a petite powerhouse vocalist who'd been on everyone's radar since finishing as her state's first runner-up at the age of eighteen.

Still, the camera loved Vanessa. Pictures of her goofing around with Muhammad Ali at a photo shoot hit the national wires. And the *New York Daily News* was clearly developing a crush. Granted, she was the home-state girl. But of all the women sent down to the beach in swimsuits Monday to meet photographers, it was Vanessa in her white maillot whom the tabloid splashed along the full length of a page—a stunning *Baywatch*-caliber image of Miss New York sprinting through the surf with a playful glance over her shoulder.

Caption: "She looks like she's in the running."

◆   ◆   ◆

History was being made at the Miss America pageant. There were four African-American contestants, the most ever in a single year: Vanessa, Suzette, Amy Keys of Maryland, and Deneen Graham of North Carolina. Pageant folks had noticed something else about them: They were *good*. Maybe this could be the year the pageant would move beyond its long, uncomfortable racial history—perhaps even crown a black winner?

For decades, race was a stubborn non-issue for Miss America—there simply weren't any black participants, because the doors were not open to them on any level, same as in many quadrants of American society. Within a couple years of Lenora Slaughter's arrival in 1935 from heavily segregated Florida, though, racism was formalized with the so-called "Rule Seven."

Al Marks would later try to raise doubts that any such formal rule ever existed, though sadly it was hardly a surprising policy for an institution in South Jersey, where schools remained segregated into the 1950s, Jim Crow practices were upheld in many public spaces into the 1960s, and black Atlantic City residents were cast in the role of King Neptune's "slaves" to pull his chariot in the parade before the 1922 Miss America contest. Some barriers did collapse early: Native American Mifaunwy Shunatona represented Oklahoma in 1941, and a woman of Chinese descent, Yun Tau Chee, came to Atlantic City as Miss Hawaii in 1948. But these were hardly indicators of a progressive awakening: As Lenora explained to South Dakota's Black Hills Indian Council in 1948, the whites-only rule was aimed specifically at keeping out black contestants, "due to the fact that it is absolutely impossible to judge fairly the beauty of the Negro race in comparison with the white race." Lenora, in later years, was vague about when it was lifted ("sometime in the middle 1950s"), but it remained documented in the literature for local pageants as late as 1949 in Wisconsin and 1955 in Utah. And a racial status quo lingered for years, thanks to the decentralized nature of a contestant pipeline that funneled through chummy small-town pageants, where organizers could set strict residency requirements or limit entry to invitation-only.

"I'll be honest, we've never invited a Negro girl," the president of the Wilson, North Carolina, chapter of the Jaycees told author Frank Deford in 1970. "But then the subject has just never come up. We've never had a Negro apply for the Jaycees either."

In her prewar push for respectability, Lenora had built a culture of aristocratic snobbery and elitism—requiring candidates until the mid-1940s to submit their family trees, for example—that did little to encourage diversity. Bess Myerson, arriving on the scene as Miss New York City in 1945, found the Atlantic City pageant culture to be intimidatingly "silver-spoonish," run by matrons in hats and gloves and upper-crust accents. Lenora recognized Bess early as a contestant to watch and tried to convince her to change her name to something, uh,

less obviously ethnic, like "Betty Merrick." Her status as the first Jewish
Miss America—and incidentally, the first winner to find enduring fame,
as a television personality and New York City political player—later became a major point of pride for the pageant, proof of its tolerant and
progressive values. It eventually became clear that Bess had blazed a
trail to little effect: Seventy-five years later, they still hadn't crowned a
second Jewish Miss America.

For African-Americans, change came gradually. In 1959—five years
after the Supreme Court's *Brown v. Board of Education* decision and
amid fitful integration efforts in the South—black women won local
crowns for the first time, in Sacramento and at Indiana University. Yet
as of 1968, no state had sent a black winner to Miss America. That
August, three weeks before Miss America, the first Miss Black America
pageant was held in Atlantic City. It was both a protest of historic ex-
clusion and a celebration of the black-is-beautiful movement. Coming
the same year as the landmark feminist protests in Atlantic City, the
oblique criticism clearly got to Al Marks. He brought on two black
board members that year and a black judge in 1969 but maintained
that it was not Miss America's fault there had not yet been any black
women in the contest.

"Look, I would love to have a colored girl here to take the heat off
this thing," he said in 1969. "But we won't fix anything"—meaning, they
wouldn't rig a state contest to make it happen—"so we just have to wait."

The wait ended a year later, when Cheryl Browne was crowned Miss
Iowa 1970. It would take another decade for a black woman to make
it to the Miss America Top 5—Lencola Sullivan of Arkansas, in 1980.
By 1983, only about a dozen African-American women had ever walked
the Miss America stage. While Vanessa and Suzette had been feted in
their home states as "firsts," the milestone was even more profound for a
North Carolinian like Deneen Graham, nineteen, a soft-spoken dancer
from small-town North Wilkesboro.

"It was a big deal," she says. "You don't realize sometimes how significant it is until you see the press the next day." She was deluged by interview requests and fan letters. But there were also threats, direct and
indirect. A local chapter of the Ku Klux Klan held a rally and threatened

to host a Miss White North Carolina pageant or burn a cross in her yard (neither happened). She had to enter her local airport through a back door on the way to Atlantic City; at the pageant, a bodyguard escorted her from her hotel lobby to the car.

It was hard to get to know her fellow contestants as she was whisked around all week. But she did strike up a little friendship with Vanessa, her neighbor in the alphabetical state lineup, and like Deneen a newcomer to this strange world—competing in only the third, and the last, pageant of her life.

✦　　✦　　✦

Yet as the most diverse pageant in Miss America history officially got underway, the biggest story in Atlantic City was about a white woman: B. Don's protégé, Miss Texas Dana Rogers.

The headlines telegraphed the blossoming national scandal: "Pageant Hopeful Admits Surgery" . . . "Pageant Entrant Admits She Had Implants" . . . "Nose Job for Miss Texas" . . .

Dana tried to sound carefree. "Some women wear their padding on the outside," she told reporters. "Mine is already there on the inside."

But it didn't matter. Cosmetic surgery was the focus of a roiling, ugly debate in pageant circles—and it had all begun a year earlier, just days after Debra Maffett was crowned Miss America 1983.

Debra was a Texas girl, too, from a forest crossroads known as Cut and Shoot, where she grew up clearing brush, scraping grease out of the doughnut-shop fryer, and hanging with the wrong crowd. Not a whole lot of self-esteem, she says, until she discovered pageants. Her first attempt, in 1978, at the advanced age of twenty-one, was a stage-fright flop. But a judge pulled her aside: "If you learn how to sing," she advised, "you might be Miss Texas." She won another small pageant, and then, even though she was a *mess*—her gown too short, her skin too tan, her press-on nails peeling off—she managed to finish in the state's Top 10. Suddenly, other local pageants were trying to recruit Debra. She transferred to a college that offered a pageant scholarship and kept polishing her act. The next year she was second runner-up. But she got crosswise with B. Don Magness, who tried to tell her what to sing, what to wear, and then she fizzled out at fourth runner-up the next year. She tried Miss Texas USA, but it turned out she had just passed the age limit. Some of those pageant officials felt sorry for her and helped her meet the right people in L.A. and get some bit parts in soap operas. And after she'd been in California just a couple months, someone from the Miss Anaheim program approached. . . .

Flash-forward several months to September 1982. Miss California Debra Sue Maffett was crushing it in Atlantic City. She was twenty-five now and heeding no one's counsel but her own. She won her swimsuit preliminary. Then two days later, she said a prayer, felt her stage fright dissolve, and went out and won the talent preliminary. The Miss California director couldn't resist taunting the Miss Texas folks: *You lost her, and now she's going to win it all for us.* Miss Texas 1982 didn't even make the Top 10. But a couple days after Debra was crowned Miss America, Texas got its revenge—spreading the word that the only reason she won was because she'd bought herself an entirely new face.

"Debbie has had extensive cosmetic surgery since she last tried our pageant," Gary Jordan, the executive director of Miss Texas, told the *Dallas Morning News*. "She had her nose done, her chin and I'm not sure what else." Rumors spread that "what else" included a thigh tuck and a lower-rib removal to shape that tiny waist. The network evening news compared her before-and-after pictures.

Debra maintained—and still does—that she simply had her nose repaired, after her last try at Miss Texas, for the "deviated septum" that ran in her family and was impeding her breathing. But in nearly every interview during her year as Miss America, the reporter asked her about plastic surgery. Newspaper columnists fretted over "truth in packaging" and "deception" at the great American beauty pageant. So as she prepared to hand over her crown, Debra gave a stern lecture to the pressroom. The national media "treated me as though I was manufactured on an operating table," she vented. "They disregarded the fact that I spent six years developing my talent and my mind."

But also, undeniably, her look. I've spent a lot of time staring at photos of Debbie Maffett. She made a lot of changes after parting ways with the Miss Texas pageant: She lost fifteen pounds. She lightened her makeup. She traded her brassy blonde for a softer shade, balanced her strong jaw with fluffy bangs, and harnessed the magic of a sun-kissed California tan. In short, she freed herself from a hard-edged 1970s aesthetic that still ruled the pageant world and conjured one that would strike the judges' eyes as fresh, contemporary, and youthful. Did that count as fakery? True, she also got a nose reconstruction that, for whatever its purpose, certainly had a refining effect on her face. But I'm inclined to believe it was her only surgical alteration. Even after her crowning, you could still see the same rawboned Texas girl from certain angles. Beauty is a skill, as Caroline Weinroth told me thirty-five years later. And Debbie mastered it.

Even while Gary Jordan was ratting out Debbie, he took pains to emphasize that of course there was nothing in the rules prohibiting cosmetic surgery. He was wise to make this point because—well, the Miss Texas program hardly had clean hands when it came to cosmetic surgery.

Dana Rogers was about ten weeks from her first attempt at the state title in 1982 when B. Don gave her figure a hard look.

"If this is how you come to Miss Texas, you're not going to win," he said.

She went on a crash diet and started working out every day. When she placed second runner-up, the consensus was that she'd gotten *too* thin; she'd lost her spark. Dana resolved to find a healthier path the next year. But she hated how skinny she looked up top; at the pageant after-party, she went to the bathroom and ripped the spongy push-up pads from her evening gown. *Never again*, she thought. That summer, she told B. Don she wanted implants.

Well, he said, Miss San Antonio was coming up: If she won there, maybe *they* would pay for her surgery? She did, and they did. And on her second try the next summer, with a bigger chest and a slightly slimmer nose, Dana was crowned Miss Texas.

But now the Debbie Maffett controversy had everyone on the lookout for surgical scars. So when a *People* magazine reporter came to interview Dana for a story about the 1983 contenders, B. Don warned her: People would ask if she'd had work done—and she should tell the truth.

Later, she questioned his strategy. It was demeaning to have to talk about her implants in interview after interview, with the implication that she had done something illicit. But you just didn't disobey your pageant director, she explains.

"He picked out my evening gown, he picked out my clothes, I wore what he told me to wear, I said what I was supposed to say." In hindsight, Dana realized that as the child of an alcoholic mother, she had found her coping strategy in pleasing and appeasing—and this was what prepared her to put up with the indignities of pageantry, the petty dictates, the invasive questions.

The backlash was puzzling. Twenty years after the first silicone implants helped take breast augmentation mainstream, cosmetic surgery wasn't particularly controversial anymore. Surgeons had sold the American public on nose jobs, hair plugs, and other tweaks by casting them as a psychological salve, a fix for whatever shortcoming made you unhappy. Meanwhile, the feminist complaint that cosmetic surgery was self-butchery in the service of pleasing men had been countered by the argument that women should be empowered to make the choice for themselves.

But cultural critics weren't ready to let pageant girls play by these new rules. Miss America had smugly held itself to a higher standard all the way back to 1921 by exalting girl-next-door "natural" beauties. For a contestant to fix her appearance felt like hypocrisy, these critics seemed to think. Or worse, it was like cheating—the equivalent of a doping athlete. The critics had a point: Miss America was both a major cultural event and a multimillion-dollar scholarship provider. If cosmetic enhancements were in the mix, could it truly promise a level playing field for its contestants? And wouldn't it foist unreasonable beauty expectations on a generation of impressionable girls?

Dana, though, felt an uglier undercurrent of judgment and accusation: *You're not "real." You're not "wholesome."* And yet, throughout that week in Atlantic City, one contestant after another approached her privately to say, *I had it done, too.* (For all the press attention Trelynda got, the secret of her surgery never leaked.)

"I never thought, 'Why aren't you telling them?'" Dana says. "I thought, 'Well, don't tell a soul.'"

✦   ✦   ✦

On Wednesday, a squad of contestants was dispatched to a hotel swimming pool for yet another photo op. The point, as always, was to get more girlie pics out on the wires and into newspapers across the country to promote Saturday's broadcast. After the photographers begged for one of them to please get in the water, Miss Oregon Stephanie Wymer gamely took the plunge. Upon surfacing, she was "horrified to discover the top of her one-piece suit had strayed and she was uncovered on her right side," to quote the Associated Press account. Because of *course* there had to be an Associated Press account of the time Miss Oregon's swimsuit slipped for a split second. Dozens of newspapers ran photos of Stephanie covering her chest as her friends gasped. Somehow, she felt obliged to apologize.

"I'm such a conservative, and it had to happen to me," she told the press. "I'm just sorry it happened."

Slow news day? In fact, the action had moved behind the scenes, to the closed-door interviews with the judging panel. The women would perform their talents and parade in swimsuits and evening gowns on the Convention Hall stage for the same judges later—but everyone knew these seven-minute sessions were the true make-or-break. Interview scores counted toward a contestant's overall tally, but the impression she made in this room had an amplified effect: Of course the judges, when trying to score something as perplexing as an evening gown competition, ended up leaning subconsciously to whomever they liked the most. And they decided that in the interviews.

Trelynda's was a disaster. She had spent the summer brushing up on politics, but instead the judges drilled down on the depth of her religious faith. If she were hosting a party and opened the door to find Jesus standing there, they asked, what would she do? "I'd invite him in," she lamely replied, boggled as to what they were looking for. The clever retort only ever materializes minutes or years later: Of course she should have asked Christ, "Red or white?"

Miss Mississippi, Wanda Gayle Geddie, went into her interview feeling confident. But that's how Wanda went into the entire week.

She had come to Atlantic City with the firm conviction that she would not be returning home to Hattiesburg. She had come to Miss America to win.

Wanda got into pageants late, but Mississippi's hothouse pageant scene whetted her competitive instincts. When she won the state title on her third try, a wave of buzz preceded her to Atlantic City. Her extraordinary looks—as if Phyllis George had borrowed Katharine Hepburn's cheekbones and Shirley Temple's smile—made her the favorite of a certain old-school contingent who were, perhaps, impervious to the excitement over potentially crowning a black winner. Wanda was also one of only three contenders who merited a mention in Vanessa's 2012 memoir, in the only anecdote from her short chapter on the 1983 pageant that betrays a hint of Vanessa's own competitive hunger. She wrote that Wanda ("who'd been in the pageant circuit forever") cautioned her about the Swarovski crystal–bedazzled knit outfit the Miss New York folks had chosen for Vanessa's show opener.

"Don't you know?" Vanessa recalled Wanda saying. "Sparkles in the opening number are forbidden."

It may have been the case, but Vanessa seems to have felt patronized by this bit of advice ("Wanda thought she could rattle me, but her plan didn't work"), even while Vanessa's pageant director immediately got to work pushing the crystals to the underside of the knit. Wanda now wonders if Vanessa confused her for someone else, since she herself was an unrepentant sequin addict. But Wanda, too, had been sizing up the competition. She sensed that she wasn't vying with fifty women. At most, she was up against fifteen. The rest were just happy to be there.

But the judges threw her off with one of their questions: "How do you feel about little boys competing in pageants?" Wanda certainly had some thoughts about this. But was this a question about the problems with kiddie pageants, or about equal rights? What was the *right* answer? She feared that if she shared her true opinion, "they might see me as a backwoods girl who wasn't open to new ideas," she says, "so I said, 'I don't have a problem with that.'" It seemed designed to make her squirm, and she felt she never succeeded in connecting with the judges. It was a far happier thing to have low expectations. Miss Nebraska, Kristin Lowenberg, a short-haired girl from a state that never, ever, won, was tickled to find that Rod McKuen, the 1960s poet/songwriter, was one of her judges, she being the last teenager in America to still read his books.

"I started to have a conversation with him about poetry in the middle of my interview," she says. "I had a really good time."

No such luck for Dana. She knew she was doomed when the poet hit her with a question that implied her surgery confession was a publicity stunt. On that Wednesday night, she was in the first of three groups competing in swimsuit. Walking across the stage, she noticed the judges tilting their heads for a better look at her bosom. The word on the street was that she would have won the swimsuit prize if not for their issues with cosmetic surgery. But who knows? She was up against tough competition: That night, it was Vanessa who took home the prize.

✦   ✦   ✦

Vanessa's swimsuit victory was big news—only the third time a black woman had won a preliminary. But the New Jersey folks in the crowd knew that Thursday was the night to see. That's when Suzette Charles would sing.

Suzette wasn't merely a hometown girl, raised just twenty-five minutes from Convention Hall, in Mays Landing, New Jersey. She was also a prodigy, who had been working in commercials and small film roles since childhood; more recently she had performed in the casino lounges, sometimes as the opening act for Lou Rawls or Gladys Knight. Born Suzette DeGaetano, the only child of a black mother and white father, she had taken her father's first name for her stage name, her eye on becoming a singing, acting, multihyphenate superstar, à la Liza, Barbra, Diana.

She handily won her talent preliminary that night with a soaring Streisand ballad, "Kiss Me in the Rain." Now it was clear that there were two African-American front-runners. "A Miss America First?" a *New York Daily News* headline proposed. But there was still one more night of preliminaries—one more chance for a contestant to break through.

Wanda was in her swimsuit and in a panic. She thought her interview had gone poorly; and in the talent prelims, her trilling soprano had hit the high notes of "More Than You Know" but lost to Miss Missouri's electric fiddle. Mississippi was legendary for winning swimsuit trophies, but this had never been Wanda's strength. She had struggled to keep the last fifteen pounds off. After she was done with pageants, Wanda would let herself go back to her old size 10 and find a happy career as a plus-size model. But at age twenty-four and peak svelte, she was not at ease walking out there in her bathing suit. Until Miss Texas gave her a talk backstage.

"Wanda, let's change the way you're thinking about this," she recalls Dana telling her. "You need to walk out there like you're the most beautiful, breathtaking creature they've ever seen. *You* are their Miss America, and you need to show it."

In the years that followed, Wanda would hear all the stereotypes about pageant girls—the legends of thrown hairbrushes and stolen shoes and all kinds of backstabbing. But that was never what she experienced. Pageant girls might gossip about one another; they might harbor a quiet envy. But for the most part, they *liked* one another. Rivals went on to become roommates, bridesmaids, pen pals, Facebook friends; seeking one another out for reunions decades after their brief shared moment in Atlantic City. Who else, after all, could possibly understand? Who else could appreciate why it ever mattered?

Dana was having a hard time, too. Though she still had one last chance, in that night's talent preliminary, she and B. Don agreed she wasn't going to make Top 10, and she had a little breakdown that night, crying by herself in her hotel room. Still, she always enjoyed the company of the other girls, especially those from the other superpower states. They all goofed around backstage, Trelynda hoisting Dana on her shoulders in a cheerleader hold, the singers harmonizing in the stairwell just for fun. So of course she gave Wanda a pep talk. "That's what we did for each other," she says.

It worked. Wanda walked on stage focused on sending a message to the judges with her face, eyes, and body: *Look at me!* And Wanda, who had never won a swimsuit competition in Mississippi, won the prize in Atlantic City that night.

Dana did not win her talent preliminary, though. Once again, the trophy for her group that night went to Miss New York, Vanessa Williams.

✦   ✦   ✦

It's that time again
There's that mountain to climb again
The challenge is there
The prize is yours if you dare!

They spilled out onto the stage in their sporty knitwear and pumps, swaying to the sounds of the Glenn Osser Orchestra, the Miss America house band of nearly thirty years, and lip-syncing one of the upbeat ditties Glenn and his wife, Edna, wrote for the production numbers every year.

And you know, yes you know
You're gonna go for it, go for it, go for it all!

This was it. Finals night. The two-hour televised culmination of a competition it had taken them months or years to reach. And it all blew by in a flash.

One by one, they walked to the microphone for a four-second self-intro. Out in the audience, B. Don stood up from his seat as Dana came up to the front. This was his secret signal to her, so she gave an especially big grin as she informed the world that her state pageant was held in Houston.

Just minutes into the show, Gary Collins pulled an envelope from his burgundy dinner jacket: the names of the ten finalists. First, Suzette. She seemed pleased but not surprised. Same with Wanda, who'd gotten her groove back with that swimsuit win. But even though B. Don had tipped her off, Dana couldn't help but clasp her hands to her face, flustered with glee. And Kristin Lowenberg, the Nebraska girl on nobody's radar, trembled with giddy shock as she was beckoned forward. Vanessa got a huge cheer when at last her name was called.

For forty other women, including Deneen Graham and Trelynda Kerr, the game was over. Trelynda was devastated. The end of a fifteen-year dream. And *now* what was she supposed to do? Today, she wishes that she had come up in pageants in the era of "platforms" and service requirements. Trelynda could have used a cause back then—something to take with her beyond pageants. Years later, after realizing she was gay and drifting away from pageant circles, but then returning as a Miss Oklahoma judge in 2016, she thought, maybe *this* was it—maybe she could be the person who helps make Miss America LGBTQ-friendly. Soon enough, of course, Miss America had bigger problems to deal with. But it remained essential to her, this thing she'd been a part of at the age of twenty-one.

"It's still," Trelynda says thirty-six years later, "the greatest thing I've ever done."

They were shunted off to the wings, to be seen only fleetingly for the rest of the show. But even the Top 10 were seen more than heard, and hardly seen enough, what with all the variety-show fluff. When they had a rare chance to speak live, during the evening gown competition, it was in corny get-to-know-me declarations.

"As a math major, I may one day design a future space shuttle!" said Miss Alabama, Pam Battles, in form-fitting white lace. "And as a music major, I will also be able to supply the piped-in music!"

At least the swimsuit competition was interspersed with ten-second excerpts from their interviews, another chance to hear accents and see faces in motion. Otherwise, it was a parade of pencil bodies, the hard-fought reward for the eight-hundred-calorie-a-day diets that pageant women openly bragged about in those days. The pale-skinned girls looked downright ghostly: It was the era before aggressive bronzing went mainstream, and even a Bain de Soleil tan got neutralized by the TV lights. But if the rest of their figures had wasted away, the bustlines remained solid—how *did* that work? The Miss Nebraska advisors, confounded by Kristin's lean, athletic figure, showed her all the tricks with padding and tape and thickly lined bra cups—because nothing, they said, absolutely *nothing* must show. So Kristin had been stunned to see Miss New York stroll into preliminaries in an unreinforced, civilian-grade bathing suit, her silhouetted nipples leading the way.

"I thought, 'Oh my gosh, this is not going to be good!'" Kristin says. But apparently it was just fine.

The talent portion was comparatively deep, each woman getting a full two and a half minutes of camera time. Dana took the stage in a billowing, high-neck gown—this time the focus would be on her voice, not her body—and began to sing.

Oh I wish I was in the land of cotton.
Old times there are not forgotten . . .

Yes, Miss Texas was singing "Dixie." Yes, in 1983, yes, at *this* historic moment for Miss America. It was Elvis Presley's version—his "American Trilogy" medley—and Dana killed it, with her lusty vibrato, weepy sighs, and glorious high notes. But she knew even then it was not a politically well-considered choice. "Why B. Don had me do 'American Trilogy,' I have no idea," she says thirty-six years later. "I did a really good 'Don't Rain on My Parade,' but he hated that song." And B. Don loved Elvis.

Pam Rigas had won a swimsuit preliminary, and she looked like a Ralph Lauren model in her peach-and-silver column evening gown. But now the elegant Miss Ohio was done up in a garish purple pantsuit, a hokey black fedora pushed over her eyes, not just singing but *dancing*, too, with much shoulder-hunched strutting and Fosse-lite jazz-hands-ing. It was "Shine It On," a little-loved Liza Minnelli number, and Lord knows, Pam was working hard, but . . . it just didn't work. "I was not a stage performer," she explains. Pam was an artist, who had won her local pageant the year before by showing her paintings, in fact. But the state pageant folks had determined that this non-singer/non-dancer should sing *and* dance. And so she did—with a handheld microphone, its white cord unspooling ominously around her spike heels.

"I was so naïve and young and trusting," she says. "I should have played the piano."

There may have been fifty young women from across the country vying to be Miss America, but they had pageant directors the age of their parents or grandparents telling them how to do it. That's why you had a twenty-four-year-old Miss Kentucky crooning about the midlife regret of "Yesterday When I Was Young," and Miss Missouri sawing through the bluegrass standard "Orange Blossom Special." Alabama played a Gershwin piano medley, Florida sang "Over the Rainbow," and Wanda's song was straight from Tin Pan Alley.

So to see Miss Nebraska in her leotard and legwarmers rolling on the floor, spinning on her bottom, cartwheeling, back-arching, and skipping to one of the biggest pop hits of the year—it was different! Her state pageant director had politely hinted that singing might be safer: Dancers never won. But Kristin was a dancer, her favorite new movie was about dancing, and she wanted to have some fun. So, she did *the* dance, the one you'd seen all that summer on MTV:

What a feeling . . .
I can have it all now I'm dancing for my life . . .

It was a ballsy choice, setting Kristin up for comparison to a gorgeous movie star of the moment and her pro-dancer body double. But if you wanted to pump up a crowd in September 1983, you could never go wrong with "Flashdance."

For singers who wanted to edge into a contemporary aesthetic without alienating the old folks, the new lodestar was Streisand. That is, if you had the chops to tackle her songs—and Suzette, who performed first, turned in by far the most virtuosic performance of the night. How was *this* voice coming out of a twenty-year-old? The only problem was the song itself: "Kiss Me in the Rain," a complex and less-than-indelible tune that never topped the charts.

Vanessa had run into the same issue. She won Miss Syracuse with "Being Good Isn't Good Enough"—another showcase for a sparkling vocalist. But Vanessa's pageant mentor urged her to switch: It was important to pick a song the judges knew. She suggested "Happy Days Are Here Again"—not the bouncy FDR campaign theme, but the sloweddown reinterpretation of it that Streisand debuted during her early rise to fame.

So there she was, the last woman to perform. On stage in a liquid silver gown, Vanessa stuck to the languorous Streisand tempo. But while the young Barbra had wrung some ambiguous melancholy out of the song—as if still scarred by the *un*happy days—Vanessa's take was bright-eyed, triumphant, and more than a little sly.

This was the song of a woman enjoying her happy days, all right, and ready for more of the same. This was quite possibly as sexy as you could ever be and still win the Miss America pageant.

The ten women returned to the stage, lined up facing the audience to hear the results.

Fourth runner-up: Miss Ohio, Pamela Rigas.

Her gracious smile betrayed just a hint of sweet relief. Pam looked more than ready to get back to law school.

Third runner-up: Miss Mississippi, Wanda Gayle Geddie.

Wanda mustered the obligatory smile. She got over it quick, crying the next day more out of release than sorrow. "*You* were supposed to be Miss America," her mother said months later, after everything blew up, but Wanda knew better. "Mom," she said, "if I was *supposed* to be Miss America, I would have *been* Miss America."

Second runner-up: Miss Alabama, Pam Battles.

At this point, Vanessa could do the math. Seven women left on the stage, and she knew the names that would definitely be called that had not yet been called. And it was an honor to come in second to Suzette Charles. . . .

First runner-up: Miss New Jersey, Suzette Charles.

Now everyone knew—even Vanessa. Rod McKuen later claimed that the panel had fought all week over Vanessa vs. Wanda until he and another judge prevailed. And yet in that crowning moment, it would feel as though the outcome had always been inevitable. Dana, standing at the far end of the line and no longer listening for her own name, leaned forward with a huge smile to glimpse Vanessa's reaction a split second before it came.

When Debbie Maffett put the crown on her head, Vanessa could only think: *There goes my junior year abroad.* It took a couple minutes for her to realize that she had become the first black Miss America, and that this would mean something to the rest of the world.

✦   ✦   ✦

Some of the media was caught off guard. The *Washington Post* had decided the previous year that no one cared about Miss America anymore and opted not to send a reporter. The *New York Times* ran a wire story in its Sunday-morning editions with a photo of runner-up Suzette—correctly identified, at least—rather than the actual winner.

They caught up quickly. Everyone did. Vanessa's crowning would go down as one of the biggest news events of the year—heralded in some quarters as a breakthrough on par with Jackie Robinson integrating Major League Baseball.

"The inherent racism in America must be diluting itself," declared Shirley Chisholm, the first black woman elected to Congress. "Thank God I have lived long enough that this nation has been able to select the beautiful young woman of color to be Miss America."

The *Times* put Vanessa on Monday's front page and opined that her victory "tells a new truth about social values in America." The *Washington Post* placed her in the context of a glorious trend of "the new black women"—burgeoning stars like Jennifer Beals and Shari Belafonte, born after the strife of the civil rights movement but reaping its rewards in what promised to be a color-blind world.

Vanessa was cheered by the press for speaking her mind on the obligatory checklist of issues—pro-ERA, anti–marijuana legalization, pro-choice, wary of the Soviets, in favor of a federal holiday honoring Martin Luther King Jr. But the politics of this Miss America were quickly resituated to a grander context. And if the world was looking for a new spokeswoman on racial progress, Vanessa intuitively delivered.

"There is nothing holding anyone back," she said in an early meeting with the press. "People can do anything they want, and be anything they want . . . Nothing has held me back." She gave credit to those who had come before her: "I know it is not half as hard to make it [now] as 20 years ago." Yet she struck a positive tone that a white audience would find reassuring. No, she did not think America was racist anymore; no, she did not experience it as segregated. She emphasized the importance of education, character, and hard work. "I'm ambitious, I have a lot of drive, and I work hard to get somewhere."

Still, there was a fraught undertone to the conversation about Vanessa. In 1983, a backlash against affirmative action was underway, with the Reagan administration trying to roll back workforce diversity measures that promoted specific "quotas" for minority hiring, and conservative pundits bemoaning the specter of "reverse discrimination." Whether or not the question was directly asked of her—*Did you win just because you're black?*—it was in the air. And Vanessa, this woman of traffic-stopping beauty and steamrollering talent, was forced to address it.

"I was chosen because I was qualified for the position," she said the day after her crowning. "The fact I was black was not a factor. I've always had to try harder in my life to achieve things, so this is regular."

"I can assure you," Al Marks added, "that this young lady got there on her merits."

Clearly, the Atlantic City impresario was pleased. There was an unarticulated upshot in all the free publicity Vanessa had brought the pageant—all the news stories, opinion pieces, talk-radio chatter, even the negative takes—that was deeply validating for him, for her, for the institution itself. The fact that it was such a big deal that a black woman had been crowned Miss America was proof that Miss America still mattered.

All Miss Americas found themselves swept up into a whirlwind of glamour and excitement—but nothing like what Vanessa experienced. Other Miss Americas got to ride on floats at the Macy's Thanksgiving Day Parade; Vanessa got to sit next to President Reagan at the White House state dinner for West Germany. Debbie Maffett dated a cute soap opera actor she met during her reign; Vanessa got asked out by Eddie Murphy, the hottest young star in the world.

She headlined a $225-a-head New Year's Eve concert at New York's Waldorf Astoria. She stood alongside Coretta Scott King and trailblazing black astronaut Guion Bluford Jr. at an MLK birthday rally in Atlanta. On a trip to Washington, where she spoke to both the National Press Club and the National Conference of Black Mayors, "people approached her with a frenzy once reserved for Mick Jagger and departed with the ecstatic smiles associated with religious experience," a reporter noted.

All the while, though, she had to deal with racial slights and various forms of blowback. "The first black Miss America was crowned," Johnny Carson joked in his monologue. "It's about time. That's really nice. [*pause*] Having Mr. T as one of the judges didn't hurt." Mary Ann Mobley, a Mississippi native, reportedly snarked to Vanessa's new pageant chaperone, "Are you ready to go to Harlem?" There were racist, threatening letters sent to her parents' home and extra security required at some appearances. Some of the most stinging gibes came from African-Americans—black commentators who dismissed the notion that her crowning was a racial breakthrough, arguing that her fair coloring and straight hair simply reinforced Anglo beauty standards. Her victory "does not mean that nappy hair, full lips and dark skin are beautiful in America," wrote the *Washington Post*'s Courtland Milloy. When it was revealed that her longtime boyfriend was white, Vanessa received vicious letters calling her a race traitor.

Six months into the job, she was frustrated that even on the best days, she was always treated as a symbol of race relations, asked to hold forth on the burning political issues of the day. "I'm only 20 years old," she told a reporter. "What qualifies me to answer?" She had taken on this gig in hopes of launching a performing career—but no one was taking much notice of her talent.

Yet by all accounts Vanessa Williams was very, very good at this job. With a grace and maturity beyond her years, she gave her handlers none of the headaches they had encountered with other young titleholders. The pageant's corporate sponsors—Gillette, McDonald's, Nestlé, American Greetings—called again and again for promotional appearances and dinners with executives. And she remained conscientious about showing respect to all the small-time volunteers at the pageants where she was called to officiate.

"She was *loved* by the Miss America people," says Trelynda, who ran into her a few times that year in Oklahoma. "She'd remember their names and be able to say, 'You look like you lost weight' . . . She had this photographic memory of meeting people that was amazing. Everyone just loved her."

✦ ✦ ✦

In July 1984, several of the past year's contestants were brought back together to perform in Atlantic City for pageant volunteers. As they gathered in a hotel suite, Dana Rogers noticed that Vanessa seemed out of sorts.

She was sitting on the floor, knees pulled to her chest, staring at the rug. Her usually gorgeous skin was badly broken out. When Dana asked, Vanessa insisted that everything was fine.

The previous Friday, Vanessa had taken a phone call from a *New York Post* reporter in her hotel room in Watertown, New York, where she had returned to crown the next Miss New York. She was nine weeks from the end of her reign as Miss America.

At first, it seemed like the typical interview she had done so many of that year. The reporter asked her about Geraldine Ferraro's selection that week as Walter Mondale's running mate, the first woman in history on a major-party presidential ticket—and the biggest barrier-breaking moment since Vanessa's crowning. But the conversation took a bizarre turn: Oh, by the way, the man asked, a source told him there would be nude photos of Vanessa in *Penthouse*—was it true?

Vanessa denied it and got off the phone as quickly as possible, horrified.

She knew nothing about *Penthouse*. But photos? They did exist.

Years later, Vanessa would describe herself as an unlikely beauty queen, an outlier in this uptight, churchy world. Growing up in affluent Westchester County, New York, where her family was for many years the only black family on the block, she was a good student and a theater prodigy. But she also smoked pot and drank beer. She had had boyfriends, and she had enjoyed sex with them. In her senior year of high school, she got pregnant and had an early-term abortion. "Vanessa as Miss America?" she recalled her theater pals joking in 1983 after she won her local title. "They have no idea who you are!"

In fact, over the previous decade, Miss America had crowned liberals, a law student, and a couple other admitted pot-smokers. But Vanessa, in her limited experience of pageants, still felt that she was different, and maybe she was—even if it was simply by virtue of being more like a typical American college junior than most of the women who still entered pageants.

She did have a rebellious streak, though, that drove her school-teacher parents up a wall. Much, much later she would grapple with the memory of the night she was molested, at age ten, by a teenage girl who was a friend of family friends and realize that this episode had left her "highly sexualized" at too young an age, angry and confused and prone to act out.

So she was both a daring nineteen-year-old drama queen and a naïve suburban kid when she replied to a "models wanted" ad at the end of her freshman year at Syracuse in 1982. It turned out that Tom Chiapel was operating his Westchester photography studio as a commonplace quasi-scam—sure, he needed models, but first she needed a portfolio, and he could offer her a *great* bargain—but in hindsight it also looks like a cruel long con. He ended up offering Vanessa a summer job as a receptionist and makeup artist. They became pals, she thought, and he impressed her with his patter about chiaroscuro and other art-school techniques. He took some "fashion" shots of her. And after a few weeks, he mentioned that a female friend was coming over to model nude, and would she like to join the shoot? *It's going to be very artsy. You won't even see your face. The photos will stay with me.*

Two summers later, her life had metamorphosed—and it soon became clear that none of Tom's glib reassurances had ever been truthful. The week-long crisis that followed would not just humiliate a young woman on the world stage and threaten to blow up her future. It would bring the entire Miss America institution to the brink of collapse.

By the time that Dana noticed her in a funk, Vanessa had learned through her lawyer that the *Penthouse* rumor was true and broached the issue with Al Marks. Accounts differ on exactly how those conversations went down. Al told reporters she apologized, "tearful to the point of hysterics." Vanessa recalled Al taking the news calmly and reassuring her that it would all blow over, which he later denied. Leonard Horn, then the pageant's general counsel, was unable to attend the meeting, but he recalls Al describing Vanessa reassuring *him* that there was nothing to worry about—yes, there were photos, but "with a drape here and a drape there" to keep it decent.

It was a couple days later, on Wednesday, that Leonard learned there was plenty to worry about. A sponsor had seen an advance copy of *Penthouse* and called Al: *We've got a problem.*

Al convened an emergency meeting of the Miss America executive committee at his home. The magazine wouldn't arrive until Friday. But that Wednesday night, Leonard says, they decided that if the photos were as bad as they were hearing, they would have to ask Vanessa to resign. And if she didn't resign . . . well, they would have to figure it out.

Vanessa was still going about the business of being Miss America. On Thursday, she made an appearance for Gillette in a Little Rock, Arkansas, drugstore. Wearing a puffy-sleeved print dress that would have looked just right on Princess Diana, she was signing autographs for kids when her chaperone whispered, "Your lawyer needs you to call." The news of the photos was breaking on Chicago's WBBM-TV. But news did not travel fast in those days, and network television was consumed with Walter Mondale's acceptance speech on the closing night of the Democratic National Convention. So at a dinner that evening with Gillette executives, Vanessa endured one more night of pretending everything was normal.

When she awoke on Friday, the story was in all the papers—"Miss America in Nudie Pix" was the *New York Daily News* headline. There were quotes from Al Marks musing that she could lose her crown. Bob Guccione, the founder of *Penthouse*, gloated that he had destroyed the "myth" of Miss America: "The vestal virgins have just flown the coop. These are real, live, flesh and blood women." Vanessa was chased to the airport by paparazzi only to find a CBS camera guy on her flight, angling for an interview.

Al had scheduled a press conference in Atlantic City for early Friday afternoon. Shortly before reporters showed up, the magazine arrived. Leonard heard the reaction of the others in the office—"Oh my God"— before he saw it for himself.

"There is no question," he says, "that this went beyond 'a drape here, a drape there.'" The decision was made to give her seventy-two hours to resign; Vanessa was still in flight, but he called her attorney. Later, Vanessa would say she was hurt that she didn't hear this request directly. But as far as Al was concerned, everything was in the lawyers' hands now.

"This is a unique and terribly difficult situation in the 63-year history of Miss America," Al told the roughly seventy-five reporters and photographers who turned out for the press conference. He said he fully expected that Vanessa would resign by Monday afternoon: "She knows that the photographs . . . are totally inconsistent with the Miss America image." He also brandished the office copy of *Penthouse* to show everyone the cover—an innocent, cutesy file photo of Vanessa with octogenarian comedian George Burns. The Miss America pageant, Al maintained, "celebrates the whole woman" and is "intrinsically inconsistent with calculated sexual exploitation."

Had Vanessa violated pageant rules? Technically not, perhaps, Leonard explained to the press—but she had signed a contract swearing "to good moral character" and pledging that she had not "engaged in acts of moral turpitude." He added, "If you don't draw the line here, where do you draw it?"

How "bad" were the photos? "Ugh. I can't even show them to my wife," Al said. There were ten photos in all. The ones in which she posed with the other young woman were indeed gauzy and backlit, her shadowed face not obviously identifiable—except if cross-referenced against the two images of Vanessa by herself, topless and gazing at the camera. Four of the photos suggested oral sex—abstracted, to be sure, but poses that the models would have had to understand were luridly erotic in their intent.

The photos were mild compared to typical *Penthouse* fare—but nonetheless, they were in *Penthouse*, considered the epitome of sleaze, far more edgy and graphic than *Playboy*, whose editors boasted about how they had nobly refused to buy the photos when offered. *Penthouse* and *Playboy* were both eager to make a splash in those days, facing the first real challenges to their business model now that the VCR revolution was allowing porn enthusiasts to bring X-rated films home. And *Penthouse* made a big profit on the $50,000 it paid for the photos, selling millions more copies than usual at a jacked-up cover price. Regardless of *Playboy*'s piety, this was a standard strategy for both publications—procuring the obscure photos a star posed for long before she became famous. It had happened to Suzanne Somers a couple years earlier; it would happen the next year to Madonna. And the fact that they would publish these photos against the star's wishes? Well, that was the point. The humiliation, the vulnerability, was the point. On top of that, these were photos of Vanessa with *another woman*. In 1984, 72 percent of Americans thought it was always wrong for same-sex adults to have sexual relations, a number that had dropped to 31 percent by 2018. Which may explain the degree of vehemence Vanessa faced. In an interview with *People*, Miss America 1944, Venus Ramey, called Vanessa a "slut."

For three full days, no one knew whether Miss America would step down. Vanessa spent the weekend holed up in her hometown of Millwood, New York, conferring with her parents, her attorney, Dennis Dowdell, and a young L.A.-based publicist named Ramon Hervey, debating whether to fight or resign. Her father, Milton, argued that resigning would look like an admission of guilt, and she had not done anything wrong. "They'll have to pull the crown off her head," he told reporters. "My daughter is a feisty young woman."

Vanessa did fight, up to a point. On Sunday, after days of silence, she gave two galvanizing interviews to the *New York Times* and the Associated Press. She alleged that neither the photographer nor *Penthouse* had legal permission to use the images.

"Right now I feel personally very violated," she said, "by *Penthouse*, by the photographer, and by the pageant officials." She said she had hoped in vain that Al Marks "would believe in me enough as a Miss America to hear my side, especially after I confided in them."

These interviews were trial balloons that failed to catch wind—but what's remarkable is that she launched them. Vanessa spoke out and pushed back. Most young women caught up in that era's sex scandals did their best to get lost as quickly as possible. Vanessa confronted her scandal head-on. It was a harbinger of the gutsy way a younger generation would grapple with news that once would have been ruinous—like Jennifer Lawrence, who in 2014 ably flipped the script when nude selfies hacked from her phone ended up on the internet, refusing to apologize for the photos and standing up for herself as the victim of a sex crime.

Al Marks, though, intensified the pressure. That same day, he put out word that no matter what Vanessa planned to do, she would not be a part of the upcoming pageant. She would not be allowed to crown her successor; her name would never be uttered.

On Sunday, Leonard got a call from Vanessa's attorney: She was not going to resign. That's when Leonard says he delivered his speech.

He told the lawyer that Vanessa had been an excellent Miss America—but that she was now also the face of the entire Miss America system. And if her image was besmirched, then thousands of demoralized little girls who once dreamed of being Miss America would want to have nothing to do with the program. And she would be responsible for this. Ten minutes later, Leonard recalls, the lawyer called back to say that Vanessa would resign.

But in Vanessa's telling, she agonized until the last minute on Monday. Her lawyer had made another compelling argument: that she would do better to prepare for her long-term future than get dragged down in a fight for a short-term job. Even before settling on a decision, she and Ramon worked out a speech intended to send the message that she would be back, that she would survive and move on to greater things. So when she finally made her decision, they only had to rewrite a couple lines.

"I wish I could retain my title as Miss America," she told a packed press conference in Manhattan. Her voice was clear and calm. She managed to smile and make eye contact. "However, the potential harm to the pageant and the deep division that a bitter fight may cause has convinced me that I must relinquish my title as Miss America."

The story trickled on for a couple more months, a spiral of sleaze. Some more nude photos came to light: a shoot from that same summer of 1982 by a different supposed fashion photographer who wheedled Vanessa into sheerer fabrics and ever tinier garb, the last a sort of S&M

bikini. (Stupid? Maybe. But you can also imagine a college freshman with modeling ambitions thinking: *Just like those edgy Helmut Newton spreads in* Vogue, *right?*) *Penthouse* got those, too. Bob Guccione played the mustache-twirling villain with insinuating faux magnanimity— offering to finance Vanessa's legal case if she fought to keep her title, offering to improve upon her Miss America salary if she joined the *Penthouse* PR team.

Vanessa sued the magazine and both photographers. The defendants fought back, arguing she had signed waivers allowing them to use her photos, and the cases chugged through court. Her lawyers, though, warned that her life would go under the microscope in deposition—and that she would be asked if she had ever been with a woman. Vanessa thought of the teenage girl who molested her, and the mixed-up shame and horror of it all came back. In 1986, she dropped the suit, acknowledging all the fine print she had failed to read when signing documents at those photo studios so long ago.

The cruel way Vanessa was treated then—by the media, by the pageant—is hard to fathom today. It was manifestly clear in 1984 just how cynically the photographers seemed to have exploited her. Why didn't the Miss America establishment fight *for* its winner, instead of shamefacedly casting her off?

More than thirty-five years later, Leonard Horn makes no apologies. He felt sympathetic to her then and still does. But she knew these photos were in her past when she signed her contracts, first with Miss New York and then Miss America, and she told no one of their potential to surface in her future.

And those who believe the pageant could have been more magnanimous and forgiving of this twenty-year-old girl? They have *no* idea, he says, just how tenuous the pageant's position was in that moment.

Set aside the sixty-three years of history and the blockbuster ratings, and Miss America was nothing more than a rickety mom-and-pop operation, unequipped for the stress of a global scandal. It still operated under an increasingly outmoded sponsorship system, in which pageant officials were responsible every year for bringing a full slate of advertisers to the network, which meant that the brands were intimately involved with the workings of the pageant—the reason why Gary Collins would hype the upcoming Taster's Choice commercial, the reason why Miss Americas found themselves riding so many Oldsmobiles and touring so many Gillette plants. If the sponsors had bailed on the pageant—well, that would have been it, Leonard says. There would be no pageant.

Eight years later, Leonard would work out a deal to free Miss America from this panicky hand-to-mouth cycle, allowing NBC to fill all the commercial spots itself and pay the pageant for the privilege of airing it. It put the organization on a steadier financial footing and liberated the Miss Americas from the circuit of supermarket and department-store appearances that Leonard felt diminished the crown. But in July 1984, Miss America was still on the sponsorship model—and at that very moment, waiting for the sponsors to send the annual checks that would pay the bills and award the scholarships for the next pageant, just eight weeks away.

"A whole pageant was on the verge of collapse," Leonard says now, "had we not handled it the way they wanted it to be handled."

He doesn't know for sure whether the sponsors would have pulled out if Vanessa had not resigned. But "they were ready to pull out," he says. After she stepped down, the sponsors called and said they would wait and see how things played out. Which was just as much lifeline as Miss America needed in that moment.

"If they had pulled out in July of that year, the pageant would have ended," Leonard says now. "We had no money."

✦   ✦   ✦

Vanessa's downfall was alarming for the women who competed against her. Many found themselves in the awkward situation of being asked to comment on the scandal by their hometown newspapers or TV news stations.

"I was more *upset* than I was ever ashamed or ticked off," says Kristin Lowenberg, who had applauded so hard when Vanessa was crowned her arms looked like they'd fly off. "I was upset it could happen to someone like that."

"I do not think she should have had to resign," says Trelynda Kerr.

"Yes, she took the pictures, but no, she didn't put them out there . . . There's a difference between someone who comes up in pageants and someone who doesn't. She didn't know what she was getting herself into."

They all knew how much Vanessa had at stake; more than any of them would have had. She had lost out on $2 million in endorsement deals that were supposed to pave her way well beyond Miss America. Her goals were bigger, her ceiling was higher; whether she wanted it or not, she had become a symbol.

"I had all of my stuff air nationally, and I didn't like it, but it didn't break me," Dana Rogers says. "But her—it broke her."

Yet their thoughts also went to Suzette Charles. The Miss America line of succession, never before tested, suddenly looked fragile.

During the weekend that Vanessa's fate hung in the balance, Wanda Geddie got a call from the Miss America staff wanting to know if she, as third runner-up, would accept the crown if it was offered to her. Pam Battles, the second runner-up, was unavailable on account of getting married in August. And as for the first runner-up . . . no one was confident Suzette would take it.

Suzette had options. The contestant with the daunting résumé—"the best talent I've ever seen," says Trelynda—had moved up from casino lounges to showrooms, performing with stars like Bill Cosby. She had just booked her first Atlantic City headlining gig, a three-night mid-September stint at the Sands Casino. Talk would soon burble up that she was in the running for a role on the hot new *Cosby Show* sitcom as the off-at-college oldest daughter.

Wanda told the Miss America folks that she'd take the job if it came to that. She doubted Suzette would ever want it. "Most of the girls who are standing there on stage are looking for Miss America to take them to the next level," she says. "But Suzette was already there." They were all mindful, too, that Suzette had been the one who had worked for years to become Miss America. That she was the one, unlike Vanessa, who really wanted it. But would she want it *this* way—a title with an asterisk, a crown for eight weeks?

But Suzette said yes. Her formal installation took place at pageant headquarters—Al Marks kissing her on the cheek and saying, "You're the new Miss America." Then she said a few words to the press. No one had a crown ready for her. When she did a photo shoot with Gary Collins, he fished his wife's 1959 crown from the closet for her.

After her brief reign, Suzette seemed primed for stardom. But a role on a soap quickly ran out its storyline. She continued to play big rooms for years, but her success in casinos never led to a breakout recording career. There were stories of inept management and a record label that went bust, a sense that the techniques that thrilled middle-aged audiences couldn't translate to a modern pop sound. By 2002, she had stepped back from touring to raise her children at home in southern New Jersey. It's never been clear whether Miss America is a plus or minus in show business—the exposure vs. the baggage—and especially so with a title as jagged as the one 1984 had to offer.

But whether it was at personal sacrifice or not, Suzette undeniably did the pageant a big favor in 1984. Could the pageant have survived taking the title away from the first black Miss America if they had not been able to anoint the second that very same day?

"My commitment," she explained a day before she stepped into Vanessa's shoes, "is to the pageant."

✦   ✦   ✦

A fast eight weeks later, the crown was on a new head, this one blonde. Miss Utah, Sharlene Wells, had the kind of clear blue eyes and glowing complexion that suggest brisk hikes in mountain air and the aristocratic kind of nose you knew matched the family photos. She sang a Paraguayan folk song, accompanying herself on the harp, and she had won the swimsuit competition in an athletic tank that exposed the barest minimum of cleavage and fewer inches of thigh than most—a "Utah" suit, they called it. If the press hadn't picked up on all the signals, she spelled it out for them the next day:

"You can be very sure," the Brigham Young University junior said, "there will be no problems this year."

She went on: "I have lived my life above reproach. . . . I have absolutely no skeletons in the closet."

Ahem. "Couldn't she just accept her crown with grace and no moral smugness?" wrote one syndicated columnist, who like many critics interpreted Sharlene's words as a jab at Vanessa. Those critics had no idea, though, the kinds of questions that had provoked those awkward comments—and no idea what it was like to compete in Atlantic City that miserable year.

The funk of the Vanessa scandal lingered for years, but it overwhelmed everything in September 1984. About 450 journalists swarmed Convention Hall to cover the pageant, up from 300 the previous year. Despite Al Marks's plea to put the "unforeseen events" of July in the past, contestants found themselves quizzed on them by every reporter they spoke to. It was a feistier and more skeptical press corps covering Miss America than a decade or so ago, thanks to the new young generation of reporters inspired by Watergate. The attitude of the press this year seemed to be that the public had been sold a bill of goods on this whole Miss America thing, and now its degree of actual wholesomeness must be interrogated.

On the first day of the pageant, United Press International broke the news that Miss Ohio, Melissa Bradley, had two years earlier pleaded "no contest" to a shoplifting charge—the kind of indiscretion that in past years may well never have been noticed. But this new era of skepticism dovetailed with the increasing digitization of court records that kept making it easier for journalists to unearth the bad behavior of the newly famous. Within a day of Miss Ohio's tearful public explanation and the pageant's legalistic words of forgiveness, though, the episode was mostly forgotten—indeed, she went on to finish as first runner-up—because, well, guess who slithered back into the spotlight.

It was Bob Guccione, of course, claiming he was in possession of 350 nude color slides of one of the fifty-one contestants. Which one, he wouldn't say—but if she won, he intended to publish the photos. Oh, and she was bound to make the Top 5, a *Penthouse* flack insinuated, because "that's how great she is."

Was it true? No such photos ever emerged, and it's hard to believe that *Penthouse* would demur from the opportunity to humiliate a Miss America also-ran in 1984 simply because she hadn't won. But the threat sent

Atlantic City into shudders of paranoia. Now it wasn't only journalists on the hunt; judges, too, asked contestants in their interviews if they had ever posed in the buff. State directors started policing evening gowns for excess sexiness. Miss Texas found herself the focus of much leering speculation because B. Don had put out a press release—condemned by a Texas chapter of the National Organization for Women—bragging that she had "all the parts it takes" to become Miss America.

The paranoia fueled a toxic sense of resentment among the young women that the contest was rigged to avoid another "Vanessa situation." Many were convinced that neither a black woman (a record six in competition that year) nor anyone with a showbiz background would be allowed to win. Much later, that year's Miss Iowa interviewed fellow contestants for a master's thesis and found they had spent years stewing over the outcome and their own misplaced sense of failure.

"They picked Sharlene because they knew a Mormon girl would never pose in the nude," one complained. "To then show their hands were not forced, they chose a shoplifter as first runner-up."

Obviously, Sharlene heard this kind of talk.

"Everyone has something to say about why you shouldn't be Miss America," Sharlene told Debra Deitering Maddox, the former Miss Iowa, in 1998. She was glad that she entered the pageant but wouldn't want to do it again. If she had anticipated the demands of the job, the backbiting, and the toll on her self-esteem, "I don't think I would do it."

It had been a year since Vanessa Williams changed the conversation about Miss America. When she won, swooning journalists suspended the condescension they typically brought to the pageant. Her ground-breaking victory reestablished that there were many interesting things to discuss with or about a suddenly famous young woman—civil rights, feminism, or global politics, say; not just sex and drugs. For a moment, it seemed that *who* won this peculiar competition and *why* could have a meaning worth parsing for the larger culture. But then Vanessa's disgrace became the entire conversation about Miss America. With her abrupt ouster, old cynicisms hardened. And honestly, there was a lot to be cynical about in pageants.

Before she was crowned Miss America 1986, Susan Akin had competed in about one hundred pageants—Maid of Cotton, Little Miss America, Miss La Petite—beginning at the age of six, a résumé that suggested pageants were a "virtual profession," one critic noted. It was hard to square with all the rhetoric about scholarships and empowerment. Susan, a wide-eyed blonde with a husky lilt in her voice, was the latest in a generation of Miss Mississippis who had moved into the home of husband-and-wife pageant boosters for the summer to train under their guidance—diet, exercise, rigorous interview prep, and current-events cramming. "I guess you could say I sacrificed a boyfriend," she said, "but that doesn't matter when you want to be Miss America."

What *other* crazy lengths were these pageant girls going to? Days after her crowning, a radio host asked Susan about padding and cosmetic surgery. Not for her, she replied: "The only thing I did was put Firm Grip on my behind so when I walked my swimsuit didn't ride up." Butt glue became *the* story of Miss America for years to come—that and all the other "secret" beauty tricks, like tape under the breasts (for uplift), Preparation H under the eyes (to reduce bags), Saran Wrap on the thighs (to sweat out water bloat), Vaseline on the teeth (to keep the lips from sticking), rouge in the cleavage (to grant the illusion of depth)—the thing that every pageant girl got asked about.

Of course, many of these techniques seem low maintenance now compared to what your typical movie starlet employs before walking a red carpet, or even a Kardashian puts on before going to the grocery store. It was a lascivious strain of media coverage—*what are these girls doing to their bodies?!?*—that pretended to raise healthy doubts about Miss America's cult of wholesomeness while at the same time perpetuating it, by ridiculing anything that smacked of trying-too-hard.

And yet, the critics had a point. It could go too far. Miss Americas were getting skinnier; Susan's body-mass index rated her as officially undernourished. In 1986, a young feminist at the University of California, Santa Cruz, embarked on a scheme to infiltrate Miss America. It took her eighteen months, but she won a local title and got as far as the Miss California pageant, where, as the winner was about to be called on live TV, she unfurled a banner on stage that read "Pageants Hurt All Women." Later, Michelle Anderson—who went on to become a legal scholar and president of Brooklyn College—described the pressures she faced to lose weight; the winner, she claimed, was anorexic and bruised from vitamin deficiency. She had no qualms about deceiving pageant officials with her stunt, because pageantry was based on deceit, she said: "To be the icon, you have to be a liar."

Fifteen years after she became the icon, Susan Akin opened up about the toll it had taken. A life devoted to winning Miss America felt terribly empty when it came time to hand over her crown. When her attempts at a Hollywood career got no traction, she started drinking heavily; injuries from a car accident led to painkiller addiction and more drinking.

"There was always something missing along the way," she told her hometown paper. "I was this title and I was that title, and there was no way I could admit I wasn't happy. What in the world would people have thought?"

◆   ◆   ◆

Vanessa finally made her Off-Broadway debut in the summer of 1985—in a ninety-nine-seat theater two years later than she had originally planned. It was a small part in a quirky little musical, *One Man Band*, and the critics were *meh* on the show—but impressed by the girl in the back. Vanessa handled "her nearly nonexistent assignment with the aplomb of a seasoned trouper," wrote the Associated Press. "She looks sensational, too. . . ."

She had hit the reset button on her career, taking a slow, dues-paying, respect-mustering pathway back into show business. No more overnight-sensation stuff. She married Ramon Hervey, the publicist who had helped her through that terrible week, and turned down the splashy, exploitative offers. She took small roles in medium-sized movies and gigs as a backup singer. She recorded a single and hustled it at music festivals, always as the warm-up act, until the song caught on. It led to a gold album, and then a second album, and then a major-mega career-defining smash hit—"Save the Best for Last," the poignant ballad that dominated the charts for a chunk of 1992.

And then suddenly no one felt the need to bring up Miss America every time Vanessa was being discussed. Instead, whenever Miss America was being discussed—which was less frequent—Vanessa's name would get mentioned. *Wasn't Vanessa Williams a Miss America?* But in a positive way.

In 1984, the Vanessa crisis almost destroyed the pageant. But a dozen years later—after the blockbuster action role and the Broadway hit and the National Anthem at the Super Bowl—her soaring career gave the pageant a shot in the arm, validation that, hey, maybe this musty old variety show actually did a decent job of cultivating talent. Maybe it was relevant after all.

Vanessa never did hit the A-plus-plus list of *Vanity Fair* covers or billion-dollar franchises, possibly because she spread her talents across so many different realms. She hasn't won the big awards, though she's been nominated for most of them. Yet she remains a beloved household name, and it's hard not to credit that in part to the Miss America title that still lurks in the background, a quiet multiplier of her fame. The scandal faded, but the aura that remained was one of redemption and endurance. It humanized this dauntingly beautiful, supremely confident, fiercely talented woman. It made you want to root for her.

"I knew once the dust settled, I would ultimately get the chance to do what I do best," she said in 1996 while accepting a career-achievement prize. She didn't have to remind anyone what the dust was from; everyone knew.

"I can be some type of a role model," she added, "for anyone that has seen some days where you think you'll never be able to see the light of day again."

7

"YOU *CANNOT* LET DOWN FOR A SECOND"

Becoming Miss America: June 2019

Chip Brown gazed proudly at his Miss Arlington. His work here was just about done.

"You know," he mused. "I'm, like, *this close* to saying don't get those extensions."

It was a Sunday in early June 2019; in less than two weeks a new Miss Virginia would be crowned. And now Taylor Reynolds stood before Chip and his partner Scott Freda and a small group of advisors who had gathered in a friend's open-plan suburban home to send her off with a celebratory brunch and a final round of coaching. She had finessed her mock interview questions about abortion law and Confederate statues; everyone had weighed in on the chandelier earring versus the hoop. As the remains of the frittata and coffee cake cooled on the counter, Chip leaned back into the couch, hands clasped over his belly, savoring the picture in front of him—Taylor, in a black, businesslike sheath dress with a single swooping white lapel that everyone joked would send a subliminal nudge to the judges to envision a sash in its place.

"I just think she looks good with short hair," Chip told the room. "But I know a lot of people like the long, glamazon look."

Taylor nodded sympathetically. She promised she wouldn't overdo it. But she needed extensions to survive the full week of competition awaiting her in Lynchburg. "This looks good *today*," she said, brushing back her pageboy, "but it won't last. Especially with the weather."

I had run into Taylor a week earlier at the annual Miss Virginia recital, an afternoon fundraising reception held in the party room of a pool club outside of Richmond. It was an odd little event. Contestants for Miss Virginia or Miss Virginia Outstanding Teen, who would perform and attended for free, made up nearly half the crowd. They were all done up with exquisite contour makeup and extra-extra lashes and the most of-the-moment summer cocktail garb: mullet dresses over hot pants, rompers cut from a dressy brocade, and so many genres of jewel-tone jumpsuit—wide-legged, one-shouldered, halter-top-with-exposed-back. And delicate rhinestone crowns on every head of course. They all looked fabulous. *Where are all the boyfriends?* I found myself wondering, lamely, like someone's out-of-touch grandma. Obviously, that wasn't the point; once again the Miss America system was providing a space for a certain kind of young woman to be among her own kind.

And whether it was my own advancing age or the fact that this was, essentially, the Miss America farm team, these pageant women were registering with me for the first time as *young*. Summer-intern young, salutatorian young. Their conversation felt effortful, though touchingly so. One discreetly asked if I was undergoing dental work; she had done the same procedure. Another asked if I knew a particular Washington journalist she had once met, and when I said I admired his work but didn't know him personally, she was almost apologetic. "I just wanted to make a connection," she said. (*And you're doing great!* I wanted to say.)

Taylor seemed like the gravitational center of this room, the one with the most confident carriage, the one that drew your eye. *It's Taylor's year*—that was the consensus. In the clamor of the uncarpeted room, she sat talking to seven or eight other young women in a voice she didn't have to raise, and they all paid attention.

About half of the women there had decided to perform. Caroline Weinroth, the guitar-playing Miss Roanoke Valley, sang along to her finger-picking rendition of "Blowin' in the Wind." ("Perhaps you've heard

it; he's a Nobel prize–winning writer.") Then a woman I hadn't met before, Miss Historic Hanover, picked up an acoustic guitar and sang the
pop ballad "Titanium" in a strong and nuanced voice. A hush fell over
the room—a spoiler in the race? Taylor had opted not to perform for the
recital, though. Better to hold something back for the competition.

When she mentioned the mock interview that Chip and Scott had
planned for the following week, I angled for a chance to sit in. Yet, as
I arrived at their suburban brunch, I worried that they would just be
going through the motions for my sake. Surely I had already missed the
key moments in the coaching and development of Taylor Nicole Reynolds. She was already the most graceful and mature young woman in
the room. There would be no Rocky Balboa moments or Eliza Doolittle
scenes today. Taylor had been to Miss Virginia six times; she could probably teach this class.

But after a couple minutes with Chip and Scott, I remembered what
we were doing here. Taylor had been third, first, and second runner-up.
But she hadn't yet won the state pageant. These guys had won Miss
Virginia seven times.

Chip and Scott had been together since their college days in the
1980s but didn't get lured into pageantry until the late nineties, when
they followed a friend's journey to a second-place finish at Miss Virginia. Unlike most of the immaculately stylish men in the pageant
world, Chip and Scott were typically turned out like middle-aged sports
bros—Washington Nationals T-shirts, cargo shorts, ball caps. Yet they
had shown a killer instinct for grooming beauty queens. Within five
years of launching Miss Arlington in 2001, they had scored their first
victory at the state pageant, and just a few more years after that, Caressa
Cameron's Miss America victory. Some rivals whispered that the duo
managed to snap up the best girls by hosting their pageant so early in the
season. But that was no strategy, Scott insisted. They just liked to wrap
up Miss Arlington in the fall, before basketball season got in the way.

Chip called the mock interview to order in a stage voice.

"Ladies and gentlemen, this is Miss Arlington, Taylor Reynolds. Hi,
Taylor!"

"Hello!" she responded brightly.

"Taylor, there's been a recent fad that pageant girls are wearing their hair natural. Why didn't you?"

Damn. He went *there*. The earnest policy questions I had offered to bring suddenly seemed like layups. But Taylor, as an African-American pageant veteran, was unfazed.

"Well, I think it's important to be yourself on stage. And if a woman feels more like herself with natural hair, then I say go for it. For me, I don't even know what I *look* like with natural hair, so that wouldn't be myself." The room burst into laughter.

A longtime pageant judge named Al jumped in: "How are you going to respond to the fact that Virginia's top medical issue is the opiate drug crisis?"

"So, as a pharmacy student . . . ," she began. This was right in Taylor's wheelhouse. "It's making sure that we are aware of the signs and symptoms of someone who is abusing the system for opioids . . . There is a database where you must look up that patient to see if they have used that same prescription throughout the country . . . It's the physicians making sure they're not dispensing or prescribing too many pills for one person. I think it's also on the pharmaceutical companies to design a mechanism in the pill that will shut off if you burn it, if you crush it, anything like that."

Nods and smiles all around.

Next question came from Bart, father of a former Miss Virginia. "What do you think is the biggest problem facing the people of Earth right now?"

"Well, I think . . ."

It was like she hit a pothole at cruising speed.

"Goodness, there's so many different things. But I think the biggest one is . . ." Taylor paused. "Sorry, I'm drawing a blank here."

She paused again. "Why can't I think of what it's called!?! Basically, we're polluting our Earth. We're not doing enough—the planet is getting hotter."

Taylor kept edging around the multi-headed existential crisis of her generation, trying to get an arm around the monster while the nomenclature kept slipping away. "I think we are basically not using our resources wisely. I think we need to reduce and reuse and not necessarily focus on the recycling aspect. . . ."

Blessedly, Al changed the subject to abortion. An easy one: "It's none of our business what a woman does to her body," Taylor said firmly. "She should talk about it with her family, her spouse, and her God. It should not be within a politician's hands." Chip's turn again: "Legalize marijuana—yes or no?" "Not yet," she fired back. "I don't think we're there yet. There actually are no studies for long-term use of marijuana." How would she assess President Trump's communication skills? "If I could grade him, I think I would give him a D," she said. Cackles all around.

Chip invited her to give a concluding statement. "I'm more than ready to grow this program using my skills that I've acquired in the last seven years," she said. "I know I can do a great job and I promise I won't let you down. Thank you."

Interview over.

"Global warming!" Taylor exclaimed. "I looked outside like, 'It's hot—what am I trying to say?!?'"

"You recovered very well," Scott assured her.

Chip had some critiques. Taylor had rambled through an answer about the lieutenant governor facing old rape allegations; he advised her to separate the moral issue from the legal ones. When she talked about natural hair, she shouldn't emphasize the importance of a woman feeling comfortable *on stage*; this was an issue bigger than the pageant world. "Everybody should just be comfortable with the way they look, period," he said.

The men urged her to deploy humor when possible. If Taylor got the question about natural hair, Bart suggested, "Look right in their eye and say, 'Well, how do you know this isn't my natural hair?'"

"That's good!" Chip howled. "You could almost flirt with them. 'How do you know this isn't my natural hair?' And they would *love* it. And *you* can carry it off!"

Taylor soaked up the feedback gratefully. Chip and Scott had done more than just run her through questions and review her dance performance and take her shopping at Georgetown boutiques. They had also introduced Taylor to next-level strategy, like reading up on the judges' bios so that Taylor would be armed with the right chitchat at the welcome reception and the smart talking points to insert into her interview. And they had advised her to choose a slot toward the end of her competition group, so that she would be among the last contestants the judges would see. Taylor had always assumed she wanted to leave a strong early impression, but Chip's tactic was to slip in at the end, after the weary judges had found the rest of the field lacking, when they were eager to be dazzled, score someone a 10, and get out of there.

As she left the room to change into her evening gown, another friend leaned toward Chip. "Why the blue shoe?" he murmured. Taylor's cobalt pumps—an unexpected choice with her black sheath.

"We wanted a pop of color," Chip said. He raised an eyebrow. "I don't want to give away my secret just yet. But—I know who I have seen wearing blue high heels with different-colored dresses."

Chip's friend knew who he meant: one of the Miss Virginia judges.

"She'll throw on a different-color shoe with every dress," Chip noted. "And you always go, 'Oh!' She's all about the shoes."

Taylor strolled into the living room in a black velvet off-the-shoulder gown, her hair pulled up loosely from her face. "*Ohhhhh*," they all sighed. "Now, for this dress," said Chip. "You know what I'm talkin' here. I want to see that hip movement."

"You look ready for Miss America," said Ella Strickland, Chip's Miss Arlington Outstanding Teen.

"Girl, I'm ready," said Taylor. "Whenever it will be."

Whenever, wherever, under whatever circumstances. Midway through the year, plans for the next Miss America pageant were entirely up in the air.

Four days earlier, Gretchen Carlson had unexpectedly resigned as chair of the Miss America Organization, after securing a 2019 broadcast slot for the pageant at NBC, its golden-age home. She was the most visible symbol of the changes wracking the pageant world, and giddy rumors erupted in the grassroots that *now* Miss America might bring back the swimsuit competition Gretchen had axed the year before. But that was unrealistic: The remaining board was one that Gretchen had installed after exiling her critics. And those who had protested Gretchen's leadership most loudly—even suing to try to block her purges—had mostly made their peace with swimsuit's demise. There was no way to rationalize bringing it back.

But while everyone had been loudly debating Gretchen's leadership, the pageant's contract with the state of New Jersey had quietly expired, as state officials declined to subsidize another costly production at the old Convention Hall on the Boardwalk. Miss America was still looking for a new venue, which meant the date for the next pageant was also uncertain. This was leaving a lot of pageant folks uneasy about the future of their beloved institution—even as they threw themselves body and soul into its seasonal rituals.

Taylor felt she was ready for Miss America—and Miss Virginia before that. But Chip wasn't done with her.

"The whole time you're on stage," he began somberly, "and I mean the *whole time*—you will look like you're having fun."

Taylor nodded. He went on.

"Because people are watching. And they'll talk about it: 'You know who looked like she was having fun up there?'"

And off stage—well, there was no "off stage" during the week of competition at Miss Virginia. People would always be watching, Chip warned. Taylor would have to fix her hair even for rehearsal. She should put on eyeliner even if she was just walking down to the Coke machine. She would have to smile and say hello every minute of the day; it wasn't enough to merely thank any volunteer who held a door or zipped a dress or fetched a cup of water for her—she should *gush*. There were secret, unofficial points to be gained throughout the week, and Taylor would need each and every one of them.

"I know it's exhausting," Chip said. "But if you're going to be Miss Virginia, you *cannot* let down for a second that whole week. Even if you feel like dog shit."

It went unsaid, but everyone knew what he meant.

Taylor might well be the most experienced contestant at Miss Virginia. She was arguably the most serious and probably, for what it was worth, the most beautiful. She had a solid talent, honed by years of training, and a noble cause to promote. And she had already come so close.

But those near-victories had been powered in part by what had once been the trump card for so many pageant queens: a killer swimsuit body. And this year—her last chance—Taylor would have no opportunity to deploy it.

✦   ✦   ✦

Taylor had cried when she heard Miss America was dropping the swimsuit competition.

Something about Gretchen's language on "not judging on physical appearance anymore"—it made *her* feel judged. She had worked hard for this body, through years of competitive dance and running track, long before pageants entered her life. Her physique helped her do well in pageants, but pageants had brought structure and ambition into her life. This decision felt like someone telling her she was no longer the Miss America type.

Taylor had won the Miss Virginia swimsuit competition in 2016, her fourth time at the pageant, which helped secure her Top 5 finish. She had won it again in 2017, when she finished as first runner-up— which then raised expectations for her in 2018. Instead, two weeks after Gretchen's world-shaking announcement, Emili McPhail came out of nowhere to win not only the last ever Miss Virginia swimsuit competition but the Miss Virginia crown. Taylor was named second runner-up, a crushing loss. But three months later, she dusted herself off and strode back into the arena to win Miss Arlington.

She never felt demeaned by the swimsuit competition. Weren't women judged on their appearance all the time? What she loved was that Miss America was *also* judged on merit. "Miss America was unique because she was the girl who could do it all," Taylor told me. "Miss USA and Miss Universe were the girls who looked great on a runway. Miss America had talent and could speak *and* had a great body."

This was the surprising thing I learned about the younger generation of women in whose name Miss America had jettisoned swimsuit. By and large, they didn't mind the swimsuit competition at all. They didn't speak of it with the dread of their elders. They had started to talk about it like a bungee jump—a terrifying, life-affirming act of daring.

"I put on my swimsuit for the first time, and I started crying because I didn't like the human I saw in the mirror," Savvy Shields, Miss America 2017, recalled. "It ended up being my favorite phase of the competition. I have never been more confident and strong. I learned to love my body not for the way it looked but the way it worked."

Of course, these were pageant girls—a self-selecting group that stuck with Miss America as pageants became a niche pursuit. But they had a different sense of the politics involved than many of the women who'd walked runways in swimsuits in the seventies and eighties, as well as the critics who had blasted Miss America as a cruel flesh parade that foisted unrealistic beauty standards on other women.

The major concern that Caressa Cameron, Miss America 2010, had with the swimsuit competition was that it exalted a specific kind of body type—slender limbs, long torsos. She still felt bitter on behalf of a super-fit fellow Miss Virginia, African-American like herself, who Caressa believed had been scored poorly because her powerful thighs veered from the traditional silhouette. But Caressa wanted to revamp the contest, not ax it.

Others questioned what, exactly, was so inherently enlightened about staying covered up. Betty Cantrell, Miss America 2016, thought the new standard seemed to assume that women were ashamed of their bodies and fearful of certain gazes. "What kind of world is this that we're telling women that they can't walk in a bikini because they might be objectified by someone?" she asked. Why not encourage women of different body types to show them proudly? "It's like they are saying if you are plus-size, we don't want to see you in a swimsuit," she added.

Yes, this could sound eye-rollingly idealistic—especially coming from a dazzling creature like Betty, who could have played the classic Miss America on a vintage cereal box. But, like Taylor, she was born in 1994. She had come of age in the era of body positivity, of Dove's "Real Beauty" campaign featuring regular women in their underwear, of Serena Williams and Jennifer Lopez on magazine covers, of plus-sized models like Ashley Graham celebrated in the *Sports Illustrated* swimsuit issue.

And they were all beneficiaries of a cultural earthquake that had quietly but fundamentally remade pageantry—and the lives of women across the country—a decade before they were born.

✦ ✦ ✦

The gym was on a commercial strip about a mile from campus. It was called the "French Riviera Health Club and Spa," and in 1985, Kellye Cash and her best friend at Memphis State were the youngest people there. They rarely went without each other—safety in numbers. The whole concept was just that exotic.

"I remember thinking, 'We're *paying money* to do this?'" she says. "I really had to be convinced."

Kellye Cash was not a pageant girl. When the fraternity guys running Miss Memphis State asked her to compete, she scoffed. She thought pageants were vapid. Her roots were in the South, but her dad's navy career had taken the family to suburban San Diego, where, in the early 1980s, pageants were simply not cool. Her goal when she walked into the French Riviera didn't involve a crown and sash. It was to tackle the pounds she had gained freshman year.

It was also a bit of an adventure: Health clubs were the new-new thing in America's booming fitness culture that year.

For more than a decade, the most popular forms of exercise had been fueled by the American desire to burn calories. Jogging took root in the late 1960s with middle-aged men looking to stave off the cardiac risks of their steak-and-potato lifestyles, before a younger generation embraced it as energizing and liberating. By the early 1980s, the quest had moved inside with aerobics-heavy Jazzercise classes, Jane Fonda workout tapes, and *The Richard Simmons Show*. A devotee who paired heartbeat-revving aerobics with rigorous dieting could achieve the fashionably slim-hipped look of Nancy Reagan or Heather Locklear, all the more striking paired with shoulder pads the size of tail fins and a *Dynasty* corona of moussed hair. This was a very big look for pageant girls in the 1980s—though in fairness, it was big everywhere.

But another new body ideal was emerging. "Slimmer than before, but it is surely stronger," *Time* magazine rhapsodized in an August 1982 cover story. "The frame, deprived of some adipose tissue, looks more sinuous. It is a body made for motion: for long, purposeful strides across the backcourt, through the mall, into the boardroom." The pursuit of visibly defined muscles had been both glamorized and demystified for many men by the 1977 documentary *Pumping Iron*, which followed a young Arnold Schwarzenegger through so many deadlifts and biceps curls on his quest for the Mr. Universe title. But it turned out that these tactics produced pleasing effects for women as well—"the powerful neck and shoulders" of Arnold's *Conan the Barbarian* love interest Sandahl Bergman, *Time* wrote, and "the mesa-flat stomach" of Mariel Hemingway, newly ripped for her role as a track athlete in *Personal Best*. Nautilus's newfangled weight-lifting machines—safer and easier to master than barbells and dumbbells—lowered the barrier of entry for women; by 1985, half of their estimated 4.2 million users were female. But machines were too bulky and expensive for home use, leading to the boom of health clubs that were rapidly opening across the country.

Kellye and her friend felt like they were stepping into a different world at the French Riviera. Health clubs drew an older cohort—affluent enough to afford the fees, mature enough not to take their health for granted. *Perfect*, a John Travolta–Jamie Lee Curtis romantic drama released that spring, captured their reputation as flirty yuppie pickup spots. "The older demographic would wear their makeup to work out," Kellye recalls, laughing.

She and her friend both gravitated to the Nautilus-type machines, and eventually, they started to see a difference. Their arms, their shoulders, their legs—everything looked firmer. Kellye wasn't involved in any sports, but for the first time, she felt like an athlete.

When she learned that Miss Memphis State got a free semester of tuition, she reconsidered that invitation from the frat guys the next year. Kellye didn't win. But a couple weeks later, she conquered the Miss Milan contest. And three months later, Miss Tennessee. Three months after that, she was in Atlantic City.

Of course Kellye Cash was going to win Miss America. She had the classic "cornball looks," as one snarky pageant correspondent put it—the blonde hair, the round eyes, the big smile, the pointy chin—and the bright, brisk way of talking, both upbeat and down-home. She also had a talent so ferocious—a big, belt-it-out, jazzy rendition of Randy Newman's "I'll Be Home," accompanying herself on piano—that pageant groupies still reminisce about it.

But there was the impact she made when she walked to the front of the stage in her white swimsuit and heels. In a crowd of pencil bodies, Kellye looked like a Greek statue. Her musculature wasn't startling; it didn't advertise her hours in the gym. She didn't flaunt the sexy little upper-arm ridge that Angela Bassett and Jennifer Aniston would debut as the must-have accessory of the nineties. But her confidence matched her physique. She clearly felt good about what she did to get there.

It took a couple of years—Atlantic City would still see a few more seasons of big hair and tiny torsos—but eventually a buff Miss America became the standard. In later years, the contestants would almost evoke bodybuilders, with their power poses, confident strides, and concave, polished-marble abs, increasingly on display once the pageant opened the door to bikinis in the late 1990s.

Studies have suggested that lifting weights can lift moods. Something to do, maybe, with the Zen-like power of a repetitive, tactile activity to anchor a roaming mind, or the immediate sense of accomplishment felt in the muscle strain. Perhaps the gym did more than get pageant girls fit; perhaps it made them happier about the process of getting there.

Kellye Cash was a fundamentally happy Miss America. Many of her predecessors in the seamy, scandal-plagued, naggingly judgy 1980s distanced themselves from the pageant after their year. Kellye had her own frustrations with the crown, but she became a devoted alumna—returning year after year to Atlantic City, hosting state pageants around the country, organizing her own local in Tennessee, and encouraging her daughters to compete.

With her grounded cheerfulness and physical command, she represented the arrival of a new generation—the happy warriors of Miss America. They were the ones who reveled in the training and the competition, the ones who took joy in mastering the fussy aesthetics without taking them too seriously, who turned rivals into friends and a youthful quest into a lifelong hobby. The ones whose only regret about their time spent in pageants would be the pageants that they lost.

✦   ✦   ✦

Whoa! Ohhh-ohhh-ohhh-oh.
This is gonna be the best day of my liiiife . . .

The twenty-four contestants for Miss Virginia 2019 sauntered onto the stage of the soaring, honey-hued theater at Liberty University to the chorus of a five-year-old pop song. This was just an afternoon rehearsal for the first preliminary, so I would hear it again that night, then at the next day's rehearsal and show, and finally at the pageant final itself.

. . . My lie-ie-ie-ie-ie-ie-iiife!

Everyone already seemed to know what to do—stroll out, smiling, arms raised to wave to the audience or in a little groove to the music, and then slide into one of two rows on either side of the stage. But of course, this was old hat: Thirteen of them had competed at Miss Virginia before, ten more than once. Three others had competed at other state pageants. Only eight were seeking a Miss State title for the first time, though some of them knew the ropes from the teen circuit.

No matter how ragged the participation had been on the local level this year, and no matter what uncertainty lay ahead for this year's Miss America cycle, the pageant people—local directors, longtime volunteers, superfans—had turned out to Lynchburg with a sense of hope, eager for the games to begin.

They were easy to identify at the campus and hotel, most of them displaying a certain care about appearances even when dressed down; the women in blown-out layers, Lily-inspired tunics, cold-shoulder tops, festive necklaces; the men in vivid blazers and bow ties. And there was a jolly lack of pretense about the effort that went into it: Young women and their moms lugged overstuffed roller bags and tiered makeup cases here and there. Some former state contestants had set up shop in the lobby selling a line of colorful high-end shapewear. Emili McPhail, who cycled through about a half dozen different red-carpet gowns on stage every night, showed up for breakfast one morning with her hair in rollers the size of soup cans.

And the drama. Delicious small-bore drama. Inevitable when everyone cares so much. In a corridor behind the stage, a young volunteer in a black T-shirt guarding the dressing room flagged down a pair of pageant matrons to plead for an intervention.

"The girls are really struggling back there," he warned. It was hot, chaotic, not enough hands to zip dresses.

The women shrugged, he pushed back—*no, really, it's bad!*—until one of them silenced him with a firm look: "We've been doing this for *thirty* years."

Same as it ever was, in other words. True, the numbers were down—twenty-four contestants compared to thirty in 2018. But the stage felt full, thanks to the presence of the next-generation brigades. The Miss Virginia Outstanding Teens and the "Teens in Training"—younger girls doing the equivalent of summer glamour camp in Lynchburg—joined a local dance academy for a high-energy dance to "I Just Want to Celebrate" in black spandex and shiny green-and-silver tops.

"These young ladies are the future of the Miss Virginia program!" the emcee intoned.

But I kept staring at the faces of the current Miss Virginia contestants during rehearsal. *Who looks like they're having fun up there?* I caught myself wondering.

Hmmm. No one?

The best day of my liiiife . . .

Then I glanced at Taylor. A moment after the music died, she was doing a joyful little extra-credit shimmy.

Good for her.

It was a journey that had taken her nearly seven years. An older generation would have been scandalized by a girl making so many runs at a state title. But now the Taylors of this world were the lifeblood of an organization, not just in Virginia but every state.

Certainly, they were the reason there were even *enough* contestants to keep the whole thing afloat. But these young women had also become the emotional hook for everyone involved. As they returned each year, they formed a tiny, familiar universe for pageant boosters to care about—a cast of characters in whom to take a rooting interest, to coach and to nurture and to gossip about, whose individual stories they could watch unfold over several seasons.

"To see them come back year after year, and to see them grow, and they're taking their LSATs and going on job interviews," Snooky Bias, who started with the Miss Georgia pageant as a Jaycees volunteer before becoming its longtime director, told me. "That's why you do it year after year."

Taylor had been stunned and gratified to encounter these kinds of people when she entered her first pageant in 2012, a high school senior looking for a place to channel her energy as her time in competitive dance came to an end. All these people offering constructive advice—a world apart from the cutthroat dance scene. "It was a culture shock," she recalls. "What is this, people want me to do *well* in this?" It began to feel like a family to her.

She was the youngest girl at Miss Virginia 2013, and she didn't place. But people on the circuit told her they could "see" her as Miss Virginia one day. And the next year, when she made Top 10, she began to see it, too.

Competing in the Miss America system meant having to cultivate an advocacy cause—or "platform," in the jargon of the moment. During her senior year, Taylor participated in a training session organized by Rachel's Challenge, an anti-bullying nonprofit, named for a victim of the 1999 Columbine High School massacre, that urged young people to start "chain reactions" of kindness in their community. Taylor fell in love with the philosophy, and Rachel Scott's story resonated with her memories of being ostracized in middle school.

"I had a good story about being bullied," Taylor told me. Which is a funny way to put it. But for pageant girls, the "good story" that demonstrated character and self-awareness was a crucial part of the package—just like their friends seeking admission to an elite college with a compelling "personal statement." So she adopted Rachel's Challenge as her platform—and while some competitors switched causes from year to year, she stuck with it, burnishing her message. She visited schools in her crown and sash to talk about it. And as she shared her own experience being bullied, she felt she was finally processing it for herself.

"I realized I was looking for someone who had been in my shoes, who could tell me what to do," she told me. And now "I just want to be that person I was looking for when I was in middle school."

She had never imagined she would be doing pageants this long. But she had earned about $30,000 in scholarships, without a substantial outlay. ("I've never spent more than $700 on a gown.") In fact, pageants were the reason she was now studying to become a pharmacist. There she had been, so young and unformed, walking into interview sessions where she knew they would ask: *What are your goals? What do you want to be?* These questions had forced her to think through her future. And eventually, she came up with an answer that just felt right. "Pageants," she said, "helped me mature."

✦ ✦ ✦

Just one night all we got
Just one night all we got

And now, it was happening: night one of the Miss Virginia pageant preliminaries. The audience, a couple hundred strong, squealed as the staccato saxophone riff of a six-year-old Fergie tune heralded the arrival of the contestants.

A little party never killed nobody . . .

As the twenty-four marched out in an array of cocktail finery, I second-guessed Taylor's choice. Her multicolored sequin romper probably looked amazing in the dressing room. But on a stage full of sparkle, it got lost in the crowd. And while her spectacular legs were on display, the overall cut was too loose to showcase her figure. *Not that that's what mattered!* Certainly not this year! But pageant judges would always respond to physical charisma. Every human did.

But you know who looked like she was having fun up there? Tatum Sheppard. Miss Piedmont Region had made a shrewd choice with her slim-cut coral jumpsuit: the solid matte color popped amid all the sequins. And she was adorable—just twenty years old and making her first appearance on a Miss State stage, but she moved gracefully through the basic group dance steps with her shiny, bouncy hair and delighted smile. Whatever "it" was, she seemed to have it.

Or was it just because I knew her backstory?

It didn't necessarily help to be the one with the backstory. Kellye Cash had learned this in 1986. In Tennessee, everyone quickly figured out the new girl at the state pageant was one of *those* Cashes. And that her grand-uncle, Johnny Cash, had paid for her $800 evening gown.

Her backstory then preceded Kellye to Atlantic City. And it put a distance between her and some of the other contestants. Some seemed to perceive her pedigree as an unfair advantage. (She knew this was absurd: Why would the Oscar and Tony nominees among the judges be cowed by the Man in Black's nephew's daughter?) After she was crowned, the knives came out. "That girl was the least-liked girl around," Miss Florida told the *Orlando Sentinel.* "She acted like she knew she was going to win." The interview opened the floodgates on a week's worth of stories—a highly unusual public airing of post-crowning frustrations. Miss Colorado claimed the judges just wanted a "country" Miss America, and Miss Ohio demanded an audit, and Miss Florida got booked on *Larry King* to reprise her complaints. *Kellye* didn't even get to go on *Larry King!*

And now, thirty-three years later, an excited whisper was going around the Miss Virginia pageant: Did you know Tatum Sheppard was one of *those* Sheppards? *Hmm-mmm.* The youngest daughter of Miss America 1987 Kellye Cash Sheppard.

"They're not going to leave Tatum out of the Top 5," one pundit confidently told me. "Not with Kellye Cash sitting in the audience."

✦   ✦   ✦

"No music! No music! No, no, no—no music!"

Half of the Miss Virginia contestants would compete this night in talent, and Dot Kelly—the Miss Arlington runner-up with the commanding voice—was shouting and pounding the boards in the same energetic tap routine I had seen the previous fall. Hallie Hovey-Murray, whom I had seen win in Manassas, did her ventriloquist act. The fellow on her left arm sang just fine, the lady on her right sounded muddy.

There was a Bollywood-tinged ballet; a not-bad Etta James song; some nice rifle-twirling to a *Hamilton* medley; and a boggy spoken-word poem. Miss Historic Hanover, whose pop vocal had dazzled at the reception, went with just-okay opera instead. Who could blame her, though? Judges swooned for the "classically trained" thing. I'd been advised to watch Miss Apple Blossom, Victoria Chuah, said to have the most charming facial expressions from the vantage of the judges' front-row perch. Her *Carmen*-inspired ballet en pointe won the night.

But the women I watched most closely were tasked this night with talking—first in an onstage question-and-answer, and then in the "social impact statements" that would accompany their evening gown modeling.

It's next to impossible to assess anyone's performance in a pageant Q&A. Answers that sound brilliant in the moment fall apart when rendered in text; answers that sound like bumbling nonsense never seem to hurt anyone's chances. In 2015, I watched Betty Cantrell hedge and flail on live TV through a question about whether Tom Brady had cheated by ordering that air be let out of the footballs in a 2015 New England Patriots game ("That's a really good question, I'm not sure. I think I'd have to be there to see the ball and to feel it to make sure if it was deflated or not deflated, but if there was any question there then yes, I think he cheated. . . ."). *Well, so much for her!* I thought—and then minutes later, she was Miss America.

So I could tell you that Tatum, when asked if the government should mandate paid maternity leave, called it "a case-by-case issue"; or that

Caroline Weinroth, asked about millennials suffering from depression, recommended drinking a cup of tea. I could tell you that Taylor got a wheelhouse question about bullying, and she exuded warmth but not specifics (". . . so we really need to be careful about what our children and our youth see").

I could tell you that Camille Schrier, the one who was getting some buzz for her "science experiment" talent, gave an answer about carcinogenic blood-pressure pills that amounted to little more than, well, *both* the manufacturer *and* the FDA are to blame. (Patient safety, she asserted, should be "a number one priority.") But she had not only the polished good looks of a traditional pageant woman (long, shiny brown hair, wide-set eyes, ample cleavage), but the quintessential talking skills as well, and in the moment, she managed to make it all sound breathtakingly erudite.

Everyone was talking around the topic and filling dead air and stating the obvious, but I'm not sure I could have done better. For all of the pageant's hype about brains and savvy and leadership, these Q&As were mostly useful as small talk. A chance for the judges to draw out a conversation a bit and gut-check decisions they had already half settled upon. To remember who they liked.

The prize this night for best Q&A went to Miss Cardinal, Katie Rose, whose response to mass shootings was to urge legislators "to address this issue of mental health and see the reason behind why people are picking up a gun and pulling the trigger" and to "educate our high school students and our community on how to handle themselves in dangerous situations."

Sure. Fine. This was never supposed to be Miss Arlington's category anyway. And Chip could see an opening. Over drinks in the hotel lobby that night, he leaned back into the sofa with a sly smile. "I think Taylor still has a chance," he said.

✦　✦　✦

The extensions looked *fine*—really, they did. Certainly doing their part to get Taylor through this week. But as she rehearsed her dance for the first time on the Liberty University stage, that nice cascade of dark hair was a little distracting. Especially when she did the aerial cartwheel, the hair whipping around with her.

Chip went backstage to confer and returned to their second-tier seats to report back to Taylor's mom, Beverly, and Scotty.

"Her shins are bothering her a little but she'll be okay," he said. "And she's going to put her hair in a ponytail."

Taylor was hitting all her marks. Her performance energy seemed a little low, but she was pacing herself—no need to put it all out there for a rehearsal. While her dance performances were always commanding, Taylor had never won a talent preliminary at Miss Virginia. It didn't seem out of the question this year, though, given the competition: There was an okay violin recital, a Bonnie Raitt song too big for the voice tackling it, a not-bad piano performance, an unmemorable country song, and there was Katie Rose doing a kicky jazz-ballet routine to "Blue Suede Shoes" with a gold-eagle capelet. Oh, and the science experiment.

Camille, a student at the same pharmacy graduate program as Taylor, came on stage in a white lab coat over slim, sparkly black pants and black heels. Stagehands pushed a wheeled table bearing oversized beakers onto a tarp in the middle of the stage, and Camille went to work, speed-narrating her efforts in a sharp, clear voice.

"Science is all around us. I've loved science since I was a little girl . . . Science is a talent. And it's my mission to show kids that science is fun, relevant, and easy to understand . . . What we're about to watch is the catalytic decomposition of hydrogen peroxide!" She donned protective goggles. "Don't try this one at home!"

Poof! Her beakers went volcanic, long columns of candy-colored foam shooting out the narrow openings—a reaction between the hydrogen peroxide–spiked dish soap in the flasks and the potassium iodide she'd dropped inside—before pooling into picturesque coils on the tarp around her table. Camille nattered on brightly about breaking the bonds of the hydrogen peroxide molecule, before closing big.

"Now the *next* time that *you* see a bottle of hydrogen peroxide, I hope you impress your friends with what you've *learned!*" she sing-songed. "And keep an eye out, because *science* really *is* all around us!"

Word was already getting around: Miss Vermont 2016 had done

the exact same demonstration—known as the "elephant toothpaste" trick—in her bid for Miss America. It was on YouTube. But if you had never seen a pageant girl do a science experiment, the stunt worked, and Camille's showmanship was undeniable.

Taylor was up next for her second run-through. She walked out in her white midriff-baring dance costume, her hair in a ponytail now. Then she stopped and frowned at her bare foot.

"There's some stuff on the ground," she advised the producer, sitting below the footlights. "And I'm wearing a white costume."

It was Camille's foam. Taylor hopped away to avoid spreading it. Half a dozen stage techs poured out to investigate, peering at the floor.

The producer tried to keep things on track. "We need Arlington out here *now*," he ordered.

"The stage is still dirty," a tech told him.

"Somehow, this thing needs to be cleaned in the next three minutes," he replied.

Up in the seats, Chip bristled. "I knew this would screw us up in some way," he groaned.

Sherri McKinney, a prolific local pageant director with four girls in the race this year—including Katie, the toe-shoed dancer who would also have to brave this stage soon—wandered over to commiserate.

"What are you thinking, Chip?" she teased.

"Evil thoughts," he muttered.

Beverly and I helplessly floated ideas: Why not push a dry mop around the stage? "That's dish soap down there," Sherri replied sagely: nothing so easily removed.

Camille's routine would require a larger tarp. In the meantime, the techs kept dabbing away at the floor. Sherri sighed. "How many Liberty students does it take to clean up a stage with Bounty?"

◆　◆　◆

Chip and Sherri's concern was legitimate: the nightmare vision of Taylor or Katie twirling onto an invisible patch of Palmolive and skidding out of control in front of the preliminary-night judges.

But it didn't matter. Now that I'd seen the entire field in rehearsal, I knew a dancer wouldn't win tonight's talent prize anyway. Holy cow, was Kellye Cash's daughter great or what? Tatum had strolled on stage in a shimmering green column dress and with a voice roughly three times bigger than her body, to tackle "Cry Me a River." Goose bumps. The rare pageant talent you might have paid money to see.

But in performance in front of the judges that night, Tatum faltered. No huge gaffe, just a weak start, her voice lost in the room until she found it at the chorus. An ordinary case of the nerves, her mother told me later.

And maybe for the best. She was still just twenty. All the pageant directors had stories of the girls who had won Miss State too soon, who would have killed it in Atlantic City with another year or two of seasoning at the local level. Maybe the Miss America centennial would be Tatum's year. Taylor, though, brought all the energy and stage presence to her dance that Chip had hoped for.

In the second night of onstage Q&A, Miss State Fair, Anna Kelly, got a big cheer when she said she would never have an abortion—and a bigger cheer when she affirmed her right to have one. No wonder that Virginia—a purple state with a population of young women fluent in both Southern charm and Beltway ambition—had made the Miss America finals ten times in the last fifteen years. They could speak to both sides. They could play this game.

Anna won the night's prize for Q&A. But if you were looking for a bellwether of Miss Virginia politics, it came with the stunning announcement of the night's talent winner. Elephant-toothpaste maestro Camille Schrier.

✦   ✦   ✦

By the time the Saturday-night finals rolled around, I had seen it all, multiple times. The cocktail-garb parade, the group dance routines, the same pop anthems sung by the same slickly wholesome Liberty alums playing emcee. *The best day of my liiife* for the third straight day in a row.

But there was a clarity in seeing the contestants in a field that had now been winnowed from the full twenty-four to the Top 12. They included Taylor, Dot Kelly, Tatum, Camille—and Caroline Weinroth.

Caroline had told me her goal was to make the Top 5—and earn enough scholarship money to make it worth her while. But really her hope had been the honor that had eluded her the two previous years—to make the finals so she could show her talent to the full house.

As the lights came up, she spun to face the audience, jerked back the neck of her Fender, and broke into a jangling opening riff.

"I go out walkin'. . . after midnight," she sang. "Out in the moonlight . . . just like we used to do . . ."

It was a rockabilly take on Virginia's own Patsy Cline—toe-tapping, nostalgic, and one hell of a crowd-pleaser. Caroline had gone all out with her costume: a spangled red chiffon jumpsuit with dramatic bell sleeves, fit for a rodeo queen. And in performance, she *brought it*— strutting across the stage with yelps and riffs and a climactic key change, serenading with sly bedroom eyes and punctuating the lines with a saucy, openmouthed Marilyn Monroe smile. Too sexy? Whatever! She ended with a blitz of the strings and a little extra jazzy patter: "I've been on my feet, I've been out on the street after midnight! I'm searchin' for yoooooouuuuuu!"

It was Caroline unbridled. On the verge of aging out, she relaxed this year and bonded with some of the other older contestants. Yet she still harbored hopes. She didn't expect to be Miss Virginia. But she had thought it possible that this year, her final year, might be her turn to win the talent preliminary.

Then the Friday-night prize for her competition group had gone to a chemistry demonstration. That was it. Caroline was *done*. She went into finals night with no more illusions, no more care, just determined to have fun and let her inner rock star come out to play. She thought to herself: *I'll show them what a fucking talent is.*

✦ ✦ ✦

And so then—I don't know how to tell you this. They called the Top 5. And Taylor was not in it.

Hindsight rushed up on me. Suddenly it became clear what was going to happen here, and more than that, I realized I had seen it coming all along.

Fourth runner-up, winner of a $3,000 scholarship . . . is . . . Miss Piedmont Region, Tatum Sheppard!

Just before this big finale, they had announced the Miss Congeniality–type prizes, for academics or volunteerism or general goodness. There was a new prize this year, $200 for "Poise and Elegance." Taylor—already off to the side with Caroline and the seventeen other women who would not be Miss Virginia this year—looked dazed when she walked up to accept it.

Soon, only three were left on stage: Dot, Camille, and Victoria Chuah.

Our second runner-up and winner of a $5,000 scholarship . . . is . . . Miss Apple Blossom Festival, Victoria Chuah!

You had to admire Taylor for her steady commitment to one cause through all those years. Yet there had been a vagueness in her presentation: "Rachel Joy Scott once said, 'It takes one person to show compassion to start a chain reaction. And I want to know: Will that be you?'"

I knew what Taylor meant. Did the audience get it? Maybe not. But perhaps, I reasoned at the time, it would resonate with the judges, who had heard her deeper discussion of the issue in her private interview. Still, bullying wasn't quite the hot-button issue it used to be. . . . And then Camille had taken the stage.

"From medication errors in the home, to the opioid epidemic plaguing our nation, it's time to start 'Minding Our Meds' and talking about drug safety and abuse prevention," she declared. Camille had a cause both ripped from the headlines and aligned with her career goals, and the kind of voice that punches a hole in the air.

And the first runner-up, with a $7,000 scholarship, sponsored in part by the Margaret R. Baker Foundation, and the Forever Miss Virginias (Miss Virginia receives a $20,000 scholarship) . . . our first runner-up . . . is . . . Miss Lynchburg, Dot Kelly!

When only two are left standing, the first runner-up is all they need to announce. Camille dropped to the ground in a crouch, mouth agape, hands on her head, hands on her face. Emili stepped from the wings to hand her a jumbo bouquet of flowers and pin the crown to her hair.

Later, I would learn that Taylor was never the sure thing I'd assumed.

Placing second runner-up the year before had been tough. That's when she had posted something on social media that some interpreted as a goodbye-to-all-that kiss-off. Of course, this was just one of her annual mood phases on the pageant circuit. "Every year I think I'm done with this," Taylor had told me, and yet every year she would come back anyway. She couldn't help herself; she got so much out of it. But there could be a cost to letting that game face slip for even a second. People would always be watching, and talking to one another.

The contestants surged forward to congratulate Camille. I couldn't see Taylor in the crowd at first. Then she emerged, making a beeline behind the cluster, headed to some unknown point on the right side of the stage. It was Dot, the first runner-up, who stepped in her path and wrapped Taylor in her arms. And the two of them stayed that way, rocking back and forth, for a long time.

8

"DO YOU THINK I'M THE FIRST WOMAN TO HAVE AN INTEREST?"

1991

It was 4 a.m., and Carolyn Sapp had barely taken the new crown off her head to catch a few hours of sleep when the phone rang in her Atlantic City hotel room in September 1991.

It was a reporter, from her home state of Hawaii. But instead of late-night congratulations, he was asking the new Miss America about Nu'u Fa'aola—her ex-fiancé, a former New York Jets running back and, until that night, the better-known half of their relationship.

"We know you accused him of domestic violence," the reporter said. "Tell us about it."

Miss America had never dealt with a Miss America quite like Carolyn Sapp before. She looked like a beauty queen from the 1940s, an hourglass knockout with the big shoulders and big face and big hair, her natural strawberry blonde dyed a rich mahogany to set off her pale skin and dark red lips (it was the nineties). But her energy was a very new thing. She had a swingy kind of walk and eyes that would pin you to the wall while her mouth stayed in constant motion, laughing, talking, smiling.

The night she was crowned, when they told her they needed a family picture, but *just with your mom and dad, okay?*—she pushed back, not for the last time, and got both her stepparents and her three half siblings and a grandmother and a couple aunts and a cousin in the photo, too. The next morning, as she posed for photos in the surf, she let the Old English sheepdog who came bounding into the frame lick the makeup off her face, and the photographers nearly died of joy. *Click-click-click-click-click.*

That energy—it could be a lot to take, and the Miss America staff didn't always know what to make of it. They tsk-tsked when she greeted sponsors with a hug and a kiss, and she had to explain it was just the Hawaii way of doing business, the Carolyn way. But the sponsors *loved* it. They loved her, loved the fact that this Miss America was so much *fun*. Carolyn loved the meet-and-greet stuff. She was always game to stay late, after the photos, after the dinner, to stay up talking and laughing, maybe even get up and sing with the band—you only have one year to be Miss America, right?—even as her dear pageant chaperone was left sitting there, waiting for her, at an hour when *she* would have much rather retired. There were clashes over this, too, high-level debates over the appropriate bedtime for a twenty-four-year-old woman, though usually phrased in terms of how *we don't want you to burn out.* . . .

But Carolyn Sapp and the Miss America Organization were on the same page in one important way, for which that extraordinary energy of hers would prove essential.

After that terrible, early-hours phone call from the reporter, she went to talk to Leonard Horn, the pageant's longtime general counsel who was now its chief executive. And she told her new boss everything about the private trauma that would soon explode into public view. Leonard listened and made some lawyerly calculations.

"You have a choice," he told her.

The story of how Carolyn Sapp became an accidental domestic-violence crusader marks the moment that a new era for Miss America came into focus—the last golden era for Miss America. The pageant had barreled out of the messy 1980s with still-formidable television ratings, a bulwark of corporate sponsorships, its identity in the public imagination secure, but also aspirations for a new relevance. Just in time for the advocacy-minded Miss Americas of Generation X.

More than twenty years after feminists protested on the Boardwalk, the first generation to enjoy all the fruits of the women's movement was coming of age, and some of its members, as it turned out, were still interested in pageants. For this new cohort of pageant girls, entering the workforce would be neither a political statement nor a fraught choice, but simply a given. They had grown up knowing they could play soccer or basketball if they wanted, watching anchorwomen deliver the news and alpha heroines take down bad guys in the movies. On their college campuses, women were already beginning to outnumber men.

The kind of women who would still choose to enter the Miss America pageant heading into the 1990s—and specifically, those chosen to be Miss America—would seize their crowns with more self-direction than the women who preceded them. And eventually, they would become the first group of Miss Americas to question why the pageant wasn't run by Miss Americas—and set out to do something about it.

✦   ✦   ✦

"Ohhhh, nooo!!! What happened???"

Leanza Cornett and the other Top 10 finalists were rushing to get ready for the evening gown competition at the September 1992 pageant, when she grabbed her red Bob Mackie gown with the puffy shoulders and metallic paisley trim, and— Wait, what??? The *zipper* was *busted!?!* Well, she would just have to wear her yellow gown instead . . . her favorite, flattering, canary-yellow gown with the white-sequined bodice.

Such a shame.

If you overlook the bugle beads and the shoulder pads, then Generation X arrived at Miss America in spirit—if not in aesthetics—the morning Miss Florida woke up and realized she really wanted to wear her yellow gown that night.

Problem was, Leanza had already filled out the form saying she would wear the red gown. But she changed her mind! She had worn her yellow one for the Boardwalk parade—accessorized with a fin, in a cute homage to her job as a Disney mermaid—and it felt so right. It was absolutely what she needed to wear in competition. The pageant staff, though, said it was too late to switch. Soooo, when no one was looking, Leanza took a pair of scissors and ripped out the zipper of her red Bob Mackie. And made a big, theatrical show of "discovering" it at the last minute.

"Nobody," Leanza laughed twenty-seven years later, finally ready to share the story, "is going to tell *me*."

Something surprising happened to the pageant with this generation. The Miss Americas were suddenly sort of . . . cool? They rocked bikinis and even short hair. They said quotable things. They were a little more willful than their predecessors, and vivid in a way that helped sustain media attention throughout the year, even as TV ratings were beginning to droop.

"We liked that you didn't need this," one of Leanza's judges later told her. They could tell: If they hadn't voted her Miss America 1993, this tiny, self-possessed twenty-one-year-old with Natalie Wood eyes would have been content to go back to starring as Ariel the singing mermaid at a Walt Disney World stage show and keep looking for her next thing.

Leanza made no bones about Miss America being a means to an end. "I want to be famous," she said, joking-not-joking, and in 1993, those opportunities could still come Miss America's way. As her reign neared an end, she won a role in a Broadway revival of *Grease*—such a plum achievement that the pageant planned a huge *Grease*-inspired song-and-dance for her farewell. Which ended up looking silly when Leanza decided at the last minute to take a job with *Entertainment Tonight* instead. Leonard Horn was *not* happy. She got to crown her successor, but he otherwise cut her out of the show.

What secured Leanza's reputation as a rebel during her Miss America year was her advocacy work. When she was headed to Miss Florida for the third time, her local pageant director asked her to come up with a "platform"—the topic she would champion if she won, part of Miss America's new service-minded initiative. She mentioned AIDS education, and her director winced: Did she have a second choice? AIDS was just *so* controversial. . . .

"You know what? I don't care," Leanza recalled saying. "If this is not okay, this is not an organization I want to be a part of."

As Miss America, Leanza visited schools across the country to talk about safe sex. She took the stage at a drag-show fundraiser in New York City and taught everyone how to do the pageant wave: "Elbow, elbow, wrist, wrist. Touch your pearls and blow a kiss!" When a rural school district in Florida refused to let her say "AIDS" during her speech, she played by their rules—and then promptly told her Rotary luncheon audience that same day how she had been censored.

"I can adhere to any school board's needs," she said at the lunch. "But I will not be an accomplice to the spread of this disease."

And oh yes, it became a big story. Soon, she was discussing the flap on *CBS Morning News*, and editorial writers across the country were hailing her moxie.

Leanza got branded as the "controversial" Miss America. Marian Bergeron, Miss America 1933, even called her "amoral." ("Being Miss America certainly isn't about condoms or whatever they are doing with them.") But in 1993, controversy wasn't so bad, as far as the organization was concerned. If a Miss America could make controversy, then Miss America still mattered.

✦   ✦   ✦

It was Kaye Lani Rae Rafko who gave Leonard Horn the idea.

Miss America 1988 seemed like the others, at first. Tall. Blonde. Conservative. Like the previous six Miss Americas, Kaye Lani had won the swimsuit contest, and she had spent six years in pageantry before winning Miss Michigan, the kind of résumé that could get you labeled a "Pageant Patty."

But there was that exotic talent of hers, which—*whew!* It was a mesmerizing, hip-quivering Tahitian dance, which she performed in a towering pink headdress, a feathered skirt, and the longest unbroken expanse of bare torso that anyone ever saw at the pageant in those pre-bikini days. And then, when she met the press for the first time in September 1987, the conversation quickly turned to . . . death?

"Death is a part of life," she said. "And my job is to work with patients and families to accept it."

At twenty-four, Kaye Lani was already an oncology nurse who hoped to open a hospice for the terminally ill, and did *she* have some stories. The reporters were rapt.

Wow, thought Leonard. *Why can't we have this every year?*

He usually hated these post-crowning press conferences, where reporters either fell back on rote questions about boyfriends and political stances or tried to make Miss America look like an idiot. (The following year, one reporter challenged Gretchen Carlson to identify which president was on a $20 bill and asked if she was a virgin.) But this beauty queen was talking about serious stuff. Hospice was a new concept in the U.S., and Kaye Lani spoke passionately about it. She fielded questions on hot topics like assisted suicide, bone-marrow transplants, and HIV transmission, which she said the public shouldn't fear from ordinary social contact.

"I have gone up to AIDS patients and held their hands and not worn gloves," she explained.

The follow-up questions were smart and respectful. The stories the next day were glowing. And so was Leonard. Was this the solution to his Miss America problems?

A couple months earlier, he had been offered a plum appointment as a New Jersey Superior Court judge. But when he called Al Marks to tell him he had to leave the board, Al begged him to stay. He was retiring after twenty-eight years as chairman and wanted Leonard to take over. Leonard agonized over the decision. But lots of people get to be a judge, he reasoned. And there was only one head of the Miss America pageant.

And yet three years after the Vanessa Williams debacle, Miss America was facing even bigger problems. Cable TV was beginning to chip away at the ratings. The stodgy old broadcast, still carrying the flavor of a 1970s variety show, needed an update. And the contestants, sad to say, were part of the problem.

He called them "Stepford Wives"—stiff and over-rehearsed, with the hairstyles and wardrobes of women twice their age. Not their fault: This was how they had been groomed and trained by the B. Don Magness generation of home-state honchos who had worked in beauty pageants since the 1950s or '60s.

"They didn't look real," Leonard says now. "And they weren't comfortable in their façade." The pageant was stuck worshipping an ideal of femininity—remote, glamorous, pristine—that made no sense for a generation of young women who had so many more options.

A glitch at the next pageant brought him another bolt-of-lightning idea. When the time came for the accountants to hand Gary Collins the envelope with the results, they weren't ready: A mathematical tie for second runner-up meant the judges had to vote again. During the eleven minutes it took to iron things out, Gary had no choice but to fill the dead air by simply *talking* with the ten finalists. On live TV! No scripts, no notes! He just asked them questions and let them answer.

"What's your favorite part of the competition?" Gary asked Miss Colorado.

"Oh, lunchtime," she replied.

Frankly, it was the most interesting thing to happen at the pageant in years, and Leonard resolved to work more spontaneous, off-the-cuff conversation into future pageants. These women had personalities, it turned out—why not show them off?

And over the next several years, he instituted a flurry of rule changes to try to break the stranglehold of the Stepford aesthetic: banning backstage stylists, so the women would have to do their own makeup; mandating that swimsuits be bought off the rack, instead of the custom-tailored girdle-like "supersuits" so popular through the eighties; opening the door to bikinis; and attempting, at least, to ban the insane practice of high heels with swimsuits. (That one didn't stick; they all just walked on their toes instead.)

But first came Kaye Lani, a Miss America who was keynoting at health-care conferences about the nursing shortage that was hobbling community hospitals, and lobbying Capitol Hill to loosen visa restrictions on foreign nurses. Wherever Kaye Lani went, she made news. Leonard was stunned. All this positive press! How'd she come up with the idea to do all this?

"Leonard," Kaye Lani recalls saying, "do you think I'm the first woman to have an interest?"

And that was it. Leonard got to work on a plan to have every title-holder devote her year to the worthy cause or mission of her choice. He had been dismayed by how much of the typical Miss America's year was spent singing in shopping malls or signing autographs in drugstores. It seemed low-rent and irrelevant. What if Miss America promoted issues and ideas instead of brands, in business suits instead of sash-wrapped cocktail dresses?

In the 1990s, this advocacy work would imbue the title with a dignity it had lacked for a while. It may well have added a decade or two to the pageant's life. That was Kaye Lani's breakthrough.

She never stopped talking that year. Sent to sign autographs at some trade show, she would end up taking the mic to hold forth on hospice care. Booked for a shopping mall fashion show, she would look for a nearby high school and invite herself in to talk up nursing careers. The 1980s were a rough time to be Miss America, mired in debates about sexual morality and physical appearance. But Kaye Lani cried when she gave up her crown, and she cries a little now, three decades later, just to think of it. "I loved every minute," she says.

The best way to change the conversation about Miss America, it turned out, was by having something to say.

✦   ✦   ✦

It was in 1989 that Leonard launched the requirement for contestants to come to Atlantic City with an advocacy "platform" to champion if they won, a plan that quickly helped his Miss Americas find meaningful footing on the speaking circuit. But at first it mostly drew only a politely mild interest from the media.

It took a pageant queen from an earlier generation—the so-called Silent Generation, ironically enough—to demonstrate Miss America's potential as a galvanizing public advocate for the 1990s.

Marilyn Van Derbur was one of the most popular Miss Americas of the 1950s, a sporty blonde from a socially prominent Colorado family—the quintessential Grace Kelly type in an era when the pageant world looked to the pearl-wearing Oscar winner–turned–real-life princess as something of a patron saint. Marilyn's pageant fame, combined with her low, calm voice and precociously assured manner, set her up for a successful career as a motivational speaker, giving life advice to rooms full of people twice her age.

Privately, though, she was grappling with a childhood of sexual abuse by her father. She suffered a breakdown in her forties, when seeing her daughter hit puberty awakened painful, buried emotions. Several years into her recovery, and after his death, her family contributed a six-figure gift to launch a program for adult survivors of incest at the University of Colorado's medical school.

Even then, Marilyn wanted to keep her own experience private. She found it just too shameful. She agreed, though, in May 1991, to speak about the new program to a closed group of survivors and staff. Unexpectedly, word got out: Even thirty-three years later, Miss America 1958 was a public figure in her home state. When she arrived for her speech, a writer from the *Denver Post* had made it into the room, too. Marilyn was mortified by the front-page coverage ("Beauty Queen: I Survived Incest"), and she prayed for the story to die quickly. But then she ran into a well-wisher who expressed how relieved she was that Marilyn's sister divulged that she, too, was a victim of their father—because it had quieted the community's doubts about Marilyn's story.

There had been *doubts*? Marilyn was horrified. If people weren't going to believe fifty-three-year-old Marilyn Van Derbur, then who was going to believe a *child*?

She launched her new life as an advocate—speaking across the country, launching a nonprofit, writing a book, spending her days talking to other survivors on the phone. A cover story in *People* brought national attention to her saga. After posing for dozens of melancholy photos, Marilyn had insisted on smiling for one of them, and that's what they used. Coverline: "Miss America Triumphs Over Shame."

Yes, she thought when she saw it. *That's exactly it.*

"That's why I won Miss America!" she said to her husband. "That's what I was put on Earth to do."

If she hadn't been Miss America, her story, tragically not unique, would never have landed on magazine covers. It helped get the nation talking about sexual abuse, and it showed other victims this could happen to anyone, that they could survive this, that they need not feel ashamed. A friend later told her that she had given "meaning and relevance" to Miss America by going public—but Marilyn knew it was the Miss America title that had granted her that power.

Her message wasn't entirely embraced at first by the pageant community. When she visited Lenora Slaughter at her retirement home in Arizona, the legendary pageant director begged her to stop speaking out.

"This is just about sex," she recalls Lenora saying, "and I want you to stop talking about it!" Marilyn also recalls an odd letter from pageant leadership wondering if she had considered the ramifications of using the Miss America name to go public. She ignored it.

Apparently, they thought better of it, too. Weeks later, they asked her to come to Atlantic City for the 1991 pageant, to serve on the judging panel that would end up awarding the crown to another dynamic young woman with a horrifying secret.

✦　✦　✦

The press didn't know what to make of the new Miss America, Carolyn Sapp.

Leonard's push to elevate the title had been helped by the crowning of three successive Miss Americas with the kind of academic credentials that dazzled the media. There was Gretchen Carlson, an honors student at Stanford; followed by Debbye Turner, who had nearly completed her graduate studies in veterinary medicine; and in September 1990, Marjorie Vincent, a third-year law student at Duke University. With the victories of Debbye and Marjorie—the first African-American winners after Vanessa and Suzette—the pageant was also able to signal to the world that its old racial fault lines were a thing of the past.

Then came Carolyn, a twenty-four-year-old rising junior from a Honolulu commuter school.

She had beaten a field that included two professional opera singers, a Phi Beta Kappa concert pianist, a classics major, and an attorney for the National Labor Relations Board. Carolyn couldn't recall her Hawaii

Margaret Gorman, a year after her 1921 crowning. In an unsettling era,
the judges swooned for the youngest but most old-fashioned contestant.

Virginia Lee (far left) maintained until her death that she was the true winner of the 1921 pageant, and not Margaret Gorman (third from left).

Deborah Bryant with her runners-up in 1965, an era of debutante stylings and puffy treatment from the press—though that was about to change.

The first Miss America crowned on television in 1954, Lee Meriwether, wrenched hearts nationwide when she tearfully spoke about her late father.

Plucked off a Texas street and persuaded to enter a pageant in 1942, Jo-Carroll Dennison had no idea what awaited her.

The "women's liberation" protest on the Boardwalk in 1968 energized a national movement—and left the pageant world deeply rattled.

"Instantly, there's something electric in the room," said a pageant judge of
Phyllis George, seen here the morning after her 1970 crowning.

Terry Meeuwsen and
Laurie Lea Schaefer
visited President
Richard Nixon in
September 1972.

Phyllis George with Bill Kurtis
in 1984 on the set of *CBS
Morning News*—a career peak and
crashing disappointment.

Rebecca King bluntly admitted that she entered the pageant to cover
law school tuition—and shockingly didn't cry when she won.

"There goes my junior year abroad," thought Vanessa Williams, as
Debra Maffett crowned her Miss America 1984.

Below: Gretchen Carlson told almost no one where she was going when she took leave from Stanford for her Miss America quest.

Vanessa Williams, center, and Suzette Charles, right, during pageant week 1983, when swimsuit photo-ops were a daily ritual.

Carolyn Sapp received her crown from Marjorie Vincent in 1991, hours before an unsettling phone call from a reporter.

Left: Vanessa fought the push to dethrone her as Miss America in 1984—until she made a strategic decision and resigned.

Nicole Johnson with Sen. John Warner and House Speaker Newt Gingrich in 1998, when the crown opened doors for advocacy-minded Miss Americas.

Heather Whitestone's 1995 crowning (here with Kimberly Aiken) launched her to national fame, and complex politics, as the first deaf Miss America.

Camille Schrier with outgoing Miss America Nia Franklin in 2019. In her words, "I only do this for a year . . . and then I go back to being a normal person."

Left: Caroline Weinroth in 2019, a rock guitarist trying to find her place in the pageant world.

Below: Camille used her talent portion to show that "Miss America can be a scientist and a scientist can be Miss America."

Taylor Reynolds, who competed seven times at Miss Virginia, in 2019.

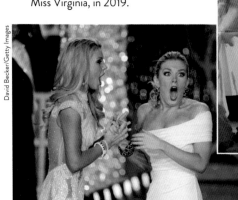

Mallory Hagan, right, the "relatable" Miss America 2013, found herself a catalyst of the email scandal that would upend the pageant leadership.

Mallory during her 2018 run for Congress in Alabama.

Former Miss Americas gathering in Atlantic City for the pageant in 2017.

Pacific University grade-point average when someone at her first press conference asked her about it.

"I'm an average student," she replied.

Journalists chalked up her victory to retrograde sensibilities. "The mob demanded a babe. It got one," sighed the *Washington Post*. "She wasn't just Miss Hawaii. She was Miss Ha-cha-cha," the *Philadelphia Inquirer* hooted. "While the other contestants promenaded down the runway, Sapp slinked . . . the sexiest Miss A since Vanessa Williams." They couldn't have known that Carolyn crushed it in her interview, with compelling stories about her sprawling multicultural family, her travels beyond Hawaii, the three jobs she'd juggled through college.

There were insinuations that Donald Trump, the Atlantic City casino owner, somehow had something to do with her win. He had nothing to do with it—a past judge, he merely swanned around the pageant that year with his fiancée, Marla Maples. At one pre-show gathering, he swaggeringly asked to see the "bodies" who had won the swimsuit competition. And Carolyn, being Carolyn, stepped forward with just as much swagger.

"I don't know if you remember me . . . ?" she said.

Everyone in the room took note.

So, this was the deal: A couple years earlier, Carolyn had traveled to New York for a PR job, and the future president of the United States chatted her up. Nothing had happened, so she had no qualms about reintroducing herself. But her air of familiarity got pageant tongues wagging; Marla described her as "very brazen." Donald and Marla broke up after that weekend in part because of his ogling commentary from the front row of the pageant, though they reconciled and wed two years later.

Carolyn didn't seem bothered by this particular strain of gossip and media criticism, though. The story about Nu'u was looming, and it blocked out everything else.

She and Nu'u had been *the* celebrity couple back in Honolulu. He was the hometown football hero who'd made it to the NFL. She was Miss Kona Coffee, Miss Waikiki, Miss Honolulu—corny-sounding titles that in fact had ushered her into rooms with politicians and CEOs and sent her across the Pacific to promote Hawaii tourism and business development in Japan and on the mainland. And for a while, everything had been fine.

Well. Sort of.

There were flares of temper, physical outbursts that she had trouble interpreting. At first, she found it oddly flattering: *He must really like me if he's this jealous!* And she had her own kind of aggressive energy, after all. But more than a year into their relationship, Nu'u was cut by the Jets in September 1989 and brooded angrily. As they walked through a park together, she said, he abruptly turned his furor her way, hitting, kicking, and threatening to kill her. It seemed so out of character, and he was so immediately apologetic, she blamed herself for not being supportive.

Months later, Nu'u was cut by another team. He and Carolyn started quarreling in the car while he was driving; she said he tried to push her out of the moving vehicle and strangle her with the seat belt. Finally, Carolyn broke off their engagement. But she felt the need to remain friends, and one night in the fall of 1990, after she had given him a ride home, she said he assaulted her again, slamming her against the wall and threatening her with a knife. That's when she got the police involved and filed for a restraining order.

It was this restraining order that journalists would find connected to her name a year later, after she became famous overnight.

"You have a choice," Leonard recalls telling Carolyn that morning after her crowning, when she told him everything: "You either figure out how to talk to the media about the abuse in a productive way, or you opt not to talk about this at all."

It wasn't much of a choice, he acknowledged: "Either way, they're going to hound you to death."

She decided to talk.

If the press didn't know what to make of Carolyn Sapp, they really didn't know what to make of domestic violence in 1991. Especially when experienced by a prominent woman. And especially when a prominent man stood accused. Though Nu'u was never criminally charged, he never denied Carolyn's stories, either, once they were forced into the open. ("The problem was me," he said at the time. "I was very aggressive and I had a temper.") If the reporters who broke the news had any hesitation about exposing the identity of a victim of violent crime—which ran counter to journalism standards then as now—this concern did not come across in the stories. They certainly didn't know what to call it. "Miss America: Old Ex-Beau Troubles" is how the *Honolulu Advertiser* wrote the front-page banner headline. Others referred to it as her "stormy relationship." Or even more darkly, her "troubled past."

Somehow, this was considered a Miss America scandal. If anything, it should have been an NFL scandal.

"There She Is, the Latest Gossip Topic," chortled the headline on a news story reckoning that "the Miss America pageant may have gotten more than it bargained for." The fact that Carolyn's ex-boyfriend allegedly beat her up got mingled in the media imagination with the unwarranted snark coming out of the pageant world—her GPA, the Trump thing, the photos dredged up from Hawaii of her "seductive poses" in "very tiny bikinis." ("Bikinis are very popular and very necessary in Hawaii," she responded dryly.) In Hawaii, some readers showed distaste for the story and seemed less troubled by the way Carolyn's privacy had been invaded than by the "sensationalism" casting a shadow on the islands at their moment of pride.

A decade or so later, it became almost a rite of celebrity passage to come clean about childhood trauma or personal struggles; but in the early 1990s, it was highly unusual to learn these things about a famous person, and those who were coming forward were often controversial or faded-fame personalities perceived to be desperate for attention, like Roseanne Barr, La Toya Jackson, or Suzanne Somers. Carolyn sometimes got lumped in with them, though she had never even volunteered her story.

"I felt like I was being punished in a sexual way for being a victim of domestic violence," Carolyn says. "I got a quick education in media."

It took a couple of days after the story broke in September 1991 for a more positive message to emerge. Advocates said that Miss America's story could help other women grapple with abusive relationships.

Hawaii's female state lawmakers hailed her for "taking charge of her life and refusing to submit to being a victim." Once again, it took a *People* coverline, just four months after Marilyn's, to fully de-scandalize Carolyn's plight:

"A BATTERED MISS AMERICA . . . How she found the courage to finally break away."

But if most of the press didn't know what to make of domestic violence in 1991, in truth, neither did Carolyn.

"The situation has been resolved," she told the *Honolulu Advertiser* as news of her restraining order against Nu'u first broke, "and we are today friends."

At every step in that early interview, she justified, deflected, diminished, and did her best to protect Nu'u.

Yes, she said, she had filed for a restraining order, but she never pressed charges, so the matter was dropped, and that was fine with her.

Yes, she had told police he beat her, but in hindsight, she told the paper, it was just "a very personal incident."

Yes, those were her startling words in the complaint describing the incident with the car, the incident with the knife, but it was "written a long time ago."

And yes, they were *friends*. She seemed determined to get this point across to every interviewer: that everything was cool with her and Nu'u, that this was not a bad breakup, that he was not an abuser, just as she had been trying to make herself believe for so long, willing it to be so.

Because at that moment, when Carolyn Sapp was tumbling into the role of celebrity advocate for domestic-violence victims, she still hadn't fully come to terms with the fact that *she* was a victim.

"I was a twenty-four-year-old that was still living it, breathing it," she says twenty-seven years later. "He was my fiancé. We were going to counseling together to try to fix his anger management and to learn how to deal with it and figure life out. I didn't know the statistics. I didn't know how deep it was. I didn't know that it was a dirty little secret."

All these things she had to learn on the job as Miss America.

✦   ✦   ✦

On the morning after she was crowned Miss America on her twenty-fourth birthday in September 1995, Shawntel Smith went back to her hotel room to pack all the things she would want or need in the three suitcases she was allowed to bring on this yearlong journey. As she laid her belongings on the floor to make her choices, she felt her eyes brim with tears.

"I don't know if I can do this," she confessed to her mother.

A petite, sunny redhead from tiny Muldrow, Oklahoma, she was a surprise winner, having made it through the pageant with no preliminary wins and the risky choice of a complex and obscure Streisand song ("The Woman in the Moon"). Pageant observers had a theory: Was this a sympathy prize for a state still reeling from the Murrah Federal Building bombing in April? Judges, though, said they were simply wowed by her darling personality and her genuine enthusiasm for the wonky cause of vocational training and apprenticeship programs for public school students.

Now it was dawning on Shawntel. She was going to have to go on the road talking about "school-to-work," as policy types called this suite of initiatives. What on earth could *she*, a beauty queen from Muldrow, impart to all the politicians and experts in this field, not to mention the young people whose lives could be affected by these programs?

Her sweet mother said all the right things, all the distilled philosophy of the pageant world about God's role and the judges' infinite wisdom in selecting her.

"Just be yourself," her mom said, "and don't lose who you are, and you'll be fine."

But Shawntel had raised a good point. This was the audacity of Leonard's overhaul of Miss America. The public might be fascinated by a Miss America who took up a stunner of a topic, like AIDS or her own domestic abuse. But would anyone listen to Miss America about cancer? Or poverty? Or school-to-work initiatives? Not every winner was going to be a twenty-four-year-old professional like Kaye Lani with a wealth of credible experience.

The essence of the whole pageant system was still, basically, college girls. Two years before Shawntel, it had been a college freshman who rocketed to the top—Kimberly Aiken, a poised eighteen-year-old who had been talked into entering her first pageant just months earlier. The chairman of the Miss South Carolina pageant had secretly tried to lobby state judges against sending Kim to Atlantic City, out of fear that she was "too young" to win there. (One of those judges suspected the chairman was simply averse to crowning Kim the state's first African-American winner.) He was wrong, obviously. With her simple chignon and un-sequined black gown, she had style mavens cheering the end of Miss America's gaudy *Dynasty* aesthetic. Yet she *was* on the young side—and desperately shy about speaking before crowds.

But the pageant organization was committed to making this experi-ment work. They flew media coaches out to train Kim. Within months, she was delivering thirty-five-minute speeches (her platform: homeless-ness) before large audiences without notes. Shawntel got coaching from John Healy, a PR man from Chicago who worked extensively with the pageant during these years and helped her gather the data and research she would need to speak credibly on her issue, though it was ultimately up to her to write her own speeches and craft her message.

And who would listen to Miss America hold forth on school-to-work? You might be surprised. Two members of President Clinton's cabinet—Labor Secretary Robert Reich and Education Secretary Richard Riley—were so thrilled that their pet issue had crossed into the pop-culture mainstream that they traveled to Shawntel's introductory press confer-ence in New York.

"You probably brought more attention to School to Work in several seconds than Bob and I have been able to do in several years," the grate-ful schools czar gushed.

The topic still drew a bit of a yawn from the press. Leonard was dis-mayed by the too-few reporters in the too-large conference room they had booked, most of them more interested in host Kathie Lee Gifford's recent abrupt announcement that she was done with the show. (She and her talk-show partner, Regis Philbin, had taken over hosting duties from Gary Collins in 1991, but now Leonard was attempting to stream-line the broadcast, greatly reducing a host's treasured song-and-dance opportunities.)

Yet the topic that bored the press was a little too hot for the corridors of Capitol Hill, where Shawntel's own home-state senator, Republican Jim Inhofe, agonized privately that his Miss America had taken up a Clinton administration initiative.

"Senator Inhofe has given me some great suggestions on different avenues to pursue," Shawntel dodged gracefully when the two of them met with reporters.

"I support Shawntel Smith," the senator asserted.

But Shawntel's calendar quickly filled up with one speaking engagement after another at education conferences across the country, earning her at least $300,000 in appearance fees for the year. In the 1990s, Miss America had tapped into a demand that no one had quite realized was there—the hunger of advocacy groups trying to find a human face for their cause, or at least a media splash, or a way to make a panel seem less old, less male, less boring. Would the *Los Angeles Times* have bothered to cover the Ventura County School-to-Career Conference that fall if Miss America, Shawntel Smith, weren't keynoting?

It was like magic, the way a rhinestone crown could open doors and secure an audience. No one seemed to care about the little advice book (*A New Job for the New You*) that twenty-three-year-old literacy volunteer Tara Dawn Holland self-published to help newly literate adults crack into the job market, until she was crowned Miss America, and suddenly every member of Congress was delighted to talk with her about it.

"I have pictures of me on Newt's balcony," she says. "Everything changed, and I was able to make a difference in a way I never could have as a normal, average American girl."

Getting a meeting may not necessarily equate to making a difference. But the established advocacy groups that shared a mission with a Miss America certainly treasured her foot-in-the-door mojo.

A decade later, Angelina Jolie's astonishingly effective humanitarian work inspired armies of celebrities to follow in her path—Ashton Kutcher fighting child pornography, George Clooney advocating for war-torn Sudan, Christy Turlington promoting maternal health—in some cases turning to philanthropic consultants adept at matching showbiz stars with the perfect causes. Miss America pioneered this model of the plug-and-play celebrity lobbyist. Did it sometimes seem contrived? To hear fifty contestants proclaiming their devotion to recycling, or allergy awareness, or arts education, or whatever, could feel a little silly. There was always the nagging question of whether a cause had been chosen solely for the purpose of wowing the Atlantic City judges.

Former Miss Indiana Shelli Yoder, a second runner-up in 1992 who later renounced pageants, was troubled by what could feel like performative do-gooder-ism. "As we struggle to alter our own body shape to achieve a culturally defined image of beauty, as we volunteer within our community not necessarily for our community's sake but to win favor from peers, a violation of the soul occurs," she later wrote.

On a certain level, though, the judges in this era seemed to have a keen radar for insincerity. Because the women selected as Miss America seemed deeply invested in the platforms they chose. It may even have been the reason they won.

Kate Shindle was a brainy, lanky Northwestern drama student who didn't fit the classic pageant aesthetic and got nowhere in her first two years trying to compete. But after stumbling into a volunteer stint at a support center for HIV-positive people, she became consumed by the AIDS cause, with the monomania of a nineteen-year-old budding activist, burning with big ideas about the need for more education and resources. When she tried pageants again the next year, she was suddenly a more interesting person, and she rocketed in a single season straight to Miss America 1998. If there was one moment when it was clear Kate would win, it was in her interview, when she held forth on the symbolic power of the AIDS Quilt and one of the judges started weeping.

Heather French's father encouraged her to give Miss America one last shot in 1999, the last year she was eligible, and to champion the cause of homeless veterans. He had taken a bullet to the arm in Vietnam and knew how hard coming home could be. It seemed an incongruous platform for a Miss America, but Heather could speak poignantly of her memories as a kid hanging out in the VA hospitals with him. It was only after she was crowned, during her year as Miss America, that the family shared more details of their experience—how her father had contended with PTSD and substance abuse, how he had spent time in treatment programs and the local jail during Heather's childhood—and her true connection to the issue resounded.

None, though, had a platform as intimately tied up in her very quest to become Miss America as Nicole Johnson.

Shortly after her Top 10 finish at Miss Virginia in 1997, one of the state pageant honchos came to Nicole with a request: Could she *please* not come back next year?

Nicole had almost died that week. Asleep in her hotel room, she had slipped into a diabetic coma. She and the other contestants were required to share a room with their chaperones, so thank God her Miss Apple Blossom director was there to hear the thud as Nicole had a seizure and fell out of bed.

She had been grappling with type 1 diabetes since she was nineteen, diagnosed back home in Florida after she fainted on stage during the 1993 Miss Sarasota/Manatee County pageant. *That's it*, the doctors said: *No more stressful situations.* She would need to regulate her blood-sugar levels through an aggressively routine schedule of food and sleep for the rest of her life. Forget about broadcast journalism as a career. Forget about pageants.

But after a bleak half year holed up in her parents' home, convinced her future was dim, Nicole began to doubt the prognosis. She went back to college—and pageants. She was on a crusade now about diabetes education, she says, "a mission to make sure people knew you didn't have to accept that negative advice." But the truth was, she still hadn't quite conquered the disease. At Miss Virginia, her medical emergency turned into a spectacle, the paramedics showing up just as her competitors were emerging from their rooms for breakfast.

Regardless, Nicole *did* come back to Miss Virginia. And when she went into the interview room at the 1998 state pageant, she lifted her suit jacket to show the judges the new technological breakthrough on her hip.

"This is my insulin pump," she said. It promised a less onerous way to regulate her blood-sugar levels. She should have worn it the previous year but had been too self-conscious about the lump it would create under her pageant gowns. No longer.

"It keeps me alive," she told them. "You are welcome to ask me anything about it."

As Miss America, Nicole lobbied for expanded insurance coverage for diabetes. She helped advocacy groups raise millions for diabetes research. In her travels around the country, she gave interviews to local media describing the warning signs and risk factors for the disease. And in an echo of the days when corporate sponsorships would land Miss America on cornflakes boxes and in soup commercials, her name and image were licensed by pharmaceutical companies, as in an Eli Lilly campaign to screen tens of thousands of people for diabetes.

Kate and Heather also ventured into the world of legislative lobbying and high-end corporate partnerships. All three had a certain anchorwoman gravitas—mature for their age, commanding yet warm—and a decade earlier, they might easily have been lured into broadcast careers like so many others before them.

Instead, their year as Miss America primed them for careers in advocacy and policy: Heather as the secretary for the Kentucky Department of Veterans Affairs; Kate balancing her own theater work with a job as president of the Actors' Equity union; Nicole as vice president of the American Diabetes Association.

"I never set out to be a scientist," Nicole says twenty years later. "I'm much happier doing this kind of thing than I would ever have been with my initial plan."

The rush of being Miss America in that era, when a young woman's voice could not just be heard but respected, would stay with these Generation X winners. Years later they would still believe in the potential of Miss America—and that it was worth fighting for.

✦　✦　✦

When the moment of truth arrived for Heather Whitestone, the breathless climax of her three-year journey to Miss America, she couldn't quite figure out what was happening.

As an almost entirely deaf woman, she had mastered a repertoire of work-arounds—lip-reading, hearing aids, an attention to body language and context clues—to contend with a highly vocal world. But they were failing her amid the lights and cacophony of Convention Hall.

There she was, one of the five finalists for Miss America 1995. But she couldn't get a clear look at Regis Philbin's lips as he read the names, over at stage right, nor could her hearing aid pick out his syllables from the ambient roar. She could only see her friends walking away—fourth runner-up, third runner-up, second runner-up—until it was just her standing there with Miss Virginia, Cullen Johnson.

And then Regis said . . . something about Miss Virginia? She could see the crowd react, but what to? Was Cullen crying? That would be the tip-off that Cullen won. . . .

But Cullen wasn't crying. She was turning to face Heather, to give her the news a second after the rest of the world heard it. She pointed to Heather and mouthed emphatically:

It's you!

The crowning of Heather Whitestone in September 1994 marked a new emotional peak for the pageant. The first Miss America with a disability triggered an avalanche of media coverage and public interest on par with Vanessa Williams's win; it coincided with a growing awareness of the potential of people with disabilities to play a major role in the workforce and public life, as the final provisions of the watershed 1990 Americans with Disabilities Act took effect.

And, holy moly, was that *amazing* television or what? In a decade when Leonard kept trying new tricks to reengage wayward viewers—allowing bikinis, letting the folks at home call in a vote—Heather's win made the show a watercooler event for the first time in years.

Who knew? It turned out viewers loved televised competitions with vivid characters, inspiring backstories, and underdog narratives, just as the pioneers of sports broadcasting had figured out thirty years earlier. Miss America could probably thank Heather for its ratings spike the following year, the last time it would score more than 25 million viewers. Heather's story was the sort of lightning in a bottle that Miss America would never again quite capture. In just a couple more years, of course, the architects of reality TV would figure out how to replicate that kind of energy and craft entire genres of it.

Growing up deaf in Dothan, Alabama, Heather often felt socially isolated. With hearing aids and lip-reading, she could get through classes in her large high school. But she couldn't always perceive it when someone said hi to her in the hallway, and so she wouldn't respond, and that made her seem standoffish.

She found solace with her faith and with ballet—a patient dance instructor taught her to count the vibrations of beats to keep up with the music—and, eventually, with pageants. When a friend suggested she take her dance skills to the Shelby County Junior Miss pageant, she was surprised to find that she felt on equal social footing with this niche of girls. When some of them struggled with the choreography for the opening number, *she* was the one who could show them what to do. She didn't win, but they voted her Miss Congeniality.

"It was *such* a big deal," she says. "I had such a good time. I felt so good."

Heather discovered a similar sense of camaraderie the first time she competed for Miss Alabama as Miss Jacksonville State. Not so much the second time. By then, she was no longer viewed as a non-threat, having scored a surprise first-runner-up finish in her debut. But this, too, was a useful social experience. Frustratingly, she came in first runner-up a second time, and she thought about giving up. But friends convinced her to travel to Atlantic City that fall so she could see the national pageant for herself. After Kim Aiken was crowned and the hall emptied out, Heather asked a stagehand if she could walk the runway, and she heard God's voice: *I want you to dance for me on this stage next year.*

And so she agreed to give Miss Alabama one more shot. The rest is Miss America history.

The inevitable post-game whispers suggesting that she only won because she was deaf missed the point in many ways. Heather was hardly the first hearing-impaired contestant—a deaf woman made the Top 10 in 1989—just as Vanessa Williams, the object of similar speculation, was hardly the first African-American.

And Heather's victory never felt like a foregone conclusion: Many, including her, predicted that her halting speech would disqualify her from a job that was becoming more about giving speeches than waving from parade floats.

"I knew I sounded different," she says. "I don't sound like an American girl."

She was, however, a drop-dead babe, classically beautiful, with Bambi eyes and long, graceful limbs, with or without her compelling backstory. Did her ballet performance get bonus points from judges in recognition of her steep learning curve? Maybe. But it was also exquisite. Did they ladle extra points onto her swimsuit score just because they were rooting for her? Probably, but that happened for a lot of contestants.

Here's the thing: Heather was *intensely* charming. And this was the part that was impossible to untwine from her deafness.

Social psychologists and management consultants argue that charisma lies at the intersection of strength and warmth. We are drawn to people who convey both. These are the people we would instinctively follow into battle. They seem like they could get the job done but also look out for us while they're doing it.

But there's another factor: presence. Heather had heaps of it.

Presence signifies how we recognize that someone is present in the moment—alert to their surroundings, listening to what we say. It's a quality we see with our finest actors, the minute emotions flickering across Meryl Streep's face, proof of a mind attuned to every bit of feedback in her environment; as well as politicians with the gift of making you feel like you're the only person in the room. Heather had to work hard to communicate, and this manifested with those huge eyes searching your face, tiny nods as she processed every word, a palpable alertness. There is nothing more seductive than a good listener, and the girl who couldn't hear was listening to you like no one else ever had.

Heather and her team made a strategic decision early on: Deafness would not be her cause.

"I felt like people were seeing me more as a disabled person instead of a person with a disability," she says.

She was also a conservative, uncomfortable with identity politics, and eager to find a topic that more people would relate to. Her mother and sister helped put together a five-point follow-your-dreams motivation philosophy for young people, and if it seemed a little vague, she believed in it deeply. "I think the worst handicap in the world is our negative attitude," she says.

And yet, against Heather's own preferences, her mother also insisted that she wear her hair in an updo during the competition, putting her hearing aid on display. Deafness might not be her message, but it was part of her brand.

Heather's victory put Miss America on some front pages for the first time in a decade and was cheered by pundits nationwide. "She will be a Miss America who educates the public and who inspires people with and without handicaps," opined the *Boston Globe*, commending the pageant "for seeing the possibilities rather than the limitations." ABC News declared her "Person of the Week."

Yet by avoiding deafness as a platform, Heather walked unaware into some of the complicated politics surrounding it.

She casually explained to reporters that she had lost almost all her hearing at eighteen months after a bad reaction to a vaccination. This wasn't actually the case, and the medical community flipped out. The American Academy of Pediatrics put out a statement, joined by Heather's old pediatrician, explaining that the Whitestone family was confused, that the pertussis vaccine had nothing to do with the childhood fever that put her in the hospital for two weeks; it was a bacterial infection, *Haemophilus influenzae*, known as Hib. Heather was no anti-vaxxer; she was dismayed to realize she had put out bad information. "I didn't know!" she sighs. "I just told the media what my mother told me."

Meanwhile, the journalists who flooded onto the campuses of deaf schools looking for celebrations were stunned to learn that the new Miss America was a highly controversial figure in the hearing-impaired world because she favored hearing aids over American Sign Language.

This was a choice that Heather's mother, Daphne, had gradually settled upon in the months and years after the devastating diagnosis. Initially she worked on teaching Heather sign language. But then she realized that her once-garrulous toddler was starting to sign rather than speak, and Daphne was determined that Heather would speak. "She wanted me to be part of the hearing world," Heather says. So Daphne found a program to teach speech to deaf children and rigorously drilled Heather through it. She recalls her mother sitting with her for hours, working on a single word: *drink, drink, drink.*

"She would not let me go until I said it correctly," Heather says. It took her six years to learn how to pronounce her own last name.

Heather attended a middle school for deaf children in St. Louis so she could master lip-reading, but then returned home to Alabama for a series of mainstream high schools. She was largely oblivious to her generation's emerging deaf pride movement. In 1988, student protesters at Gallaudet University, the college for deaf and hard-of-hearing people in Washington, D.C., shut down the campus to protest the hiring of yet another non-deaf president and succeeded in getting a deaf one instead. The movement asserted that deafness wasn't a disability, just a different way of life, and that American Sign Language was not merely an accommodation but the centerpiece of the deaf community's vibrant culture. Heather, as a merely proficient signer who relied on hearing aids, was perceived by some critics to be turning her back on this culture, a sellout to the hearing world.

A relatively sheltered twenty-one-year-old, Heather was blindsided and devastated by the backlash, the subject of numerous national news stories. Her Miss America handlers labored to reassure her that she would survive these stories just fine.

"Heather!" one of them told her. "It's *publicity!*"

Politics aside, Heather's unique status brought her endless opportunities. She was appointed to the President's Committee on the Employment of People with Disabilities; she presented an award to Hillary Clinton at the White House; she performed the National Anthem in sign language at the Super Bowl and a ballet on Kathie Lee Gifford's TV Christmas special—the kind of prime-time spotlight that had become more scarce for Miss Americas since the extinction of variety shows in the late seventies. She became friends with disabled veteran Bob Dole; and she met her future husband during an official Miss America visit to Capitol Hill. For years after she gave up her crown, she toured the country giving speeches and was handsomely compensated for it.

Yet some of the most valued connections she would make through her Miss America experience were with her fellow Miss Americas. They would cluster in the hospitality suites when they returned to Atlantic

. City, and they would ride together on the floats in the famously kitschy Boardwalk parade. Heather cultivated friendships with them individually, across a wide age range, and was quick to sign up when they started organizing annual retreats in 2015.

With them, she got the same warm feeling she got from those Junior Miss girls she'd met at her first pageant, after a childhood feeling socially unmoored. With the Miss Americas, she felt at home.

✦   ✦   ✦

Kate Shindle had a secret.

Not a bad one! Yet she was profoundly aware, as she visited schools during her Miss America year to talk about sex—or specifically AIDS, and how not to get it, all the way down to the gritty details like avoiding oil-based lubricants that could degrade a latex condom—that every kid in the room was wondering about Miss America's own sex life.

And at that point, just turning twenty-one that year, she had not even come *close* to having sex. Nothing to be ashamed of! Still, she lived in horror of this biographical data point going viral, metastasizing into a nightmare headline: "Virgin Miss America Gives AIDS Talk at Area School."

So she had prepared herself for the smirking questions. Even before she won the crown, Kate had traded notes with Leanza Cornett about AIDS advocacy, and Leanza offered a couple suave, well-polished shutdowns:

"I've never had unsafe sex."

Or, more simply: "I practice what I preach."

They may have been cool girls, and they were certainly beautiful girls, with the body-confidence to stroll across a stage in a swimsuit. But with a few exceptions, the Miss Americas of this bold new generation were not getting laid.

This had a lot to do with the brutal logistics of being Miss America. Through the glory years of the pageant, Leonard's team liked to brag that Miss America traveled twenty thousand miles every month. Realistically, this meant she was rarely spending more than two nights in a single city, in constant motion with only a handful of days off over the entire year.

And of course, she was trailed everywhere by one of her "traveling companions"—the team of two Atlantic City matrons who traded monthlong shifts on the road, tasked with sticking by her side. The tradition had started during the Lenora Slaughter years, in part to uphold certain notions of propriety, but also at a time when most Miss Americas were unworldly eighteen- or nineteen-year-olds, both in need and want of some adult assistance. The traveling companions were more staffers than chaperones—the people who kept track of the schedules, remembered the names, shooed away the clingers, helped carry the bags.

Still, there were certain Miss Americas in the seventies and eighties infamous among pageant staff for the steady boyfriends who would follow them from town to town and sneak into their hotel rooms. Another particularly daring Miss America managed to sneak out a few times during her year to meet a fling—no easy thing when your room adjoins the chaperone's. Fortunately for this Miss America, one of her traveling companions had a habit of saving the mini liquor bottles from their first-class flights and enjoying a nightcap or two . . . so this Miss America would wait with her ear to the door until she heard the sounds of snoring, and then make her way to her booty call.

But in the 1990s and onward, it seemed increasingly that sex was not in the conversation for a lot of Miss Americas. Pageants were becoming more of a niche culture: Fewer women competed, but those who did were far more intent on it. These were women who didn't do *anything* casually. It wasn't simply that pageantry left them with little time to date; it was also the case that pageants were now dominated by the self-selecting group of young women who simply hadn't yet met the special-enough fellow to distract them from this consuming postadolescent hobby.

Of course, religious faith was a factor, too.

"You press, you're not going to have any dish on me," Tara Dawn Holland teased the journalists at her post-crowning press conference in 1996, "because I have lived my life to be ready for this moment."

She didn't spell it out, but they got her point: At twenty-three, she was a virgin. Her quip may have left the impression that it was because she feared sex would disqualify her from being Miss America. That was not the case. "I had always been staunchly committed to sexual purity," she says now, "and obviously, you have to be committed to it. It's definitely a decision."

Five months into her reign, she was flying from Washington to Omaha for a literacy event when a fellow passenger stopped her in the aisle. Returning to her seat, Tara murmured in a side-whisper to her traveling companion, Bonnie Sirgany: "I just met the *greatest guy*." He was Jon Christensen, the newly single young Republican congressman from Nebraska—and within a few weeks, he was her long-distance boyfriend.

Chastity may have been a commonality with many of the Miss Americas of this era, but for the most part, it remained a private lifestyle choice. The days when every new Miss America was obliged to present her philosophy on premarital sex to the press were over. No one was overtly self-branding as a virgin—at least not until sex unexpectedly became an issue in Jon Christensen's campaign for governor.

The young congressman was immediately drawn to the statuesque brunette with the Nancy Kerrigan smile on his Nebraska flight who turned out to be Miss America. Ten months later, he dropped to one knee at the White House Christmas Ball and proposed.

"The Lord knew exactly what I needed, a person who has a strong faith," the lovestruck politician shared with a reporter a couple days later. "She is a very disciplined woman who has saved herself for marriage. She talks the talk and walks the walk."

Until then, Tara had not put herself out there as an abstinence advocate. Literacy was her topic. But Jon's interview came as he was seeking the Republican nomination for governor, and a year after his first marriage ended in divorce, with his ex-wife filing an affidavit acknowledging her infidelity as the reason for their split. So now the *Omaha World-Herald* blasted him for oversharing: "Imagining their fiancés publicly bragging about their sexual decisions is enough to make most women cringe," a columnist wrote. "A man announcing that his betrothed is a virgin sounds backwoods." Talk radio picked up on it, with one cynic dubbing him "the virgin slayer."

"It became a citywide and therefore statewide topic," Tara sighs. "I had sophomores in high school coming up to me and saying, 'We talked about you during social studies!'"

But then James Dobson, the evangelical broadcaster, invited the couple onto his radio show to discuss chastity, and Tara just decided to lean into it. She believed strongly in chastity and was happy to turn her personal choice into a public crusade and cottage industry. The abstinence movement, championed by organizations like True Love Waits, was on the rise and eager for attractive young spokespeople. By the time she returned from their honeymoon, Tara was booked for the next year and a half, the start of a ten-year career of public speaking, sharing her story of being the Miss America who waited.

✦   ✦   ✦

And then there was Miss Ha-cha-cha.

Some in the pageant world winced at how Carolyn Sapp rounded out her year—by starring in a made-for-TV movie about her own domestic-violence saga.

Leonard argues that they had to sign on to the development of the NBC drama. The networks were nuts for ripped-from-the-headlines stuff, churning out movies about wife killers, murderous cheerleader moms, and a tragic switched-at-birth saga; in 1992, three networks raced to air their own version of the exploitative "Long Island Lolita" scandal. There was a fear the same flock of vultures could descend on Carolyn's story if Miss America didn't endorse a specific project. So Carolyn worked out a life-rights deal with NBC and insisted that Nu'u get paid as well. But then she surprised everyone by auditioning to play herself. She got the part.

The critics were not very kind to *Miss America: Behind the Crown*. It certainly didn't launch a big acting career for Carolyn. But making the obligatory press rounds to promote it gave her another chance to talk about domestic violence. She would keep traveling and talking about it for years, grateful for the words that were said back to her: *Thanks to you . . . You made me realize . . . If you got out, then I knew I could, too.*

Of all the things that were said about her, Carolyn was hardly offended by being called the sexy Miss America. She knew nothing of the pageant's demure white-glove history or the unspoken expectations the culture had of Miss America. She couldn't see the lifted eyebrow in statements like that. So she took it as a compliment.

Never mind that fabulous swagger, that voracious energy, the pro-baller boyfriend—Carolyn was not the worldly creature she seemed. At twenty-four, she had never lived on her own; even when she left the family home on the Big Island for college in the city, her Filipino stepmom's devoutly traditional parents insisted she live with them in Honolulu. She had dated very little before Nu'u. When she visited him in New York, she would decorously arrange to stay with married friends. And even after they broke up—well, good luck trying to find a guy in Hawaii brave enough to date Nu'u Fa'aola's ex-girlfriend.

They were broken up. But they remained in each other's orbit. Even after the police report. Even after she became Miss America. Even after it made the news, and even after she told her story on the cover of a national magazine.

She still cared about him. She worried about him. She wanted to help him. She was only twenty-four and still thought this was a thing she could fix.

On an official Miss America trip back to Hawaii, Carolyn hosted a surprise birthday party for Nu'u. They also went out to dinner to-gether—just friends, of course. They were *friends*, she believed, and everything was *fine*. (Bonnie, the veteran Miss America traveling com-panion, joined them, and Leonard hit the ceiling about it later. "Leon-ard," Bonnie said, "would you rather she had gone without me?")

Today, Carolyn still feels bad about Nu'u, who never got hired to play football again, who had many hard years after that. Nu'u, who later joined a class-action suit with hundreds of other players blaming the NFL for the repeated head trauma that left them with neurological symptoms such as depression, confusion, and aggression—an epidemic no one could yet perceive in 1991.

But she also looks back and thinks: *Thank God for Miss America.*

It was easy for her to see later, with wisdom and maturity and every-thing she came to learn about domestic violence, how bad things could have ended up if she had stayed in Hawaii. Winning Miss America got her out of Hawaii, and out of Nu'u's orbit.

And when they called her the sexy Miss America? Well, that was a *highly* useful data point to learn about herself at the time. She found it empowering. It made her realize that other interesting men would be interested in her, in a big world filled with opportunities and adventures that she now had the courage to pursue.

It definitely paved the way to a sexual awakening. She had far more fun heading into her thirties than she could have imagined in her naïve early twenties. But it also gave her the confidence to stand up and talk about domestic violence to groups of women far older than her. A decade later, she read an article about female Walmart employees suing the company for workplace discrimination, and she got mad and made a call and ended up as the group's celebrity spokesperson and professional rabble-rouser. One thing led to another, and there she was, Miss America 1992, addressing a rally of the National Organization for Women. Years later, looking back from a quieter vantage, in a sunny L.A. home, with a handsome stuntman husband and three beautiful children, she could finally see it clearly:

Miss America saved her life.

9

"I WANTED TO BE A LITTLE OUT OF THE BOX"

Becoming Miss America: November 2019

G ood morning, guys! How *are* you?"

"Good!" replied Miss Virginia's Friday-morning audience.

"You guys can do a whole lot better than that!" she teased, in a bouncy voice. "How *ARE* you this morning?!?"

And so the assembled kindergarten- to fifth-grade population of Lacey Spring Elementary School stepped it up:

"*GOOOOOOOODDDD!*"

"Hey guys, so I'm Camille. I'm Miss Virginia. I came all the way from a city called Richmond today. Has anyone ever been to Richmond?"

Four months earlier, Camille Schrier, a twenty-four-year-old graduate student, had emerged from out of the blue to win the Miss Virginia pageant, and now this was a typical day in her new life. She had arrived at the rural school that morning lugging cardboard boxes filled with educational activity books, practically blown in by the sharp November wind coming off the mountains. Camille was the school's big event of the week, or perhaps the month, and the teachers had led the kindergarteners into the gymnasium early—"so they can get used to seeing her," one explained.

For a Miss America contender on official business, Camille was somewhat dressed down this day. On stage in Lynchburg, she'd looked like an Italian movie star. Today, wiped clean of the smoky eye and bronze glow, in her bell-sleeved black dress and nude pumps, she would have blended into the background of any D.C. lobbying shop—the junior staffer hauling binders into the boardroom for her boss. But in Rockingham County, at a school flanked by cow pastures and a soothing view of the Blue Ridge Mountains, where teachers dressed in jeans and fleece, she was probably the fanciest person in a fifty-mile radius, even before she donned her crown and sash. And Lacey Spring was honored to have her.

"We just like to get anyone in from outside of here," a school administrator told me, "to show our girls what they can do."

In five weeks, Camille would be heading to Miss America. After months of uncertainty, following the expiration of key contracts that had bolstered the pageant's finances, the 2019 competition had finally been scheduled for the Thursday before Christmas—three months later than usual, an inconvenient weeknight sure to dampen enthusiasm and ticket sales.

Discontent still burbled in the grassroots: The decision to end the swimsuit competition, never widely popular in the pageant world, had done little to inspire the return of sponsors, viewers, or even contestants. Gretchen Carlson, who ushered in that change, had stepped down as chair of the Miss America Organization five months earlier, but it was still being run by her allies, who remained committed to her vision of "modernizing" the contest. Now, reinforcing Gretchen's pledge that the pageant not judge women based on physical appearance, the organization announced there would be no more evening gown competition.

Granted, contestants would still *wear* gowns for the opening introductions; they just wouldn't be *judged* on them. And they could wear whatever they pleased for the crowning ceremony—even the business garb ("what you would wear to give a TED Talk or corporate presentation," a memo advised) required for the talkier parts of the pageant. Traditionalists shuddered at the vision of Miss America 2020 receiving her crown in a pantsuit. But for the young women involved, the supposed freedom to "wear what you want" merely presented yet another high-stakes decision to contend with in the ultimate contest of strategic self-presentation.

In the meantime, Camille had some extra months to spend as Miss Virginia, doing Miss Virginia things, as she explained to the under-twelve set sitting on the flecked tile floor around her feet.

"So, I get to do this really cool job where I go around to seventy-two different schools like yours and talk to people about making healthy choices. You guys like to stay healthy?"

"YEAAAAHHH!"

Camille cajoled the kids to volunteer their healthy-living tips—veggies, hand-washing, a good night's sleep—before she eased them into the lesson for today.

"Someone said one thing that's really bad for us is drugs and alcohol?" she said, echoing a suggestion offered by one of the children. "It's something that affects this really cool thing behind your head and in between your ears that helps you learn: your *brain*. . . ."

It was a charming scene, and a nice community-service gesture. But it was also an unofficial part of the training and auditioning for Miss America—a process that had become more complex and sophisticated over the past generation.

In 2019, beauty queens still rode in parades, reigned over county fairs, and mingled at charity golf tournaments. But visiting schools, as a sort of role model of the day, had become one of the most visible ways for a Miss State to perform the work of being Miss State. In Virginia, the practice had been formalized for the past decade by the Alcoholic Beverage Control Authority, which paid Miss Virginias to visit schools across far-flung corners of the commonwealth on a mission to discourage kids from substance abuse. Camille's schedule that month had taken her from the Washington, D.C. suburbs to the North Carolina line, from rustic mountain enclaves to port cities. A Miss Virginia typically covered more than thirty thousand miles in a year.

But paid or not, public appearances also played a key role in the months of prep leading up to Miss America, in consort with the regimen of triceps dips, dress fittings, spray-tanning, hair-extension appointments, and talent rehearsals that occupied a Miss State's time.

These public appearances were their own kind of rehearsal. If a Miss State was going to compete for Miss America, if she was going to *be* Miss America, she would have to get comfortable talking to a new group of strangers every day.

And in return, going out in the world and meaningfully interacting with the public like this would help any Miss State worth her sash derive some life lessons to share with the judges, like those high school mission trips that help children of privilege gain life-altering insights for their college applications.

Camille, though, was doing something else that struck me as extremely shrewd.

"This game is called 'Pills Versus Candy,'" she told the kids brightly, unveiling a series of near-lookalike images. "Raise your hand if you think this is the candy? . . . Okay, *this* one is cinnamon candies . . . and *this one* is acetaminophen!"

As she spoke to the youngsters about the difference between good medicine and bad drugs, things you can put in your mouth and things you should not, I realized that she had deftly customized her state-funded speech to mesh with the "Mind Your Meds" advocacy platform on drug safety she would take to the pageant—which in itself meshed nicely with her pharmaceutical studies.

It was all perfectly on-brand.

✦　✦　✦

In the summer of 1978, Miss Georgia let a *Wall Street Journal* reporter observe her preparations for the Miss America pageant—or her "plotting," as he put it. Twenty-one-year-old Deborah Mosley was dieting, jumping rope to stay fit, and working on her tan every day, a veritable "training camp." She had chosen a brown evening gown as a "strategy," the reporter wrote, to pop on an Atlantic City stage that would be crowded with pastels. And she was reading two newspapers and several magazines a day, clipping stories on current events such as Jimmy Carter's scandal-plagued budget director Bert Lance and the Equal Rights Amendment, then letting her pageant mentors quiz her.

Debbie wasn't just doing mock interviews, the paper revealed; she was recording them at the local TV news studio and playing back the tapes to look for the distracting mannerisms or lapses of poise she needed to bring under control.

There was an implicit eyebrow-raise in the story: Was Miss Georgia *trying* too hard to win Miss America? But Debbie made no apologies.

"This could be a million-dollar deal for me," she said.

Debbie wanted to be a sportscaster; the crown could be her springboard. "That's why I entered in the first place," she told the paper. "Something like this could determine my whole future."

But after the story was published, Debbie sensed a backlash. In Atlantic City, the judges never asked her about Bert Lance or the ERA. Instead, they asked about the much-read *Journal* story and a slew of other media accounts of her meticulous preparation. The clear implication was that she had received too much publicity for her own good. Crushingly, she failed even to make the Top 10.

"Maybe I worked too hard," she said, once she was back home in Dunwoody, Georgia. "Maybe I came across too professional."

Forty years later, it was hard to gauge whether the judges were scandalized by how much work Debbie put into pageant prep, or just by the fact she had revealed this to the press. Women were finally being encouraged to exercise their ambitions in public life, and the pageant celebrated this. Yet it was clear from the tone of the *Wall Street Journal* coverage that the outside world considered it gauche that a young woman would *work* at becoming Miss America—a betrayal, somehow, of old ideals of unadulterated merit and aw-shucks virtue.

In truth, they were *all* working at it, and working *hard*—dieting, exercising, knowledge-cramming—perhaps just more quietly than Miss Georgia. Pageant girls transferred schools to better devote themselves to being Miss State; they moved into their pageant directors' homes for summers of intense coaching. It could take a village to turn a small-town girl into a polished Convention Hall contender—hair, makeup, talent coaches, shopping trips, gown fittings, etiquette lessons. Even states with a far more laid-back approach managed to leave their mark on a girl. In 1983, some New York state pageant sherpa didn't bother to ask permission before grabbing the hairspray and scrunching Vanessa Williams's hair more than it had ever been scrunched. In 1974, the Miss

Florida team prescribed that Delta Burke tweeze her eyebrows down to a pencil line and go get some sun.

And even as the ranks of pageant volunteers began to thin in later years, there would still be experts standing by, ready to help.

On a Saturday morning in June 2012, Bill Alverson, a suave and garrulous native of Andalusia, Alabama, got a text from one of his clients. Miss New York City was competing in the finals of the state pageant that night, but she was freaking out. She felt disconnected, he recalls her saying, almost an out-of-body sensation.

"Go to the bathroom," he typed back to her, "and slap your pussy."

Bill didn't mean for Mallory Hagan to take the order literally, of course. The point, he says, was that his words "shocked her out of her damn self," and got her to focus and relax. She won the Miss New York pageant that night, and seven months later was crowned Miss America. Bill tells the story to demystify his misunderstood profession. When you hire a private pageant coach, he says, "you're really going to a life coach."

In the early 1990s, Bill was a decade into his career as a trial attorney when a choir director friend asked him to meet with a local high school girl competing in a Junior Miss pageant: She needed more practice talking with grown-ups. After a highly productive conversation with Bill, she won. And word began to get around to other girls in the area. Bill turned out to have an eye for hair and wardrobe—his day job had schooled him in the art of making the right impression before a jury of strangers. But it was his insights into how a young woman should prepare herself for a pageant interview—not so different from a courtroom cross-examination, really—that set him apart as he built a thriving sideline in this growing field.

It's a question of "what's the best way to communicate the information she wants to communicate," he says. "How do we sell the argument that is *you* to the jury?"

Bill had become a legend by coaching three consecutive Miss Americas—Mallory, Nina Davuluri, and Kira Kazantsev. He had even had a hand in the training of Miss USA 2019 Cheslie Kryst, the attorney with the cloudburst of natural hair. Cheslie was *so* smart, he said, that she ran the risk of talking over the heads of her judges. So Bill coached her on how to discuss politics and popular culture without intimidating them. Progressive politics were not a dealbreaker in pageantry, even with conservative judges. "But if you make someone feel defensive," he said, "you're not going to enlighten them."

Bill's trademark tactic was to help his clients craft a personal brand. This meant establishing consistency in their self-presentation. A contestant who led with her Christian faith and morality would want to avoid the low-cut, high-slit gowns: "Either we're going to sell sex or sell Jesus, but in a short pageant, you can't sell both." For another, it might mean wearing a pantsuit to her interview when everyone else was wearing dresses. And it meant finding a message—preferably one that could be boiled down to a sentence—that cohered with her look, her résumé, her cause.

In 2013, he met with Nina Davuluri, a lushly beautiful aspiring doctor born to Indian immigrants. Her talent was a Bollywood-style dance, but she began to worry the judges would see her as Miss India instead of Miss America.

"Honey, you walk in the *room*, you're Miss India," Bill told her. Nina could not avoid the first impression of her ethnicity, so why not lean into it? And so she did, adopting "celebrating diversity" as her platform. And when she happened to mention something to him about how "the girl next door is an evolving face," he thought, "Oh my God, that is *gold*" and urged her to work it into her interview. In fact, she used it on stage, on live TV. When a question came up about an anchorwoman who had cosmetic surgery to make her eyes look less Asian, Nina said she disapproved. "I've always viewed Miss America as the girl next door, and the girl next door is evolving as diversity in America evolves," she added. "She's not who she was ten years ago, and she's not going to be the same person come ten years down the road." Seven minutes later, Nina was Miss America.

Yet the concept of pageant coaching still raised suspicions, just as the efforts to prep Debbie Mosley had—and all the more so now that it had gone professional. The Miss America Organization even tried to curtail professional coaching at one point, out of concerns that it gave an unfair advantage to the women who could afford it. Bill scoffed at this. Pageantry was inherently expensive, and "I'm the cheapest person they use," he maintained. "They spend more on hair and makeup than they do on me." A few hours consulting with him might cost less than $1,000—nothing compared to what they would have spent on years of dance or piano lessons.

Beyond the cost, though, judges were said to be wary of a contestant who sounded "too coached"—too rehearsed, too compulsively on point. But Bill maintained he was actually breaking his clients out of those patterns, by teaching them critical thinking and communication skills that would empower them to think on their feet and speak naturally. These were skills that would help them in their professional life well beyond pageantry and that they would be grateful to have acquired even if they lost.

Like Debbie. She never became Miss America. But a couple of broadcasting execs in Arizona saw this forthright young woman with a Southern accent on TV talking about how she hoped to jump from pageants to TV news. And they called the Miss Georgia office to let them know they'd be interested in hiring her. That's how Debbie Mosley became the top-rated anchorwoman in Phoenix in the 1980s.

Besides, Bill said, *everyone* at Miss America was getting *some* level of coaching, even if it came courtesy of a parent, a friend, or a state director rather than a hired gun. There was a word for contestants who went to the pageant without a coach, after all.

"They're clappers," he said. Because that's all they get to do.

✦   ✦   ✦

As the December 2019 pageant approached, the Bill Alverson philosophy started to make sense. Only a small number of contestants were getting any serious buzz on the online Miss America fan forums, and each one of them had a definite *brand*.

There was Miss Oregon, Shivali Kadam, who had the looks of a model, but more to the point, a job in semiconductor manufacturing as a chemical engineer, and a mission of encouraging women to work in science. This consistency in personal messaging seemed to dovetail with optics the pageant yearned to project: Gretchen Carlson's talk of "women of substance," and a decade of efforts before her to attach to the STEM-for-girls cause.

But there was also Miss Georgia, Victoria Hill, a serious opera singer with sapphire eyes, but more to the point, short and *spiky* black hair, a look that signaled a break from the pageant's heavily moussed past. And there was Miss Alabama, Tiara Pennington, who had an inspiring pedigree—her mother had been the first black woman to win a preliminary at Miss Alabama—but more to the point, her name was Tiara, and how perfect was that?

Branding *mattered*. The story the next Miss America could tell about herself could also help a struggling institution rebrand—and hopefully survive into its next century.

And that's why the world of pageant obsessives—the former contestants, volunteers, and superfans who congregated online to talk about Miss America year-round—had put Miss Texas on the top of their lists the moment she won her state title in June.

Chandler Foreman was a bonfire of charisma. She rocked an explosive Afro and a conspicuous Lauren Hutton gap in her front teeth. Her Miss Texas crowning had been a viral sensation: Astonished to hear her name called, she collapsed to the ground, in a near-face-plant, and pounded the floor with her fist as her rivals cheered ecstatically for her. The theory about Chandler was that her curvy physique had kept this dynamo personality from winning in previous attempts at Miss Texas. So there she was—living proof of the argument for getting rid of the swimsuit competition.

No one was talking much about Camille Schrier, though. And this surprised me.

Yes, Miss Virginia was a conventionally beautiful white woman. But her trick with the erupting rainbow foam had proven a public-relations smash—highlighted over the summer not only by local media but by *Inside Edition* and the *Daily Mail*. Camille was even flown out to L.A. to perform her "chemistry demonstration" on the nationally syndicated *Kelly Clarkson Show*. The hook was the way it bucked stereotypes: *Not what you expect from a pageant queen!*

And Lord knows, she was *working* it, just as hard as Debbie Mosley four decades earlier. Camille sold her chemistry demonstration as a radical statement—a blow for both science and self-actualization.

"As someone who is breaking the boundaries and breaking stereotypes for what talent looks like at Miss America, I wanted to be a little out of the box," she told a local reporter after she was crowned Miss Virginia.

Scientist. Inspiring. Breaking stereotypes. Authentic. You probably didn't even need Alverson-tier coaching to tell you how to do this anymore. This was the legacy of growing up on social media, where a few well-chosen words and images could telegraph precisely whatever identity you wanted. On the placards that the Virginia folks would wave at the national pageant, Camille wore her protective laboratory goggles; her mother, in the audience, wore a white lab coat in homage.

But this was not Camille's first attempt at establishing a brand. She had tried out a couple others.

Fit Like a Queen was the name of the blog she started in her senior year of high school. It was devoted to "healthy living, fitness, and eating well," from the perspective of a teenage beauty queen—Camille herself, captured in Disney princess mode, with a sunny smile, a tumble of light brown hair, a strapless white bodice, and a rhinestone crown.

As Miss Virginia, Camille sometimes gave the impression of being a newcomer who only entered pageantry after Miss America dropped the swimsuit competition. But she had a history with pageants, going back to when she was fifteen and competing for lesser-known titles like National American Miss and Miss High School America—and here on the blog she shared her winning diet tips.

"My AP Bio class went into town for lunch to celebrate being done with APs!" she shared in a typical entry from her senior year, in 2013. "I got grilled salmon with tomatoes and basil, on top of a fresh green salad! No dressing necessary!"

Or: "The hot food at my school is usually fatty or fried so I stick to the salad bar!" she wrote on another day.

She had hashtags for #weightloss and #paleo, recipes for "guilt-free" oatmeal pancakes and "cookies" made from protein bars. But then one day, an explosion of pure anguish: Camille had regained some lost pounds and couldn't zip into a competition gown.

"I felt like a hypocrite for being a girl with a health food blog who couldn't fit into her dresses," she wrote. "I was so upset with myself."

Two years later, the public-facing Camille had a sophisticated new look on the internet—sleeker, blonder, with a skeptical arch to her brows and red, wryly pursed lips. She had joined the ranks of young women seeking to become social-media "influencers" in the field of beauty. "I am thrilled to finally announce my partnership with Essence Cosmetics, Europe's #1 cosmetic brand!" she announced—essentially a gig that would get her makeup freebies in exchange for plentiful social-media plugs. She was also showing off the professional-caliber makeup sessions she was doing for her pageant friends.

Camille no longer had the pageant-girl look, though. Because she had stopped being one.

College had hit her like a ton of bricks. From the outside she was thriving, graduating from the elite Hun School of Princeton, near her home in the Philadelphia suburbs, to enter the highly ranked engineering program at the University of Michigan, where she joined a sorority. She was one of the beautiful people on campus, her photo highlighted on a hot-coed website called Big10Tens, her name called out more than once on a Twitter feed compiling the secret crushes of Michigan students. "You were like a celebrity on campus," an admirer-from-afar commented on one of her blog posts, ". . . in a good way."

And yet, she was struggling socially, she would later say. There were panic attacks, a slew of illnesses, and a gradual acknowledgment that she was suffering from an eating disorder. It had started with pageant-driven crash diets of six hundred calories a day, followed by food binges—a habit that continued into college. Camille kept up a positive façade as she withdrew from Michigan in the fall of her sophomore year, maintaining in a blog post that "I am succeeding here" and merely wanted to pursue a line of studies not offered at Ann Arbor. A year later, though, she would reveal that she had been in the grips of deep depression, lying on the floor in a fetal position, crying because she believed she was a failure. She went home to Pennsylvania, where her parents got her into treatment. By the next summer, she felt she had reclaimed her life.

This was the story she shared, in bits and pieces over a year and a half, in a series of heartbreakingly candid posts on *Fit Like a Queen*. This was the truth, she finally admitted, behind the exuberant glamour-girl image she had presented to the world for so long. Camille had come to realize that "everyone is struggling with *something*, whether you see it or not," she wrote. "PLEASE seek help. It will save your life."

Things seemed to pick up for Camille after she transferred to Virginia Tech—assuming, of course, you can ever really understand what's going on with someone from social media. The makeup tutorials and pageant sashes vanished from her Instagram, replaced by a happy chronicle of her college life: pledging Kappa Delta, finishing her thesis, growing hyacinths, trying goat yoga, playing with her cats. She also highlighted her mother, Cheryl, who was on her own sequined journey through a circuit of "Mrs." pageants. Camille didn't seem to be selling anything anymore. Both the teen-queen brand and the beauty-influencer enterprise had been shelved. But other than a couple references to homework or the PCATs, she wasn't exactly foregrounding her interest in science.

So if you had known Camille Schrier in college, at least by her online presence, you might have encountered a personal brand that was blurrier, and more human, than those that came before or after—that of a young woman who had battled demons and emerged stronger, who had come to terms with the teenage rat race and the female cult of perfectionism, who was unashamed of her struggles and eager to help other people with their own.

By late 2019, though, she had deleted the entire blog.

✦   ✦   ✦

I was eager to see how the kids at Lacey Spring would respond to Camille's chemistry demonstration. But of course, the elephant-toothpaste trick, requiring insulated mitts and half a dozen stagehands, was impractical for elementary schools. She showed them a video of it instead. But the kids barely murmured, even at the money shot, kids being accustomed to all kinds of pyrotechnics on screens. Camille carried on brightly, sharing a picture from her *Kelly Clarkson Show* appearance where she had created a volcanic cloud of mist by pouring hot water into liquid nitrogen, wearing a crown atop her protective visor.

"I've gotten a lot of really cool opportunities being Miss Virginia and being a scientist Miss Virginia especially," she told them. "I would have never had that opportunity if I had just been a girl who went out and danced or sang at Miss Virginia. Because that wouldn't have been authentic to who I was."

That last thought of hers didn't quite track. No one gets booked on a talk show for being "authentic." Camille got booked for being *different*. But talking points can trip you up that way. They create their own wheel ruts.

The kids had questions. How did she keep her crown on? How old was she? Where did nitrogen come from? And finally: *Are you a real princess?*

"Am I a real princess?" Camille repeated. "It depends on your definition of what a real princess is. But no, I'm not. I only do this for a year . . . and then I go back to being a normal person."

10

"EVERYONE WANTED SOMETHING FROM ME THAT I COULDN'T GIVE THEM"

2007

The stylists offered the Miss America hopeful some radical advice. Her long, thick blonde hair, the anchor for so many elegant updos? Yeahhhh, she should chop it off. A sassy bob was *just* what she needed to put her look over the top, they said.

As she wandered into the room where her fellow contestants were sitting down to dinner, this Miss State agonized over her decision. Did she dare make such a dramatic change just two months before the pageant? What if she hated it?

"Oh my gosh," she murmured. "I cannot eat when I'm nervous."

A male voice broke in.

"Hey, let's get that again," he said. "Can you walk back in and say that again?"

That was no ordinary styling session, and this was not just dinner. All of it—and all the camaraderie and the tension—was being captured on camera for *Miss America: Reality Check*, the eighty-seven-year-old pageant's attempt to join the reality-television revolution.

All of that year's contestants had convened a couple months before the 2008 pageant at this Italianate mansion in the hills north of Los Angeles. They bunked together for ten unpaid days, sharing a mere seven bathrooms, submitting to makeovers and coaching, competing in obstacle courses and trivia quizzes, and sitting down, fully miked, for the kind of heavily edited heart-to-hearts that had become the connective tissue of virtually every reality hit of the new century.

Pageant brass had lately tried to claim that Miss America was "the first reality TV"—but everyone knew that it had lost ground to the new generation, shows like *American Idol*, *Survivor*, and *The Bachelor*, with their addictive, season-long story arcs and delicious cultures of conflict.

It wasn't just a matter of ratings: It was an essential fame quotient that no longer accrued to Miss America. Once, her overnight stardom would earn her a feature in *People* and a visit to *Today* or *The Tonight Show*. Now even the semifinalists of *Dancing with the Stars* were seizing the magazine covers, and reality television was churning out so many insta-celebrities that there was no guarantee Miss America could get herself booked.

So now the idea was to juice the audience's flagging interest in the big annual broadcast with a four-episode series on Discovery's TLC channel showcasing the sparky personalities that always flew by too fast on finals night and dramatizing their intense behind-the-scenes preparations. TLC was the home of leading-edge reality programming, such as *Jon & Kate Plus 8*, which in 2008 was still a quirky look at a family with sextuplet toddlers and not yet a portrait of a disintegrating family burned by reality-TV fame. Despite the trepidation of state pageant directors, Miss America leadership handed over the keys to TLC's producers.

But *Miss America: Reality Check* also tried to target viewers who had lost interest in pageants—by mocking pageants.

"Your sequins are burning my retinas, *aagghh!!!*" screamed host Michael Urie as he greeted contestants in the first episode—a set-up ripped off from *The Bachelor*, with a parade of women arriving by night to the romantically spot-lit villa.

The gibe was a little unfair. Leonard Horn had spent the previous decade knocking the mid-century stiffness out of Miss America. But this new show presented itself as the change agent. "Miss America is getting a makeover!" chortled the voice-over guy. "This year, Miss America will be a new type of woman: relatable, real, inspiring. . . . You'll see who can make that change—and who just can't get that pageant training out of their system!" Runway sergeants drilled the women on a supermodel swagger, and stylists tackled their helmet hair or dated lipliner. "Big hair, big dresses—ladies, big mistake!" groaned the host, familiar from TV's *Ugly Betty* as the conniving assistant to the fashion editor played by, small world, Vanessa Williams.

Reality Check lifted brazenly, going so far as to patch in the snarky hosts of *What Not to Wear*. (Stay away from polyester, they chided Miss Pennsylvania: "It's for strippers.") In fairness, the show did manage to evoke some of the backstage energy that had hooked so many contestants and volunteers over the decades: the coaching and grooming that transformed a grad student into a goddess; the unexpected sweetness of this all-girl tribe. And with the theatrically fabulous style gurus hired to sass them into fighting form, there was at last a symbolic nod to the legions of gay men who had long been running the pageant from behind the scenes as local organizers, coaches, and superfan volunteers.

But it was 2008. Fabulous gay men had staked out turf all over reality TV. Miss America couldn't bring much new to the table.

And then there were the contestants. On paper, they seemed made for reality TV—peppy, super-fit young women who craved competition and rocked a sparkly gown. And yet, they were still pageant girls. They didn't want to win some catfighting, scavenger-hunting reality show; they wanted to win Miss America. They played it safe: no loose lips, no acting out, no drama. Women like this, they *did* come here to make friends.

The 1990s were over, but these women still carried some of the DNA of that decade's alpha Miss Americas. They came to the pageant with résumés and causes of the heart and a poised, direct manner of communicating.

They wanted fame but the *right* kind of fame, and they were no dummies: They'd seen how cruel reality TV could be to pretty young women like themselves.

They were women like Miss Michigan, Kirsten Haglund, just turned nineteen, a former ballerina from the suburbs of Detroit. The Miss Americas of this era all seemed to take after the new archetype in girl culture—the thick-haired, narrow-faced, doe-eyed Disney Princess—and Kirsten had the look. (Princess Aurora, in her case.) But there was a wry savvy in her deep brown eyes that signaled she had your number. Kirsten was sitting in the mansion's dining area as her fellow Miss State fretted over the haircut advice. When she heard the director ask her friend to repeat the comment about being too nervous to eat, Kirsten knew she had to say something.

"Hey, can you actually *not* shoot that?" she asked him.

"What?" he said, confused.

Kirsten had studied dance for years, a joyful experience until puberty, when she grew frustrated with her body's refusal to match the long, lean ideal. She had dieted obsessively, falling deeper into depression. At fifteen, her family recognized she had a problem, but it took months for her to acknowledge it, and months more of intensive outpatient treatment to get better. Eventually she realized that the culture of ballet was exacerbating her eating disorder, so she quit. And now, having chosen eating-disorders awareness as her platform, she was an expert on treatment strategies and risk factors. She had learned how to talk about her own struggle without dishing the grisly details—the number of lost pounds, the old calorie-avoidance tactics. Those kinds of specifics could be triggering, she knew, even aspirational for a young person with anorexia.

Her face reddened as she confronted the director. To have a slender and gorgeous Miss State on television proclaiming how she doesn't eat when she is nervous could glamorize the habit, she warned; it could plant unhealthy ideas in the mind of a vulnerable young viewer.

"I think that's a really bad message to send to girls," Kirsten told him, "and I don't want it on camera."

And that was it. They didn't film it. Simply because the teenage girl who wasn't yet Miss America convinced them not to.

Television was essential to Miss America's survival—and Lord knows, Miss America would do whatever she could to make this relationship work. In Kirsten's year, producers tried to rev up the broadcast with man-on-the-street interviews, edgy questions about Britney Spears and binge drinking, and a zhuzhed-up swimsuit competition with as much twirling, hair-tossing, and hip-cocking as a Victoria's Secret Fashion Show.

Television was the source of Miss America's funding, of her brand identity. Everything Miss America had come to represent in the American century was because of television. Yet as they headed into the new millennium, there would be some places she just could not follow it.

✦ ✦ ✦

In the spring of 1954, Lee Meriwether was finishing her freshman year at City College of San Francisco when the dean of women called her in. A fraternity, she informed Lee, had nominated her for the Miss San Francisco contest.

"Do I have to?" Lee asked, confused.

"Well, my dear," the dean replied, "I'm afraid a lot of people would be disappointed if you don't."

Lee was no wallflower. A tall brunette about to turn nineteen, she had a frame-filling face and a sly Lauren Bacall quality, and she had set her sights on an acting career. Still, it was a mysterious proposition, so she telephoned her father from the dean's office. A local grocer, he made a few calls of his own and called her back.

"This is all on the up-and-up," he told her. The Junior Chamber of Commerce had taken over the city pageant, so it seemed respectable enough. Lee would need a talent, he said, but she was taking drama classes, she could figure it out.

Miss America had been an institution for three decades at that point, covered by the newswires, by *Life* magazine, by the newsreels shown between features at the movies. But Miss America remained a glamorous cipher for most of the population because they'd never seen the pageant. That was about to change.

Several weeks later in Atlantic City, Paul "Pops" Whiteman headed to a business meeting at the Penn-Atlantic Hotel. The veteran bandleader, now in his sixties, was in town to host *On the Boardwalk*, a weekly teen talent search broadcast live from the Steel Pier; the reigning Miss America, twenty-one-year-old Evelyn Ay, sat on his judging panel. But Pops also had a side gig as a vice president for ABC. And it was in that role that he caught up with Hugh Wathen, the local gas company executive and former stage actor who had just been voted president of the pageant.

It was time, Pops advised Hugh, to put the pageant on TV.

It couldn't have happened much sooner. Television was introduced at the 1939 World's Fair, in time for Miss America's eighteenth birthday. But no one really started buying TVs until ten years later, once the war's end allowed factories to mass-produce affordable sets, and Milton Berle's debut on *Texaco Star Theater* finally gave Americans something they wanted to watch. In 1949, 2.3 percent of households owned a TV. By 1952, 34.2 percent did.

The schedules filled out to meet the audiences, shows like *You Bet Your Life* on NBC, *I Love Lucy* on CBS, *The Adventures of Ozzie and Harriet* on ABC. But these were filmed, and the pioneers of this new medium craved more live programming. Live shows had energy and urgency. They were also cheaper. And they were the one thing TV executives knew they could do better than Hollywood studios when it came to loading up the airwaves of the local stations they were trying to lock down into their growing national networks. By the early 1950s, the coaxial cable that could transmit live, coast-to-coast, was snaking its way from the major markets to midsize cities.

ABC, the youngest, smallest, and hungriest of the three TV networks, had made a first pass at Miss America in 1953, offering $5,000 to air that fall's pageant. But the pageant folks freaked out, petrified of losing ticket revenue if fans could simply watch from home. They tried to insist on a blackout of the Philadelphia–Atlantic City market. ABC backed away.

"You guys are crazy," Pops told his network colleagues. They simply hadn't tried hard enough. It would be a cinch to put the pageant on air. His crew was already in town, and the microwave technology was now in place to send a signal from Atlantic City to Philly, and then onto the coaxial cable. Meanwhile, Pops knew what Hugh needed. He called his friends at Philco, a leading manufacturer of television sets with whom he also had a consulting gig, and got them to write a check for $10,000 to become Miss America's first TV sponsor.

The deal would soon propel Miss America's fame and finances to never-imagined heights. But as far as Hugh and Lenora Slaughter were concerned, ABC was a half-tolerated guest that first year, invited merely to cover the festivities as a news event. The network kept its five cameras to the side of the stage, out of the sightlines of the Convention Hall audience. The celebrity hosts, newsman John Daly and Bess Myerson, anchored from a backstage studio, their commentary only heard by viewers at home.

ABC's presence was so downplayed, in fact, that Miss California Lee Meriwether had no idea they were on television at all, not until well after she spotted the camera allowed backstage as part of the pageant's most significant concession to ABC.

Lee was standing there with the other finalists, confused about what was happening. The rituals and clichés of Miss America were even a little mysterious for the regulars at Convention Hall, where in the early years the winner was crowned backstage, her identity revealed to the audience only when she walked out in full regalia. And now Lenora was giving the finalists a little speech about how wonderful they all were, and suddenly one of the girls was pulled away.

Oh, she's it, Lee thought. But then someone called, "Lee, come here," and all she could think was: *Did someone fall? Do they need my help?* That's when Lenora told her she was Miss America 1955.

Lee burst into tears. She still had no idea she was on television.

"I hope Daddy knows," she said, casting her eyes upward. Her beloved father had died suddenly in July, after seeing her crowned Miss California. She wept harder. "I hope he's proud."

And an entire nation wept with her.

Lee was still crying minutes later after she completed her runway walk and retreated backstage to be interviewed by Bess Myerson. "Stop your sniveling," said her mother, who still had no idea they were on air, and this, too, was clearly audible to the folks at home. It sounded rather cold—but also excitingly *real*.

"There have been few such real emotion-packed moments on TV," the *Des Moines Register* declared. "Something no script writer could have foreseen and injected into the show," marveled a Los Angeles critic.

Miss America, the TV show, was a hit. It captured 27 million viewers and 39 percent of the national audience that night, without harming the pageant's precious ticket sales. Philco came around again the next year, hoping for a deal, but a young board member drove a hard bargain. It was Al Marks, who extracted $25,000 from the sponsor and began his ascent to the top of the pageant he would run for nearly three decades. By 1958, the show had moved to CBS and won an estimated 60 million viewers and two-thirds of all TV sets. In 1966, when NBC won it in a bidding war, CBS tried to counterprogram with the NFL season opener. Miss America beat the game in the ratings by a 3–1 margin. Five times in the 1960s, Nielsen ranked the pageant as the most watched show of the year.

That wonderful, weepy moment Lee shared with the nation transformed her life. Her scholarship prize paid for acting classes in New York, and her overnight celebrity won her roles on scores of TV dramas—and eventually, in the 1966 film version of *Batman*, where her memorable portrayal as Catwoman capitalized on the slinky sophistication that had pulled all the focus on that Atlantic City runway. Lee was close to forty, though, when she found her stride with her Emmy-nominated role in the hit detective series *Barnaby Jones*. It can take a while for Miss Americas to reach the age that matches the gravitas they seem born with.

But her televised crowning didn't just launch Lee to fame. It altered the very identity of the pageant, turning it into a television show *about* launching young women to fame, and heightening the expectations for those who wore the crown.

As if they weren't high enough already.

✦   ✦   ✦

In February 2002, Miss America Katie Harman returned to Atlantic City headquarters, after months of growing tensions, for a clear-the-air summit. As usual, she was the youngest person in the room by decades.

Bob Renneisen, the CEO of the Miss America Organization, walked in and dropped a stack of papers on the table in front of her.

"This," he said, "is your contract."

He flipped to the signature she had made five months earlier on the morning after her crowning.

"This organization does *not* work for you," Katie recalls him saying. "You work for *us*." He reminded her that by accepting the crown, she had agreed to follow the pageant's orders. And if she didn't, "we will replace you."

Katie couldn't see what an empty threat this was, that it would take a Vanessa-level transgression for the Miss America Organization even to *want* to dismiss a Miss America, nothing like the petty accusations that had been flying in recent months. But she was a doe-eyed twenty-one-year-old, far from home and ready to burst into tears.

It would take years for her to grasp everything that had led to that confrontation—the financial strains on an organization in flux, the brutal grown-up politics, the conflicting stories and paranoia, and, yes, her own immaturity. Then she could make her peace with it. But at that moment, the Miss America experience was tarnished for her.

"I thought, 'This means nothing. There's no value to this. I'm a pawn, I'm a toy,'" she says eighteen years later. "Everyone wanted something from me that I couldn't give them."

Leonard Horn had left three years earlier. The trial attorney–turned–pageant impresario had steadied Miss America's financial footing by letting the networks do the work of finding sponsors and getting the state to underwrite production costs. But he had clashed with his board, made up almost entirely of South Jersey natives who chafed at proposals to change anything about a pageant they still saw as a community pet project. The final fight came in 1997, when he says none of them bothered to warn him that board member Gordon Shindle's daughter had started competing—what were the odds that little Miss Lake County, Illinois, would go anywhere?—until it was too late, and then reporters were questioning him and his new Miss America about conflict of interest. Kate Shindle's highly successful reign focused on AIDS advocacy quickly silenced any insinuation of a rigged contest. But Leonard, furious the pageant had endured the mere appearance of scandal, stepped down with two years left on his contract.

Ever since, the Miss America Organization had skipped from mini-

crisis to mini-crisis. Anxiety within its ranks seemed to rise as the television ratings sank.

While it remained one of the most watched TV shows, the ratings had fallen far from the estimated peak of 80 million viewers who
watched Phyllis George's crowning in 1970. Leonard had introduced
a flurry of gimmicks—call-in polls on whether to keep the swimsuit
competition (viewers always said yes) or which contestant should be a
"viewer's choice" finalist, and opening the door to bikinis. But the pageant, like all network TV shows, was vying for attention with hundreds
of cable channels and bountiful video-rental options.

In 1990, the pageant was the most watched program of the week it
aired, reaching 16.6 million homes. Even as late as 1997—Kate Shindle's year—Miss America drew 12.3 million households, more than
Friends or *ER* that week and standing nearly as tall as *Monday Night
Football* in the ratings. But the next year—Leonard's last—the pageant
lost 2 million households. And two years later, another 2 million.

Leonard's replacement, Robert Beck, was the first outsider tapped to
run the pageant since Lenora Slaughter in 1935. But his backstory was
poignantly attuned to the new Miss America sensibilities—a business
executive who had segued into advocacy as the head of Mothers Against
Drunk Driving, after a drunk driver killed his son. The new chief exec
understood that everything hinged on a TV broadcast in desperate need
of an overhaul. For the September 1999 pageant, he hired Donny and
Marie, then enjoying a nostalgic revival, to replace the generic soap
opera stars who had succeeded Regis Philbin as host. He moved the
start time to 8 p.m. Eastern Time to capture more prime-time eyeballs
and hook a generation of kids with strict bedtimes. And he axed the
hokey production numbers in favor of Oprah-style chats with the finalists. He even got ABC to run a full hour-long special of "Up Close &
Personal" stories on each contestant. But in a dire break with tradition,
he also slashed the number of televised talent performances from ten
to five—a cold acknowledgment that the arias and jazz-tap routines into
which fifty-odd women had poured hearts and souls no longer met base-
line definitions of "entertainment."

Yet it was a far stealthier change that doomed Rob Beck. It came after he convinced the board to revise the standard contestant contract, eliminating a couple of Lenora-era provisions that might run afoul of New Jersey's anti-discrimination statute—namely, requirements that the women had never been married or been pregnant.

In practice, these changes would have meant next to nothing. Miss America would have remained a title reserved for the single and child-less, just with fewer questions asked about the contestants' past. Yet in stark headline form, the upshot of the new wording detonated like a hand grenade: Miss America was opening the door to *women who'd been divorced* and *women who'd had an abortion*! State pageant organiz-ers headed to court to challenge it.

"Miss America has a long history of high moral standards and tradi-tions," the director of Miss Kentucky told reporters, "and I'm opposed to anything that changes that." Two days later, the board voted to scrap the contract changes. The old prohibitions would stand. And then they fired Rob Beck after less than a year. He had overseen exactly one new-and-improved pageant. And the ratings had stayed flat.

His replacement, Bob Renneisen, was an Atlantic City guy, a for-mer hotel and casino manager, who had long observed the pageant cy-cle's ebb and flow. He had some of Leonard's brash PR instincts, and a tendency to say the quiet parts out loud. "Bob could recognize what changes needed to be made," one board member said, "but he wanted to get them all made tomorrow."

Miss America's bankbook looked healthy, thanks to a $15 million surplus Leonard had left behind. But every year, it was costing more to retrofit ancient Convention Hall with the basic equipment for a live TV show. And as it sank in the ratings, the pageant could no longer command network fees big enough to cover its costs. Every year, Miss America was losing money.

Bob's first Miss America was Angela Perez Baraquio, the first Asian-American winner—an effervescent, shaka sign–flashing phys-ed teacher from Hawaii who played keyboard in an all-girl band. He sent her out on a media charm offensive, confident that word of the pag-eant's new look and mission would win back corporate sponsors. But two months after he started the job, CBS debuted a new series that would change the game for everyone. *Survivor* was half game show, half sociological documentary, starring a scrappy yet telegenic crew of strangers struggling to survive in a tropical wilderness for a $1 million prize. From day one, it was a watercooler phenom, fetching ratings reminiscent of Miss America's old days. Bob suggested adding some reality-TV elements to the pageant broadcast. He also broached much bigger changes, like leaving Atlantic City. Other cities had newer, well-wired arenas all set to serve as broadcast venues. One dream scenario he explored would not just have moved the pageant to Orlando but handed over control to the solid-gold marketing machine of Disney.

So in late 2001, the former casino manager made a high-stakes gamble. He threatened that if the Atlantic City community didn't boost its financial support, which had never gone much beyond free hotel rooms and a discount rental rate on Convention Hall, Miss America would leave. His trump card: a lucrative offer to move the pageant to Connecticut's Mohegan Sun casino. The change was set to save hundreds of thousands in production costs and make Miss America profitable overnight. But his own board rebuffed him and pledged to stay at the shore for at least another year. Bob, humiliated and furious, told board members they were in "breach of their fiduciary duty."

It went downhill from there—the kind of toxicity that can brew in any organization where there is little money to fight over, just faded prestige and a small-pond sort of power, and yet everyone cares so very, very much. With the exodus of the last high-end sponsors, Waterford and Clairol, Bob suggested licensing the Miss America name to casino slot machines, and this enraged the traditionalists. Tensions boiled over at a meeting with state directors, where Bob accused his critics of undermining him and told them to "get the hell out."

And caught up in the middle of it all was the small, radiant, fragile receptacle for everyone's fixations—the reigning Miss America, Katie Harman.

She seemed laboratory-bred for this new era of Miss America, a serious young woman from a conservative, working-middle-class family in Portland, Oregon, who had pursued studies in medical research before her dynamic soprano diverted her to performing. Katie had stumbled into pageants barely a year earlier to pay for college, but she opted for a sleek, anti-pageant Carolyn Bessette Kennedy aesthetic—minimalist black jersey gown, low ponytail, no false eyelashes. It worked. She was the first blonde Miss America in thirteen years.

Her year blasted off with dizzying emotional momentum. She and her fellow contestants had arrived in Atlantic City on September 10, 2001. Two days later, Bob Renneisen and the show's producers gave them the choice: Should we call off the pageant? The fifty-one women voted to carry on. It was the first live television event after 9/11, a more stripped-down and sentimental pageant than usual—and yes, the ratings even bounced up a little. Visiting Ground Zero days later, Katie chatted up some firefighters, and one told her how glad he was to watch the show.

"I needed to see Miss America," the fireman said, and what he meant was everything Miss America symbolized—something nostalgic and sweet, glamorous yet familiar. A return to something normal.

But being Miss America was hard. Just turned twenty-one, the farthest she had ever been from home, Katie felt she was flying blind, frustrated by a lack of guidance as she traveled the country. She showed up to a red-carpet event in a business suit and to the Winter Olympics opening ceremony in dress pants, when everyone else was in sporty ski wear. She had crying jags and fits of exhaustion that tested the patience of her handlers. "I was a self-absorbed Miss America," she says now, but she may just have needed more nurturing than they were equipped to give at a challenging time. Terrorism fears canceled many of her bookings, and she was bumped from the traditional Miss America spot in the Macy's Thanksgiving Day Parade, replaced by Miss Universe (either because Macy's needed to promote a new store in Puerto Rico or because Donald Trump, who had bought the rival pageant five years earlier, pulled some strings).

Her parents, meanwhile, were freaked out by 9/11, frustrated when they couldn't reach her, and struggling to make sense of the baffling paperwork they had to handle on her behalf. And they made a nuisance of themselves with their calls to Miss America headquarters.

Word of their distress reached some of the state pageant directors who had been clashing with Bob. They urged the Harmans to put their frustrations in a letter.

"Katie is your Miss America," Glen and Darla Harman wrote to Bob in February 2002, "and I can't tell you how many times she is in trouble for things that are not her fault." They complained that the pageant wasn't getting Katie booked enough and that she had been billed for alterations to her official pageant wardrobe and a post-crowning victory party someone else hosted.

Katie didn't know her parents were writing the letter. Her parents didn't realize that it would be weaponized in the tense climate they were sending it into—right at the time four state pageant executives were headed to Atlantic City to demand major changes or Bob's head. Bob saw the letter as part of a coup attempt—"the rebellion of the beauty queens," he called it. He went on the offensive and released the Harmans' letter to the press.

"Miss America's Whine List," teased one tabloid headline. Katie was pulled off the road. That's when Bob confronted her with her contract and scheduled a press conference, where she realized she had no choice but to say that she was never mistreated, never mismanaged—that everything, contrary to Glen and Darla's letter, was *fine*.

"Miss America vs. Parents," blared the *New York Daily News*.

Katie went home to Portland for a day and cried for a night, and then picked herself up and flew off to her next appearance as Miss America. "I was terrified to do anything out of step," she says now. "If I had the experience and knowledge I do now, I would have spoken out." The episode left her distrustful and wary; it took years of therapy to rebuild her family relationships, to stop watching her back, to find a place in her heart for her Miss America experience.

In many ways, Bob Renneisen would end up on the right side of history: The pageant would soon start chasing reality-TV trends and revenue sources more questionable than slot machines—and yes, it would leave Atlantic City, not once but twice. But two weeks after that awkward press conference, he abruptly parted ways with the pageant. So there would be only one crucial lesson from his short tenure:

Don't get on the wrong side of a Miss America.

✦   ✦   ✦

There would be one last scandal before the world stopped paying much attention to Miss America.

It was a juicy, meaningless multiweek media sensation that *almost* made the pageant sexy enough for the new Young Hollywood era—the paparazzi-driven moment in our culture when there was no more burning question than whether or not Britney and Justin had *done it*—except that it also exposed the pageant as insultingly out of step with the lives of the young women involved.

Rebekah Revels had been Miss North Carolina for a month in 2002 when her board called her in for a meeting. She was twenty-four, a high school English teacher, with a lush, dark-eyed beauty reminiscent of Ava Gardner, the original Tar Heel bombshell. A member of the Lumbee tribe, Rebekah was only the second Native American to win the state title, a focus of community pride. She expected a routine meeting. Instead, a board member showed her a printout of an email with a familiar address: her college ex-boyfriend. His message—sent to Atlantic City and forwarded to North Carolina—warned that Rebekah did not have the "moral standards" for the Miss America crown, as he was in possession of nude photos that could fetch top dollar.

Rebekah felt the walls closing in.

"Are you going to fight for me?" she asked.

No, they said. If she didn't resign, they would fire her.

She was cryptic when reporters first inquired, saying only that she had quit because of an ex-boyfriend's "attempt to defame my character." Rebekah was so terrified of bringing shame to her tribe that she resigned fast to make it all go away. It took about a week for Rebekah to get mad. Those photos, she realized, were *nothing* to be ashamed of—shirtless candids snapped by someone she once loved who had betrayed her; photos she'd assumed would never see the light of day. Hardly the stuff of *Penthouse*. And nobody's business but her own.

She got a lawyer, who made the case her resignation was coerced, and she opened up on national TV about her ordeal. And Rebekah went to court, where a state judge agreed she had been terminated without cause in a breach of contract—and temporarily reinstated her as Miss North Carolina, days ahead of the national pageant.

Of course, the Miss North Carolina board had already handed the title to Rebekah's first runner-up. And now *she* had a lawyer, too. But Rebekah got a preliminary injunction, and the Miss America Organization conceded that, for now, they would just have to welcome *two* Miss North Carolinas to Atlantic City.

Two Miss North Carolinas! "Beauty Queen Cat Fight," hollered one New York tabloid. "Miss-Mosh at the Pageant," yelled another.

"Now to the tiara tussle at the Miss America pageant!" began Greta Van Susteren on Fox News one night. "The fur is flying in North Carolina over who is the reigning queen. . . ." On NBC: "Are we going to have two Miss North Carolinas at the pageant?" anchor David Bloom asked poor Katie Harman, who of course got dragged into this one, too, in the final days of her reign. "It's awkward," she said brightly, but pageant girls could cope with awkward. It was just more preparation "for the job of being Miss America."

The story hit at just the right time in the news cycle: two days after the debut season of *American Idol* came to an end.

Idol had conquered the nation that summer of 2002, a televised star-factory competition like Miss America, but with higher stakes (a $1 million recording contract), a longer story arc, and a clearer sense of the game. Instead of asking fans to parse the murkily weighted intangibles (swimsuit, interview) that factored into some TV judge's decision, *Idol* got viewers invested by asking *them* to help settle, with a call-in vote, one simple question: Who's the best singer? Or boiled down to its essence: Who do you *want* to hear sing again? Miss America had always been a contest of charisma, but *Idol*, by stretching the contest out longer, took viewers along on a searching investigation into the very nature of charisma. It was mesmerizing television. That summer, Kelly vs. Justin vs. Nikki vs. Tamyra was a debate you could enjoy with almost anyone—your kid, your bus driver, your boss, your grandma. Everyone watched *Idol*.

But once it was done for the year, Miss North Carolina filled the vacuum. Never mind that this was essentially a matter of contract law.

Two beauty queens scrapping over one title awoke some slumbering synapse in the collective unconscious, a reminder that Miss America had always offered the rich drama of women in competition, the same delicious catfight overtones as *The Bachelor*, the other new reality show blowing minds that year.

Miss America officials welcomed Rebekah to the pageant with as much graciousness as they extended to the fifty-one women who weren't suing them. She joined them for rehearsals and meals, even posing for photos with Misty Clymer, the other Miss N.C., on the beach in matching white bikinis. The other contestants were frosty to her, though, and Rebekah understood. They had worked so hard to get there only to be upstaged by the girl with the topless photos.

"It just totally changed the face of Miss America that year," she says. And yet, couldn't they sympathize with what she had been through? She had worked just as hard to get there. The only difference is that she'd had a rat of an ex-boyfriend lying in wait to humiliate her.

The media mostly treated the saga as a piece of a quirky subculture; it was the court hearings that got creepy. Rebekah argued that she hadn't violated any morality clause because she never consented to these photos. She was getting dressed in the dorm room, her boyfriend called her name, she turned, and *click*. Yet the state pageant boss countered that her very presence in that room was problematic. "The pictures were taken in an intimate situation," he testified. "The fact of the nude photos was immoral, immodest, and in bad taste."

And that was it in a nutshell: The pageant world could not bring itself to stand up for a victim of what would soon become known as "revenge porn," because she had been intimate with a longtime boyfriend—and sex was still incompatible with the decades-old ideal of Miss America they continued to exalt.

Ultimately, four days before the preliminary competitions kicked off, a federal judge refused to restore her to the pageant, and Rebekah, who is now a married mom and community college administrator, had to watch from the sidelines as her fellow Miss States competed, fully aware that she was hardly the only one of them to have been involved in an intimate relationship.

"I'm probably not the only one," she says, "who had pictures, either."

✦   ✦   ✦

The call from Donald Trump came at one of the darker hours for Miss America.

The buzz over the Year of Two Miss North Carolinas had done nothing to juice the 2002 ratings. In 2003, they lost another million and a half viewers.

In September 2004, the crown went to Deidre Downs, a Miss Alabama who might well have been the apotheosis of Leonard Horn's dreams—a Rhodes Scholar finalist and former Division I volleyball player with Bette Davis eyes, a runway-model frame, and a spot waiting for her at a top medical school. (Fourteen years later, when she wed her girlfriend, Deidre would make history as the first former Miss America to come out as gay.) Yet for the first time, fewer than 10 million watched. A month later, ABC announced it would no longer carry the pageant. No other network stepped forward. The long-feared nightmare was coming true: Miss America had no home on TV.

Donald's call in early 2005 was not entirely surprising. While Miss America's fortunes were sagging, Miss USA had seen a strong uptick that past April, winning 13 million viewers the same week that the first finale of Donald's new reality show, *The Apprentice,* topped the ratings. Perhaps it was time to reunite the rival pageant communities?

The casino mogul was happy to tell reporters all about the conversation he'd had with Miss America's new chief executive, Art McMaster, its fourth since Leonard Horn left in 1998. Donald expressed sympathy for the pageant's plight.

"It's tough. The networks don't want to put it on," Donald told the Associated Press. "I'd like to do whatever I can to help them out."

Miss America execs were far more circumspect when reporters asked about the Trump talks. Because truth be told, the newly minted reality-TV star's offer of help was a big nothing. As it was relayed to the board, the offer pretty much amounted to: Well, he'd be glad to take it over! In exchange, he promised to keep it on TV—something that was well beyond his power, as would become clear a decade later, when NBC severed ties with his Miss USA franchise.

And the volunteer board members that ran Miss America didn't just care about keeping the pageant on TV—they wanted to preserve the brand, expand it, raise more scholarship money for the girls, keep it classy, keep it respectful, and keep it in Atlantic City. A simple wish list that was becoming harder and harder to reconcile.

Meanwhile, a stealthier VIP intervention was proving far more consequential. The Miss Americas were starting to organize.

One day in February 2004, Kate Shindle, Gretchen Carlson, and Debbye Turner piled into a car in Manhattan and headed to Atlantic City. It was unusual for former Miss Americas to get together outside of September; for years, they mostly saw one another at the pageant, sitting together in the audience and mingling in the hospitality suite.

Now, though, email made it that much easier to keep in touch. And the Miss Americas started emailing one another like crazy in early 2004, spurred by reports that ABC—at that point still trying to make the broadcast work—was angling to eliminate the talent competition. Research showed it was a drag on ratings, the point at which viewers grabbed the remote. This was intolerable for the Miss Americas. Talent was what set Miss America apart from Miss USA and other hot-girl contests. But the three women who set off to storm a meeting of the Miss America board had a bigger agenda. They had high-level contacts and big ideas to reinvigorate an institution they loved.

"We don't want to take over. But we also don't want to hang around on the sidelines, waiting to be trotted across the stage once a year," Kate later explained. "We want to do more than look pretty and sit in the corner while the grown-ups talk."

It was a meeting thirty-five years in the making, and a culture clash waiting to happen.

The Miss Americas born alongside the women's movement were hitting the peaks of their careers now, seizing the opportunities that had come harder for their baby-boom sisters and fulfilling the Leonard Horn vision of what a generation of ambitious, outspoken, service-minded winners could do for the pageant's reputation. Gretchen and Debbye both had big on-air jobs with CBS News at the time; Kate's Broadway acting career had taken off.

But this had triggered a fundamental power shift. Once, the pageant had been run by the pillars of a thriving Atlantic City who could take a paternal stance toward the very young women who passed through the system. Now, though Miss America alumnae were, on the whole, a higher-powered group than the South Jersey locals who made up the board, its members remained wary about getting Miss Americas involved, for fear they would shift the focus from business to pageantry.

When the three reached Atlantic City, they were joined by two other especially beloved winners—Evelyn Ay, '54, the last of the pre-television Miss Americas, and Heather Whitestone, '95, the last of the high-ratings Miss Americas—to help make their case. And yet the meeting was a flop. The board responded coolly to their suggestions of potential sponsors to pitch and a showbiz-savvy marketing firm to hire. Some apparently perceived the Miss Americas' *let us introduce you to our contacts* offer as *please hire our friends.* "They're not used to hearing a lot of outside opinions," Gretchen dryly assessed later. It wasn't an entire waste: The board agreed for the first time to reserve two seats for former Miss Americas. And both parties were galvanized to push back on ABC to keep the talent competition, at least for what would turn out to be the network's final broadcast before dumping the pageant. Still, the meeting left a mutual smolder of distrust between the people who ran the pageant and the women who had worn its crown.

✦ ✦ ✦

In her ball cap and ponytail, Lauren Nelson looked more like a high school kid than the reigning Miss America as she welcomed a nervous-looking guy at the door.

"Stay right here," she said, leading him into the house. "I've got to grab the phone."

As she stepped away, a gray-haired man in a leather jacket entered the room.

"What are you doing here?" he asked the visitor.

"Hanging out with friends," the younger man said.

"Just friends?" John Walsh replied, skeptically. "You didn't come to have sex with what you thought was a fourteen-year-old girl?"

There was actually a decent rationale for Miss America to guest-star on Fox's *America's Most Wanted*, Walsh's long-running crime-solving show, in 2007. Lauren, a honey-haired undergrad from Oklahoma (whose Disney doppelganger would have been Cinderella) had a platform of promoting internet safety for children. So she was a legitimate choice for producers trying to reenergize an old show with a new stunt lifted from NBC's popular *To Catch a Predator*—a hidden-camera sting operation helping police target would-be child sex abusers. Lauren had lent a photo of herself as a fourteen-year-old to the operation, which lured men to a house on Long Island for what they had been led to believe was a sexual assignation with an underage girl; she even spoke with them on the phone. And then she greeted them at the house before they were arrested on camera; eleven men in all.

But if Lauren was doing a public service, Fox was certainly returning the favor. It was a rare and welcome opportunity to get Miss America's face on prime-time television during some strange years of exile and limbo.

After the breakup with ABC, the pageant spent months looking for a new home before finding it on Country Music Television in time for the 2006 broadcast. Suddenly as few as 3 million viewers were watching the live show—great numbers for basic cable, but a jarring new reality for Miss America.

And the pageant had finally left Convention Hall and relocated to Las Vegas. Even in an Atlantic City that had become bloated by boxy casinos in the 1970s and '80s, Miss America still loomed over the town. But that would never be the case during the pageant's eight years on the teeming Vegas Strip. Even if you walked straight into the Planet Hollywood Resort & Casino on finals night, you might have no indication that Miss America was being crowned in the theater up above the acres of slots and roulette and fine dining and shopping. She was simply swallowed by the scale of it all.

The crown, though, still turned heads and still opened doors. The women who wore it just had to hustle a little more than their predecessors.

"We had to keep Miss America alive, which meant getting creative," says Katie Stam, Miss America 2009 (and that decade's Belle avatar). It meant partnering with "unique sponsors," as she gracefully puts it—such as a company selling an acupuncture magnet you stuck in your ear to wipe out your urge to smoke—and saying yes to every invitation. She sang "America the Beautiful" at the Indy 500, walked red carpets at movie premieres, lit up the faces of hundreds of sick children in the hospitals she visited. She also smiled through a brutal twelve-hour autograph session in a California grocery store, wedged between mountains of onions.

Jennifer Berry, the first Miss America crowned on basic cable, still got to appear on *Good Morning America* after her win, merrily pinning her crown on the weatherman's head. Yet it seemed no one knew what to talk about with Miss America anymore. On an MSNBC political gabfest, Tucker Carlson asked if she put Vaseline on her teeth. On CNN, she was quizzed about Miss USA Tara Conner, whose cocaine-and-nightclubs descent into the gossip rags had inspired Donald Trump's days-long public deliberations over whether to fire her. (He did not.)

"Miss America and Miss USA are two very different organizations," Jennifer replied with gritted-teeth graciousness. "So, I didn't really keep up with what she was doing. . . ."

Increasingly, though, the interviewers went for the jugular: They asked if the pageant was still *relevant*.

"It is your sense then that the Miss America thing continues to thrive and all that?" Neil Cavuto asked Caressa Cameron in 2010 when she was booked on his Fox News show to discuss, for some reason, Earth Day.

"As long as there are people who want to make a difference," Caressa affirmed, "there is a place for Miss America."

It remained a uniquely challenging job. After a busy year in the spotlight, both Lauren Nelson and Kirsten Haglund lost interest in the Broadway careers they once aspired to. "I realized I don't want to live so far away from my loved ones," says Lauren, now a minister's wife and mother in Houston who hosts a TV show promoting Oklahoma tourism. "My dreams just changed."

And Kirsten—who had grappled with an eating disorder and stared down reality-TV producers on her journey to becoming Miss America 2008—grew uncomfortable with the unexpected burden of being the young, attractive, semi-famous woman in the room.

"There are some circles you're in," she says, "they just look at you and treat you like a sex object."

When she was Miss America, there were men who would put a hand on her butt while posing for a group photo. But there were also the comments focused on her appearance or undermining her message, even from the lawmakers she met on Capitol Hill to discuss mental-health issues.

"Oh, you don't look like you had an eating disorder!" some would say to her. Or they would pat their bellies and joke, "I wish *I* had an eating disorder."

As a Miss America fluent in mental health, Kirsten was invited to discuss it on cable news. And for several years following Miss America, bookers kept calling her on a wider array of issues—politics, policy, faith, culture. "They like the fact you're young and pretty and can talk," she says, "and it just took off from there." Fox News, in particular, brought her on air frequently, and she realized that she was being cast in a specific role: the attractive young woman who votes Republican. Once she came out as Never-Trump, the bookings dried up.

"I began to feel a cognitive dissonance between what I felt I was expected to say on Fox and what I really felt," says Kirsten, who now lives in Switzerland with her husband and works in business development for eating-disorders treatment centers. "You get into the business of TV, and then you realize how ugly that business is."

✦   ✦   ✦

What would happen when the high-energy, blazingly ambitious, ever-more-liberated women who had been on the rise in pageantry for forty years made it to the pinnacle of Miss America—and realized Miss America just wasn't all *that* anymore?

In September 2009, the fifteenth season of *The Amazing Race* debuted. It featured the usual motley group of regular-folk contestants on an around-the-world sprint for a $1 million prize: a med student, a lawyer, a couple of musicians, two obscure Harlem Globetrotters, a pair of yoga teachers—and Miss America 2004.

Six years had passed since Ericka Dunlap's epic crowning. She had flipped out—bouncing, gasping, swooning so much that they could barely pin the crown on her head; a full thirty seconds of hands-waving, earring-losing *ohmygods* until she lassoed an arm over Tom Bergeron's neck for support.

She was Miss America 2004, the host reaffirmed. "How does it sound?"

With perfect timing, Ericka dropped her voice a sultry half octave: "Please say it again."

YouTube wouldn't launch for another year, or Ericka would surely have gone viral. She was the seventh black Miss America, but of all past winners she most brought to mind Lee Meriwether, with those wide-set cat eyes and that fabulously emotive quality. She strolled down the runway like she owned it, arms outstretched to her public.

Yet this creature so clearly born for celebrity just couldn't quite hit the next level of it. Granted, she picked a tough path—country music, which rarely welcomed African-American women. So Ericka and her husband decided to audition for *The Amazing Race* in a bid to renew her fame. They were the show's first interracial couple. Perhaps Miss America was once a bigger deal, but *The Amazing Race* would be viewed by more people, and for twelve weeks instead of one night.

"I figured with fourteen million viewers a week, I've got to get at least a million of them to want to buy my album," she says.

Yet all her experience in the spotlight did nothing to prepare her for the world of reality television in 2009. As Miss America, she had walked into rooms where people were eager to see her; when the camera light went on, she could charm by being herself. On *The Amazing Race*, thirty days of filming were boiled down to twelve frenetic hours of television and a narrative beyond her control. Ericka brought the same spontaneity and competitive drive to the race that she had to pageantry, but the editing team used that energy against her. ("Don't get me pissed off!" she shrieked at her husband during one tense obstacle challenge where they fell behind the other teams.)

"I came across as a bitch," she sighs. Meanwhile her passive, amiable husband was set up as her foil. "I wasn't a nag," she insists. "He just wasn't listening to me."

They made it to the season finale, finishing third. But viewers reacted poorly to her, a shock after her rosy Miss America experience. She went to therapy for the first time and came out of it resolving to leave both the music business and her marriage. "The realities of being on that show were too much for me," she says.

Miss America's grip on the culture had eroded slowly for a couple decades, but with the explosion of reality TV, it all but crumbled. If you wanted a good old talent show, *American Idol* imitators were mutating across the airwaves. If you craved the frisson of feminine competition, the stars of the dating shows were always bikini-ready and game for a catfight. Makeover shows, like *America's Next Top Model*, satisfied armchair scholars of charisma and poise. And evening gowns were practically their own programming category now, with the ever-sprawling red-carpet broadcasts preceding the Grammys and the Oscars and newer awards shows the networks kept patching together.

Teresa Scanlan never even watched Miss America when she was growing up. She was only eleven the last time it had aired on network television, in 2004. So pageants got their hooks in her the old-fashioned way—the volunteer-driven network of small-town contests that had nourished Miss America long before TV. As a twelve-year-old homeschooler in tiny Gering, Nebraska, she was intrigued by an ad for a teen pageant at the county fair, with a $200 scholarship prize. Pageants coaxed her out of her shyness. One title put her, at age sixteen, on a local United Way board. She was terrified to walk into that first meeting, but the adults in the room took her seriously. So she, too, began to take herself seriously.

She set a long-term course for Miss America, assuring her dad that her $300 gown purchase would be amortized over seven years of pageants through college and law school. She was just as efficient when it came to grooming: After she wrecked her hair by over-bleaching, she invested in a couple of high-quality wigs—perfect waterfalls of Jessica Simpson–blonde tresses that caught her some grief on social media.

"People thought it meant fraud, I guess," Teresa says. But weren't they all wearing fake nails, fake tans, fake lashes? And not just in pageants. Everywhere.

Teresa's pageant hobby was cut short, though, when she unexpectedly won in her very first attempt at Miss Nebraska—and soon she was Miss America at not-yet-eighteen, the youngest in more than seven decades. Which meant that she was suddenly a *former* Miss America at not-yet-nineteen. And while life never slowed down for her, she felt an absence.

It didn't matter that she had already won the ultimate crown. She just really missed *competing* for it.

So in 2015, she went for Miss World.

"People were very mad," says Teresa, of the furor in Miss America circles that followed. "The idea that this was diminishing the brand . . . I had not really thought about that much." Miss World had some cachet overseas but next to none in the U.S. Many Miss America also-rans had competed. But for an *actual* Miss America to enter Miss World felt like an inexplicable step down: Miss World wasn't even on *television*.

But what did Teresa know? She was born in 1993. Whatever Miss America meant to an earlier generation, it meant something else to her. Fame wasn't the point; being on TV wasn't her priority. Why *not* be Miss America and then Miss World and maybe even Miss USA, too—like a Triple Crown? Otherwise, it was like asking a marathoner to quit after her first medal.

In the end, Teresa maxed out as first runner-up at the Miss World America precursor pageant and did not make it to the Miss World stage. But that was fine. By twenty-five, she was juggling single motherhood, UC-Berkeley law school, and Air Force National Guard duties. Her year as a teenage Miss America had shown she could handle more than she realized, and she had resolved to carry that mentality through her life.

"It's this feeling that I never want to let an experience go by, a goal go by, without trying," she says. "It's the reason some of us go for Miss America and become Miss America. Part of that year is realizing your potential, and you never lose that. And you think, 'I'm going to do it all and be okay.'"

11

"YOU DON'T LEVERAGE THE GODFATHER"

2017

In January 2017, nearly twenty years after Kate Shindle was crowned Miss America, she was contacted by Regina Hopper, a former member of the pageant's board of trustees. She wanted to talk.

Regina had thrived in professional worlds far removed from pageants, first as a CBS correspondent and now a Washington lawyer-lobbyist who had run two trade associations. But with her thick blonde hair and command presence, a faint Southern accent punctuated by practiced cadences and dramatic pauses, you could still see a bit of the Miss Arkansas 1983 in her.

She had left the board the previous summer, unhappily. Kate, meanwhile, was now the president of Actors' Equity, but also someone you'd want to share your frustrations about the pageant with. In 2014, she had published a memoir that slammed the pageant's recent leadership—the wobbly finances, the sexist reality-TV tropes, the reluctance to give the Miss Americas a seat at the table.

They met in Las Vegas, where Kate was starring in a national tour of the musical *Fun Home*. According to people who spoke to them later, Kate argued that nothing about the pageant could be fixed if its current

CEO, Sam Haskell, a powerful former Hollywood agent, remained in place. And eventually, the conversation turned to the secret emails she had heard about, in which Sam disparaged some former Miss Americas. Herself included, it would turn out.

It had been fifteen years since Bob Renneisen griped about a "rebellion of the beauty queens"—an overstatement at the time, but something of a prediction. It was like the old dorm-room debate: What happens if the robots become self-aware? Except this time it was: What happens if the Miss Americas start to question the system that made them Miss America and try to make it their own?

Here's what happened: The Miss Americas would succeed in pulling off a coup, only to see it collapse into a civil war they weren't prepared to fight. And they would discover the kingdom they were fighting for wasn't quite what it used to be—and was rapidly less so once they seized it.

✦   ✦   ✦

While Kate and Regina stewed over the future of Miss America, the pageant by all outward appearances was healthier than it had been in years. Case in point: the triumphant return of Vanessa Williams barely a year earlier.

> *Oh how the years go by*
> *And oh how the love brings tears to my eyes . . .*

Vanessa returned to the Miss America pageant as a judge in September 2015, after a thirty-one-year exile mostly of her own choosing—but she made her entrance singing one of her old hits, with a twelve-piece choir backing her up.

> *All through the changes*
> *The soul never dies . . .*

At fifty-two, she looked exquisite. Her gown was form-fitting satin in a color-blocked ombre crossed by bold black stripes and winging off to one side, like she was wrapped in the flag of her own sovereign queendom.

"I want it to look different," she had told the designer, Christian Siriano, "than all the other dresses at the pageant."

As Vanessa sauntered down the runway toward her rapturous public, photos flashed behind her that hammered home the catharsis of this moment—showing not just her 1983 crowning and her meeting with President Reagan, but then the heartbreaking press conference and the brutal headlines, and then the platinum albums, the Broadway roles, the hit films.

We fight, we laugh, we cry
As the years go by

But everyone knew: This moment was far more about Vanessa choosing to validate the pageant than it was about the pageant welcoming her back, which it would have done long ago if she'd have let them.

And Sam Haskell made it happen.

There he was, at the front of the stage now, an arm around Vanessa, ready to deliver the words an amped-up arena longed to hear, the words necessary to make it all happen.

"I have been a close friend of this beautiful and talented lady for thirty-two years," the pageant CEO said, beaming at Vanessa. "You have lived your life in grace and dignity, and never was it more evident than during the events of 1984, when you resigned. . . ."

Convention Hall felt ready to explode. Vanessa blinked hard, emotion held in by pressed lips. Sam continued:

"Though none of us currently in the organization were involved then, on behalf of today's organization, I want to apologize. . . ." Sam raised his voice over the rising cheers. "I want to apologize for anything that was *said* or *done* that made you feel any less the Miss America *you are*, and the Miss America you *always will be!*"

Sam had made this happen, as he had made so many small miracles happen for Miss America over the past decade. It helped that as a former top executive at the William Morris Agency, he knew everyone, understood what levers could be pulled. Sam had met Vanessa back in

1984 when he got Miss America a deal for a Diet Coke commercial.
He had approached her gently about returning now as a judge, courting
her pageant-fan publicist to serve as a preliminary judge, and only *then*
asking about the star herself, gamely agreeing to her requests for a live
band and her A-team of stylists.

A flurry of excited TMZ reports had buzzed about the preparations:
Will they apologize to Vanessa Williams? Not everyone in the pageant
world was happy when they did. For Leonard Horn, long since retired,
and a few (not all) of her fellow contestants who had suffered through
1984, it felt like a betrayal. But the emotion of the moment played beautifully on TV. It even generated a rare uptick in the ratings, just in time
for Sam to negotiate a new three-year contract with ABC.

"Miss America is back, y'all!" cheered one of the Top 10 finalists
on the stage that night, bantering with the evening's tuxedoed host,
reality-TV royalty Chris Harrison of *The Bachelor*. Miss America was
back on network television, back in Atlantic City, and frequently, back
on the pop-culture radar. "Your leadership, your integrity," Vanessa told
Sam, "you bring this pageant back to what it ought to be."

To get Miss America back to this place—or at least, the place it
seemed to be—had not been easy. The finances, for one thing, were far
more delicate than in the days when Gillette spent as much to sponsor
the pageant as it did the World Series, and the networks vied for the
honor of broadcasting it. But that was all the more reason for the pageant to treasure Sam, perhaps the only person with the show-business
experience—and, crucially, the inclination—to run the Miss America
pageant in this era.

Sam had scaled the ranks of Hollywood power by engineering the
deals behind some of the hottest sitcoms of the 1980s and '90s, but he
knew pageants. He went way back with Phyllis George, to the summer
of 1974, when Phyllis was just another former Miss America, not yet a
star, hired to host the Miss Mississippi pageant, and Sam was an Ole
Miss sophomore recruited for the Miss Mississippi chorus. They hit it
off, two people-pleasers with heat-seeking instincts and big-city dreams,
and she was the first of the celebrity friends he would make and keep on
the way up, in an industry built on relationships.

He, too, was a small-town Southern kid. In Amory, Mississippi,

Sam played football to try to please his aloof dad but studied every issue of *TV Guide* like a sacred text. Switching from pre-med to theater not long after arriving at college, he got his start by producing the Miss University of Mississippi pageant. In his senior year, he nudged his girlfriend Mary Donnelly to enter, and she went all the way to Atlantic City that summer as Miss Mississippi. Five years later, they were married.

Sam rose rapidly from the mailroom of the legendary William Morris Agency, disarming clients like Ray Romano and Dolly Parton with his Mississippi drawl and courtly manners. He built on his web of colleagues-turned-friends while packaging the talent for shows like *Everybody Loves Raymond*; he nailed down the deal to launch *The Fresh Prince of Bel-Air* on NBC in the middle of his son's second birthday party, thanks to so many of the key players being there as guests. But Sam was as much a creature of William Morris as of Amory, Mississippi. In his world, there were agents who might fling their lunch entrée against the wall just to make a point, and he understood dark power dynamics. When the *Raymond* cast attempted a sick-out in 2003 to cadge a bigger slice of syndication profits, he was the one to dissuade them from what he could see was a losing strategy.

"You don't leverage the Godfather," he later explained, referring to CBS chairman Les Moonves. "He will be good as gold if you play by the rules, but if you try to screw or pressure him, he ain't gonna respond."

But after a quarter century navigating Hollywood minefields, Sam eventually landed on the losing side of an agency power struggle in 2004. Once in line to become William Morris president, he cashed out his ownership stakes and left. He was weighing his options, including a political run in Mississippi, when Phyllis called. It was the dark days of 2005, when the pageant needed a new TV home and a showbiz sherpa to help it find one.

Would he please join the board? she asked.

Soon, Sam was working his magic, helping to get Miss America a berth on Country Music Television, and then two years later, on TLC. A grateful board made him their chairman—and eventually CEO.

Sam brought a bit of the William Morris style to the old pageant, ruffling a few feathers along the way. When traditionalists sniped behind his back about his decision to put the contestants in the TLC reality show, he confronted them head-on at a meeting of state directors.

"The girls get it," he told them. "You'd better be getting it too, because this train has left the station."

Sam's Hollywood relationships paid off. In 2009, he reconnected with a former junior agent from William Morris who had written a gushing letter praising Sam's new memoir. Billy Goldberg was launching his own consultancy, and he had ideas for how to help Miss America. By the end of their breakfast meeting, they had started hashing out a deal: Billy's Buckeye Group would hunt down new licensing and sponsorship deals for the pageant, in exchange for a one-third cut.

This was an edgy new business model for Miss America, materializing at a crucial time. Sam was desperate to get the pageant out of the basic-cable wilderness, but the only way a network would consider taking on the pageant again was through a "time buy." Meaning, Miss America would have to pay *the network* to put it on the air, not the other way around.

"We needed to change the perception of Miss America," Sam later said in a court deposition, "and being back on network would help do that."

Billy's sponsor-hunting made it possible. Within months, he signed Amway for $750,000 and the DSW shoe store chain for $2.4 million, among several other smaller-dollar deals—more than enough to pay ABC the $1 million it was demanding to air the 2011 pageant.

The ratings weren't stupendous, but with 6.6 million viewers, it was far more exposure than basic cable. Sam later said he felt in the moment that, once again, "the sky was the limit" for Miss America.

When DSW didn't stick around for a second year, Billy introduced Sam to another partner who could help them come up with the cash to stay on the air in 2012 and 2013. The Infinity Group, a New York–based brand management firm, proposed licensing the Miss America name and logo to product manufacturers—clothing, shoes, makeup, whatever. Sam was a little hesitant: It seemed that Infinity specialized in buying rights to near-extinct brands: Polaroid, The Sharper Image, Bugle Boy. "And I didn't look at us as a brand that was failing," Sam said later.

But Infinity was willing to pay Miss America up to $2 million a year. Enough to keep the pageant on TV, and for Sam to start getting compensated for what had, until then, been an unpaid board chairmanship.

Suddenly, Miss America was *back*, y'all. In January 2013, 7.1 million viewers tuned in to the crowning of Mallory Hagan, the spunky, tap-dancing Miss New York coached to the title by Bill Alverson—not bad for a Saturday night opposite an NFL playoff. And by the time they had to negotiate a new contract with ABC, the network was once again willing to pay Miss America for the privilege.

Sam was a natural at public relations, and during these years, Miss America tickled the news cycle with proud stories about the first visibly tattooed contestant—Miss Kansas 2013, Theresa Vail, an archery and riflery enthusiast who didn't win but did get her own Outdoor Channel show—and the first out lesbian, Miss Missouri 2017, Erin O'Flaherty. The crowning of Nina Davuluri as Miss America 2014 triggered a small but nasty social-media backlash from no-name racist trolls grousing on Twitter about a brown-skinned Miss America, some wildly misidentifying her ethnicity. ("Congratulations Al Qaeda," wrote one. "Our Miss America is one of you.") But the backlash to the backlash was far louder, as social-justice warriors and millennial media typically too cool for pageants, like *BuzzFeed* and *Jezebel*, rushed to her defense, and TV bookers clamored to ask Nina about the "controversy."

"It's unfortunate," Nina told one interviewer brightly. "But that's why my platform is so timely. . . ." Five years later, she was still traveling the world giving speeches on diversity.

Even New Jersey wanted Miss America back. After Hurricane Sandy pummeled the shore in 2012, the state offered financial incentives to lure the pageant away from Las Vegas the following year to signal to a nation of TV viewers that Atlantic City was once again open for business.

The irony was that Miss America barely belonged to Atlantic City anymore. Sam had gradually replaced the locals who had traditionally filled its board with out-of-towners who had corporate connections and ties to national media, the kind of people who could make things happen with a phone call. Regina Hopper, the Miss Arkansas–turned–Beltway lobbyist, was one. Gretchen Carlson was another.

✦   ✦   ✦

Gretchen told almost no one where she was going. Not even her sorority sisters.

She just picked up and left Stanford University at the end of 1987, right in the middle of her senior year. It was like she had disappeared. But there was no way she could have explained it to them. The dean had scoffed ("the most ridiculous thing I've ever heard") when Gretchen said she was taking leave to try to become Miss America. Pageants carried gauche stereotypes for the people she knew at Stanford, and Gretchen didn't want to have to explain herself.

Also, "I didn't want to set myself up," she later wrote, "in case I failed."

She had been studying abroad in England in the spring of that year when her mother called from Minnesota with the idea. In Gretchen's recollection, her mother had just read a news story about Leonard Horn, the new director of the Miss America pageant.

"He says they're changing direction this year," she recalled her mother saying. They wanted contestants from top schools now, women who had spent years honing a talent. Gretchen had been a violin prodigy, who once competed in the same circles as future classical-music superstar Joshua Bell.

"I think this is your year," her mother said.

Memory is a funny thing. In fact, Leonard didn't take over the pageant or make news at all until the fall of 1987. It wasn't until well after Gretchen launched her Miss America quest, at the Miss Cottage Grove pageant, that he spoke of his plans to get Miss Americas more involved in substantial service work. But whatever their conversation or the impetus for her decision, Gretchen's mother was right: It *was* her year.

Back home in Anoka, Minnesota, she began a grueling season of two-hour daily workouts, twelve-hundred-calorie diets, three-hour daily violin rehearsals, relentless reading up on current events. With the help of a pageant coach, she even practiced how to walk. Gretchen was already looking past the Miss Minnesota pageant, preparing for the big runway nine months away. This lonely regimen resonated on some level with a woman who had given so many teenage weekends to high-pressure music competitions, who had set out to become valedictorian and nailed it.

"I had an undeniable quest to persevere and excel," she later wrote. "I believed in pushing myself beyond my limits, no matter what. Being a perfectionist was intrinsic to my personality."

And so, months later, meeting the press with her new Miss America crown, she told the truth about how she'd won. No false modesty, no making it look easy.

"This wasn't luck," she told them.

That debut press conference was classic Gretchen. She recounted for reporters that morning how she had been twenty pounds heavier in high school, that her brothers called her "blimpo" and the high school jock she liked refused to date her—until, of course, she lost the weight, and then she turned *him* down. Gretchen was hardly the first Miss America to approach it like a competitive sport. But she was the first winner to be so open about it, to make that steely intensity part of her brand, and she could sound like Michael Jordan giving a Hall of Fame speech, still savoring the wounds and nursing the grudges that fueled her.

Her 2015 memoir smoldered with these sorts of embers: the seamstress who told her no one could win with a pink swimsuit or a violin, the coach who told her she couldn't pull off this quest in one year, and later, the news director who scoffed at the idea of hiring a former Miss America. Until, of course, he did. She also recalled her quiet fury at the reporter in Atlantic City who humiliated her with all the questions that so dismayed Leonard: Did she know whose face was on the $20 bill? A decade later, Gretchen ran into the woman, a local TV news reporter, on assignment in New York and reintroduced herself.

"I'm the Miss America you demoralized in 1989," she recalled saying, "and I'd just like to let you know that I still made it. I'm a CBS News correspondent, and you're not." (The woman later said she did not remember Gretchen confronting her.)

The young woman who yearned to win Miss America while simultaneously feeling too embarrassed to tell her friends about it had similarly conflicted feelings about *being* Miss America. She loved meeting President Reagan, visiting with schoolchildren and wounded veterans, playing violin with regional orchestras and even at a gala honoring American Nobel Prize winners. Yet her reign seemed shot through with indignities and frustrations. Years later, she would remember the Nobel laureate who slammed the choice of a Miss America for the dinner entertainment. And the emcee at a corporate event who introduced her as "a five-foot-three, 108-pound gal with green eyes"—nothing about her music or academic honors. She chafed at the stereotypes that came with the title: airhead, bimbo, beauty queen, victim of an exploitative system. And sudden fame and prying media left her jaded and wary.

"I could never wake up on the wrong side of the bed," she wrote. "People had incredible expectations of who they thought Miss America should be."

The happiest part of the year for this parent-pleasing perfectionist seemed to be the interlude that revealed her rebellious side. At a corporate event, she met Bill Farley, the dashing forty-five-year-old chairman and CEO of Fruit of the Loom, and they started dating. The company was a pageant sponsor, and Bill had been one of her pageant judges—a barely averted scandal that shocked her friends and parents and triggered media inquiries, especially when they showed up together at a 1989 Bush inaugural ball. Her pageant chaperone once apprehended Gretchen trying to sneak out of her hotel room to meet Bill. But she felt at ease with him, despite the age difference. She spent most of her time that year with older people, and they, like Bill, "seemed to get me in ways that my peers could not," she wrote. "It was a great release to feel understood."

Even though she kept her romantic life under wraps, Gretchen found herself more scrutinized than any Miss America other than Vanessa. It may have been her brand as the "smart" Miss America—something advisors tried to warn her away from—that put a target on her back. One news story documented her supposed "uncooperative, unfriendly behavior," a line of coverage that is painful to imagine an only mildly famous twenty-three-year-old having to read about herself.

"A Beauty of a Mistake," declared the cover of *TV Guide* with her photo on it: "Miss America—Was Last Year's Voting Suspect?"

"Suspect" was an unfair word choice. But the judging process was certainly irregular that year, the magazine revealed. Leonard Horn had set up a new system of two separate judging panels: one to judge the preliminary competitions, the other to judge the televised finals. (He wanted VIP judges for the broadcast but couldn't get celebrities to commit to a week in Atlantic City.) The accidental upshot was that the backstage interview conducted by the preliminary judges, the all-important test of X factors like ease, gravitas, and plain old likeability, was not considered by the finals judges picking Miss America.

This didn't dawn on anyone until after Gretchen's victory. Yes, she had thrilled the finals judges with her flawless violin rendition of Pablo de Sarasate's *Zigeunerweisen*. But the preliminary judges who personally met with everyone were less wowed, *TV Guide* claimed.

"She was very smart; she was academically very skilled," one told the magazine. "But there were very many women who did better on the interview." The pageant later tweaked Leonard's new system to carry over the interview scores to the finals.

Gretchen's final Miss America indignity came a year after she gave up her crown, when one of those preliminary judges, William Goldman, the Oscar-winning screenwriter of *All the President's Men* and *Butch Cassidy and the Sundance Kid*, published a memoir charting his midlife crisis across the year he judged both the pageant and the Cannes Film Festival. He found Gretchen a smug "Sunday School teacher" type: "*Real* bright. Chunky. Self-possessed. Not a lot of humor," he recorded in his judging notes. *Chunky?* Hard to know what he meant. Like all of them, she was waifish walking the stage in a swimsuit, fifteen to twenty pounds lighter than a year earlier. He also called her "Miss Piggy," seeming to mean her upturned nose, satisfied smile, and twinkly close-set eyes, not her figure, but Muppet comparisons rarely flatter. (As it happens, Eva Gabor, one of the finals judges, is said to have favored Gretchen because Gretchen resembled Eva Gabor.) By his closing pages, the writer came around, as the haters always do, admiring the new Miss America's charm and grace at a post-show reception. But a quarter century later, in the opening pages of her own book, Gretchen punched back at the man who implied she should never have been Miss America: "This kind of degrading talk is what keeps young women from being fully themselves—or even trying."

Another lesser public embarrassment came with a silver lining: the time Ed McMahon and Dick Clark's *Super Bloopers and Practical Jokes* decided to trap Miss America into having to explain some piece of technology she knew nothing about in front of what turned out to be a make-believe live TV audience. Gretchen stayed so cool and ad-libbed about the mystery product so artfully that the clip became part of the reel she sent out to land a broadcast news job when she abandoned the law-school path.

She would need a strong reel: By 1990, there would be no Phyllis George–style catapult to the top; the airwaves were already filled with former Miss Somethings. Gretchen spent a decade climbing through small and then larger markets—Richmond, Cincinnati, Cleveland, Dallas—before snagging a network job reporting for CBS News. By 2011, after she was well established as host of Fox News's national morning show *Fox & Friends*, she was asked to join the Miss America board.

And as the Miss America who had carried the brand of the "smart" one, who had heard herself called "chunky" and not worthy of the crown, she would have a lot of ideas about how to do things better.

◆   ◆   ◆

Outwardly, Miss America was the picture of health as Vanessa Williams reprised her historic walk down the Convention Hall runway in 2015. Internally, it was a mess.

In an industry built on relationships, CEO Sam Haskell's relationships seemed to be fraying left and right.

The deal with Infinity Group—the rainmakers who four years earlier had promised up to $2 million a year for the right to license the Miss America name—was riven with strife. When Sam and Miss America president Art McMaster clinched the deals with ABC and New Jersey, the guys from Infinity flipped out, maintaining that they were supposed to play a role in negotiations, and slashed payments to Miss America by 25 percent.

Lawyers exchanged angry letters, each side accusing the other of defaulting on their agreement. But Infinity's gripe seemed rooted in regret that it had ever signed on in the first place. The Miss America team had resisted Infinity's suggestions for cultivating a cooler, more modern image. And no one, it turned out, seemed eager to license the Miss America brand anymore.

"The only license agreement that we've ever done that we didn't make money," Infinity's chief executive Ike Franco fumed later in a deposition. "And lost money."

In May 2014, Miss America and Infinity Group broke up, a bitter semi-unwinding that allowed Infinity to continue managing the brand and keep Ike on the board, but without paying Miss America a seven-figure up-front fee anymore.

Which was a problem. Because Miss America was supposed to pay Sam's old friend Billy Goldberg $300,000 a year. That was the revised deal Sam had to work out when Billy's Buckeye Group got squeezed out by the Infinity contract. Now, though, Sam argued that Buckeye's fee was contingent upon Miss America getting paid by Infinity. But that was not Buckeye's understanding.

As tensions rose, Sam made a last-ditch effort to mend fences, calling Billy to commiserate over the debacle and ask him to help Miss America sue Infinity.

"I was ready to be friends again," Sam later said. Instead, the Buckeye Group sued the Miss America Organization for breach of contract.

Miss America's greatest asset was its storied name and glorious past. Again and again, it drew entrepreneurs eager to help prop up its illusion of a comeback, only to find precious little payoff in return.

"Every step of the way, everyone fooled themselves into believing Miss America could be more of a moneymaker," says someone who worked closely with the pageant through most of Sam's era. "They overvalued the brand and thought they could do a much better job of exploiting it. When there wasn't much money there, they got mad and started spitting at each other."

But that was only half of the reason for the anxieties curdling the dynamics within this strange, one-of-a-kind little organization, creating the toxic brew that would soon be weaponized against it.

And again, it came down to relationships.

◆   ◆   ◆

Mallory Hagan and Sam got along great at first, two Southerners who had both set a path for the big city at a young age.

Miss America 2013 had been Miss New York, but she was originally from Opelika, Alabama, and while she had lost the accent, she maintained a down-home appeal: throaty voice, easy laugh, comfort in her own skin. The word was that the pageant wanted a "relatable" Miss America that year, and they got her: Instead of an opera singer or classical pianist, Mallory was the first tap dancer in a half century to take the crown, with a swaggering routine set to James Brown's "Get Up Offa That Thing."

When the tabloids gawked over paparazzi photos showing Mallory at the beach looking slightly less ripped in her bikini than she had at her crowning a month earlier, she let it roll off her back, while also making a point about realistic body standards.

"Well, you know, I think that I am human," she told a talk-show host. "I like to equate getting ready for the Miss America pageant to getting ready for a boxing match . . . We get in shape, and then afterwards life goes back to normal."

And yes, she added, she struggled with fitness. Just like a lot of women.

"I'm *real!*" she said.

It was a smart message for a Miss America to be making in this moment. By 2013 celebrity snark culture was finally waning; the public was beginning to question the scorn, masquerading as witty commentary, heaped upon Lindsay Lohan, Britney Spears, and so many other famous young women for what they wore or how they looked. Sam was known to refer to Mallory at the time as "one of our best Miss Americas."

But then Mallory started dating Sam's top deputy, Brent Adams. And everything changed.

Or at least, that was the explanation Brent hinted at in the cataclysmic story that would later prompt the resignation of Sam and his entire board.

It was a little more complicated than that.

✦　✦　✦

Brent started working for Sam as a personal assistant in 2012, right out of Ole Miss. He was fair-haired, handsome, a small-town athlete. On stage at the Miss America pageant, he and Josh Randle, another of Sam's protégés, delivered floral bouquets into the arms of the runners-up. Off stage, his work was divided between Miss America and Sam's own production company, Magnolia Hill. Within two years, he had been given the title of director of development at both organizations.

If Sam thought of his Hollywood colleagues as dear friends, he cultivated a family vibe in his Miss America world. Brent joined the Haskell family at home to watch *Gone With the Wind* and went fishing with Sam's same-age daughter, Mary Lane, an NYU theater grad. Like all his Miss Americas, Mallory was a visitor to the home, too. Shortly after her reign ended, she posted on Instagram a photo of herself with Sam, Mary Lane, and Brent at a festive restaurant table. "Good to see the fam last night!" she wrote.

This was October 2013, around the time Mallory and Brent officially started dating. She moved to Los Angeles that fall to look for television work, and a couple months later, he relocated as well, to work for Sam from the West Coast. With Miss America on his arm, Brent stepped up his own look, trading his Southern-gentry wardrobe and side part for a sleek, urban-vagabond aesthetic and bristly hipster haircut.

Sam was vehemently opposed to the relationship. The explanation Brent would later share with a *HuffPost* writer was that Sam wanted him to date Mary Lane instead. Friends of Sam say they do not believe a connection between those two was ever in the cards. Sam's disapproval, they say, lay in a more abstract notion of how he thought things should be, and the world he envisioned for Brent—not to mention the uncomfortable optics of a Miss America staff member romancing a very recent Miss America.

But there was also the incident that occurred in Mallory's final weeks as Miss America. It happened in August, when the pageant world gathered in Orlando for the annual Miss America's Outstanding Teen competition. Mallory went with friends to a bar; she was twenty-four but didn't have her ID with her to prove it, and bar staff caught her with the drink that a companion covertly bought for her. According to people within the organization at the time, pageant security got involved to finesse her hasty exit, and police were never involved.

The internal frenzy set off by this incident spoke to the inherent weakness at the very core of Miss America, a company whose highly visible face was chosen by outsiders and changed every year; and who, by virtue of the job description, was necessarily *young.*

Can't-rent-a-car young. Living-at-home young. Sowing-wild-oats young. Still-dealing-with-her-shit young.

Over the coming months, there were more reports of Mallory's drinking in public and aggressively flirtatious behavior; though none became widely known, some were elevated within a small subset of the organization to potential public-relations crises. And this hardened sentiment against her, especially for Sam. He asked friends to "warn" Brent about her. Brent clearly didn't care for this advice. But when they broke up, a friend says, Brent shared details with Sam that would further embitter Sam toward Mallory. And then the couple got back together. In early 2015, Brent left both the Miss America Organization and Magnolia Hill.

Mallory's first pass at the TV business did not pan out, and she expressed some wistfulness in a group email to other former Miss Americas that the pageant didn't do more to prepare winners for life after the crown. Word of this got back to Sam, who had set her up with an agent and unsuccessfully lobbied the producers of *Dancing with the Stars* to cast her. He brooded over this as if it were a personal attack.

Mallory moved back east and started a pageant coaching business with a fellow former Miss New York. But she eventually found herself thwarted, the work drying up as she learned that there were lists of Miss America–approved coaches, and that she was not on them.

✦   ✦   ✦

Gretchen Carlson had some ideas. Her fellow board member Regina Hopper did, too.

Many had to do with what kind of young women the pageant should recognize and reward, according to fellow former board members. Regina, who had financed much of her law degree competing in pageants, was keenly focused on scholarships as the way to differentiate Miss America from other contests. Gretchen spoke of returning to the days when talent counted for half the score, as it was her year, and of creating a separate scoring category for academic achievement, perhaps even tied to a contestant's GPA.

She had floated the same idea in 1988 as the newly crowned Miss America with the 3.5 at Stanford, but Leonard Horn shot it down. ("There are a lot of successful people whose GPA wasn't that enviable," he said.) It raised obvious questions: How on earth to measure academic achievement in a competition that pitted eighteen-year-olds against grad students, and Harvard alums against junior-college matriculates?

Sam was happy to have them championing academics, assigning both women to seek corporate donors; Miss America introduced a series of new scholarships during these years recognizing academic achievement. Yet he could also be brusque when board conversations veered from the business of putting on a TV show to more philosophical questions about pageantry and how it should be judged. Getting along with Sam could take work, according to one board member who was happy to put in the effort but notes that not everyone did. More assertive personalities, like Gretchen and Regina, "got under his skin."

By 2014, Sam was attempting to place restrictions on pageant coaches; Gretchen initially argued against this, noting that she owed her Miss America crown to the guidance of a good coach. But Sam had come to believe that coaching granted too big an advantage to young women with the deep pockets to hire one. There were reports of coaches masquerading as stylists or hiding in bathroom stalls to confer with contestants in the middle of competitions. And he didn't like that a couple of former Miss Americas had entered the coaching game—trading on their title, as he saw it. Friends say it may have especially bothered him that one of them was Mallory; another was Kate Shindle.

Sam had consolidated power, having quietly maneuvered Art McMaster out of the role of president a couple years earlier and taken on the chief executive role for himself; with the departure of Art's short-term successor, Sam became the sole boss, paid nearly $400,000 a year on average, far more than Art had earned. But the drama with Infinity left finances tight, and the *Press of Atlantic City* had started asking questions about the "arrangements between friends" that governed the non-profit. Raising similar questions was Kate Shindle's 2014 book, which spotlighted a controversial aspect of the creative new financing keeping the pageant afloat: It turned out that only about half the funds contestants were required to raise for Children's Miracle Network under a new-ish initiative stayed with the hospital charity. The other half was returned to Miss America's own scholarship fund—a setup Kate called "borderline fraudulent." Pageant officials didn't comment on her accusation at the time but privately seethed, maintaining that the arrangement was aboveboard—and essential. "It sustained the viability of the scholarship fund," one insider argued.

Regina, as vice chair of the board and president of its new fundraising arm, clashed with Sam's protégé Josh Randle, like Brent a product of Ole Miss, hired as chief operating officer at twenty-seven. Regina and Josh's final battle came in the summer of 2016 with an obscure spat about the timing of a media announcement, according to board members, but it triggered a big internal blowup, in which key board members took Josh's side and agreed to ask Regina to leave. She was smart and hardworking but too often in conflict with others, some said.

Gretchen had already left of her own accord months earlier. She had bigger issues to deal with heading into 2016.

Fox News had demoted her from its popular morning show to a sleepy afternoon slot in 2013, after she complained about a condescending cohost. So she had started covertly recording her conversations with Roger Ailes, the network's powerful cofounder, whose advances she had rebuffed and who she later said continued to harass her. "I think you and I should have had a sexual relationship a long time ago," she said he told her when she complained about her marginalization at the network. "And then you'd be good and better, and I'd be good and better."

In June 2016, two days past her fiftieth birthday, Fox dropped her after eleven years. But Gretchen was ready. She sued Roger for sexual harassment, and within weeks, he was forced to resign after more than a dozen women came forward with similar stories. By summer's end, Gretchen had both an epic $20 million settlement and an exceedingly rare public apology from Fox. Also, a new mission, and personal brand, as a crusader for women in the workplace.

✦   ✦   ✦

A couple weeks after she was crowned Miss America in the fall of 2016, Savvy Shields was interviewed by Mario Lopez, the former nineties teen star and occasional Vegas-era pageant host, for his syndicated radio show.

"Do you have a boyfriend?" he asked, midway through their chatter.

"I am focused on my year right now," Savvy replied carefully.

Mario got the picture. He moved on to other topics. But as soon as the taping ended, she recalled, he shot back at her knowingly: "How long have you guys been dating?"

Yes, Savvy had a boyfriend. But she had been instructed by her handlers not to acknowledge him publicly, so as not to disturb the illusion of . . . whatever the Miss America illusion was supposed to be in 2016. One handler advised her to reply with "I'm America's sweetheart." Ugh.

She had no idea of the stresses rippling through the top ranks of the Miss America Organization. She just knew there were so many rules. So many trip wires. She was warned, without explanation, not to reach out to former Miss Americas, though she could have used their advice. Her ideas for promoting the Miss America brand on social media were second-guessed and resisted. On conference calls, board members would tell her how she could be doing her job better.

Savvy had felt so ready for all of this. Flaxen-haired, bubbly, and driven, she had competed in teen pageants but waited until she was twenty to try for the big title, when she knew she was "mentally, emotionally, spiritually ready for the job." She may have been more sensitive than some to the ups and downs of the position. Savvy was one of those people who savored the full range of human emotion. When she spoke at an orientation for Outstanding Teen contestants in Michigan, the girls slipped a note under her hotel room door. She snuck out to visit with them, and they all stayed up talking in their pajamas until 4 a.m. It touched her heart like nothing else that year.

Still, she spent it in constant fear of getting in trouble. When she asked if her mother could stay with her in Atlantic City for the final two weeks of her reign, three staff members took turns chewing her out for being needy and immature, she says. (She finally appealed to Sam, who made it happen.) She had no way of knowing how much of this was normal. And no inkling that she would be the very last Miss America to have anything close to a "normal" Miss America experience.

✦   ✦   ✦

In February 2017, Regina reached out to a former state pageant director with a deep grasp of Miss America's business structure. She explained her frustrations with Sam's leadership—a tendency to hoard information about finances and lash out at board members who asked too many questions—and her desire to bring about change. She also confided that she had access to some astonishingly damaging emails.

"What's your endgame?" the former director recalls asking her.

Regina said she wanted to run the Miss America Organization herself.

Her goal may have been high, but Regina's abiding interest in the pageant was not unusual, even among the women who never won Miss America. Competing for the title was a profound experience, where they developed lasting friendships, crucial career connections, or just a sharper sense of the world outside their hometowns, and the roles they might play in it. Many former Miss States ended up running state or local pageants. A few were among the deep-pocketed donors who helped keep the whole thing solvent in later years—or the loudest voices in the looming fight over its future.

The former state pageant director that Regina approached was glad to advise her. But in the following months, this advisor would pose other questions to Regina, soon to be joined in these conversations by Gretchen Carlson, Brent Adams, Kate Shindle, and, eventually, Mallory Hagan:

Do you really want to do this? Do you know what you're taking on? And are you sure you can do a better job of running it than Sam?

The plan hinged on getting the attention of the pageant's TV producing partner, Dick Clark Productions, the latest in the series of business interests that had thrown a lifeline to Miss America. The production company, which specialized in glitzy live events such as the Academy of Country Music Awards and the Golden Globes, hunted down sponsorship deals and oversaw marketing and other creative decisions; it also arranged for Miss Americas to attend other televised events and red carpets to promote the brand.

And it was a far more generous partner than those that preceded it. The company paid off nearly $5 million of the mounting debt that threatened to swamp Miss America while also agreeing to stabilize its annual budget, in exchange for the lion's share of profits from the TV broadcast. Some wary board members became convinced that the company had notions of seizing greater control of the pageant—two of its executives were now on the board—and there were frequent clashes over production decisions. But it was essential to Miss America's struggling business model.

Regina's first appeal to Dick Clark Productions came in April 2017, according to a memo the company later sent to the Miss America board outlining the chain of events: She met with its executives in L.A. and shared her ideas for the pageant organization. But the concerns she raised about Sam's management were lacking in the specifics the executives needed.

Four months later, Regina called again. Now, she told the executives, she had evidence of wrongdoing by Sam.

She flew again to L.A. in August, this time with Brent Adams. The two of them shared a series of emails traded by Miss America board and staff, from 2013 to 2015—and warned the executives that these emails could end up being aired publicly, by other unspecified persons, unless there was a leadership change at the Miss America Organization.

✦   ✦   ✦

The least of the emails were basically just snotty.

In one, Sam referred to a business frenemy as a "major bitch." In another, a writer for the show expressed condolences about the death of Miss America 1959 Mary Ann Mobley, but under the snarky subject header: "It should have been Kate Shindle."

The show writer was Lewis Friedman, a veteran showbiz utility player who had penned material for awards shows and roasts as well as a raunchy movie script for the creators of *South Park*. Emails suggest he was among the colleagues that Sam would vent to about the melo-dramas consuming the organization, and who, in turn, would attempt to jolly Sam out of a funk or calm him down.

"Even in my sadness you can make me laugh," Sam replied to Lew-is's email.

But some emails went far beyond petty; they were brutally unkind. Sam casually shared secondhand gossip about men Mallory had sup-posedly slept with. In a sequence from early 2015, he mocked a recent photo of her: "OMG she is huge . . . and gross . . . why does he want that??????" Josh Randle replied: "She's a healthy one!! Hahaha."

It was a kind of back-channel bitchiness that many of us would be ashamed to find in our inbox, and probably have. But this particular bitchiness came from the head of an organization, aimed at the much younger woman who had been the face of the organization, a job that, by description, was supposed to accord her an official measure of respect. Miss America—your ideal.

The most bizarre emails seemed to take a conspiratorial and re-sentful tone toward Mallory, but also toward other, unnamed Miss Americas as well. "Malcontents and has-beens who blame the pro-gram for not getting them where they think they can go," longtime board member Tammy Haddad, a well-connected media consultant and former cable-news producer who had finessed numerous meet-ings for contestants and winners in Washington's power corridors, wrote to Sam in May 2014: "80% of the winners do not have the class, smarts and model for success . . . You don't need them. They need you. We also have to punish them when they don't appreciate what we do for them."

In another thread, in December 2015, Sam wrote to several board members: "If Hagan was viciously and cruelly attacking you and your family every single day, would you REALLY just ignore her? Isn't there some way to stop her?" Tammy responded: "I think u should hire an investigator to get something on her. Or a lawyer to call her and threaten her with legal action." And Lynn Weidner, a former Miss New Jersey and a casino executive's wife who had worked in television and tourism and donated hundreds of thousands of dollars to the pageant, wrote, "If we can prove a direct connection between MH and specific instances of cyberbullying, we could at least threaten her with a lawsuit, right? I do believe that our anti-coaching initiatives are already impacting her business. And that our policy of ignoring her is driving her crazy."

What on earth was going on? The excerpts were incredibly damning. Read in full, many of these emails revealed a more complex dynamic. Sam's colleagues were trying to cajole, commiserate, and reassure. Sometimes it seemed they articulated wild-sounding suggestions more for the purpose of ruling them out.

"If you ignore it, it will go away," Tammy wrote. "Don't fuel the madness that has been such a burden for your family."

"No matter what course we choose," wrote Lynn, "this issue has the potential of blowing up in our faces if we are not very cautious and judicious in our actions."

"Whatever is decided," Josh wrote, "I think we must maintain the positive good will we have worked so hard to build."

Why did they need to talk Sam off a ledge?

Ever since the internet had taken off in the late nineties, a generation of pageant women had been driven low-grade insane by reading the bitchy anonymous commentary about themselves on pageant-fan message boards. And now the chairman himself had landed in these crosshairs—a phantom attack that seemed to consume Sam during much of 2014 and 2015.

According to a confidential report commissioned by the board to investigate the email controversy, several posts appeared on one popular site mocking the looks of his daughter and insinuating that Sam was gay and that his marriage was a sham. In one of his intercepted emails, Sam fretted that his assailant was promoting a story that he wanted Brent to date Mary Lane—the same story Brent would later tell *HuffPost*. The postings were anonymous, but the deeply personal tone apparently led Sam to believe they were placed by Mallory. She later denied any involvement.

The email exchange that would eventually capture the most attention was another shared by Sam and Lewis, during the preparations for the September 2014 pageant.

"I have decided that when referring to a woman who was once Miss America, we are no longer going to call them Forever Miss Americas," Sam wrote, nixing the cloying honorific he had devised a couple years earlier. "Please change all script copy to reflect that they are Former Miss Americas!"

The comedy writer riffed: "I'd already changed 'Forevers' to 'Cunts.' Does that work for you?"

"Perfect . . . Bahahaha," Sam replied.

✦ ✦ ✦

Regina's hope, according to people who spoke with her, was that Dick Clark Productions would use its influence to convince the rest of the board to deal with the Sam situation. The company went for a more arm's-length strategy, though.

Three days after the September 2017 pageant, and several weeks after receiving Regina and Brent's cache of emails, Dick Clark Productions sent a sharply worded letter to the board demanding an investigation.

It took two months for the lawyer the board tapped for the job to come back with a report. Its focus was mostly on improving email protocols and forming a committee to contend with anonymous chat-forum flare-ups.

Sam delivered an emotional apology and kept his job. Lewis was fired.

But Dick Clark Productions was already gone. The company had severed its Miss America contract a month earlier, with an attorney-drafted letter chiding the board for moving too slowly on the investigation and for seeming to show more concern about how the emails were obtained than about what they contained, according to board communications.

With Sam still ensconced at the top, but Dick Clark Productions no longer involved, Regina and Gretchen and their allies reconsidered the option that some people they spoke with say they were initially reluctant to pursue—going public with the emails.

A revolution had happened since Regina and Brent brought the emails to the producers. Blockbuster stories in the *New York Times* and the *New Yorker* that fall revealed how the Hollywood producer Harvey Weinstein had sexually harassed and assaulted women in show business for decades. Suddenly, other women were inspired to share their stories about powerful men, and journalists were emboldened to investigate them. Career-crippling accusations hit Charlie Rose, Matt Lauer, Louis C.K., Dustin Hoffman, Garrison Keillor, Russell Simmons, Al Franken, and dozens of other prominent men.

There was an appetite for stories of young women wronged by sexism, but there was also a surplus of these stories—and a couple of media outlets took a pass on the complex Miss America saga, which revolved around words rather than actions. It wasn't until December that the story ended up in the hands of Yashar Ali, a former Democratic political operative who had started breaking big stories about media and celebrity culture, including Fox News's sexual harassment scandals, and who occasionally picked Twitter fights defending Gretchen's honor.

On a Thursday evening four days before Christmas, his story about the Miss America emails was published on the *HuffPost* website. And then everything started happening very fast.

Gretchen, the subject of one of Sam's bitter email exchanges, called for the immediate resignation of "every MAO executive and board member who engaged in such crude behavior and signed off on it." She asked pageant women to "join me in a collective effort to fight for the dignity of this great institution."

By noon the next day, forty-nine of the sixty-four living former Miss Americas signed a letter demanding the resignations of Sam, Josh Randle, Lynn Weidner, and Tammy Haddad, the board members on the most problematic emails. Leonard Horn and the mayor of Atlantic City soon echoed their call.

Tammy stepped down immediately. Sam fought back, even as the board voted to suspend him. He apologized but called the story "dishonest [and] deceptive" and said the emails reflected impaired judgment: "I was under stress from a full year of attacks by two Miss Americas . . . This was a father whose family was being attacked, and a man whose character was being assassinated daily."

The statement was utterly cryptic to the world that didn't follow anonymous pageant forums, and the former Miss Americas found his apology inadequate. With fifty-six of them now signing, they renewed their call for resignations via a statement released on social media: "In this #MeToo cultural revolution, victim shaming is no longer accepted as a defense. . . . We stand up for our sisterhood and for women everywhere with zero tolerance for this kind of behavior." State and local pageant organizers started to circulate their own petitions, a hint of the revulsion arising in the all-volunteer army that nurtured the pageant from the grassroots.

On Saturday afternoon, Sam resigned, and Lynn resigned, and Josh resigned. But Gretchen put out a statement with Kate Shindle: "This is not over yet."

They demanded the resignation of the *entire* board.

This was a coordinated campaign that displayed an impressive political deftness and media savvy.

It began in the hours before the *HuffPost* story was published, as Regina and Gretchen's allies tracked down email lists for former Miss Americas and Miss States whom they could rally for support. The Roger Ailes scandal at Fox News had demonstrated the power of a drip-drip of negative stories to force change, and Mallory threw herself into the holiday news vacuum, getting booked on *Good Morning America* to discuss the scandal on December 26. The next day, she delivered a fiery monologue via Facebook Live that would log a hundred thousand views, blasting the twelve remaining board members who had "stood by and allowed these people to act this way."

"They thought they could weather this storm," Mallory said. She paused for effect. "I *am* the storm. You're not weathering it." She read emails from state pageant folks explaining how Sam's team had warned them not to associate with her. The next day, she was online again, reading more damning email excerpts that hadn't made it into the *HuffPost* story, calling out the board members cc'd on them.

The beleaguered board devised a plan. It needed new leadership, so it proposed that a committee of Miss Americas and state directors help select it. Phyllis George, a longtime board member, was dispatched to communicate this offer to Gretchen.

But the Miss Americas loudly rejected it: An *entirely new board* should select new leadership, they said.

This was the plan they had been formulating for months now. Among the core group, there had originally been talk of having Gretchen and Kate serve as co-chairs, in part because Gretchen, busy promoting a new book that fall, was reluctant to take a lead role. But after the *Huff-Post* story broke, sentiment seemed to be accumulating in the emails traded among the larger group of Miss Americas that Gretchen should take the lead role, and she let the others know she was interested in serving as solo chair.

The logistics of the coup remained murky. Legally, an entire board could not resign without dissolving the company. But the board wearily conceded: Instead of an ad hoc committee, it would add the Miss Americas straight to the board.

On New Year's Day, just eleven days after the email scandal broke, the Miss America board announced that it had voted Gretchen Carlson as its new chair. Kate Shindle was also added to the board, along with Heather French, Miss America 2000, and Laura Kaeppeler, Miss America 2012, now married to reality-TV superproducer Mike Fleiss.

And once these new members were in place, most of the original board members submitted their resignations, as they had agreed to do in behind-the-scenes negotiations.

But not Phyllis.

And so on the evening of January 1, Gretchen called Phyllis to ask her to resign.

Why get rid of an entire board, with its deep pockets, valuable contacts, and institutional memory? Even some of the Miss Americas who had charged the barricades were uncomfortable with this, especially if it meant purging four of their beloved fellow Miss Americas.

The argument for a full purge was that those board members, even if they were never cc'd on Sam's emails, had known about them since the fall and yet chose to stick with Sam, at the cost of losing the all-essential Dick Clark contract. But it was never that stark a decision, former board members say. They thought they were complying with Dick Clark Productions' orders, but then the production company severed the contract before they could weigh Sam's fate. Some believed it had all been a pretense to cut the pageant loose after two years of declining ratings, and that Dick Clark Productions might have done so even if the email scandal hadn't provided an easy out.

Still, most board members were ready to leave by that point. Phyllis was not.

She had a philosophy she liked to call PNP: "positive-negative-positive." If you have a criticism or negative message to share, Phyllis would often say, sandwich it between praise or optimism.

"I have been inspired by the outpouring of emotion from each of you," she wrote to her fellow Miss Americas the next day. "While this has been a turbulent time, our collective love and caring for this organization is what makes us great and will propel us forward."

Then Phyllis confided how gravely ill she had been in recent years, and that she regretted not being more active on the board. She wrote of how Miss America had launched the groundbreaking career that she hoped had inspired other women. How she wished to stay on the board until the centennial, which would be the fiftieth anniversary of her own crowning. "However," she added, "yesterday Gretchen Carlson called and asked me to resign with her reason being it was what you wanted."

Is that really what you want? Phyllis would not put it so bluntly, but her question was clear. She did not get the response she was looking for. And she, too, resigned.

✦ ✦ ✦

Five months later, in June 2018, the new chair of the Miss America board appeared on *Good Morning America* for a big announcement.

"We are no longer a pageant, we are a competition," Gretchen said, smiling. "We will no longer judge our candidates on their outward physical appearance. . . . And that means we will no longer have a swimsuit competition."

It was in the weeks after Gretchen's announcement that her fragile new organization began to pull apart at the seams, so when the stories of this conflict were written, it was often framed as a battle over swimsuits and a century-old institution's struggle for a modern identity.

But it was a little more complicated than that. Or perhaps a whole lot less.

Miss America's public image in the first days of 2018 was triumphant, a girl-power phoenix rising from the ashes of a MeToo dumpster fire. That was the battle-weary but forward-looking mood that pervaded the January 2018 Miss America retreat in Florida. The Miss Americas were running Miss America! It felt like a wild extension of Leonard Horn's vision, or the future signaled in 1973 when a long-haired feminist won the crown. (Never mind that that winner, Rebecca King, was *already* on the board, toppled in this coup, along with Phyllis and fellow Miss Americas Donna Axum and Debbie Bryant.)

"Please stay tuned," Gretchen said, "because I plan to make this organization one hundred percent about empowering women."

Behind the scenes, though, her small board was at odds from day one. Gretchen made the case that she should be named not just chair but executive chair, with power, at least in the short term, to make certain crucial day-to-day decisions for a decimated organization that suddenly lacked a CEO. Kate and Laura, wary of enabling another all-powerful chair like Sam, opposed this idea, but Gretchen had Heather's vote.

For a tiebreaker, Gretchen called the one carryover member from the old board. The new team had not sought Ike Franco's resignation, apparently under the belief that Infinity Group's vestigial deal meant they were contractually obligated to keep him in place. Sam's old antagonist picked up the phone while in an airport on a family trip and agreed to vote Gretchen's way.

With her new authority, Gretchen made two key executive hires. One was Regina Hopper, tapped as consultant-CEO. The other was Brent Adams.

This small team had their work cut out for them trying to piece together the next pageant and pin down the organization's financing. The latter was no easy thing, when they owed budget-straining severances to both Sam and Josh. There was also a seven-figure debt to Billy Goldberg, from the settlement of his lawsuit several months earlier.

A lot of big decisions started getting made very quickly, and not always with much input from the small board, according to some of its members, an expanded group that now included two former Miss States and two former state pageant directors.

Instead of a nationwide search, Regina was officially hired as the permanent CEO—albeit unpaid for now—during an Easter-weekend board meeting at which no other candidates were presented. A marketing firm was signed with no board input, and many were surprised when a second production team was hired for $200,000.

An independent market-research report helped make the argument to finally drop the swimsuit competition after nearly fifty years of hand-wringing. Yet some board members and state pageant directors would later say that they were most compelled by a dire warning from Gretchen and Regina that no TV partners in this fraught era would have anything to do with a pageant that judged the bodies of young women.

In other words, as they understood the warning, keeping the swimsuit contest could keep the pageant off television. And what would Miss America be without television?

But two days before Gretchen's scheduled *Good Morning America* announcement, they were still figuring out how to craft their message about the overhauled competition. Board members say Gretchen and Regina unexpectedly began spitballing ideas for dropping the evening gown competition or encouraging women to parade in attire suited to their profession—for example, Regina suggested, a marine biologist could walk out in scuba gear. Baffled board members cut the conversation short.

So they were surprised when Gretchen, after announcing the end of the swimsuit competition on live TV, continued on to say: "We'll also be revamping our evening gown competition phase. . . ." Her comments were hazy enough, but they rattled the world of super-involved pageant volunteers, not to mention the board members who hadn't yet approved such a plan. It was the same with her declaration that the pageant would "no longer judge . . . outward physical appearance." Though some of her allies would later argue that this was the logical upshot of eliminating swimsuits, to some board members it was an overreaching declaration they hadn't signed off on.

"It was a disaster publicly because they had not thought about the pageant community at all," says one of the board members, Jennifer Vaden Barth, a program manager for Google who was Miss North Carolina 1991. The messaging seemed geared to impressing pageant skeptics, the people who had always thought that parading young women on a competitive stage was unseemly or tacky.

But would *this* bring them into the fold? Would anything?

"They were speaking to an audience that did not exist," says Jennifer, "and would not exist."

✦　　✦　　✦

One key person was often missing from this conversation.

In many ways, reigning Miss America Cara Mund seemed like an exemplar for the new-era Miss America everyone seemed to want to cultivate. She was a Miley Cyrus lookalike from North Dakota who had graduated from Brown with her eyes set on law school and politics but still retained a likeable small-town grit.

"There was a realistic component to her," says one pageant judge who pulled for her.

But her relationship with the new pageant leadership was tense from the start. They rescinded her access to Miss America social-media accounts, she later said; they criticized her wardrobe and called her the wrong name in public; they pushed talking points on her that leaned a little heavily on the importance of Gretchen Carlson and the MeToo movement. (Her bosses called these "mischaracterizations" and "unfounded accusations.")

And during an unusually high-profile year for the organization she represented, Cara seemed to vanish from public view. When Gretchen went on *Good Morning America* to discuss the future of the program, Miss America herself was left waiting in the wings. (ABC's choice, the pageant's leaders said.) When Gretchen flew to Cannes Lions to promote the Miss America brand, Miss America remained home in Bismarck.

One theory offered by a pageant insider: Cara was brainy and hardworking, happy to keep signing autographs until the janitor turned off the lights. Yet she also savored the old-time princess sensibility of Miss America—the sparkle, the spray tan, the extra-extra lashes. And this was not the aesthetic that the new organization was eager to project.

But it was how a lot of young women styled themselves in 2018. Including a lot of the young women who were still interested in pageants.

◆   ◆   ◆

It was time, the Miss Americas sadly decided, for another pageant coup.

By late spring, board members had begun to panic. The pageant had not yet secured new sponsors, and none of them knew what the finances looked like. They felt that Gretchen was treating them as a rubber-stamp board, turning hostile whenever challenged.

State pageant organizers were threatening to revolt, frustrated by a lack of direction for September's pageant. The pro-swimsuit grassroots were still grumbling. And now, through a showbiz source of Laura Kaeppeler's, these board members learned that ABC had never put any pressure on the pageant about dropping the swimsuit competition. (Gretchen and Regina later said their concern had been with other financial backers of the broadcast, not necessarily the network.) They began to feel they had been railroaded into this dramatic, overnight change.

But Gretchen had scolded and berated them during their earlier attempts to form committees to take on more of the organization's work—a move to claw back control, essentially—and Gino Serra, an attorney for the organization, blocked their every motion, maintaining they didn't have the power. Now they decided they had no choice but to strike at the head.

On June 16, six of the board members got on a call with Gretchen.

Kate Shindle laid out a series of proposals to curtail Gretchen's power and called for a vote. She, Jennifer, Laura, and a fourth member, Valerie Clemens, Miss Maine 1980, had discussed it in advance. They all planned to support it.

But as the vote began, Gino spoke up again.

"Hang up the phone," he instructed Gretchen. The vote had been improperly introduced, he argued, and the official agenda was now complete. Gretchen hung up.

✦ ✦ ✦

The irony of the swimsuit debate was that it had so little to do with who got to be Miss America.

Undeniably, swimsuits posed an optics problem for Miss America that it needed to confront in 2018. "The misperception is that we have *made* these young women do it to participate for scholarship money," Heather French told me that summer.

But no one was winning or losing Miss America based on swimsuit anymore. The killer bodies hadn't reigned in a big way·since the early nineties. To the extent that swimsuit determined anything, it was in the same way as the interview, which, face it, was never about who's the smartest anyway. Both stood in for a way to measure the amorphous quality that makes you take heed of someone—who are you inclined to listen to, who would you follow into battle, who do you *like*? Charisma, in other words. The pageant that was accidentally reenergized by the women's movement had bred a generation of forceful, vivid Miss Americas who were all bonfires of charisma. And now they were hitting their prime and ready to deploy their powers.

But what did charisma get you, exactly? Did it teach you how to manage or inspire, to read a room or assuage conflict? If people perceived you as a leader, did it mean you could lead? Or was that a quality no pageant could measure?

✦ ✦ ✦

The coup that failed when Gretchen hung up the phone kicked off a season of bloodletting and open feuding.

Kate and Laura quit the board and went public with their concerns in letters shared with the pageant community on social media. Gretchen clapped back in a Facebook post that accused them of harboring unspecified conflicts of interests and plotting a power grab. And she deployed a loophole that allowed her to push her two other adversaries, Jennifer and Valerie, off the board.

Shocked state pageant directors demanded Gretchen and Regina's resignations. Gretchen responded by releasing a letter with the names of thirty fellow former Miss Americas expressing their support. It backfired. "I did NOT give you my approval to use my name!" wrote seventy-six-year-old Maria Fletcher, Miss America 1962, in a furious Facebook post.

And then some of her fellow Miss Americas began to turn against Gretchen, two dozen of them stepping forward to demand her resignation, signing petitions and echoing the message in cable-news spots. "It's all about her," said Heather Whitestone, in one particularly withering TV interview. "She wanted to be the face of the Miss America Organization." It was hardly unanimous, though. Elizabeth Ward, '82, criticized the anti-Gretchen forces as troublemakers who would "keep the Miss America pageant sliding down the slope of irrelevance and mockery." Bitter arguments broke out in the sisterhood's private Facebook group, and there were many unfriendings. Plans for the next Miss America retreat were quietly scrapped.

With the encouragement of Miss Americas who opposed Gretchen, Cara went public with her complaints of mistreatment—a galvanizing moment for the pageant world. There was talk of boycotting the pageant, but everyone knew the states would always blink first: This was the moment they worked all year toward, the one and only shot for the girl who wore their sash. They couldn't bear to miss it.

But just before that September's pageant, another cadre of Miss Americas quietly attempted to convince Gretchen to step down. This time, according to friends who communicated with them at the time, it was Debbye Turner, Gretchen's longtime colleague at CBS News, who had filled one of the board vacancies just months earlier, and Heather French, who had stood by Gretchen during the last ouster attempt; they were concerned about Gretchen's health and morale after months of scathing criticism and threats. But Gretchen still did not resign, and soon both Debbye and Heather left the board.

Gretchen's team yanked the licenses of four state pageant organizations whose leaders had been most outspoken against her team and threatened action against three others. The move essentially exiled these volunteers, whose unpaid labors had helped maintain the pipeline of contestants that kept this entire system going, from their longtime hobby. The official reasons were arcane and varied, but it sent a strong message to all the rest.

Several of them joined a lawsuit, spearheaded by ousted board member Jennifer Vaden Barth, accusing Gretchen and Regina of orchestrating an illegal takeover of Miss America. In response, the defense accused them of attempting to seize power and thwart progress. It dragged on for a few months until the plaintiffs lost an initial round, ran out of money, and withdrew their case.

Gretchen almost never again spoke publicly or even tweeted about Miss America after that last pageant. When she finally did step down, the following spring, there was little celebrating, even among her fiercest detractors.

Only one Miss America remained on the board; there had been four when Sam was still in charge.

The rebellion of the beauty queens was over. And nothing had been won.

12

"THAT TITLE ISN'T GOING TO WIN EVERYTHING"

2018

Mallory Hagan and her campaign manager tumbled into her Auburn, Alabama, headquarters on a burst of adrenaline, bleary from a two-hour road trip but energized by a new battle plan.

"We'd really like to find this young girl who's eighteen," said her campaign manager, Jacob Ray, consulting the thick stack of documents they had retrieved from the state capital. "She's listed as inactive, but she's never voted! This was supposed to be her first vote!"

It was a week until the election. The previous day, Mallory, now the Democratic nominee for U.S. Congress in Alabama's 3rd district, had gotten into a Twitter spat with the state's Republican secretary of state. He testily replied that the voter-registration documents her campaign had been requesting were waiting at his office. So they jumped in the car, drove to Montgomery, and came back with the names of sixty-seven thousand people recently purged from the district's voting ranks.

Voter-roll purges were the hot issue across the South that fall of 2018. Stacey Abrams, the Democrat running for governor in Georgia, galvanized her base by highlighting the outsized number of African-Americans erroneously struck from the rosters. When Alabama announced it had cleared out 658,000 ostensibly "inactive" voters, Mallory's suspicions went into overdrive. And so did her political instincts.

Was the state purging *her* voters? Could this be an issue for her, too?

Yes, she was Miss America 2013, the golden girl returned home and offering herself up for public service. But she was also a first-timer going up against an eight-term Republican in a district that had voted for Trump by thirty points two years earlier. She needed a way to break through.

There was a good energy around her dark-horse campaign. Horror over Trump's election had energized young liberal voters, and here she was in a district with eleven college campuses that, who knew, might turn out to vote this time. Pollsters barely bothered with this district, but that helped. No dire numbers to distract her youthful staff from the positive indicators they saw everywhere on the ground: the voters won over at small-group events; her opponent's sudden, nervous splurge on ads; the upbeat coverage by national media.

And now they were going out with a video camera to try to find citizens shocked to learn they had been struck from the rolls without warning.

"I'm going to knock on doors," Mallory said.

With any luck, they'd get a viral video, a little dose of righteous outrage to rally the progressive faithful well beyond eastern Alabama. *This* was why you ran someone like Mallory Hagan for Congress. Or rather, this was why a party activist would spot a former pageant girl on TV speaking out about the Sam Haskell controversy and think: *This* is a born politician.

Like generations of Miss Americas before her, Mallory had a natural poise, a dynamic speaking voice, and the ineffable strength-warmth-charisma combo that makes people like you before they even know you. Pertinent to 2018, she also had a knack for stagecraft, a taste for a Twitter feud, and a precociously thickened skin.

"We'll just make as much noise as we can," Jacob said as they prepared to hit the streets with a two-man video crew. "This is her issue."

✦   ✦   ✦

Before everything went downhill, Gretchen Carlson had unveiled a new motto for Miss America: "To prepare great women for the world, and to prepare the world for great women."

Lofty as it was, it also articulated the earnestness of the pageant world since at least the 1970s, when it became possible to imagine that a Miss America might move on to something greater than Miss America.

It was the sense that the crown wasn't just meant for the girl of the moment, but the woman of the future. Potential, in other words. But potential for what?

When a former Miss Wasilla, Sarah Palin, electrified American politics in 2008, the nation was put on notice: The beauty queens wanted a seat at the table of power, and they were ready to use their telegenic dark arts to get it.

In fact, they had already been trying for half a century.

In 1951, Miss America 1944 ran for the Kentucky state legislature. Venus Ramey was the first woman to run for office in Lincoln County. Even her husband was opposed to her candidacy, and one female voter wrote and told her to "stay home and take care of your children." She came in fourth in the Democratic primary. Her title had done nothing to help.

"The men figured I was too young to be a representative," she said, "and besides, many of them actually believed the old canard that beauty and brains don't mix."

There were the beauty queens who became activists, from various points of the political spectrum. Cheryl Prewitt filmed a scathing GOP television ad in 1984 taking aim at Geraldine Ferraro. ("Sure, I'd like a woman as vice president," she said, "but a woman of unquestioned integrity.") More typical was Heather Whitestone, who campaigned for Bob Dole and delivered a warmly inspirational testimonial at his 1996 Republican convention. Bess Myerson, the first Jewish Miss America in 1945, had an early political awakening when sponsors snubbed her and country clubs turned her away.

"I was expected to understand . . . expected to remain sweet and dignified and calm," she said later. "Outwardly that is exactly what I did. Inwardly, I felt a rage that has never left me." She transformed her reign into a speaking tour for the Anti-Defamation League, preaching against anti-Semitism and racism.

And after a national surge of women into elected office in the 1990s, it suddenly seemed plausible that Miss Americas could serve as more than just supporting players. There was an attempt to draft Kaye Lani Rae Rafko to run for the Michigan state legislature and talk of Phyllis George running for governor of Kentucky. Some Alabama Republicans pondering strategies to take the state's U.S. Senate seat back from Democrat Doug Jones tried to lure home-state heroine Heather Whitestone into the 2020 race.

By the time Cara Mund told reporters after her crowning that her goal was to become the first female governor of North Dakota, no one seemed to find the idea of a beauty queen politician especially mockable anymore, let alone surprising. Politics and pageantry had slid onto converging tracks, with the pageant demanding its contestants display commitment to social causes and savvy about the world, and the political parties turning to candidates with compelling backstories, camera-ready looks, and an ease with a sound bite.

Politics had become "a never-ending judged performance," wrote sociologist Hilary Levey Friedman, the daughter of Miss America 1970 Pam Eldred—"and beauty queens are uniquely prepared for the scrutiny."

In September 2002, my friends and I stayed home and watched the pageant from one of our living rooms rather than travel to Atlantic City. But we still analyzed all the contestant bios on the Miss America website, and we had our eye on Teresa Benitez, the Miss Nevada who was scooping up the interview prizes and resembled a cross between Maria Shriver and Maria Bartiromo. If she won, she would have been the first Latina Miss America.

We winced at first when she took the stage to perform. Uh-oh—a monologue. Dramatic recitations were wildly popular in the 1950s, when Grace Kelly was every pageant girl's idol, and six of the decade's Miss Americas won by showing off their thespian skills;* nowadays,

---

* These came in many flavors. Sharon Ritchie, '56, recited an Edna St. Vincent Millay poem; Marian McKnight, '57, did a Marilyn Monroe impersonation; and Lynda Lee Mead, '60, hammed it up in various hats and accents in a skit called "Schizophrenia."

monologues were generally unwatchable, a fallback for the most talent-challenged contestants.

But it turned out that Teresa, who had worked as a teenage community organizer before the promise of scholarships drew her into pageants, was attempting a different kind of theater here.

"I loved my son and was proud of him," she recited, her voice cracking with emotion. "He wasn't my gay son. He was *my son*, who happened to be gay."

It was taken from the speech that Dennis Shepard delivered to the court weighing the fate of the men who killed his son, Matthew, near Laramie, Wyoming, in 1998, a horror that galvanized LGBTQ activism and spurred hate-crime awareness. As Teresa sent her voice to the rafters of Convention Hall, her act felt like the kind of inspirational interlude we were now seeing a lot of at the political conventions: the stirring tributes to first responders or soldiers or AIDS patients, meant to signal the values of a party. By that yardstick of talent, Teresa was crushing it up there.

Teresa didn't win in Atlantic City. But she returned home to find that her fourth-place finish had made her a celebrity in northern Nevada. She did at least two hundred speaking events that year and shook a thousand hands and met with community leaders twice her age. A decade later, when she first explored a bid for the Nevada statehouse, her team's polling discovered her name recognition was already quite high and positive, thanks to her old pageant title.

So even as she rose to the position of Democratic majority leader of the Nevada legislature, she was fine with the fact that her rhinestone past would always be the second thing mentioned about her. *Teresa Benitez, comma, former Miss Nevada, comma* . . . Pageantry, she says, "was a great training ground" for a political career.

Though beyond the meet-and-greet, pageantry could also be a venue to exercise sharper-elbowed skills.

Erika Harold, the woman who beat Teresa for the Miss America 2003 crown, was drawn to politics as well. Two weeks after she was crowned, she went to Washington to speak at the National Press Club.

As she took questions, a reporter, who had been tipped by "an acquaintance" of Erika's, asked a pointed question:

Was it true that Miss America officials were trying to block her from advocating her favored cause: sexual abstinence?

"There were pressures from some sides," Erika said, confirming the rumor before uttering the sound bite that went national:

"I will not be bullied," she said.

A brainy, biracial Miss Illinois with a spot waiting at Harvard Law, Erika was devoted to the cause of abstinence education. She had spent her college years working with a conservative organization promoting a just-say-no-to-sex strategy for teens (one that eschewed lessons on contraception and disease prevention) and amassing a network of prominent fellow activists.

But the Illinois state pageant wanted all its winners to champion the cause of youth violence. Erika paid lip service to the issue through the chase to become Miss America. When she was crowned, she made it clear to Miss America officials she intended to resume her abstinence crusade.

They were irritated by what one observer called a "bait and switch," and then blindsided by the stories about their disagreement. But Erika had savvily outflanked them, and they backed off.

The kerfuffle established Erika as a heroine in A-list conservative circles. And after law school, she plunged into politics, starting with a bold challenge to a first-term Republican in a congressional primary. She lost, but four years later, in 2018, handily won the GOP nomination for state attorney general.

Ultimately, Erika lost that race, too. Though still a star within a shrinking Illinois Republican Party, by age forty she had not yet achieved public office. And she was hardly alone.

For all their well-honed charisma and competitive thirst, pageant women had been slow to notch electoral successes. Bess Myerson's advocacy work led eventually to a seat in New York mayor John Lindsay's cabinet and then her chairing of Ed Koch's winning 1977 mayoral campaign. But when she ran for U.S. Senate from New York, she flopped in the Democratic primary. Voters saw her as "too glamorous," and were reluctant to take a Miss America seriously, her campaign manager concluded.

"I have 35 years of public service," she protested.

Several former Miss States sought state office during the Obama years, but very few won. Teresa Benitez observed this trend with some surprise as her own political career took off. She didn't believe the crown carried a stigma. But she wondered if it set her fellow pageant veterans off on the wrong path—Erika in particular, whom she admired from across the partisan divide. Why did she try to win statewide so soon, a Republican in a place where the numbers were stacked against her?

"She is so smart, she would be amazing at this. So I have no idea why she is running a race that is so upside down," Teresa says, nearly eighteen years after they shared the stage in Atlantic City. She theorized that pageant women were getting lured into nearly unwinnable races by minority parties that hoped their native charm and residual fame might squeeze an extra ten points out of a tough district.

"You certainly have to run a race you can win," Teresa said. "That title isn't going to win everything."

◆   ◆   ◆

Mallory was behind the wheel of her black Honda Civic as she and Jacob went off in search of disenfranchised voters through a semi-rural neighborhood of scrubby pines and low-slung homes, their eyes peeled for the addresses they had marked in the registration files. Her staffers Josh and Chad trailed in another car with the camera.

The first house looked promising, a slightly dingy one-story home with a "Christ Is Alive" poster out front. Jacob was eager to capture Mallory's full approach on tape. She hesitated.

"Ahh, I think it would be better to have the conversation first," she said, imagining an unsuspecting homeowner's reaction on opening her door to a camera crew.

This was Mallory's hometown. And while she had been gone eight years before returning to Opelika for a TV news job, she retained a gut feeling of what it would take to connect with citizens here. She was skeptical of the national Democrats who urged her to rely on social media or certain messaging gambits; so many of the under-tapped voters here were older African-Americans, less likely to respond to the scripted tweets or text messages that were all the rage in Washington, more likely to be swayed by their neighbors and their churches.

"It's me getting out in the community," she said. "It's word of mouth."

Mallory had ventured out for this mission in a dynamically efficient outfit: slim-fitting black pants, a bright royal-blue turtleneck sweater, hair pulled back into a casual ponytail but face fully made up. Many women in politics now relied on this kind of perfectly appropriate business-casual uniform—all those jewel-tone blazers over neutrals—but it had been perfected by Miss Americas, the twentysomething interview queens starting in the 1990s who traveled from speech to speech in their St. John Knits. Mallory would appear utterly professional if a press conference unexpectedly happened in the middle of her day, but not intimidatingly fancy for greeting a working-class voter. Mallory was also about forty pounds heavier than in her Miss America prime. But it gave her an earthiness and gravitas beyond her twenty-nine years, like the nice doctor at the local hospital or the friendly bank manager, instead of some twinkly pageant girl.

"Hey, Miss Mary. I'm Mallory Hagan. I'm running for Congress." The middle-aged black woman who answered the door was not the voter they were looking for, who was off at work that morning. They made a note to follow up and moved on.

They were having a hard time finding anyone at home in the late morning. But as they rolled down a quiet street of tidy split-level homes, a little jolt went through the group: Their next address had a couple of cars with "Hagan for House" stickers.

"If we nail this one, we've got all the video we need!" Jacob exclaimed. Chad researched the address on his phone. Josh cross-referenced the homeowner's name on Facebook: He was a friend of a friend.

"Oh!" Mallory exclaimed, recognizing the name. "He's the union guy!" Could it be? Someone at the home of an identifiable active Democrat—a Hagan voter, no less—who had been thrown off the rolls? Mallory dialed his number and left a voicemail.

From a young age, Mallory had realized that if she wanted something, she might have to make it happen herself. She was the only child of very young parents who were working hard and not always together during her youth. That gave her a certain brash confidence, the kind of kid who'd tell her mom, "You're not the boss of me!"

Later, as Miss America, she would hint at some larger sadness behind this self-reliant childhood when she took on the platform of child sexual abuse. In her interviews, she said that every female relative of hers had been a victim of assault at some point—"a blanket over our family for a long time," she told a reporter—though "fortunately not me," she always made a point of adding.

But it was a little more complicated than that. Six years later, speaking to an audience during the week of festivities before the Miss America pageant in 2019, Mallory acknowledged that she, too, had been sexually abused as a child, as it turned out.

"And I didn't figure that out until I became Miss America," she said ruefully. "Talk about some mental gymnastics there."

She had gotten herself out of Opelika at age nineteen, when she moved to Brooklyn with $1,000 in her pocket, beckoned by the energy and comfortable with the culture. Spending time at her mom's hair salon and dance studio had exposed her to people more liberal than most of her hometown. In New York, she waited tables, chipped away at a marketing degree—and, to make friends in a big city, gravitated back to pageants, which she had done in Alabama.

The move back home to Opelika just three years after her Miss America reign was a nonscheduled detour, after the hostilities with Sam Haskell and the end of her relationship with Brent Adams. The TV news job turned out to be a successful life reboot, but she didn't love it. Knocking on the door of the family whose kid got shot was unsettling; anchoring from a studio was dull. Most of what she was hoping for out of a TV career anyway was a way back into the high-profile advocacy work she had enjoyed as Miss America.

Basically, she was like any twenty-nine-year-old grappling with a quarterlife career crisis, except with the option of running for Congress. This was the kind of extraordinary opportunity that could still, sometimes, land in an ex–Miss America's lap.

Back in the car later, her phone rang. It was the union guy.

"Hey! I just had a random question . . . ," Mallory said. "You live on Rocky Brook? Okay, so Stephanie? Is that your wife?" Long pause. "Ohhhhhhh, okay. Well, that makes more sense." The union guy had gotten divorced. His ex-wife had moved out. The state had legitimate reason to rescind her registration at his address. Mallory invited him to her election-night party and got off the phone.

The viral-video quest was looking futile; the time would be better spent on old-fashioned retail politics. She set off to knock on doors in a working-middle-class black community. "I'm as independent as they come," a middle-aged tax preparer cautioned, but he promised to consider her. "And I'll spread the word, too!" On a side street, a woman reeking of weed looked up from the front seat of a parked truck as Mallory brightly asked her if she would be voting. "Nope. Didn't register," she said sullenly. Then her face lit up: "I saw you on Facebook!"

At one house, two men putting up drywall with a couple drinks in them chanted, "Trump, Trump, Trump." At another, a woman opened the door and shrieked like she'd spotted a long-lost friend.

"Hey! I'm voting for you! I got you!" she cheered. "The other people call me, I say, 'No, I'm voting for Mallory!' I got you, girl!"

And so it went all afternoon. Bursts of enthusiasm, blank stares, dead-end chitchat, occasional tiny victories. It could have been any underdog campaign anywhere. Miss America never came up.

✦   ✦   ✦

If any Miss America could get elected to public office, it was Heather French Henry. She had been laying the groundwork for twenty years.

When she was Miss Kentucky, she started dating Lieutenant Governor Steve Henry, and after her reign, she had gone straight home to marry him—no big-city detours or anchor auditions for her. At twenty-five, she turned the overlooked role of "second lady" into a thing, focused on the veterans' issues she had championed as Miss America. After an upgrade to first lady didn't come through, when Steve lost his gubernatorial race in 2007, she made her own way into government, as commissioner of the Kentucky Department of Veterans Affairs. In 2019, she entered her first race, for secretary of state.

But on Election Day, she lost by four points. The Democrat at the top of the ticket, Andy Beshear, was the only one who eked out a victory, over wildly unpopular Republican governor Matt Bevin. Six weeks later, as Heather made her annual trip to witness the crowning of a new Miss America, she was mulling the lessons of the race.

The Miss America title had certainly opened doors for her over the years. During the state's push to get the Medal of Honor for one of its war heroes, she'd had no trouble reaching the major players at the Pentagon.

"There are fifty state secretaries of veterans affairs out there," she said. "But when you leave a message saying, 'This is Heather French Henry, Miss America 2000. I'd like to talk to you'—you always get a return phone call."

But even after twenty years in and around government, after overseeing a $102 million departmental budget and hundreds of staffers, it always came up. News stories would dive deep into her opponent's list of credentials, she felt, but she remained *former Miss America* and *wife of former lieutenant governor*.

Heather began to feel that it wasn't just about being Miss America; it was about being a woman. She woke up one morning and thought, "Holy cow! We *still* have not come far enough."

Then again, Heather's frustrations would have rung true for many politicians that year, male or female. Politics seemed increasingly divorced from the skill sets that got them into this field. The ability to work with folks across the aisle, as she had for so many years? Not particularly valued anymore. The art of connecting with voters and building your reputation—call it the pageantry side of politics—had been jettisoned for the game of kicking the other guy's ass.

✦   ✦   ✦

I never expected Mallory to win: Her district was the epitome of "upside down." And yet I did imagine that she would give the GOP a scare. Not because of the Miss America title, of course, but because of some combustion between the qualities that had won it for her—the charisma, the grit, the voice—and the feisty, feminist spirit of the moment that seemed poised to deliver a Democratic wave.

But the blue wave of 2018 didn't make a splash in Alabama's 3rd. On Election Day, Mallory won 36.2 percent of the vote, only a little better than the no-name Democrat who had run there two years before. In a fiery concession speech, she lit into the state party for leaving millions of dollars unspent in a weak get-out-the-vote effort.

"Don't be mad at the Republican Party," she said. "Be mad at our own, and don't stop fighting for our state, because we deserve leadership that cares about us."

Yet her campaign also never got the media attention that I assumed would put a spirited, liberal ex-beauty queen on the radar of national donors. Of course, if you were a pumped-up Democrat looking to open your wallet that year, you had options. There were many charismatic underdogs with inspirational backstories and stirring viral ads, in addition to the numerous Democratic challengers who actually *could* win their races that year and did.

In 2018, a record number of women were elected to Congress, and this was the irony: In its many fumbling ways, Miss America had been half-consciously trying for decades to help populate this cultural moment. All those evolutions the pageant had gone through since it was first confronted by the women's movement—the scholarship hype, the advocacy of causes, the concern for diversity, the eternal chase for respectability—had not just cultivated a new breed of pageant queen but contributed to an entire new template for young women trying to succeed in a world of older men. How to carry yourself, how to dress, how to project your voice to be heard.

But by the time the doors fully opened for women in politics, there were so many other women standing in the vestibule that no one needed a Miss America type to tackle the job anymore.

It wasn't just politics. It was all public life now. For so long, it had just been Miss America standing up there alone, the singular young woman upon whom the nation could focus its slightly unhealthy fascination with girls on the cusp of adulthood. Now and then there might be a White House daughter or a fleeting starlet to share the scrutiny. Yet for much of the twentieth century, Miss America had carried the gravitas of one who had been carefully vetted and judged as *the best,* whatever that meant—and that's what had made her so potent, so aspirational.

But now it didn't matter if Miss America was demanding that we take the ambitions of dynamic young women seriously. We already did, and now they were *everywhere*. In sports, in show business, in Silicon Valley, in civic life.

Beyoncé and Taylor Swift were multimillionaires and global influencers long before they hit the Miss America age max; Jennifer Lawrence won her Oscar at twenty-two. It was an era when a young woman might take the poise she'd gained in dance class to help her climb the corporate ladder, like Marissa Mayer at Yahoo, instead of getting a foothold in pageantry; when a throaty voice and preternaturally calm demeanor could help a smart twenty-six-year-old like Brianna Keilar land a CNN anchor seat, forget about a crown. Opportunities were everywhere they had not been before. Teenage girls won six-figure science prizes and it barely made the news anymore. A young woman no longer had to adopt a specific glossy style standard to command an audience of millions, as did anti-gun activist Emma González and climate-crisis oracle Greta Thunberg.

And the political world had settled upon its Miss America for 2018 anyway. She was also unusually young and beautiful and just as merrily combative as Mallory. She, too, had dared to skip the usual steps before running for Congress and could communicate with fluid hipness on social media and an energetic calm on TV. She pulled herself together with simple elegance—the jewel-tone shifts and tidy buns—that evoked the girlishly businesslike style perfected by the cause-championing Miss Americas of the 1990s and early 2000s. But Alexandria Ocasio-Cortez had probably never even given a thought in her life to entering a pageant.

Mallory, meanwhile, was an outlier: In the new century, more Miss Americas were actually pursuing the earnest career goals they'd professed to be interested in when they walked across that stage. Deidre Downs had become an obstetrician. Kim Aiken was an accountant. Angela Baraquio was a principal of a Catholic school in a working-class neighborhood of Orange County, California. There were roles for all that excess charisma in places other than in front of a microphone.

It didn't seem impossible, though, that Mallory would continue in politics—she seemed to like it on a gut level—but in a different way than a Bess Myerson or Phyllis George.

As I left her headquarters that night a week before the election, volunteers were pouring in to strategize and mingle. But Mallory was holed up in her office, a blanket around her shoulders, frowning at a computer screen.

She was updating her campaign website and checking the latest fundraising tally. This was politics, too, and someone had to do it.

13

"THERE SHE IS . . ."

Becoming Miss America: December 2019

Well, *this* wasn't so bad! Right?

There had been so much angst over the possibility of the pageant leaving New Jersey once again, and the idea of a casino in eastern Connecticut had seemed especially bleak. But now that everyone had convened at the Mohegan Sun for pageant week in December 2019, it was fine. More than fine. Clean, modern, well-appointed. No more navigating the Boardwalk on spike heels; even if you were staying off-site at a cheaper hotel, a free shuttle would dump you directly on the carpeted infinity of the casino complex, where you could find Vegas-y fine dining (a Bobby Flay, a Todd English) and decent shopping (did Atlantic City even *have* a Sephora?). And now the competition was in full swing. Who's ready for a little speed-painting? On the convention hall stage, Miss Kansas was wearing a slinky black jumpsuit—what else?—as she dabbed at a jumbo canvas to the beat of an inspirational spoken-word track about feminism—naturally!—and now she was rotating her finished work to reveal . . . a portrait of Ruth Bader Ginsburg.

LOL. I had to text my friends about this.

It didn't take long into night one of the preliminary competition for my notes to go off the rails. I had come here to chronicle what I recognized could be the final days of Miss America. Heroic efforts had kept it alive over the past twenty years, but the viewers and sponsors kept drifting away. The organization's tax filings had been recording losses in the six figures or more for most of the past fifteen years, and two years of strife had eroded the foundations of goodwill from the donors, rainmakers, TV partners, and others who had come to the rescue over the years. The signs of trouble were all around—the Christmas-week time slot, the last-minute announcement of judges and hosts, the scarcity of former Miss Americas on hand, and the number of tickets still available for Thursday night's finals. Not to mention the two rows of empty seats before me right now, only midway back from the stage. An usher dithered in the darkened aisle, trying to find the assigned seats on the comped tickets of a couple in sweatpants and knit caps who had apparently just wandered in from the casino floor.

No worries, the man told the usher: "We're only going to be here a few minutes anyway."

And yet the notes in front of me looked exactly like scratch pads from happier times—the girls' weekend trip to Las Vegas in 2013, or the one to Atlantic City in 1999, or even the old scrap paper I'd recently found from 1983, on which my sister and I had recorded our picks from the night we watched Vanessa Williams win.

> IA—*meh opera. Cute! Saucy*
> Okla—*too sexy? Jazz dance, in booties*
> HI—*played Grieg on piano, good*
> NC—*fun tap dance!*

If this was the end of Miss America, I might as well savor the final tournament.

So, here was my top five:

Miss Texas, Chandler Foreman, turned out to have a mesmerizingly husky voice to go along with the gap-tooth and the Afro and all her other intriguing texture. Also, a compelling story about enduring homeless-ness as a child. As Miss America, she said, she would "prove you don't have to come from a certain socioeconomic background." Her fans were wearing "Go With the 'Fro" shirts.

Miss Georgia, the spiky-haired Victoria Hill, turned out to have a powerful operatic soprano. And her singing costume—a sleeveless, midriff-baring take on a nineteenth-century European military uniform—revealed a ripped physique, if that still counted for anything. If nothing else, it marked her as a student of queenmaker Bill Alverson, who insisted his clients pump iron as if they still had to wear a swimsuit. "It subconsciously makes you work on your current events and everything else," he explained.

Miss Maine, Carolyn Brady, evoked an impish Sasha Obama, but all grown up and ready to join the foreign service; her cause was refugees. "With immigration being one of the most divisive and polarizing issues of today, we need a unifying voice," she said, gleaming like an Oscar statuette in gold sequins. "Miss America could be that voice." But I also loved the way she had ranted so indiscreetly in an Instagram video about a maddening new Miss America essay contest.

Miss Michigan, Mallory Rivard, was a vivacious Busy Philipps lookalike, already working an actual job teaching first grade, which gave her a real-world rootedness reminiscent of Kaye Lani Rae Rafko. "MI—good talker!" I wrote. But I also admired her thick-but-not-overdone eyebrows and her fuchsia pantsuit.

And of course, Miss Virginia. To my dismay, no one else was buzzing about Camille Schrier. But bless her, she was leaning in on this science thing. Many women here were headed into science careers—Camille hadn't even made the final five in competition for a special $5,000 STEM scholarship—but she remained on-brand, talking rapid-fire in her onstage interview about how little girls had dressed as her for Halloween, in lab coats and tiaras.

"Miss America needs to be someone that can educate every single person, no matter their background or education level, and be able to inspire them," she said on stage. She vowed to show the world that "not only can Miss America be a scientist, but a scientist can be Miss America."

For decades, the Miss America pageant barely let its contestants speak at all from the stage. Now they were making up for lost time. Evening gown had become an earnest wear-what-you-want Q&A; swimsuit was replaced by a TED Talk–style speech.

"Welcome to the digital world," Miss Nebraska intoned, "where everything you like, comment, share, or retweet becomes a part of your personal brand. A world of technology addiction and social validation. . . ."

She roamed the stage in a sleeveless red jumpsuit and black heels; her backdrop projection showed a hand wrestling a blob of ectoplasm from a laptop screen.

"My mission," she continued, "is to create a network of socially secure users. . . ."

Theoretically, this was all very useful. Entertaining? That was another question. With all this talking, though, we finally had a chance to glimpse the energy, the poise, the charisma that everyone knew was the special sauce of Miss America.

But then . . .

Turn the beat around
Love to hear the percussion . . .

. . . Miss Missouri came out juggling three batons all the way through a perfect forward flip. And I no longer cared what any of them had to say.

✦   ✦   ✦

Somehow baton twirling had become one of the enduring clichés of the pageant, and an unkind one at that—like the joke about all the girls in updos simpering that their greatest desire is for world peace.

Twirlers always made an outsized impression when they showed up, like Mary Lee Jepsen, the 1962 Top 10 finalist who kept her cool even when one of her flaming batons escaped her grip and skidded right up to the precipice of the orchestra pit. (She caught it in time. And the pageant quickly banned onstage combustibles.)

But its influence was overstated. No baton twirler had ever become Miss America. They rarely made it to the pageant anymore and almost never made it far enough to twirl on national TV.

Still, there was no denying that baton twirling and pageantry—rare fields of competition that had welcomed young women in mid-century America, a spotlight for girls to claim when they had so few others—shared a certain cultural DNA.

The fire chief of Elkhart, Indiana, is said to have crafted the first modern baton in 1927 when he cut down a pool cue for his drum majorette daughter. She needed a lighter mace to keep up with the boys who had taken up this mesmerizing stick-tossing routine, a callback to the rifle-spinning displays from European military parades.

American marching bands were awash in the sex appeal that would later belong to rock bands, so you can imagine the cachet of being the girl of the group. In the late 1930s, high-stepping majorettes beamed from magazine covers and movie screens, the ultimate cool-girl icon. Twirling surged during the postwar years when every town had a football team and a band and the need for someone to lead a parade. By the 1960s, so many girls were twirling that it became its own competitive sport, as cheerleading would, too, decades later. Yet because it was so popular—an affordable, blue-collar hobby—or perhaps because it was the domain of girls, it attracted snark, condescension, concern. In 1949, the year at least three baton twirlers competed at Miss America, nationally syndicated columnist Inez Robb bemoaned how majorettes, with their shimmying steps and short skirts, had gotten football "inextricably mixed up with vaudeville, if not burlesque."

Just a generation later, the 1972 passage of Title IX opened a world of other athletic opportunities for girls; by the end of that decade, twirling's ranks had been decimated. And yet the stale cliché of the baton-twirling pageant girl lingered. "Good Looks and Baton Twirling Are Not Enough to Capture the Tiara in Today's Beauty Pageants" was the headline some wit slapped on the top of a 1989 *L.A. Times* article, in which baton twirling was not mentioned at all.

No one who had seen Simone Esters twirl would ever consider baton "not enough."

The convention hall of the Mohegan Sun came alive, responding to her like no other act this night. Simone twirled through perfect aerials, she juggled batons with her elbow, she sent them spiraling thirty feet high and snatched them in sync with the music's pumping beat.

She was the real deal. This was not a talent you could fake your way through, like the pageant girls who take a crash course in piano and master exactly one song. Miss America might have lost all the best vocalists to *American Idol*, but Simone was at the top of her field—the acclaimed feature twirler for the University of Missouri's Marching Mizzou and second-best collegiate twirler in the nation.

There was a lot to like about Simone if you were wish-casting the perfect Miss America for 2020. She had a compelling backstory as a biracial child who had only recently reconciled with her long-absent dad. She had done good work as a mentor to middle-school girls. And there was her powerful athletic frame that she carried comfortably in her skimpy yellow dance costume—what better way to signal a split from the narrow beauty standards of the past?

Fearless, accomplished, strong, relevant, inclusive—all the buzzwords the new Miss America Organization had been promising to live up to.

Mostly, though, I just liked the *idea* of crowning a twirler. It was nostalgic, subversive, and overdue. If Miss America was going to demand respect, why not start by extending it to another community of female competitors who never got their due? It could be the perfect way to reconcile this institution's century of complexities, this business of celebrating women by way of judging them.

Obviously, everyone in the room had to be thinking what I was thinking:

Simone Esters is going to win.

✦   ✦   ✦

And now an important question for Abbie Kondel, Miss Washington.

"You told us you want to create a 'culture of tomorrow,'" said a businesslike judge glancing at a page through reading glasses. "What does that mean and how do you achieve it?"

They were no longer asking current-events questions at Miss America. The reason for this went back to the night in 2007 that a beautiful young woman from South Carolina stood on a stage in a shimmering gown and tried to answer a question about why so many Americans couldn't find the United States on a map. "I personally believe that U.S. Americans are unable to do so because, uh, some, uh, people out there in our nation don't have maps, and uh . . . ," Caitlin Upton began. It all went downhill from there. "I believe that our education, like, such as in South Africa and, uh, the Iraq, everywhere, like, such as, and I believe that they should, our education over here in the U.S. should help the U.S. . . ."

Caitlin's cataclysmic word salad was the most talked-about pageant moment of the decade, with 70 million mocking views on YouTube. And a dozen years later, it still cast a shadow over the Miss America pageant—even though it didn't even happen at Miss America! Caitlin was competing that night at Miss Teen USA. But who knew the difference anymore?

This made me sad. I loved the current-events questions. Yes, in part because they held the nail-biting potential for a Caitlinesque disaster—good TV, in other words. But the redeeming part was that Miss America women rarely melted down. The questions were impossible, all but demanding that these people-pleasers take a stand on a divisive issue, so the fun was watching them skate through the perils. In 2016, you had to admire the deft footwork of Miss New York finessing a question about Donald Trump: "I think that he's a bright reminder of how our country needs to come together. If you don't agree with his message, then it's time to decide where you stand in this debate. . . ." Indeed!

But the new pageant leadership wanted every beat of the competition to focus on a woman's *substance*. Which seemed to mean questions about *herself*.

"You said your dream role was to play Charlotte in *Charlotte's Web*," another judge was asking Miss Nevada. "Why did it mean so much to you?"

The onstage questions, in fact, were now all drawn from topics that had come up during the backstage interviews. Which meant that the judges were tossing softballs, inviting contestants to regurgitate some entirely too well-polished talking point.

"Tiara Pennington, Miss Alabama! You said in your interview that your friends say you're 'chill.' What is the advantage of being 'chill'?"

"I would have to say the greatest advantage to being chill is . . ."

My notes went dead.

Meanwhile, from what I had seen so far in these preliminary rounds, things weren't looking great for the dark horse I had bet on.

Camille's strength was talking. That's basically what her "chemistry demonstration," the thing that had won her Miss Virginia, the thing that got her booked on *Kelly Clarkson*, was all about. But she had won no prizes on night one, when she had competed in the very talky phases of interview and Q&A. And on night two, another credentialed woman of science was coming in fast along the inside rail: Shivali Kadam, the elegant Miss Oregon and semiconductor manufacturer, who was up on stage now, holding forth on the lack of diversity in the engineering professions. . . .

Important stuff, to be sure. But I was beginning to wonder how I had ever gotten hooked on the Miss America pageant. Until:

"Up next, clogging to '9 to 5' is Jordan Hardman, Miss Wyoming!"

Whew. At least there was still a talent competition. At least there was still a good old-fashioned clogger in a teal lamé jumpsuit with white fringe. And an exuberant hip-hop dance from Miss New Mexico. And Miss Louisiana daring to sing "I Will Always Love You," hitting every note without making the room cringe even once.

And now here was Chandler doing a flute medley of seventies pop songs, perhaps the most conventionally Miss Texas–ish thing we'd seen from her so far. And then Miss Idaho showing off her ceramics skills, of all things, on a pottery wheel, with moody lighting and the backing track of "Paint It Black" for a little performative flair. Different! And then also, of course, the usual array of pianists and Irish step dancers and comic monologists—some strong, some weak, just as always.

And that's what was suddenly feeling so off about the whole enterprise.

It wasn't all the talking. It was the talent. Or rather, the jarring collision of the two. On night one, Miss Washington had strolled the stage in a long blazer and pained expression, holding forth on drug addiction: "One friend told me she used meth to compensate for emptiness, unfulfilled desire, and a lack of love. . . ." Now on night two, she was pounding the boards and shimmying through her "power tap" routine to a funk-pop tune in a sparkling mini and a fierce ear-to-ear grin.

What on earth were we asking of these women now?

The mission of Miss America had gone so lofty—*preparing great women for the world, preparing the world for great women*—it was hard to justify keeping a spotlight on C-grade talent, beyond some strained notion of "well-roundedness" lifted from the elite-college admissions playbook.

And yet talent remained the most watchable portion of this show. Even when it was bad. Maybe especially.

It was the heart of this whole enterprise. Some women spoke of the bravery and confidence that swimsuit had required. But I could not watch talent without rooting for them, fearing for them.

Of course, the swimsuit competition had always been unfair, with the advantages conferred by genetics. But what was the real bungee jump: walking on stage in a bikini when you weren't born with Karlie Kloss's body, or walking out to sing "I Will Always Love You" when you weren't born with Whitney Houston's voice?

When it was her turn to perform, Camille hit all the same notes I'd heard before. ("Science is all around us! I've loved science since I was a little girl! . . . Now, you've probably seen a bottle of hydrogen peroxide . . .") So I was surprised by the muted response from the audience when her rainbow plumes erupted toward the ceiling. In Lynchburg, the room had hollered with surprise. But as a pageant savant explained to me, "Everybody's already seen it on YouTube."

The stunned reaction would come instead at the end of that evening— when the judges announced Camille as that night's talent winner.

✦   ✦   ✦

For the contestants, behind the scenes had always been the best part of Miss America.

Or so the class of 2019 had always heard. That's where generations of pageant girls had bonded with their own kind, had found their future roommates and bridesmaids and pen pals.

But in 2019, behind the scenes was where a beleaguered, possibly dying, institution's seams were beginning to show.

In snowy Connecticut, the contestants were shuttled from private meals to rehearsals to meetings and back to their rooms. There were no giddy outings, no concerts, no shopping trips, no swimming. Some had brought a wardrobe of sponsor-provided outfits with the hope of being photographed in them. But they were all dressed up with nowhere to go. The Miss America hostess committee—the fleet of Atlantic City volunteers who for decades had escorted contestants where they needed to go and tended to their needs, even through the Vegas years—had been quietly disbanded.

Some days the contestants found themselves just sitting for hours on the carpet of a conference room, waiting for the next thing. The experience, one Miss State told me, was like wandering into a store that was going out of business.

"I thought they would tell us, 'Look, we're broke—let's make the best of it.'" Instead, she said, everyone was pretending as if everything was normal.

It wasn't a *terrible* week; she made new friends, as she had hoped. "But was it better than holiday pay at Nordstrom Rack?" she added, mentioning the job she might have been working instead. "I would say seventy-five percent of it was not."

And yes, many were dumbstruck when Camille won talent. Not because they didn't think she had done a good job. But because they knew it was a trick any of them could have pulled off—in *addition* to their performing talents.

Clearly, they were working with an outdated rule book. The leaders of this pageant now sought to make every beat of the competition focus on a woman's substance, and Camille seemed to have intuited this before the rest of them.

I love science! No flute solo or tap dance would telegraph your brand so concisely, no matter how many years you'd put into it.

"She was playing a game," this Miss State told me, "that none of us had signed up for."

◆　　◆　　◆

Simone knew she would be in the finals of Miss America. She always had a sense of how things would land.

She had picked up baton twirling at age six, in an after-school program back home in western Pennsylvania, which was still baton country. "You stay with twirling, you're going to win a lot of trophies one day," her first coach said.

From early on, she had that intuitive sense of where she was, that if she threw her baton in the air and then danced around, she would still be in the right place to catch it when it fell.

So she knew where she stood with Miss America. Everything she had done had landed her in the right place. Her bootstrapping childhood, her volunteer work, her incredible athleticism, even her journalism major—Lord knows, Miss America could use some media strategy.

"Everything they're looking for," her local director had told her, "you have it."

And now there she was. And it was all happening at the speed of a tumbling baton.

✦   ✦   ✦

The 2020 Miss America pageant was moving so fast I could barely keep up with my notes. No sooner had the fifty-one contestants been introduced to TV viewers—live on NBC!—from the stage of the brightly lit Mohegan Sun arena than their ranks were cut to fifteen. Then boom, just like that, Mario Lopez, our host for tonight, was telling the audience that they were ready to cut the fifteen candidates down to seven. Even though no competition to winnow them had happened on air.

Fast, fast, faster. The traditionalists *hated* this. But it was the TV viewers who mattered. And Miss America dared not give them a second to pick up the remote.

I had only managed to predict eight of the Top 15 correctly. No Michigan or Oregon, despite them having claimed interview prizes—and wasn't that supposed to be the key to it all? No Miss Maine, either. At least Chandler, the gap-toothed Miss Texas, made the Top 15, but no further.

But Camille had made the Top 7. And so, thankfully, had Simone.

Here was something else the traditionalists hated: There were only three judges, a risky number that could allow whims to overwhelm consensus. But they had been promoted to an on-air stature on par with Bert Parks—or perhaps Simon Cowell.

"There's so much focus on empowering and giving extra support for our young girls," the singer Kelly Rowland, radiant in a deep-plunge gown and her own spotlight, was asking Miss Colorado, Monica Thompson. "Do you think that it's fair to our young boys?"

Not a bad question. Monica parried by sticking to her talking points about the need to support young girls and nodding confidently.

"So, acting is your biggest passion?" asked another judge, sitcom actress Lauren Ash. "Do you think it's more important to *act* the role of Miss America—or to be your most genuine self, even if that means showing flaws?"

"Oh, absolutely, being your most genuine self," Monica gushed. "Authenticity is everything!"

Sigh. In the new era of Miss America, it felt like the buzzwords were always escaping the marketing brainstorm and flying wild around the room. Again and again, I had heard the contestants tout their own "authentic moments" or their ability to be true to their own selves; outgoing Miss America, Nia Franklin, was on Instagram praising her would-be successors for being "so vulnerable, so polished." Of course, that was the essence of likeability—but to speak of it this way made it sound like "vulnerability" and "authenticity" were performative skills.

And maybe they were now. Miss America was beginning to feel like a sport where the skill you had to practice the hardest was "being yourself."

"Can you quickly describe yourself in one word?" Kelly Rowland asked another finalist. Ohhh, I knew the answer to this one. . . .

"Chill," Miss Alabama, Tiara Pennington, replied brightly. "Definitely 'chill'!"

In fact, there was only one truly chill contestant in the finals.

Miss Georgia, Victoria Hill, had a glow, and not all of it came from a spray bottle. She had piercing blue eyes and always looked as though she had just emerged from a good laugh. She was already a serious student of opera when the ladies from the Miss Cobb County pageant heard her singing at a fundraiser and chased her into the parking lot to recruit her.

The girl was *relaxed*. At twenty-one, she seemed like the grown-up in the room, and it wasn't just the sporty soccer-mom hair. She was speaking to the judges like they were peers. One of them, reality-TV regular Karamo Brown, asked her opinion on adoption agencies that refuse to work with single women or gays.

"No, *everybody* needs to adopt!" Victoria cheered, drawing applause. She had a warm, musical, enthusiastic voice. *"That's* the biggest problem in our world right now, that we don't have enough homes certified to foster. So we need everybody to open their doors and their hearts to love these children in need."

Camille, by contrast, seemed far more tightly wound than at the state pageant. Was it her look? In Lynchburg, she had loose, sexy hair and a cheerful display of décolletage; here, a prim chignon and necklines that hugged the clavicle. When Kelly asked her how she would handle "those who might make fun of Miss America," Camille made clear that self-deprecating humor was not part of the arsenal.

"I think that what I'm doing by being a woman of science in redefining what it means to be Miss America in 2020 is how I deal with those people," Camille began.

She was speaking very, very fast.

"Miss America is someone that needs to educate and be able to communicate with everyone and *that* is what I do as a woman of science." Her voice kept climbing and picking up pace.

"And we need to show that *Miss America* can be a *scientist*! And a *scientist* can be *Miss America*!"

◆　◆　◆

Only the Top 5 moved on to talent this year, and it all blew past in an instant. Each contestant was allotted a mere ninety seconds to perform—half the length of a generation ago.

Miss Oklahoma jazz-danced in a silver onesie that covered barely more ground than the swimsuits of yore. "For someone who started dancing recently, you done great," Karamo offered gently. Otherwise, nothing but reinforcement from these judges. Miss Connecticut, a childhood leukemia survivor, warbled an inspirational tune. "Because of your story, I felt the emotion," murmured Lauren.

Miss Georgia poured her years of training into her aria, and the judges enthused that it was "effortless." Camille's science routine: "Such an interesting idea!"

Simone took the stage. I nudged the two friends who had joined me for the finals: *This is the one!*

But as she began twirling, we realized something was wrong. Horribly wrong.

The music was pumping, and Simone was dancing—in the dark. The stage lights were impossibly dim. We could barely see her.

In the old days, a finalist would have had a chance to rehearse on the big stage before she went on national TV. But not in 2019, at a pageant fraying around the edges, shoehorned into a busy venue. The Miss America team couldn't get access to the well-booked arena before the big night and had to use a smaller stage for rehearsals and preliminaries.

Simone had warned that she needed to test the lighting to make sure she could see what she was doing. They had reassured her that she would be fine: This crew had lit Beyoncé! So she just asked for lighting that wouldn't blind her as she tried to eyeball her flying batons—and instead they made it so dark she couldn't see them.

She caught every one of them, though, because of course she did. But who could even tell?

✦   ✦   ✦

Another brutal elimination, and then it was down to three: Camille, Victoria, and Simone. All three would deliver their TED Talk–style presentation of their "social impact statement," or advocacy cause.

There was one last bit of weirdness.

It came after Victoria strolled the stage like a top-dollar motivational speaker, beseeching her audience to help foster kids ("When you *serve* and *love* and *invest* in children in foster care, you're changing their world!"), but before Camille blitzed through her talking points about pharmaceutical safety ("Did you know that every eight minutes, a parent or caregiver makes a medication error that affects a child?").

It came as Simone walked out to deliver her speech about mentoring children. With a glance at a nearby teleprompter, she realized that the game was already over.

She doesn't know if the line of script she saw was meant for the hosts or the judges. But it seemed to indicate that the top two finalists would be Virginia and Georgia. Leaving her to believe that it was already decided. Even before she competed in this latest round.

Simone went on to deliver her speech flawlessly. "I was just another black girl growing up in a single-parent home raised by her grandparents," she told the room, "and I *needed* a champion, and I *found* one!"

But the instant it was over, you could see her deflate. She turned and started to walk off stage, forgetting that she still had to take follow-up questions, until one of the judges called her back.

A sloppy bit of dummy text? Or a cruel spoiler alert? Simone had her theories about what she saw on the screen. But honestly, she didn't care. She had told her friends before the pageant that she wanted to be second runner-up. And that's exactly where she landed.

"I love my life right now," she said. "I knew if I won, my life would change forever."

✦   ✦   ✦

I had gone into this week boldly predicting, when no one else was, that Miss Virginia Camille Schrier could win it all.

And now we were down to two—Camille and Victoria. But Camille was disintegrating in front of my eyes. The rapid speech, the choking voice, the tensed neck, the pursed lips. My heart went out to her. This wasn't her game after all.

The final competition was another novel concept: Victoria and Camille would now debate each other.

"What do you believe the limit should be," Karamo was asking Victoria, "on what Miss America can or cannot post on social-media accounts while on the job as Miss America?"

Well, of course, Victoria replied, Miss America needed to be very careful online. "Something could be taken out of context, and so we need to use discretion and think ahead. Miss America is a representative of youth and adults everywhere."

Camille nodded. "I think Victoria's right." In fact, she added, Miss America should "consult with the organization" before posting anything.

"I absolutely agree," said Victoria.

The producers should have known they wouldn't get reality-TV fireworks from today's eager-to-please pageant girls—if that was the point of this segment. Or was the pageant leadership, still pissed about Cara Mund going public with her grievances, trying to extract an on-air loyalty pledge?

Lauren asked Camille about the rule prohibiting Miss America from being married or having children—should they keep it?

Yes. The single-ladies rule was "part of the homage to the tradition of Miss America," Camille said. "That is something that should be kept."

Victoria concurred even harder: "I think it's important she not be dating anyone, so she can be fully committed to her job."

"I absolutely agree," said Camille.

And now they were standing before the judges waiting for the final verdict, holding hands. Victoria looked like Wonder Woman up there, with her sculpted shoulders and a long, tanned leg peeking from her strapless royal-blue gown. Camille looked nervous as a cat. She swallowed hard. Her neck muscles tightened. She looked like she was about to throw up.

After all my years of trying to crack the formula, I had overthought it once again. How often had I placed all my chips on the girl with the most serious résumé, the most zeitgeisty issue, a certain kind of face? A Camille type, a Simone type. But that's not what this game had ever been about. And there was Victoria up there, radiating an energetic calm, radiating joy. Just to look at her could lower your blood pressure. Whatever "it" was, she had it.

Victoria Hill was going to win.

✦　　✦　　✦

Later, trying to understand what happened next, I paid $75 to stream a video compilation of the Top 15 finalists in the private ten-minute interviews conducted by the preliminary judges.

Camille was businesslike in a white pantsuit. She seemed to make good eye contact, leaning in toward the judges. She was a little revved up but not nearly as tense as she would appear on stage.

But this time, I was struck more by what she said than the way she said it.

"I got a really awesome amount of media attention," she was telling the judges. "It's been able to show that our world is currently craving a Miss America to be a woman of science. It's brought visibility to the organization . . . And that's actually turned into dollars."

Camille went on.

She spoke of Fortune 500 companies that "wanted to sponsor me because I'm a woman in STEM." She said she had "deals on the back burner"—from TV producers who wanted her to do a demo reel, from a toy company that wanted her to design science games for girls.

In fifty-one interviews that week, the judges would hear so many compelling backstories. Illness, poverty, underdog victories, family tragedies—the kinds of plot points that we now look for in the lives of the political candidates we decide to vote for or the celebrities we choose to like. Of course these stories flourished in pageants, too.

But Camille shared a personal narrative that would resonate with the people now charged with keeping the pageant alive.

"I had never competed in this organization until April," she told them. She had always wanted to be Miss America, but the swimsuit competition had always deterred her. "I had recovered from an eating disorder," she explained. "Swimsuit would not have been mentally or physically healthy for me." Now that the pageant had an entirely new mission, she'd felt empowered to join.

And then she took the conversation back to money—and how she could help bring it in.

"Because we need to do things to pay the bills here," she said. "We need to fund scholarships."

✦   ✦   ✦

No one sang "There She Is." As iconic as the song was, the songwriter's estate could drive a hard bargain, and some years the pageant just skipped it.

Victoria waved her hands in Camille's direction and managed to look absolutely delighted as she went in for a hug. First runners-up are good at that.

The next day's headlines would emphasize that a "biochemist"—Camille's undergraduate major—had been crowned Miss America, with a "science experiment for talent." I had to admit, that probably drew far more curiosity than "New Miss America Is Opera Singer" or "Baton Twirler Wins Pageant Crown" would have.

Of course Camille Schrier was going to win. She had said the things a dying institution wanted to hear and needed to believe—that a new generation of dazzling young women was out there waiting to enter the pageant, if it could just find the tweak to make it *relevant* again . . . that this time, one of those young women might be the one to throw it the lifeline it so badly needed.

Camille put her hands to her head, then her hands to her mouth. She bent nearly in half, like the wind had been knocked out of her. When she came up for air, her mouth stayed twisted in something like a cry, something like release. And then the confetti fell.

EPILOGUE

The Miss Americas sat around the dressing room in a circle as they waited for rehearsal. It was the first time many of them had seen one another in a year and a half or more. There was much to catch up on, and logistics to discuss. Such as: *What's everyone going to wear tonight?*

Kellye Cash made a pitch for formalwear. "Heather and Nicole just brought gowns," she said. "So I don't want them to be the only ones wearing gowns."

"If anyone needs a gown," offered Carolyn Sapp, "I can run back to my house. Because I have gowns *galore*. And I have been *every* size!"

It was a pretty good group they had pulled together, considering the short notice—a dozen of them already here this first day, ranging from Miss America 1962 Maria Fletcher, to Miss America 2018 Cara Mund. Others were set to make appearances during the weekend, including Lee Meriwether. This was Cara's first time among the former Miss Americas; the newest and youngest by more than a decade, she smiled but spoke only occasionally. "For the first hour I was just soaking it all in," she explained later. "Oh, that was me for my first five *years* as a former," Katie Harman reassured her.

Katie had put out the invitation just a couple weeks earlier. The Portland band Pink Martini, with whom she had often performed, was booked for a three-night stint at the Hollywood Bowl, and bandleader Thomas Lauderdale had a vision for an ensemble of Miss Americas to join them on a song. Katie first planned just to recruit those who lived in Southern California. But Thomas wanted a *lot* of Miss Americas. And once they heard the offer—a chance to sing, on stage, at the Hollywood Bowl, *together?*—she didn't have to twist arms.

Thomas was known for set lists that resuscitated neglected gems from many genres—lounge, jazz, big band, Brazilian samba, French pop, classical—and concerts infused with quirky guest stars. He wasn't deeply grounded in Miss America, but Katie could see why he was drawn to it. "It's old, it's a cultural phenomenon, it's something that's interesting to the public but very misunderstood."

So the Miss Americas were in a safe space with Pink Martini. This band wouldn't treat the crown like a punchline. And they would have a chance to ease their way back into one another's company, a year after the hostilities that had ruptured their shared world. They would soon be glad they did.

✦   ✦   ✦

Full disclosure: I've doubled back on our timeline a bit. It was in August 2019 when the Miss Americas met at the Hollywood Bowl, still four months before Camille Schrier's crowning moment. But the strife within the organization had disrupted the usual rhythms of the pageant cycle, and this was making it harder to find the usual closure, whether you were a contestant awaiting your shot at the title, a superfan awaiting the big show, or a former Miss America awaiting her next chance to commune with the sisterhood.

For many, this felt like a loss, and if that's hard to understand—well, remember what 2020 would soon do to the rest of the world's hobbies and rituals.

Camille started her reign with a spot on *Today* and a smattering of cable-news chyrons. But the media attention quickly died down amid a presidential impeachment and a highly eventful campaign. On New Year's Day, she won the kind of national-TV exposure that had eluded Miss America lately—a spot on the grand-finale float in the Tournament of Roses Parade, along with the band Los Lobos. While they performed "La Bamba," Camille held a bouquet of roses and waved. It could have been a picture out of 1960. But Miss America was a job, as everyone kept saying—and on this day, that's what the job called for.

The pageant's ratings had been a disaster: Only 3.6 million viewers had tuned in, a record low for a Miss America network broadcast. At the end of January, the pageant board of directors announced in a brief statement: "Regina Hopper is no longer with the organization." She had been volunteering in the job, working without pay, for two years. Mallory Hagan went back into politics—this time behind the scenes, as the Alabama communications director for the Mike Bloomberg 2020 campaign. But that lasted only as long as his presidential hopes, and she returned for a while to her prior work, handling public relations for the pageant. Her ex-boyfriend Brent Adams, whose email leak had turned an entire organization upside down, remained in place as its vice president and executive producer long after Gretchen Carlson's exit in 2019.

Two months into her new job, Camille was getting a lot of bookings, especially from science museums, a pageant insider told me. Then the coronavirus struck.

Camille was grounded. Local pageants and state pageants were canceled or postponed. In May came the announcement: There would be no Miss America pageant in 2020.

Some hoped that this pause would give the organization a chance to find its footing before its 2021 centennial—especially as the sudden end of the fundraising partnership with Children's Miracle Network raised doubts about the future of the scholarship reserves. Others feared this pause would snuff the last embers of enthusiasm that kept the thing alive. But the emotional upheavals of 2020 were just beginning.

In their regular group chats and Zooms that spring, the young women who had competed for the 2020 title were also discussing the racial-justice protests that were spreading across America. Some were concerned that others among them seemed less concerned, and they were most troubled by the reigning Miss America's public silence and her absence from their discussions.

Eventually, Camille wrote on Instagram that her silence signified that she was "listening, watching, hearing, and processing." This was an inadequate response, in the view of several of her pageant classmates, who chimed in to say she had let them down by not using her platform to support her black friends.

"I just don't understand," Brianna Mason, the first black Miss Tennessee, commented in the thread, "why it's so hard for people to simply say it: Black Lives Matter."

Camille eventually deleted the entire post. Meanwhile, the nine black women who had worn the Miss America crown, frustrated by the pageant's vague statement against racism, put out their own message: "We too have felt the pain of NOT BEING HEARD and even facing racism during our reign/year of service."

That same spring, in May 2020, Phyllis George died of the rare blood disorder polycythemia vera at age seventy. She had been sick for decades but had only ever hinted at it two years earlier when she asked her Miss America sisters to keep her on the board. That the woman whose groundbreaking career had validated the mystique of the Miss America title died so near the centennial and the fiftieth anniversary of her own crowning weighed heavily on the pageant world, a community forever intoxicated by nostalgia for its better days.

An even larger shock came in October of that year when Leanza Cornett died of a head injury at forty-nine, after slipping and falling at home. The fireball AIDS activist had had some rough years before that, including a devastating divorce. But she had made peace with the fact that the fame she once yearned for, that seemed within her grasp, had evaporated so quickly after her Miss America days.

"People are interviewing you, and you're on every radio show and TV show—and then it disappears, and it's someone else's," Leanza told me earlier that year. "I went through some PTSD over that: 'What just happened? Doesn't anyone else want to take my picture?' . . . But that's just reality. You move from space to space."

❖　❖　❖

They returned to the Hollywood Bowl that night dressed and ready for the show—evening gown, razzle-dazzle cocktail, dressy going-out pants, sparkly mother-of-the-bride, a range that would blend well on stage. Thomas greeted them backstage with warm double handshakes and a courteous enthusiasm ("Ah, yes, Jackie Mayer, Miss America 1963") that suggested he had been doing his reading. And then they sat in their circle again and waited.

They traded notes on breakups and kids, cancer scares and new jobs, the custom gowns some still owned and the regional theater productions some had starred in. Kellye caught them up on how sick she had been earlier in the year, her husband letting her ringing phone go unanswered until the day he saw Kaye Lani's name pop up, and *then* he picked it up.

"Well, Miss America was calling!" he explained to her later, and Kellye exclaimed, "But *I'm* Miss America!"

They laughed a lot. They joked about buying a Miss America château, or should that be a Miss America commune, or continuing-care facility? They avoided talking about the whole business with Gretchen. Things got loud, but in a good way. Laurie Lea Schaefer looked around the room and sighed happily.

"This is fun," she said.

This room reminded me of something, but I couldn't quite figure out what. I had interviewed celebrities in backstage settings, I had mingled through parties where everyone else was famous and more attractive than me, and this was that, but also something else. And then I realized:

It reminded me of book club.

It reminded me of my loud, smart, casual, all-female book club, and reunions of my all-girls high school, where we also had a tendency to get loud, even as we were all beyond trying to impress one another anymore. It reminded me of some ordinary group lunches with female journalists in the office break room that had managed to boost my afternoons. It reminded me of listening to my grandmother and aunt gossip about neighbors I never knew, but enjoying it so much anyway.

"We're just normal people," one of the Miss Americas had told me a few months earlier. But now they were getting up from their chairs to go do something I never could.

Katie introduced them on stage in reverse chronological order, the jumbo screen showing vintage photos of each woman in her crowned heyday as she walked out. Cara, Ericka, Nicole, Heather, Carolyn, Kellye, Elizabeth, Laurie, Vonda, Jackie, Maria. And then Katie took the first few bars of the song.

I am woman, hear me roar
In numbers too big to ignore
And I know too much to go back and pretend . . .

No, thank God, Pink Martini had not trotted them out there to sing "There She Is" before a packed house on this gorgeous Los Angeles summer night. Too on-the-nose for Thomas. The song was Helen Reddy's 1972 hit "I Am Woman"—an anthem of the women's movement back at a time when the movement saw Miss America as Public Enemy Number One.

'Cause I've heard it all before
And I've been down there on the floor
No one's ever gonna keep me down again . . .

The choice surprised me. I was too young to remember it from its radio days; by the time I first heard it in the eighties, it had gone from radical to cornball. "I am woman, hear me roar"? It had been memed and mocked to death, encumbered by kitsch. But listening to it now, it was almost unbearably lovely. This was a phenomenon the Miss Americas could probably relate to, and they all came in for the chorus.

Oh yes, I am wise
But it's wisdom born of pain
Yes, I've paid the price
But look how much I've gained
If I have to, I can do anything
I am strong
I am invincible
I am woman

I caught myself scanning their faces: Who looked like she was really having fun up there? Dumb question: They all did.

ACKNOWLEDGMENTS

I would not have known the joy of writing this book if not for the two key people who put the whole thing into motion. It took a call from a stranger, Julia Cheiffetz of Simon & Schuster, to suggest that a topic I had been thinking about for twenty-five years might make an interesting book. She had an idea for a new history of Miss America, and I can't thank her enough for it. Meanwhile, I had the good fortune to have met the man who would become Washington's best literary agent all the way back in college. For more than fifteen years, Howard Yoon had been encouraging me to write a book, and when the right opportunity appeared, he was there to show me how to do it. More than an agent, he's an editor, advocate, coach, and friend.

Thanks to Shayla Thiel Stern and Tripp Evans, the pageant-curious friends who joined me on that first trip to Atlantic City in 1996, when we walked into Convention Hall and discovered a new world. Thanks to the friends who helped turn the return trip into a tradition—including Anne, Caitlin, Laird, Adriana, Mary Beth—but especially Jennifer Mendelsohn and Linda Perlstein, who stuck with it the longest and poured as much mental energy as me into handicapping the field every year.

I'm grateful to my colleagues and bosses at the *Washington Post*, especially Liz Seymour and David Malitz, for their patience and accommodation as I took time off to write. And to Roxanne Roberts, a fellow celebrity chronicler, with whom I spent many instructive years batting around theories about the nature of charisma and stardom. And friends like Peter Kaufman, Gray Wheeler, and (once again) Linda Perlstein, who volunteered to read chapters-in-progress, shared their suggestions, and helped me feel like I was beginning to get somewhere.

So many people in the pageant world have been kind and helpful, but I am especially grateful to Freeman Stamper, officially the archivist for Miss California but really a one-man clearinghouse for Miss America history and knowledge. And anyone writing a book on any subject should call Geraldine Sealey. Her edits of my manuscript were brutal, clarifying, and lifesaving.

And then there were the Miss Americas (and a few women who were *almost* Miss America). I hope it's obvious from reading this book how generous they were with their time and their memories. Many of them, though, gave me more than just a great interview. They shared their more expansive thoughts about the pageant that broadened my understanding of this institution. They opened doors and made connections that helped me probe deeper. And they entertained me with late-night texts, old photos, and vintage YouTube clips that reconnected me with the joy of pageant culture whenever this project threatened to drag me under.

I will be forever grateful to Pamela Brown for introducing me to her amazing mother, Phyllis George, and ever more grateful to her and her brother, Lincoln, for sharing their thoughts with me at a sensitive time and helping to illuminate some of the hidden corners of her extraordinary life.

Many thanks to my parents, my brother and sister and their families, and my mother-in-law for helping to pick up the slack during this endless process. But most of all, to Bill and Eliza, for their love, support, infinite patience, and many great dinners.

NOTES

INTRODUCTION

xvii *They, too, had traveled from across the country* Karen Heller, "The Year Women Refused to Stay Silent, Tossed Their Bras and Redefined Politics," *Washington Post*, May 23, 2018, https://www.washingtonpost.com/national/the-year-women-refused -to-stay-silent-tossed-their-bras-and-redefined-politics/2018/05/23/bf37606e-495c -11e8-827e-190efaf1f1ee_story.html.

xviii *"forced daily to compete for male approval"* New York Radical Women, "No More Miss America!" August 22, 1968, New York City, archived at Redstockings.org, https://www.redstockings.org/index.php/no-more-miss-america.

xviii *These were women who had marched* Heller, "The Year Women Refused to Stay Silent."

xviii *"You could spend six months leafleting"* Robin Morgan as told to Allison McNearney, "I Was There: The 1968 Miss America Pageant Protest," History.com, September 7, 1968, https://www.history.com/news/miss-america-protests-1968.

xviii *"Up Against the Wall, Bert Parks"* United Press International, "Protesters Hit Miss America Pageant Goals," *Atlanta Constitution*, September 7, 1968, https://www .newspapers.com/image/398558784/.

xviii *a pile of brassieres* Heller, "The Year Women Refused to Stay Silent."

xviii *Bras in the trash can* Ibid.

xviii *"no more Miss America"* Ibid.

xviii *the brilliant stunt stole* Charlotte Curtis, "Miss America Pageant Is Picketed by 100 Women," *New York Times*, September 8, 1968, https://www.nytimes.com /1968/09/08/archives/miss-america-pageant-is-picketed-by-100-women.html.

xx *As many as eighty thousand young women* Valerie Bauerlein, "Miss America's Finances Uncertain as It Fights for Relevance," *Wall Street Journal*, August 3, 2018, https://www.wsj.com/articles/miss-americas-finances-uncertain-as-it-fights-for-rel evance-1533288600.

xxiii *A bright and forceful Alabama beauty* Adam Bernstein, "Yolande Betbeze Fox, a Miss America Who Rebelled, Dies at 87," *Washington Post*, February 25, 2016, https:// www.washingtonpost.com/national/yolande-betbeze-fox-a-miss-america-who-rebelled -dies-at-87/2016/02/25/32374126-dbda-11e5-81ae-7491b9b9e7df_story.html.

xxiii *"The leg shows were all right back"* Associated Press, "Talent Favored Before Leg

Show, Says Yolande," *Huntsville Times*, March 22, 1951, https://www.newspapers
.com/image/554865432/.

CHAPTER ONE

2   *"It is not about kneeling"* Des Bieler, "Miss America Contestant Asked About NFL
Protests, Wins Prize for Answer," *Washington Post*, September 7, 2018, https://www
.washingtonpost.com/news/early-lead/wp/2018/09/07/miss-america-contestant
-asked-about-nfl-protests-gets-prize-for-answer/.

5   *He was a statistician* Jay Woodruff, "Miss America Correctly Predicted," *Computerworld*, October 1, 1979, https://books.google.com/books?id=H7yqUDsDixAC&p
g=PA12.

5   *"I've watched the pageant on and off"* Associated Press, "'Weightlift' Label Costly,
Says Picker," *Asbury Park Press*, September 14, 1981, https://www.newspapers.com
/image/146034897/.

6   *He and a fellow NIU statistician* Woodruff, "Miss America Correctly Predicted."

6   *At the annual meeting* Ibid.

6   *And she most likely played the piano* Peter Mattiace, Associated Press, September 9,
1979, Nexis.

6   *"The Anatomy of Miss America"* Joseph McLellan, "Statistics Can Be Vital—That's
Why There's Strength in Numbers," *Washington Post*, August 16, 1979, https://
www.washingtonpost.com/archive/1979/08/16/statistics-can-be-vital-thats-why
-theres-strength-in-numbers/7d26e1da-e4b7-465f-9117-754db7e6fe84/.

6   *She was Miss Mississippi* Donald Flynn, "Beauty Is in the Eye of—Computer,"
Daily News (NY), September 5, 1979, https://www.newspapers.com/image/48408
2627/.

7   *"Miss Mississippi had a 25 percent chance"* Mattiace, Associated Press.

7   *He looked pretty much like* Marguerite Zientara, "There She Is, Miss . . . Oklahoma?"
Computerworld, September 15, 1980, https://books.google.com/books?id=rO0QAc
SJpQUC&pg=PA10.

7   *The pageant was viewed by* C. Gerald Fraser, "CBS-TV WINS RIGHTS TO
BEAUTY PAGEANT: Miss America Program, Carried by NBC for 11 Years, Draws
Consistent High Ratings," *New York Times*, December 13, 1976, https://www.ny
times.com/1976/12/13/archives/cbstv-wins-rights-to-beauty-pageant-miss-america
-program-carried-by.html.

7   *A year later, he doubled down* United Press International, "Professor, with Computer's Help, Says Miss Kansas Will Win Title," *St. Petersburg Times*, September 1,
1980, https://www.newspapers.com/image/319472157/.

8   *his computer told him Miss Oklahoma* Billy Cox, "Computing Miss America,"
Florida Today, September 16, 1980, https://www.newspapers.com/image/125006
142/.

8   *In 1981, he gave 6–1 odds* Associated Press, "Professor Makes Pick for Pageant," *Kansas City Star*, September 7, 1981, https://www.newspapers.com/image
/678379005/.

8   *"There's quite a bit of prejudice"* Associated Press, "'Weightlift' Label Costly, says
Picker."

8   *In 1982, his algorithms* Jim Fisher, "Miller Won't Go Public This Year," *DeKalb
Daily Chronicle* (IL), September 7, 1983, https://www.newspapers.com/image
/126808421/.

8 *George predicted Vanessa Williams's victory* Jim Fisher, "Professor Picks Miss New York as Next Miss America," *DeKalb Daily Chronicle* (IL), September 18, 1983, https://www.newspapers.com/image/126814772/.

8 *In 1987, George didn't see Kaye Lani Rae Rafko* Joyce A. Venezia, Associated Press, "Forecaster Stops Predicting Winner of Miss America Pageant," September 7, 1989, Nexis.

8 *Susan Akin* Anne McGrath, Associated Press, "Professor's Computer Picks Miss Mississippi to Win Miss America," September 5, 1985, Nexis.

8 *Kellye Cash* Joyce A. Venezia, Associated Press, "Odds Are on Miss Arkansas," *Hackensack Record* (NJ), September 6, 1988, https://www.newspapers.com/image /496756682/.

9 *"She deviated the least"* Penny Spar, United Press International, "Statistics Favored Miss Mississippi All the Way," September 15, 1985, Nexis.

9 *Patti Thorn of Arkansas* Venezia, "Odds Are on Miss Arkansas."

9 *Classical violin, a Convention Hall first* Joyce A. Venezia, Associated Press, "New Miss America Says She's An Overachiever," September 11, 1988, Nexis.

9 *"The interview counts for 30 percent"* Venezia, "Forecaster Stops Predicting."

9 *he was ready to move on to a more* Ibid.

9 *As early as 1970* Judy Klemesrud, "A Tradition on Way Out at Contest?" *New York Times,* September 10, 1970, https://www.nytimes.com/1970/09/10/archives/a-tra dition-on-way-out-at-contest.html.

10 *So in the 1980s* John Carman, "Miss America's Achilles' Heel," *San Francisco Examiner,* September 10, 1989, https://www.newspapers.com/image/461395688.

10 *"Miss America 2.0"* Gretchen Carlson, interview by Amy Robach, *Good Morning America,* ABC, June 5, 2018, https://www.goodmorningamerica.com/culture/story /miss-america-scrapping-swimsuit-competition-longer-judge-based-55638426.

15 *In 2014, the comedian John Oliver* "Miss America Pageant," *Last Week Tonight with John Oliver,* HBO, September 21, 2014, https://youtu.be/oDPCmmZifE8.

15 *Miss America later acknowledged* Amy Kuperinsky, "Following John Oliver Critique, Miss America Organization Shares Review of Scholarship Program," *Newark Star-Ledger,* September 4, 2015, https://www.nj.com/entertainment/2015/09 /following_john_oliver_critique_miss_america_shares.html.

CHAPTER TWO

19 *With minutes to go* Fred Rothenberg, Associated Press, "NFL Today Soap Opera Continuing," *Tampa Tribune,* December 3, 1980, https://www.newspapers.com /image/335658333/; Val Adams and George Maksian, "TV Scene: Schedule Drama on Last Days of Hitler," *New York Daily News,* November 26, 1980, https://www .newspapers.com/image/485775079/.

20 *she had even heard worse* Phyllis George, *Never Say Never: 10 Lessons to Turn "You Can't" into "Yes I Can"* (New York: McGraw-Hill, 2003), 130.

20 *old, unhappy business dealings* Bob Oates, "A CBS Sex Object? No, By George," *Los Angeles Times,* September 3, 1981, https://www.newspapers.com/image/387 473507/.

20 *bitterly intended to wound* Phyllis George interview, *ESPN 30 for 30: The Legend of Jimmy the Greek,* ESPN, directed by Fritz Mitchell, 2009.

21 *"I'd won the swimsuit competition"* "Phyllis Tells Pageant Story," *Denton Record-Chronicle* (TX), July 29, 1969, https://www.newspapers.com/image/27005312/.

21 *Her general understanding* Phyllis George oral history transcript, June 15, 2018, interview by Gaylon Finklea Hecker and Marianne Odom, Briscoe Center for American History at the University of Texas at Austin.

22 *"power posing"* Amy Cuddy, *Presence: Bringing Your Boldest Self to Your Biggest Challenges* (New York: Back Bay Books/Little, Brown and Company, 2015), 193–248.

22 *"that electric something flashes"* Norton Mockridge, United Features Syndicate, "Georgeous Phyllis George," *Baltimore Evening Sun*, October 4, 1976, https://www.newspapers.com/image/371805819/.

22 *most Miss America contestants boasted roughly the same* Nancy Etcoff, *Survival of the Prettiest: The Science of Beauty* (New York: Anchor Books/Random House, 1999), 192.

23 *Miss Americas may well exemplify this* Ibid., 145.

23 *"The face seems familiar"* Ibid., 149.

23 *we are more likely to help pretty people* Ibid., 45–48.

23 *"Ah jus' like to drink Dr Pepper"* Norton Mockridge, United Features Syndicate, *Scranton Tribune*, September 25, 1970, https://www.newspapers.com/image/529369478/.

23 *"The day he finally crawled out"* Associated Press, "Phyllis George '71 Miss America," *Fort Worth Star-Telegram*, September 12, 1970, https://www.newspapers.com/image/643088305/.

23 *"so deep a scoop of rocky road"* Robert Evans, *The Kid Stays in the Picture* (New York: Hyperion, 1994), 285.

24 *She did commercials for Jergens* Karen Kelley, "Ex–Miss America Keeping Busy Making Commercials," *Scrantonian* (PA), August 25, 1974, https://www.newspapers.com/image/529293526/; George, *Never Say Never*, 27.

24 *There was a guest spot* "Phyllis George Named Emcee of Miss Wisconsin Pageant," *Appleton Post-Crescent* (WI), June 14, 1973, https://www.newspapers.com/image/290733069/.

24 *Three years after giving up her crown* Shirley Davis, "Former Queens," *Quad-City Times* (IA), September 5, 1974, https://www.newspapers.com/image/300542610/.

24 *Bob's challenge in November 1974* Gary Deeb, "Wussler Gets Top CBS-TV Sports Post," *Chicago Tribune*, July 2, 1974, https://www.newspapers.com/image/383950803/.

24 *"the thrill of victory"* Mike Meserole, "Arledge Created Monday Night Football," ESPN.com, December 6, 2002, http://www.espn.com/classic/obit/arledgeobit.html.

24 *Bob saw no reason why CBS* Leonard Shapiro, "TV Sweepstakes: From Wrist-Wrestling to Barrel-Jumping, ABC and CBS Fight to Bring It to You" *Washington Post*, January 26, 1975, https://search.proquest.com/docview/146218032/D90EDBE413A04861PQ/1.

24 *"There just aren't enough of them"* Hubert Mizell, "New CBS Sports Czar Declares War on ABC," *St. Petersburg Times*, November 8, 1974, https://www.newspapers.com/image/318602322/.

24 *He telecast women's tennis tournaments* United Press International, "CBS to Air Women's Pro Tennis," *Tampa Times*, November 21, 1974, https://www.newspapers.com/image/332854465/.

24 *He invested in ladies' golf* "Ladies Championship Golf Slated to Air," *Staunton News Leader* (VA), December 22, 1974, https://www.newspapers.com/image/288295012.

25 *"At least one of them will be a woman"* Mizell, "New CBS Sports Czar Declares War on ABC."

25 *"living embodiment of 'Semi-Tough'"* Melissa Ludtke, "More Than a Pretty Face," *Sports Illustrated*, August 11, 1975, https://vault.si.com/vault/1975/08/11/more-than-a-pretty-face.

25 *"so damned pretty it makes your eyes blur"* Dan Jenkins, *Semi-Tough* (New York: Atheneum, 1972), 19.

25 *"I've dated athletes"* Skip Myslenski, "Phyllis: CBS's Gamble Is Paying Off," *Philadelphia Inquirer*, November 11, 1975, https://www.newspapers.com/image/173053409/.

25 *"I was out on the field"* Kathleen Maxa, "Phyllis Is a One," *St. Petersburg Times*, November 21, 1976, https://www.newspapers.com/image/332249364/.

26 *"She sure can't announce football"* United Press International, "Fans Blitz Jane Chastain," *Miami Herald*, October 14, 1974, https://www.newspapers.com/image/626839691/.

26 *"bundle of giggles"* Jerry Langdon, Gannett News Service, "TV Sports," *Fort Myers News-Press* (FL), February 23, 1975, https://www.newspapers.com/image/214088947/.

26 *"because they know this is the last leg"* Steve Wulf, "CBS Cashes Winning Ticket," *Fort Lauderdale News*, June 9, 1975, https://www.newspapers.com/image/231563026/.

26 *Did he want to get married* George, *Never Say Never*, 4–7.

26 *"Articulate and bright and clever"* William Carter, "CBS Goal: To Upstage ABC Coverage," *Baltimore Sun*, May 18, 1975, https://www.newspapers.com/image/377436492/.

27 *"You know, I enjoy sex"* Roger Staubach interview by Phyllis George, *NFL Today*, CBS, 1975, https://youtu.be/nXE8fs5yzfg.

27 *it made for great television* George, *Never Say Never*, 67-69.

27 *they bonded over a favorite face cream* Maxa, "Phyllis Is a One."

27 *"Phyllis is prettier than Frank Gifford"* Jack Craig, "Self-Promoters Become Boring," *Boston Globe*, October 27, 1975, https://www.newspapers.com/image/436638087/.

27 *"Don't you think, Brent?"* Maxa, "Phyllis Is a One."

27 *Phyllis became the first woman to cohost* Louise Montgomery, Knight Newspapers, "Phyllis Wins Over Critics," *Charleston Daily Mail*, January 16, 1976, https://www.newspapers.com/image/36807996/.

27 *"I'm not a feminist in any way"* Ibid.

28 *"Just not my style"* Paul Jones, "No Locker Room Interviews for Phyllis," *Atlanta Constitution*, August 8, 1975, https://www.newspapers.com/image/398611308/.

28 *threatening to sue stations* Marlene Sanders and Marcia Rock, *Waiting for Primetime: The Women of Television News* (Chicago: University of Illinois Press, 1988), 123–127.

28 *"She would have had more news"* Chan Lowe, "News and Televiews: Jive Alive," *Daily Oklahoman*, April 23, 1978, https://www.newspapers.com/image/452123113/.

28 *"one of the few bright spots"* Chan Lowe, "News and Televiews: Staff Changes at KOCO-TV," *Daily Oklahoman*, January 7, 1979, https://www.newspapers.com/image/452110970.

29 *ended up signing Barbara Mougin* Kay Gardella, "Phyllis Scores Super TD," *New York Daily News*, March 7, 1978, https://www.newspapers.com/image/483110403/.

29 *"This is a role for a personality"* Val Adams, "TV SCENE: She'll Carry the Ball for CBS Sports," *New York Daily News*, August 3, 1978, https://www.newspapers.com/image/492965909/.

30 *"happy talk"* Myrna Oliver, "William C. Fyffe; Helped Pioneer 'Happy Talk' on TV Newscasts," *Los Angeles Times*, October 21, 2000, https://www.latimes.com /archives/la-xpm-2000-oct-21-me-39955-story.html; Frank Sanello, "Eyewitness Sleaze: It's TV Sweeps Time in Los Angeles," *Chicago Tribune*, November 11, 1988, https://www.newspapers.com/image/388752740.

30 *"I knew these people wouldn't be knocking"* Steve Weinstein, "Alive, Well and Anchoring in L.A.," *Los Angeles Times*, January 29, 1998, https://www.latimes.com /archives/la-xpm-1998-jan-29-ca-13158-story.html.

30 *she started exploring movie roles* Lewis Grossberger, "Phyllis George, Benched but Still Buoyant," *Washington Post*, December 12, 1978, https://www.washingtonpost .com/archive/lifestyle/1978/12/12/phyllis-george-benched-but-still-buoyant/90f 72b1c-a81c-4cb8-98a3-ee137e957466/.

31 *"Ego was what motivated my perversity"* Evans, *The Kid Stays in the Picture*, 286.

31 *"I like to go to church on Sundays"* Myra MacPherson, "Phyllis George and the Kentucky Fried Candidate," *Washington Post*, March 15, 1979, https://www.washington post.com/archive/lifestyle/1979/05/15/phyllis-george-and-the-kentucky-fried-can didate/d0cf2cee-f757-4ff0-98fa-0c307fb8b36e/.

31 *On St. Patrick's Day 1979, they were married* Judy Klemesrud, "Phyllis George: Half of a Glamorous Campaign," *New York Times*, October 30, 1979, https://www.nytimes .com/1979/10/30/archives/phyllis-george-half-of-a-glamorous-campaign-taken -state-by-storm.html.

31 *"You remind me sooo much of Jack!"* George, *Never Say Never*, 38–39.

31 *"We are"* MacPherson, "Phyllis George and the Kentucky Fried Candidate."

31 *"I was not just a tea-and-coffee person"* Phyllis George interview by Leta Powell Drake, September 1984, https://www.youtube.com/watch?v=U9jZBbBLG7U.

32 *Whispers of a potential White House run* Marie Brenner, "John Y. and Phyllis—Kentucky-Fried Style," *New York Magazine*, November 16, 1981, https://books.google .com/books?id=LOQCAAAAMBAJ&pg=PA44.

32 *She also managed to go back to work* Fred Rothenberg, Associated Press, "State's First Lady Rejoins Her Old Gang on 'NFL Today,'" *Paducah Sun* (KY), October 6, 1980, https://www.newspapers.com/image/426240729/.

32 *"We all considered her like a kid sister"* George Puscas, "The Greek Says Tigers Are Dead," *Detroit Free Press*, April 28, 1977, https://www.newspapers.com/image /98841639/.

32 People *magazine recycled it for page filler* "Chatter," *People*, May 23, 1977, https:// people.com/archive/chatter-vol-7-no-20/.

32 *derisive comments with sexual overtones* George, *Never Say Never*, 130–131.

33 *photographed while pregnant* Phyllis George interview with Leta Powell Drake.

33 *Jimmy punched Brent in the jaw* John Carmody, "Jimmy the Greek Swings at Musburger in Post-Show Punchout," *Washington Post*, October 29, 1980, https://www .washingtonpost.com/archive/lifestyle/1980/10/29/jimmy-the-greek-swings-at -musburger-in-post-show-punchout/5bd2d164-f4b8-464f-beba-d123062c75e2/; Claudia Cohen, "Greek vs. Musberger: More on the First Ave. Shootout," *New York Daily News*, October 31, 1980, https://www.newspapers.com/image/486019976/.

33 *"Face that Launched a Barroom Brawl"* Ed Ryan, "Inglorious Finale Awaits Lame-Duck Congress," *Louisville Courier-Journal*, November 9, 1980, https://www.news papers.com/image/110446598/.

33 *Brent wearing boxing gloves* George, *Never Say Never*, 133.

33 *Years later, Phyllis would express sympathy* Paul Hendrickson, "The Losses of Jimmy the Greek," *Washington Post*, May 5, 1989, https://www.washingtonpost.com/archive /lifestyle/1989/05/05/the-losses-of-jimmy-the-greek/11ee675c-860c-4521-9bbe -aa8c774c3de1/; Leonard Shapiro, "Jimmy 'The Greek' Snyder Dies at 77," *Washington Post*, April 22, 1996, https://www.washingtonpost.com/archive/local/1996/04/22 /jimmy-the-greek-snyder-dies-at-77/86b847d7-fedd-4f50-ac46-ff4f5793a7fd/.

33 *She gave interviews letting it be known* Sy Ramsey, Associated Press, "Mansion, Promoting Crafts, Take Priority over TV," *Madisonville Messenger* (KY), March 5, 1981, https://www.newspapers.com/image/530920803/.

33 *She pointedly took a substitute-host gig* Tom Dorsey, "Good Morning, Where's Phyllis? Here, There—Almost Everywhere," *Louisville Courier-Journal*, April 3, 1981, https://www.newspapers.com/image/109478971/.

33 *And only then did she sign* Fred Rothenberg, Associated Press, "Greek Forced to Go to the Tapes as Phyllis Returns," *Asbury Park Press*, August 26, 1981, https://www .newspapers.com/image/146036076/.

34 *The Greek was relegated* Oates, "A CBS Sex Object?"

35 *Their push for zippier graphics* Sanders and Rock, *Waiting for Primetime*, 190–192; Tony Schwartz, "Inside CBS," *New York*, November 4, 1986, https://books.google .com/books?id=7McBAAAAMBAJ&pg=PA36.

35 *Diane Sawyer, the future broadcasting legend* Ed Joyce, *Prime Times, Bad Times* (New York: Anchor Books, 1989), 52–60.

35 *"already known to viewers"* Ibid., 398.

35 *"It's the last straw"* Sally Bedell Smith, "Phyllis George Hired by CBS News," *New York Times*, December 4, 1984, https://www.nytimes.com/1984/12/04/arts/phyllis -george-hired-by-cbs-news.html.

35 *a bright, casual gabfest* George, *Never Say Never*, 116.

35 *Never mind that Fernando* Lorenzo Lamas interviewed by Oprah Winfrey, *Oprah: Where Are They Now*, OWN-TV, August 2014, https://youtu.be/jRrXkwRL648.

35 *She was chided for cutting off* United Press International, "Pauling Cut Short by Phyllis George," *Los Angeles Times*, January 17, 1985, https://www.newspapers .com/image/390408955.

36 *"Jesus Christ Superstore"* Tom Shales, "CBS's Morning Glory: Phyllis George, Sunny Side Up for the A.M. News Battles," *Washington Post*, March 5, 1985, https://www.washingtonpost.com/archive/lifestyle/1985/03/05/cbs-morning-glory /af70ee4f-d901-408a-ac91-4d465ab38019/.

36 *"Am I the kind of person people"* Shales, "CBS's Morning Glory."

36 *And her anxiety about this would manifest* Joyce, *Prime Times, Bad Times*, 420–421.

36 *she found religion and came forward* David Remnick, "Making Right Her Wrong: Cathy Webb's Public Mission After Recanting the Rape Tale," *Washington Post*, April 17, 1985, https://www.washingtonpost.com/archive/lifestyle/1985/04/17/mak ing-right-her-wrong/ea57367c-fa9c-4436-b894-2eeff3cf8c2a/.

36 *When he was released from prison* Kevin Klose, "Governor Frees Dotson in Recanted Rape Case," *Washington Post*, May 13, 1985, https://www.washingtonpost .com/archive/politics/1985/05/13/governor-frees-dotson-in-recanted-rape-case /df355a2f-8ca0-4585-90be-c1b30809be97/.

36 *all three networks vying to book them* Edwin McDowell, "Key Figures in Illinois Rape Case Appear on TV," *New York Times*, May 16, 1985, https://www.nytimes .com/1985/05/16/us/key-figures-in-illinois-rape-case-appear-on-tv.html.

36 *Phyllis was pushed in front of a camera* George, *Never Say Never*, 139–140.

36 *she* had *been pestering her bosses* Joyce, *Prime Times, Bad Times*, 465.

36 *"go a different route"* George, *Never Say Never*, 139–140.

37 *"Perhaps only Phyllis George"* Tom Shales, "Invitation to a Hug: Phyllis George's Gaffe with Dotson & Webb," *Washington Post*, May 16, 1985, https://www.washingtonpost.com/archive/lifestyle/1985/05/16/invitation-to-a-hug-phyllis-georges-gaffe-with-dotson-38/abd90ef2-c53a-4785-947a-56709e47d0b5/.

37 *this was probably the first big rejection* Joyce, *Prime Times, Bad Times*, 497–498.

CHAPTER THREE

41 *"and entered into a series of liasons"* Shirlee Monty, *Terry* (Waco: Word, Incorporated, 1982), 120–128.

41 *a pamphlet extolling God's power of love* Ibid., 22–26.

42 *"I've never been a brunette"* Associated Press, "Miss America Begins Busy Year," *Tampa Times*, September 9, 1968, https://www.newspapers.com/image/329015341/.

43 *she divulged her hopes for becoming a pediatrician* "Kansas Girl Named Miss America," *New York Times*, September 12, 1965, https://www.nytimes.com/1965/09/12/archives/kansas-girl-named-miss-america.html.

43 *"I just love hamburgers"* Associated Press, "Was Chubby at 12, Says Miss America," *Hackensack Record*, September 13, 1965, https://www.newspapers.com/image/491158428/.

43 *"Non-Chubby Debbie Still Has Freckles"* *Tallahassee Democrat*, September 13, 1965, https://www.newspapers.com/image/244171828/; *San Rafael Daily Independent Journal* (CA), September 13, 1965, https://www.newspapers.com/image/74267065/; *Lansing State Journal*, September 13, 1965, https://www.newspapers.com/image/208342008/.

43 *"She's not the president"* "Miss Kansas and Miss A—Then Miss Diplomat," *New York Daily News*, September 14, 1965, https://www.newspapers.com/image/3938 12287/.

44 *"I'm a firm believer in authority"* Associated Press, "Miss America 'Can't Get Any Dates,'" *Asbury Park Press*, September 8, 1969, https://www.newspapers.com/image/144255307/.

44 *"The people who were voted into office"* *Time*, September 19, 1969, http://content.time.com/time/subscriber/article/0,33009,901459,00.html.

44 *"Down in Texas we don't hear much about it"* Anthony Burton, "Where Was Women's Lib?" *New York Daily News*, September 15, 1970, https://www.newspapers.com/image/395060957/.

44 *she had competed an astonishing three times* Associated Press, "Ohio Beauty Miss America," *Allentown Morning Call*, September 12, 1971, https://www.newspapers.com/image/281677191/.

46 *"I am a conservative"* Jean Crofton, "Miss America a 'Conservative & Proud of It,'" *New York Daily News*, September 13, 1971, https://www.newspapers.com/image/464592990.

46 *building that housed the ROTC supply closet* Robert D. McFadden, "College Strife Spreads," *New York Times*, May 8, 1970, https://www.nytimes.com/1970/05/08/archives/college-strife-spreads-over-100-schools-closed-and-up-to-350-struck.html.

46–47 *"Certainly the war should end"* Associated Press, "She Reigns," *Green Bay Press-Gazette*, September 13, 1971, https://www.newspapers.com/image/189355183/; Jonathan Takiff, "There She Goes in 2 Directions at Any Time," *Philadelphia Daily News*, October 26, 1971, https://www.newspapers.com/image/185010940/.

47   *"Every woman should have the right"* Ibid.

47   *"The first Miss America to give her views"* United Press International, "Laurie Speaks Up," *Philadelphia Inquirer*, November 25, 1971, https://www.newspapers.com/image/179918599/.

48   *beach resort in wool suits* Kathy Begley, "Pageant Melts Miss America's Plastic Image a Trifle," *Philadelphia Inquirer*, September 5, 1972, https://www.newspapers.com/image/179997813/.

49   *"My dad calls me a kooky freak"* Ewart Rouse, Associated Press, "Miss Vermont Sugar, Spice and Also a Bit of Salt," *Marysville Journal-Tribune* (OH), September 5, 1972, https://www.newspapers.com/image/328923686/.

49   *every reporter at the pageant put in a request* United Press International, "Miss Vermont's Views Shake Up Status Quo," *Camden Courier-Post*, September 6, 1972, https://www.newspapers.com/image/181291735/.

50   *Miss America's "plastic image"* Begley, "Pageant Melts Miss America's Plastic Image."

50   *"one of the few contestants"* Kathy Begley, "Miss Vermont Calls Rebel Role Scary," *Philadelphia Inquirer*, September 7, 1972, https://www.newspapers.com/image/180000084/.

51   *only six other women competed* "7 Girls to Enter State Pageant April 29," *Burlington Free Press*, April 21, 1972, https://www.newspapers.com/image/200325422/.

51   *the perfect "new generation" ambassador* "Is Miss Vermont Broke?" *Burlington Free Press*, August 14, 1972, https://www.newspapers.com/image/199176422/.

51   *"The best thing to happen to Atlantic City"* "There She Is: Ms. America," *Philadelphia Inquirer*, September 8, 1972, https://www.newspapers.com/image/180001126/.

51   *"I'm not really in it for myself anymore"* Begley, "Miss Vermont Calls Rebel Role Scary."

51   *she sobbed before taking the stage* Lorna Lecker, Gannett News Service, "Vermont Beauty Deeply Hurt," *Camden Courier-Post*, September 9, 1972, https://www.newspapers.com/image/181295325/.

52   *"used the stage presence"* "Meet New Miss America: You Whistle It Meeuwsen," *New York Daily News*, September 10, 1972, https://www.newspapers.com/image/465554783/.

52   *"Terry seems to have more personality"* Pamela Swift, "Keeping Up with Youth," *Parade*, January 14, 1973, https://www.newspapers.com/image/304960902/.

52   *"represent the changing values of our society"* Ed Wilcox, "Is It Miss . . . or Myth America?" *New York Daily News*, September 6, 1970, https://www.newspapers.com/image/395001091/.

52   *"an outright insult to women"* "Pageants Insult Women," *Daily Tarheel*, June 22, 1972, https://www.newspapers.com/image/71312403/.

53   *"We were badly used"* Joanne Omang, "'Not So Congenial Any More,'" *Washington Post*, February 20, 1973, https://search.proquest.com/docview/148506018/DDA23257475E4812PQ/1.

53   *"they can exploit me any day"* Kathy Begley, "Improved Miss America Image Sought by New Titleholder," *Philadelphia Inquirer*, September 11, 1972, https://www.newspapers.com/image/179992467/.

53   *"What qualifies Terry Meeuwsen"* Patricia Shelton, "Miss America Has Broken the

Mold—and Enjoys It," *Orlando Sentinel*, January 17, 1973, https://www.news papers.com/image/223049140/.

53 *Terry was on track to earn* Swift, "Keeping Up with Youth."

53 *nearly half a million* Peter Mattiace, Associated Press, "Seen but Not Heard: Miss America Avoids Disputes, Earns $65,000," *Louisville Courier-Journal*, August 18, 1977, https://www.newspapers.com/image/110307937/.

54 *Call me 'Ms.'! Miss America 1974*, NBC, September 8, 1973, https://youtu.be/ubB mp7ZBFi8.

54–55 *she was also a Republican* Associated Press, "Miss America a Cool Cookie," *Bridgewater Courier-News* (NJ), September 10, 1973, https://www.newspapers.com /image/222595361/; David Behrens, "Miss America: She's in It for the Money," *White Plains Journal News* (NY), September 19, 1973, https://www.newspapers .com/image/163209695/.

55 *"She's in It for the Money"* Ibid.

55 *"I don't feel like crying"* Associated Press, "Colorado Beauty Wins Miss America Crown," *Arizona Republic*, September 9, 1973, https://www.newspapers.com/image /117925143/.

55 *turn his investigatory powers* United Press International, "Watergate Probe Urged of Miss America Pageant," *Philadelphia Inquirer*, September 19, 1973, https://www .newspapers.com/image/180343915/.

55 *typical of Al Marks* Michael Kelly, "There He Is—Mr. Miss America," *Hackensack Record*, August 31, 1980, https://www.newspapers.com/image/493932742/.

55 *her dress, which plunged to the navel* Peter B. Flint, "Albert A. Marks Jr. Is Dead at 76; Ex-Chief of Miss America Pageant," *New York Times*, September 25, 1989, https://www.nytimes.com/1989/09/25/obituaries/albert-a-marks-jr-is-dead-at-76 -ex-chief-of-miss-america-pageant.html.

56 *"undue pressure" put on young women* Carlo M. Sardella, "Miss America Faces Ms.," *New York Times*, September 1, 1974, https://www.nytimes.com/1974/09/01 /archives/miss-america-faces-ms-miss-america-faces-ms-marks-warily-confident .html.

56 *Security guards escorted the state queens* Judy Klemesrud, "For Miss America '75 the Questions Get Tougher," *New York Times*, September 9, 1974, https://www .nytimes.com/1974/09/09/archives/for-miss-america75-the-questions-get-tougher -masters-degree.html.

56 *"Two coon tickets to Africa"* United Press International, *Orlando Sentinel*, September 5, 1975, https://www.newspapers.com/image/300924137/.

56 *Miss Washington was at odds* Associated Press, "Miss Washington Resigns," *Spokane Spokesman-Review*, November 14, 1974, https://www.newspapers.com /image/571160035; United Press International, "'Spying' on Beauty Claimed," *Spokane Chronicle*, November 15, 1974, https://www.newspapers.com/image/56 4801555/.

57 *"My body is the temple of God"* Klemesrud, "For Miss America '75."

57 *deliberately styled her hair* United Press International, "Runnerup Charges Miss America Aided by Pageant Officials," *Waxahachie Daily Light* (TX), September 8, 1974, https://www.newspapers.com/image/84185428/.

57 *"old-fashioned hairdo"* Associated Press, "Denton, Tex. Produces Another Miss America," *El Paso Times*, September 8, 1974, https://www.newspapers.com/image /434404888/.

58   *I believe in my own God"* Ellen Karasik, "There She Is—Against the Odds," *Philadelphia Inquirer*, September 8, 1975, https://www.newspapers.com/image/1730 06019/.

58   *refused to wade into controversial topics* Mattiace, "Seen but Not Heard."

58   *the churches wanted to book the pious Midwesterner* Ibid.

58   *"I don't mind speaking out"* Diane Dorrans Saeks, "Susan Perkins Plans to Make It as Singer," *Dayton Daily News*, September 21, 1977, https://www.newspapers.com /image/405522714/.

CHAPTER FOUR

65   *a mere four thousand in 2019* Bauerlein, "Miss America's Finances Uncertain."

65   *it was a competition* Carlson interview by Amy Robach, *Good Morning America.*

65   *"'Wow, this is for me'"* Gretchen Carlson interview, *Variety*, June 21, 2018, https:// variety.com/2018/film/news/gretchen-carlson-roger-ailes-lawsuit-bill-cosby -1202853904/.

69   *a solitary female guitarist* "Ragnar Kjartansso—Woman in E," Hirshhorn, https:// hirshhorn.si.edu/explore/ragnar-kjartansson-woman-e/.

71   *"We've heard from a lot of young women"* Catherine Thorbecke and Katie Kindelan, "Miss America Is Scrapping Its Swimsuit Competition, Will No Longer Judge Based on Physical Appearance," *Good Morning America*, June 5, 2018, https://www.goodmorningamerica.com/culture/story/miss-america-scrapping-swim suit-competition-longer-judge-based-55638426.

71   *"We never really messaged correctly"* Nancy Tartaglione, "Gretchen Carlson: Laments 'Highly Sexist' Reactions to 'Miss America' Swimsuit Nix—Cannes Lions," *Deadline.com*, June 22, 2018.

73   *"I'm going out on a limb"* Cara Mund interview by Hoda Kotb, *Today*, NBC, September 7, 2018, https://www.today.com/video/miss-america-cara-mund-speaks-out -pageant-leadership-needs-to-change-1314940483665.

73   *Gretchen strongly denied* Dino-Ray Ramos, "Gretchen Carlson Responds To Miss America Cara Mund's Bullying Claims," *Deadline*, August 18. 2017, https://dead line.com/2018/08/gretchen-carlson-cara-mund-miss-america-bullying-1202448262/.

73   *"52% OFF No Swimsuits No Ratings"* Lauren Carroll, "Anti–Political Correctness Group Claims Responsibility for Miss America Sign," *Press of Atlantic City*, September 7, 2018, https://pressofatlanticcity.com/missamerica/anti-political-cor rectness-group-claims-responsibility-for-miss-america-sign/article_f69b1973 -b6c2-5c21-9256-af8ac75c320f.html.

73   *"What that says is"* Tartaglione, "Gretchen Carlson: Laments 'Highly Sexist' Reactions."

74   *Cheslie Kryst cut a confident* Scott Sonner, "North Carolina Lawyer Cheslie Kryst Named Miss USA 2019," Associated Press, May 3, 2019, https://apnews.com/arti cle/dc364316d3ef4432934a132c26f04923.

74   *authored a fashion blog* Cristina Bolling, "Here's How Miss NC USA Cheslie Kryst Is Using Her Crown for Good in Charlotte," *Charlotte Observer*, April 23, 2019, https://www.charlotteobserver.com/living/fashion/article228731679.html.

75   *"stereotypes can be corrected"* Christine Emba, "Why Having Black Beauty Queens with Natural Curls Matters," *Washington Post*, May 9, 2019, https://www.washing tonpost.com/opinions/why-having-black-beauty-queens-with-natural-curls-mat ters/2019/05/09/1f98b4d0-7283-11e9-9eb4-0828f5389013_story.html.

75   *Miss North Carolina* "Peacock Crowned Miss NC 2015," *Sampson Independent* (NC), June 23, 2015, https://www.clintonnc.com/news/1586/peacock-crowned-miss-nc -2015.

75   the reigning Miss America's *attorney* Bolling, "Here's How Miss NC USA Cheslie Kryst Is Using Her Crown."

CHAPTER FIVE

77   *"They are bound to tell you"* Michael G. Fitzgerald and Boyd Magers, *Ladies of the Western: Interviews with Fifty-One More Actresses from the Silent Era to the Television Westerns of the 1950s and 1960s* (Jefferson, NC: McFarland and Company Inc., 2002), 144–145.

78   *Scholars of pageantry have reached back to antiquity* A. R. Riverol, *Live from Atlantic City: The History of the Miss America Pageant Before, After and in Spite of Television* (Bowling Green, OH: Bowling Green State University Popular Press, 1992), 2–4.

78   *P. T. Barnum tried to get a beauty contest* Lois W. Banner, *American Beauty* (Chicago: The University of Chicago Press, 1983), 255–256.

78   *a "Miss United States" contest* Frank Deford, *There She Is: The Life and Times of Miss America* (New York: The Viking Press, 1971), 108–110.

78   *the story has been debunked* Dave Hugg, "'Rehoboth Beauty Contest' Story Disputed," *Wilmington Morning News,* July 15, 1987, https://www.newspapers.com /image/159768284/; Emerson Wilson, "Miss Delaware Story Adds to Myths in State History," *Wilmington Morning News* (DE), October 2, 1971, https://www .newspapers.com/image/156493769/.

78   *no record of the event* Simon J. Bronner, *Following Tradition: Folklore in the Discourse of American Culture* (Logan, UT: Utah State University Press, 1998), 336– 337, https://www.jstor.org/stable/j.ctt46nqtf.12; Dan Klepal, "Historian Spearheads Hunt for Buffalo," *Sunbury Daily Item* (PA), April 12, 1993, https://www.newspa pers.com/image/482984365/.

78   *first spun the tale* "Pennsylvania Girl Winner of First Beauty Contest," *Danville Morning News* (PA), November 20, 1952, https://www.newspapers.com/image /552292069/.

78   *dissipated, small-time beauty contests were popping* Banner, *American Beauty*, 255–258.

78   *She was simply the best girl* Ibid., 250–254.

78   *The concept was reimagined in the U.S.* Elizabeth Leavitt, "Southern Royalty: Race, Gender, and Discrimination During Mardi Gras from the Civil War to the Present Day," https://civilwarwomen.wp.tulane.edu/essays-4/southern-royalty-race-gender -and-discrimination-during-mardi-gras-from-the-civil-war-to-the-present-day/.

79   *"Fall Frolic"* Riverol, *Live from Atlantic City*, 12–13.

79   *It quickly became the most popular beach* Nelson Johnson, *Boardwalk Empire: The Birth, High Times and Corruption of Atlantic City* (Medford, NJ: Medford Press, 2002), xiv, xxxiii, 59–60.

79   *the Frolic kicked off the first week* Riverol, *Live from Atlantic City*, 13–16.

79   *The festival organizers' great PR trick* Deford, *There She Is*, 112.

79   *American newspapers had been sponsoring these contests* Banner, *American Beauty*, 256–257.

79   *the new craze for photography* "Prints and Photographs: An Illustrated Guide," Library of Congress, https://www.loc.gov/rr/print/guide/port-2.html.

79   *sixty-one young women, each deemed the fairest* Helen Dare, "Pulchritude of Ameri-

can Beauties Enthralls City," *San Francisco Chronicle*, June 18, 1915, https://www
.newspapers.com/image/27621850/; "Los Angeles Hails Capital Girl as Queen,"
Washington Times, June 14, 1915, https://www.newspapers.com/image/79924163/.

79 *Ruth Maria Purcell of Washington, D.C.* Ruth Purcell, "'Madness of the Movies'
Is Decried by Prize Beauty," *Washington Times*, September 23, 1917, https://www
.newspapers.com/image/79950452/; "National Beauty Is Cured; Quits 'Movies,'
Returns to Old Job," *Washington Times*, December 19, 1915, https://www.newspa
pers.com/image/79989471/.

79 *the Fall Frolic put the whole* town Riverol, *Live from Atlantic City*, 17–18.

80 *a streamlined onesie ending at mid-thigh* Banner, *American Beauty*, 267.

80 *John Zehntbauer and Carl Jantzen* Riverol, *Live from Atlantic City*, 10.

80 *the place to go for a naughty good time* Johnson, *Boardwalk Empire*, 83–87.

80 *"I most certainly will not roll 'em up"* "Bare Knee Strike by Jailed Novelist Defies
Shore Rule," *Philadelphia Inquirer*, September 4, 1921, https://www.newspapers
.com/clip/27768644/louise-rosine-rolled-stockings-1921/.

80 *The winner would be announced* "Atlantic City Bows to King Neptune," *Philadelphia
Inquirer*, September 8, 1921, https://www.newspapers.com/image/170735463/.

80 *Two front-runners quickly emerged* "Maxim, as Neptune, Rules Fall Pageant at Atlantic City," *New York Tribune,* September 8, 1921, https://www.newspapers.com
/image/100111999/.

81 *just turned sixteen, and barely 108* "Miss Margaret Gorman Now 'Miss Washington,'" *Washington Herald*, August 29, 1921, https://www.newspapers.com/image
/76052151/; Deford, *There She Is*, 113.

81 *"She has a wealth of golden hair"* "High School Beauties Seek Honor of Becoming
Miss Washington," *Washington Herald*, August 1, 1921, https://www.newspapers
.com/image/76050587/.

81 *descended from* those *Lees of Virginia* Fitzgerald and Magers, *Ladies of the Western*,
141–145.

81 *Virginia later recalled that she was tapped* Ibid.

81 *"The decision of the judges"* "Maxim, as Neptune, Rules Fall Pageant."

81 *She had been deemed a "professional"* "'Miss Camden' Wins Three Prizes in Beauty
Tourney," *Camden Courier-Post*, September 9, 1921, https://www.newspapers.com
/image/479093460/.

81 *a dozen credits to her name* Virginia Lee at IMDb.com, https://www.imdb.com
/name/nm0498419/.

81 *no restrictions explicitly laid out* "Awaiting 'Miss Washington,'" *Washington Herald*, August 19, 1921, https://www.newspapers.com/image/76051687/; "Extra! All
About Contest to Find Most Beautiful Girl," *Camden Daily Courier*, August 19,
1921, https://www.newspapers.com/image/478773176/.

82 *"The ideal Christy girl"* "Virginia Lee Is Afraid to Come Home Because 11 'Fiances'
Are Waiting Here," *Muskogee Daily Phoenix and Times-Democrat* (OK), June 28,
1921, https://www.newspapers.com/image/608069246/.

82 *her mentor Howard was even* "Reelograms," *Pittsburgh Gazette Times*, April 27,
1919, https://www.newspapers.com/image/85629843/.

82 *Some news accounts suggested* "Parade, Revue and Ball End Pageant at Atlantic City," *New York Tribune*, September 9, 1921, https://www.newspapers.com
/image/87164853/; "Atlantic City Crowns District Queen Most Beautiful Girl in
America," *Washington Herald*, September 9, 1921, https://www.newspapers.com

/image/76052563/; "Washington Girl Is Beauty Winner," *Camden Morning Post* (NJ), September 9, 1921, https://www.newspapers.com/image/447338311/.

82   *"I won it hands down"* Fitzgerald and Magers, *Ladies of the Western*, 141–145.

82   *Change was in the air* Sarah Banet-Weiser, *The Most Beautiful Girl in the World: Beauty Pageants and National Identity* (Berkeley: University of California Press, 1999), 37.

83   *little Margaret Gorman was a tonic* Kimberly A. Hamlin, "Bathing Suits and Backlash: The First Miss America Pageants, 1921–1927," in *"There She Is, Miss America": The Politics of Sex, Beauty and Race in America's Most Famous Pageant*, ed. Elwood Watson and Darcy Martin (New York: Palgrave MacMillan, 2004), 35.

83   *"original bias"* Deford, *There She Is*, 114.

83   *she became . . . "Miss America"* "Scores of Beauties Headed for Pageant," *New York Times*, September 5, 1922, https://www.newspapers.com/image/20359782/.

83   *she blatantly tried to rebrand herself* Edward P. Beach, "Nature Scores Biggest Hit in Bathers' Revue," *Atlantic City Daily Press*, September 8, 1923, https://pressofatlanticcity.newsbank.com/doc/image/v2:14829479D3F9166E@NGPA-NJPAC-17B100976722D8C2@2423671-17609ACAB1B62B96@20-17609ACAB1B62B96@.

83   *"You have been my choice"* "15,000 People at Coronation of New Queen," *Atlantic City Daily Press*, September 8, 1924, https://pressofatlanticcity.newsbank.com/doc/image/v2:14829479D3F9166E@NGPA-NJPAC-17B100A2DF6D5080@2424037-17609AB934321BC6@18-17609AB934321BC6@.

84   *eighteen-year-old Norma Smallwood* Hamlin, "Bathing Suits and Backlash," 43.

84   *she cashed in her new title* Debbie Jackson and Hilary Pittman, "Throwback Tulsa: Ex–Miss America's Divorce Case Scandalized Tulsa in '34," *Tulsa World*, May 28, 2015, https://tulsaworld.com/news/local/history/throwback-tulsa-ex-miss-americas-divorce-case-scandalized-tulsa-in-34/article_e4a9da7b-6100-5004-9807-eb25366e163e.html.

84   *"Many of the girls who come here"* Deford, *There She Is*, 129–135.

84   *the town hosted only one* Ibid.

84   *try to work off the debt* Ibid., 151.

84   *Pageant organizers were looking to neutralize criticism* Angela Saulino Osborne, *Miss America, The Dream Lives On: A 75 Year Celebration* (Dallas: Taylor Publishing Company, 1995), 75–77; Susan Dworkin, *Miss America, 1945* (New York: Newmarket Press, 1987), 95.

84   *Her work organizing a festival parade* Dworkin, *Miss America, 1945*, 95.

85   *fly-by-night local pageants* Deford, *There She Is*, 149–153.

85   *Lenora banished from the judging* Ibid., 63.

85   *"I had to get Atlantic City to understand"* Osborne, *Miss America, The Dream Lives On*, 86.

85   *her Miss America duties negotiated down* Ibid.,140–146.

85   *Lenora formalized the mandate* Osborne,Ibid., 86.

85   *"be of good health"* Deford, *There She Is*, 250; Osborne, *Miss America, The Dream Lives On*, 100.

85   *Lenora latched on to it* Dworkin, *Miss America, 1945*, 98.

85   *"We can get the class"* Ibid., 96.

86   *chapters of the Junior Chamber of Commerce* Deford, *There She Is*, 154–155.

CHAPTER SIX

87   *Everyone called him B. Don* Shelby Hearon, "The Sweet Smile of Success," *Texas Monthly*, October 1974, https://www.texasmonthly.com/articles/the-sweet-smile-of -success/.

87   *he was a balding, roly-poly fifty-something* Jeannie Ralston, *The Unlikely Lavender Queen* (New York: Broadway Books, 2008), 19–20.

88   *"so flat it looks like a cat's"* Jeannie Ralston, "Mister Miss Texas," *Life*, September 1990.

88   *"you can't win the Kentucky Derby"* Lee Wohlfert-Wihlborg, "Here She Comes . . . ," *People*, September 19, 1983, https://people.com/archive/here-she-comes-vol-20-no-12/.

88   *there were eighty-two of them that year* V. R. Bowles, "Miss Texas Pageant Brings Together 82 Women with a Common Goal," *Tyler Morning Telegraph*, July 6, 1983, https://www.newspapers.com/image/588859961/.

88   *No. 69* Ralston, "Mister Miss Texas."

88   *The final straw came* Ibid.

88   *That's when he was forced out* Hollace Weiner, "Magness Resigns, Cites 'Black-mail,'" *Fort Worth Star-Telegram*, November 21, 1990, https://www.newspapers .com/image/642071940/.

88   *"she had one of the most fantastic bodies"* Associated Press, "Ambition Pays Off for New Miss Texas," *Victoria Advocate* (TX), July 11, 1983, https://www.newspapers .com/image/438705549/.

88   *the network of state directors* Lisa DePaulo, "The War Between the States," *Atlantic City*, September 1985, 51.

88   *"We'll come back again"* Debra Deitering Maddox, "The Miss America Pageant's Influence on the Self-Construction of Its 1985 Contestants," master's thesis, University of Nebraska at Omaha, 2001, 48, https://digitalcommons.unomaha.edu/cgi /viewcontent.cgi?article=2920&context=studentwork.

89   *"For better or worse"* Vanessa Williams and Helen Williams, *You Have No Idea: A Famous Daughter, Her No-Nonsense Mother, and How They Survived Pageants, Hollywood, Love, Loss (and Each Other)* (New York: Gotham Books, 2012), 280.

90   *A quarter of the nation's homes* "Emmy Awards Top TV Ratings," *New York Times*, September 12, 1979, https://www.nytimes.com/1979/09/12/archives/emmy-awards -top-tv-ratings.html.

90   *never again the estimated 80 million* Rubye Graham, "The Miss America Game," *Philadelphia Inquirer*, September 19, 1971, https://www.newspapers.com/image /180346080/; Ben Gross, "Tuning In TV, One Finds Things Have Not Changed," *New York Daily News*, September 28, 1970, https://www.newspapers.com/image /463781820/.

90   *"the most reassuring phrase is"* *Miss America 1980*, NBC, September 8, 1979, https:// youtu.be/kbleUxNI93Q.

90   *Someone knockin' on the do'oh* "Bert Parks Sings Wings," https://youtu.be/nJBDcb 7kq_g.

91   *the usually PR-savvy chairman* Associated Press, "'There He Goes,' Not Near for Bert Parks," *Asbury Park Press*, September 7, 1979, https://www.newspapers.com /image/144113590/.

91   *Al decided to fire Bert anyway* Phil Roura and Tom Poster, "Bert Parks Out as 'Mr. America,'" *New York Daily News*, January 3, 1980, https://www.newspapers .com/image/396385014/.

91   *Bert heard about his firing* Tony Kornheiser, "After 25 Years, It's Bye-Bye Bertie," *Washington Post*, January 4, 1980, https://www.washingtonpost.com/archive/life style/1980/01/04/after-25-years-its-bye-bye-bertie/213bc312-d647-48af-b4de -f3a4091851d9/.

91   *"We Want Bert" campaign* John Hicks and Noel Holston, "Marks and Parks Show Goes On Amid Fanfare and Fanfire," *Orlando Sentinel*, January 10, 1980, https:// www.newspapers.com/image/300899479/.

91   *81 percent wanted the pageant to stick with Bert* Ceci Vandervoort, "Back Him or Sack Him? The Votes Rolled in the Bert Parks Poll," *Orlando Sentinel*, January 20, 1980, https://www.newspapers.com/image/227520927/.

91   *"I wanted the show to be sexy"* Tony Kornheiser, "It's Runaway Roulette," *Washington Post*, October 16, 1981, https://www.washingtonpost.com/archive/lifestyle /1981/10/16/its-runaway-roulette/54546e80-50f6-43ba-95c9-2861c119f5b8/.

91   *"folksy," as Al described him* Ibid.

92   *"Thank you, Lord, I am walking!"* Associated Press, "New Miss America to Be Chosen Tonight," *Rocky Mount Telegram* (NC), September 8, 1979, https://www.news papers.com/image/337087386/.

92   *Ada Duckett "supersuit"* Anne McGrath, Associated Press, "Ada Duckett's Swimsuits Get Results That Count at Miss America Pageant," *Times and Democrat (Orangeburg, S.C.)*, September 13, 1986, https://www.newspapers.com/image /344368815/.

92   *"evil and evil only"* "Resolution on Beauty Contests," Southern Baptist Conference, 1926 Annual Meeting, https://www.sbc.net/resource-library/resolutions/resolution -on-beauty-contests/.

92   *She asked the Quaker wife* Mandy McMichael, *Miss America's God: Faith and Identity in America's Oldest Pageant* (Waco, TX: Baylor University Press, 2019), 90–91.

92   *church communities came to see pageants* Ibid., 97.

92   *swimwear-clad temples* Mandy McMichael, "Why Weren't Christians the Ones to 'Ruin' Miss America?" *Word & Way*, June 12, 2018, https://wordandway.org /2018/06/12/why-weren-t-christians-the-ones-to-ruin-miss-america/.

93   *"I do not consider my Bible"* Miss America 1965, CBS, September 12, 1964, https:// youtu.be/J5B-vMiLIXU.

93   *the pageant dropped the gag order* McMichael, *Miss America's God*, 112.

93   *By the end of the sixties* Ibid., 104.

93   *Her victory as a woman of faith* Ibid., 101, 119.

93   *A devastating car accident* Cheryl (Prewitt) Salem, *A Bright Shining Place* (Cathedral City, CA: Salem Family Ministries, 1989), 119–120; "Notes on People: The New Miss America Reflects on How She Got There," *New York Times*, September 10, 1979, https://www.nytimes.com/1979/09/10/archives/notes-on-people-a-prince-at -williams.html; Henry Mitchell, "Miracle of Beauty," *Washington Post*, September 10, 1979, https://www.washingtonpost.com/archive/lifestyle/1979/09/10/mira cle-of-beauty/3243bf4f-1666-491b-bbee-1bc0453d22e9/; Associated Press, "Miss America Will Give 10% of Fees to God," *Asbury Park Press*, September 10, 1979, https://www.newspapers.com/image/144117089/.

93   *the jaded pageant press corps* Frank Ross, "Being Miss America Is, to Her, Proof of Miracle," *Philadelphia Inquirer*, September 10, 1979, https://www.newspapers .com/image/174919560/.

93   *"It's the darndest thing"* Salem, *A Bright Shining Place*, 247.

93 *"It's my life"* Tony Kornheiser, "There She Is . . . ," *Washington Post*, September 8, 1980, https://www.washingtonpost.com/archive/lifestyle/1980/09/08/there-she-is /0918c472-a402-421e-83dd-a0d14ba12ea6/.

94 *"It's not right for me at this time"* Associated Press, "Oklahoman Miss America Sings of Her Ambitions," *Central New Jersey Home News*, September 8, 1980, https:// www.newspapers.com/image/317135960/.

94 *pop culture was still only just beginning* Elana Levine, *Wallowing in Sex: The New Sexual Culture of 1970s American Television* (Durham: Duke University Press, 2007), 5–6.

94 *A few of TV's hottest babes* Ibid., 137–157.

94 *Daisy Duke or Chrissy Snow* Ibid., 162–165.

94 *"An hourglass to make the Steuben people proud"* David Remnick, "The Winning Package," *Washington Post*, September 14, 1981, https://www.washingtonpost.com /archive/lifestyle/1981/09/14/the-winning-package/5727c2ea-30d8-4de2-8294 -26847a31040b/.

95 *"premarital sex is not for me"* Eleanor O'Sullivan, "Miss America Says the Contest She Won 'No Beauty Pageant,'" *Asbury Park Press*, October 13, 1981, https://www .newspapers.com/image/145948645/.

95 *neither would consider living together* Peter Mattiace, Associated Press, "New Miss America Is Ready to Be Seen and Not Heard," *Arizona Republic*, September 14, 1981, https://www.newspapers.com/image/120278570/.

95 *one-night fling with then governor Bill Clinton* Helen Kennedy, "Ex–Miss America Says Encounter Was Consensual," *New York Daily News*, March 31, 1998, https:// www.newspapers.com/image/478159628.

95 *apologized for fifteen years later* Associated Press, "Woman Alleging Tryst Apologizes to First Lady," *Washington Post*, April 25, 1998, https://www.washingtonpost.com/ archive/politics/1998/04/26/woman-alleging-tryst-apologizes-to-first-lady/1a4ea34f ee5f-4701-9a45-7b8bd779e976/.

96 *knowing from the start* Elizabeth Gracen, "The Battle for Miss America," *Flapper Press*, August 21, 2018, https://www.flapperpress.com/post/the-battle-for-miss-am erica.

96 *Trelynda's state directors had lavished* Vicki Jarmulowski, "There She Is . . . Behind All the Glamour, the Miss America Pageant Is Grueling for Contestants," *Pittsburgh Post-Gazette*, September 17, 1983, https://www.newspapers.com/image/897 89122.

97 *The UPI guy highlighted her* United Press International, "Pre-Pageant: Grins and Giggles," *Scranton Tribune*, September 12, 1983, https://www.newspapers.com/image /565166932/; United Press International, "Beauty Pageant Entrants Work Hard to Compete," *Petoskey News-Review* (MI), September 13, 1983, https://www.news papers.com/image/554964163/; United Press International, "They Keep Smiling When the Sweet Life Sours," *Alexandria Town Talk* (LA), September 14, 1983, https://www.newspapers.com/image/216139994/; United Press International, "Calorie Counting Part of Pageant," *Kilgore News Herald* (TX), September 16, 1983, https://www.newspapers.com/image/612416047/.

97 *"She has long, light-brown hair"* Dan Geringer, "Beauty and the Beast: Miss Georgia Would Rather Be Horsing Around with Her Pony," *Philadelphia Daily News*, September 14, 1983, https://www.newspapers.com/image/185942188/.

97 *another young woman* Robert Wade, Associated Press, "Flight Foul-Up Foils Pag-

eant Tradition," *Central New Jersey Home News*, September 10, 1983, https://www
.newspapers.com/image/321389686/.

97 *she figured: Why not?* Williams, *You Have No Idea*, 21–23.

97 *she still thought she would* United Press International, "She'll Try for Broadway
Before Miss America," *Rochester Democrat & Chronicle*, July 18, 1983, https://www
.newspapers.com/image/137850264/.

97 *the limited-run musical* Mel Gussow, "Stage: Revue of Burton Lane Songs," *New
York Times*, August 31, 1983, https://www.nytimes.com/1983/08/31/theater/stage
-revue-of-burton-lane-songs.html.

97 *getting fitted for sequins* Williams, *You Have No Idea*, 24–26.

98 *junior year abroad, graduation, Yale drama school* Ibid., 23.

98 *a petite powerhouse vocalist* Cece Lentini, "She Hopes to Fulfill Dream at Pageant," *Camden Courier-Post*, July 11, 1983, https://www.newspapers.com/image
/182117997/.

98 *Pictures of her goofing around with Muhammad Ali* Associated Press photo, "We're
So Pretty," *Fort Lauderdale News*, September 12, 1983, https://www.newspapers
.com/image/234083142/.

98 *"She looks like she's in the running"* "Atlantic City: Silver Strand, Golden Girls,"
Daily News (NY), September 13, 1983, https://www.newspapers.com/image/48927
7835.

98 *Vanessa, Suzette, Amy Keys* Associated Press, "4 Blacks, Hispanic Trying to Become
Miss America," *Asbury Park Press*, September 14, 1983, https://www.newspapers
.com/image/148500770/.

99 *"Rule Seven"* Osborne, *Miss America, The Dream Lives On*, 100.

99 *Al Marks would later try to raise doubts* Associated Press, "4 Blacks, Hispanic"; Deford, *There She Is*, 250.

99 *Jim Crow practices were upheld* Giles Wright, *Afro-Americans in New Jersey: A Short
History* (New Jersey Historical Commission, Department of State, 1988), https://
nj.gov/state/historical/assets/pdf/topical/afro-americans-in-nj-short-history.pdf.

99 *1922 Miss America contest* Deford, *There She Is*, 249.

99 *Mifaunwy Shunatona* Ibid., 250.

99 *Yun Tau Chee* Elaine Woo, "Yun Tau Chee, 73; Miss Hawaii of 1948, First Asian
in Miss America Pageant," *Los Angeles Times*, March 2, 2002, https://www.latimes
.com/archives/la-xpm-2002-mar-02-me-chee2-story.html.

99 *"due to the fact"* "Allow Indians in Beauty Event," *Huron Daily Plainsman* (SD),
April 25, 1948, https://www.newspapers.com/image/31322443/.

99 *"sometime in the middle 1950s"* Associated Press, "4 Blacks, Hispanic"; Deford,
There She Is, 250.

99 *it remained documented in the literature* "To Conduct Miss America Pageant
Here," *Green Bay Press-Gazette*, March 16, 1949, https://www.newspapers.com
/image/186306060.

99 *1955 in Utah* "Fair Board Sets Rules for Contest," *San Juan Record* (Monticello,
Utah), June 23, 1955, https://www.newspapers.com/image/544663971.

99 *organizers could set strict residency requirements* Deford, *There She Is*, 13.

99 *"the subject has just never come up"* Ibid., 21.

99 *Lenora had built a culture of aristocratic snobbery* Ibid., 248–249.

99 *"silver-spoonish"* Dworkin, *Miss America, 1945*, 90.

100 *"Betty Merrick"* Ibid., 92–93.

100 *black women won local crowns* Deford, *There She Is*, 250.

100 *in Sacramento* Associated Press, "Student, 18, Becomes First Negro Miss Sacramento," *Fresno Bee*, April 24, 1959, https://www.newspapers.com/image/7024 24581/.

100 *at Indiana University* Associated Press, "South Bend Negro I.U. Queen," *South Bend Tribune*, May 15, 1959, https://www.newspapers.com/image/515571148/.

100 *the first Miss Black America pageant* Robin Givhan, "'You Can Be Unapologetically Black': How Miss Black America Has Endured 50 Years," *Washington Post*, August 28, 2018, https://www.washingtonpost.com/lifestyle/style/you-can-be-un apologetically-black-how-the-miss-black-america-pageant-has-endured-50 -years/2018/08/28/91436a58-a49d-11e8-8fac-12e98c13528d_story.html.

100 *"we just have to wait"* Deford, *There She Is*, 251.

101 *"Pageant Hopeful Admits Surgery"* Associated Press, "Pageant Hopeful Admits Surgery," *Elmira Star-Gazette* (NY), September 13, 1983, https://www.newspapers .com/image/275542675; Associated Press, "Pageant Entrant Admits She Had Implants," *Asbury Park Press*, September 13, 1983, https://www.newspapers.com/image /148500437; Associated Press, "Nose Job for Miss Texas," *Rochester Democrat and Chronicle* (NY), September 13, 1983, https://www.newspapers.com/image /137897384/.

101 *"Mine is already there on the inside"* Ibid.

102 *"She had her nose done"* Associated Press, "Miss America Reportedly Improved Appearance with Surgery," *Galveston Daily News*, September 16, 1982, https://www .newspapers.com/image/17053935/.

102 *"what else" included a thigh tuck* Bill Kent, "This Miss, Too, Faced a Bit of Controversy," *Philadelphia Inquirer*, August 24, 1984, https://www.newspapers.com /image/174092926/.

102 *"deviated septum"* Arnold Rosenfeld, "Is Miss America Too Beautiful? It's My Deviated Septum, She Replies," *Dayton Daily News*, September 26, 1982, https://www .newspapers.com/image/411853312/.

102 *"treated me as though I was manufactured"* Denise Foran, "It Wasn't All Roses for Miss America," *Pottsville Republican* (PA), September 16, 1983, https://www.news papers.com/image/467190505/.

103 *the consensus was that she'd gotten too thin* Associated Press, "Ambition Pays Off for New Miss Texas."

104 *the feminist complaint that cosmetic surgery* Elizabeth Haiken, *Venus Envy: A History of Cosmetic Surgery* (Baltimore: Johns Hopkins Paperbacks, 1999), 270–275.

105 *"horrified to discover"* Associated Press, "Pageant Contestant Gives Photographers An Eyeful," *Longview Daily News* (WA), September 15, 1983, https://www.news papers.com/image/576715572.

106 *"Sparkles in the opening number"* Williams, *You Have No Idea*, 27.

107 *Lou Rawls or Gladys Knight* "Mays Landing Girl Scores for the Garden State," *Vineland Daily Journal* (NJ), September 16, 1983, https://www.newspapers.com /image/280997715/.

107 *a singing, acting, multihyphenate superstar* Lentini, "She Hopes to Fulfill."

107 *"A Miss America first?"* United Press International, "A Miss America First? 'Impressive' Black Candidates for Crown," *New York Daily News*, September 17, 1983, https://www.newspapers.com/image/488690183/.

109 *it all blew by* Miss America 1984, NBC, September 17, 1983, https://youtu.be /1U7HSZTLlNM.

110 *it was a parade of pencil bodies* Associated Press, "'Pageants Are a Priority in My

Life,'" *Galveston Daily News*, July 11, 1983, https://www.newspapers.com/image /13433295/.

112 *the slowed-down reinterpretation of it* Williams, *You Have No Idea*, 25–26.

113 *it was an honor* Ibid., 29.

113 *the panel had fought all week* Lisa DePaulo, "Miss America—Was Last Year's Voting Suspect?" *TV Guide*, September 2–8, 1989, 4–7.

113 *this would mean something* Williams, *You Have No Idea*, 30–31.

114 *The* New York Times *ran a wire story* Associated Press, "Miss New York Takes Title; Is First Black Miss America," *New York Times*, September 18, 1983, https://www .nytimes.com/1983/09/18/nyregion/miss-new-york-takes-title-is-first-black-miss -america.html.

114 *one of the biggest news events* Associated Press, "Black Leaders Praise Choice of First Black Miss America," *New York Times*, September 19, 1983, https://www .nytimes.com/1983/09/19/nyregion/black-leaders-praise-choice-of-first-black-miss -america.html.

114 *"Thank God I have lived long enough"* Ibid.

114 *The* Times *put Vanessa on Monday's front page* Susan Chira, "To First Black Miss America, Victory Is a Means to an End," *New York Times*, September 19, 1983, https://www.nytimes.com/1983/09/19/nyregion/to-first-black-miss-america-victory -is-a-means-to-an-end.html.

114 *"tells a new truth about social values"* "Larger Triumph, Larger Loss; American Beauty," *New York Times*, September 20, 1983, https://www.nytimes.com/1983/09/20/opin ion/topics-larger-triumph-larger-loss-american-beauty.html.

114 *burgeoning stars like Jennifer Beals* Jacqueline Trescott, "Her Crowning Achievement," *Washington Post*, September 20, 1983, https://www.washingtonpost.com /archive/lifestyle/1983/09/20/her-crowning-achievement/edb843b5-d7ad-4f42 -b96e-29aae0293af7/.

114 *Vanessa was cheered by the press* Jacqueline Trescott, "Miss America's Winning Ways," *Washington Post*, September 19, 1983, https://www.washingtonpost.com /archive/lifestyle/1983/09/19/miss-americas-winning-ways/1c191460-2db2-4bbd -97fc-03a85619dc92/.

114 *"I know it is not half"* Trescott, "Her Crowning Achievement."

115 *"I'm ambitious, I have a lot of drive"* Chira, "To First Black Miss America."

115 *"quotas" for minority hiring* Mary Thornton, "Affirmative Action Found To Diversify Work Force," *Washington Post*, June 20, 1983, https://www.washingtonpost.com /archive/politics/1983/06/20/affirmative-action-found-to-diversify-work-force/0e 8ae6d1-a234-4a1c-9459-de91a66e42c5/.

115 *"reverse discrimination"* Justin Gomer and Christopher Petrella, "How the Reagan Administration Stoked Fears of Anti-White Racism," *Washington Post*, October 10, 2017, https://www.washingtonpost.com/news/made-by-history/wp/2017/10/10/how -the-reagan-administration-stoked-fears-of-anti-white-racism/.

115 *"I was chosen because I was qualified"* Chira, "To First Black Miss America."

115 *Vanessa got to sit next to President Reagan* Williams, *You Have No Idea*, 48–51.

115 *Vanessa got asked out by Eddie Murphy* Ibid., 48.

115 *She headlined a $225-a-head* John S. Wilson, "Pop/Jazz Who's at Cabarets, What You'll Pay," *New York Times*, December 30, 1983, https://www.nytimes.com/1983 /12/30/arts/pop-jazz-who-s-at-cabarets-what-you-ll-pay.html.

115 *She stood alongside Coretta Scott King* Michael Szymanski, "King Celebration Is

Extended," *Atlanta Journal*, January 12, 1984, https://www.newspapers.com/image /399067376/; Vanessa Williams, "Astronaut Guion Bluford was the 1st African American to fly into space on my left and the majestic Coretta Scott King to my right with #MLK shining above. What an honor to be afforded monumental moments in my life," Instagram, January 18, 2021, https://www.instagram.com/p/CK NAh87BsSW/.

115–116 *"people approached her with a frenzy"* Lloyd Grove, "Vanessa Williams: Today's Attraction," *Washington Post*, October 19, 1983, https://www.washingtonpost.com /archive/lifestyle/1983/10/19/vanessa-williams-todays-attraction/0f94a812-42bf-4 7d5-95b2-326e6c02eb9a/.

116 *"It's about time"* Johnny Carson, *The Tonight Show Starring Johnny Carson*, NBC, September 20, 1983, CarsonEntertainmentGroup.com.

116 *"Are you ready to go to Harlem?"* Williams, *You Have No Idea*, 44.

116 *There were racist, threatening letters* Ibid., 32–33.

116 *"does not mean that nappy hair"* Courtland Milloy, "Black Beauty," *Washington Post*, September 22, 1983, https://www.washingtonpost.com/archive/local/1983/09/22/black -beauty/54a35e78-44fb-4dac-a237-79bd95f240ee/.

116 *vicious letters calling her a race traitor* Williams, *You Have No Idea*, 44–45.

116 *"What qualifies me to answer?"* Susan Chira, "First Black Miss America Finds Unforeseen Issues," *New York Times*, April 3, 1984, https://www.nytimes.com/1984/04 /03/nyregion/first-black-miss-america-finds-unforeseen-issues.html.

116 *she gave her handlers none of the headaches* William Goldman, *Hype and Glory* (New York: Villard Books, 1991), 277.

116 *Gillette, McDonald's, Nestlé, American Greetings* Chira, "First Black Miss America Finds Unforeseen Issues."

117 *But photos? They did exist* Williams, *You Have No Idea*, 7–9.

117 *her family was for many years* Ibid., 90.

117 *She had had boyfriends* Ibid., 7–8.

117 *she got pregnant* Ibid., 136–137.

117 *"They have no idea who you are!"* Ibid., 8.

118 *She did have a rebellious streak* Ibid., 1–4, 115.

118 *"highly sexualized"* Ibid., 104–106; Vanessa Williams interview, *Nightline*, ABC, April 17, 2012, https://abcnews.go.com/Entertainment/vanessa-williams-pens-book -molested-child-abortion-high/story?id=16151650.

118 *it also looks like a cruel long con* Williams, *You Have No Idea*, 11.

118 *he impressed her with his patter* Brad Darrach, "Vanessa Fights Back," *People*, September 10, 1984, https://people.com/archive/cover-story-vanessa-fights-back-vol-22-no -11/.

118 *The photos will stay with me* Williams, *You Have No Idea*, 12.

118 *"tearful to the point of hysterics"* Elizabeth Kastor, "Miss America Asked to Resign," *Washington Post*, July 21, 1984, https://www.washingtonpost.com/archive/lifestyle /1984/07/21/miss-america-asked-to-resign/864209e3-3482-4402-b042-9a21c5df ccca/.

118 *Vanessa recalled Al* Darrach, "Vanessa Fights Back."

119 *a puffy-sleeved print dress* Associated Press, "About People," *Miami News*, July 20, 1984, https://www.newspapers.com/image/302604535/.

119 *"Your lawyer needs you to call"* Williams, *You Have No Idea*, 39. Her book places this event on July 20, but wire photos and subsequent events establish it as July 19.

119 *The news of the photos was breaking* United Press International, "Miss America '84 to Appear Nude in 'Penthouse,'" *Nashville Tennessean*, July 20, 1984, https://www .newspapers.com/image/112319391.

119 *Vanessa endured one more night* Williams, *You Have No Idea*, 40.

119 *"The vestal virgins have just flown"* John Randazzo and Stuart Marques, "Miss America in Nudie Pix," *New York Daily News*, July 20, 1984, https://www.newspapers .com/image/488072489/.

119 *Vanessa was chased to the airport* Williams, *You Have No Idea*, 40–41.

119 *the magazine arrived* Ellen O'Brien and Eric Harrison, "Williams to Be Cut from Pageant," *Philadelphia Inquirer*, July 23, 1984, https://www.newspapers.com/image /176232374/.

120 *everything was in the lawyers' hands now* Elizabeth Kastor, "Miss America Says Photos Were Private," *Washington Post*, July 23, 1984, https://www.washington post.com/archive/lifestyle/1984/07/23/miss-america-says-photos-were-private /ffe8b9fd-1dd6-4539-b965-3a17c1f50c56/.

120 *"She knows that the photographs"* Associated Press, "Miss America Asked to Give Up Her Crown," *Asbury Park Press*, July 21, 1984, https://www.newspapers.com /image/145994306.

120 *"celebrates the whole woman"* Kastor, "Miss America Asked to Resign."

120 *"to good moral character"* Ibid.

120 *"If you don't draw the line here"* Associated Press, "Miss America Asked to Give Up Her Crown."

120 *"I can't even show them to my wife"* William Plummer, "Haunted by Her Past," *People*, August 6, 1984, https://people.com/archive/cover-story-haunted-by-her-past -vol-22-no-6/.

120 *the models would have had to understand* Tom Chiapel, photographs, "Here She Comes Miss America," *Penthouse*, September 1984, 67–75.

120 *editors boasted about how they had nobly refused* Plummer, "Haunted by Her Past."

121 *It had happened to Suzanne Somers* Lois Armstrong and Barbara Kleban Mills, "Naked Came the Danger to Suzanne Somers' Career, but She Had an Ace Up Her Sleeve," *People*, January 21, 1980, https://people.com/archive/naked-came-the-danger-to-suz anne-somers-career-but-she-had-an-ace-up-her-sleeve-vol-13-no-3/.

121 *It would happen the next year to Madonna* United Press International, "Nude Photos of a Model Madonna," July 11, 1985, https://www.upi.com/Archives/1985/07/11 /Nude-photos-of-a-model-Madonna/9490489902400/.

121 *72 percent of Americans* General Social Survey, NORC at the University of Chicago, https://gssdataexplorer.norc.org/trends/Gender%20&%20Marriage?measure= homosex.

121 *1944, Venus Ramey* Plummer, "Haunted by Her Past."

121 *Vanessa spent the weekend* Williams, *You Have No Idea*, 42–43.

121 *Milton, argued that resigning* Kastor, "Miss America Says Photos Were Private."

121 *"They'll have to pull the crown"* Plummer, "Haunted by Her Past."

121 *she gave two galvanizing interviews* Esther B. Fein, "Miss America Denies Giving Consent to Run Nude Photos," *New York Times*, July 23, 1984, https://www.ny times.com/1984/07/23/us/miss-america-denies-giving-consent-to-run-nude-pho tos.html.

121 *and the Associated Press* Dolores Barclay, Associated Press, "Penthouse Photo Use Disputed," *Hackensack Record*, July 23, 1984.

121 *"would believe in me"* Fein, "Miss America Denies Giving Consent to Run Nude Photos."

122 *Jennifer Lawrence, who in 2014* Sam Kashner, "Both Huntress and Prey," *Vanity Fair*, November 2014, https://www.vanityfair.com/hollywood/2014/10/jennifer-law rence-photo-hacking-privacy.

122 *her name would never be uttered* O'Brien and Harrison, "Williams to Be Cut from Pageant."

122 *she agonized until the last minute* Williams, *You Have No Idea*, 43.

122 *her long-term future* Darrach, "Vanessa Fights Back."

122 *they only had to rewrite a couple lines* Williams, *You Have No Idea*, 43.

122 *"the potential harm to the pageant"* Elizabeth Kastor, "Miss America Resigns Amid Controversy; Runner-Up Assumes Title," *Washington Post*, July 24, 1984, https://www.washingtonpost.com/archive/politics/1984/07/24/runner-up-assumes-title/4e31c625-b51a-42b1-8a15-8a566f4bacab/.

122 *more nude photos came to light* "Williams Reports She Posed for Other Nude Photographs," *New York Times*, August 24, 1984, https://www.nytimes.com/1984/08/24/nyregion/williams-reports-she-posed-for-other-nude-photographs.html.

122 *a different supposed fashion photographer* Williams, *You Have No Idea*, 14–16.

123 Penthouse *got those* Jonathan Michael Aaron, photographs, "Bound for Glory," *Penthouse*, January 1985, 53–60.

123 *Bob Guccione played the mustache-twirling villain* Kastor, "Miss America Resigns Amid Controversy"; Bob Guccione interview, *Penthouse*, January 1985, 66.

123 *if she joined the* Penthouse *PR team* Associated Press, "Miss America Asked to Give Up Her Crown."

123 *Vanessa sued the magazine* "Williams Reports She Posed for Other Nude Photographs."

123 *the mixed-up shame and horror of it all* Williams, *You Have No Idea*, 67–68, 106.

123 *she dropped the suit* Barbara Goldberg, "Former Miss America Vanessa Williams Dropped Lawsuit," July 3, 1986, https://www.upi.com/Archives/1986/07/03/Former-Miss-America-Vanessa-Williams-dropped-a-lawsuit-against/3830520747200/.

125 *the second runner-up* "State Pageant Director Backs Decision on Miss America," *Montgomery Advertiser*, July 22, 1984, https://www.newspapers.com/image/258021369/.

125 *"the best talent I've ever seen"* "Bill Cosby, Suzette Charles at the Sands," *Vineland Daily Journal* (NJ), February 29, 1984, https://www.newspapers.com/image/280918931/.

125 *her first Atlantic City headlining gig* Esther B. Fein, "Miss America Gives Up Her Crown," *New York Times*, July 24, 1984, https://www.nytimes.com/1984/07/24/nyregion/miss-america-gives-up-her-crown.html.

125 *she was in the running for a role* Shirley Eder, "Suzette Charles' Short Reign Is Long on Options," *Detroit Free Press*, September 13, 1984, https://www.newspapers.com/image/99113311/; Stuart D. Bykofsky, "'Cosby': A Chance for Family Fun," *Philadelphia Daily News*, September 20, 1984, https://www.newspapers.com/image/184728270/.

126 *"You're the new Miss America"* Kastor, "Miss America Resigns Amid Controversy."

126 *he fished his wife's 1959 crown* Michael E. Hill, "Gary Collins: Defending 'Miss America,'" *Washington Post*, September 9, 1984, https://www.washingtonpost.com/archive/lifestyle/tv/1984/09/09/gary-collins-defending-miss-america/b5dbcff7-e6b4-4ee7-bdaa-b76dc417c4ea/.

126 *Suzette seemed primed for stardom* Hank Gallo, "On the Set with Suzette Charles," *New York Daily News*, November 11, 1984, https://www.newspapers.com/image /488137197/.

126 *the techniques that thrilled middle-aged audiences* Alissa Wolf, "Suzette Charles Plugging Away, Wanting It All," *Asbury Park Press*, April 3, 1988, https://www.news papers.com/image/144153279/; Chuck Darrow, "Suzette Charles Finds Voice in Jazz," *Camden Courier-Post*, January 15, 1989, https://www.newspapers.com /image/183064923/.

126 *By 2002, she had stepped back* Marc Schogol, "From Miss America to 'Taxi Mom,'" *Philadelphia Inquirer*, January 6, 2002, https://www.newspapers.com/image/1992 30383/.

126 *"My commitment"* Kastor, "Miss America Says Photos Were Private."

126 *a "Utah" suit* Elizabeth Kastor, "Winning with Tradition," *Washington Post*, September 17, 1984, https://www.washingtonpost.com/archive/lifestyle/1984/09/17/win ning-with-tradition/39cdb1fb-9dc9-4567-9107-f4b89cb7f52f/.

126 *"there will be no problems this year"* Ibid.

126 *"I have lived my life above reproach"* Associated Press, "Utah Student Wins Miss America Title," *Sacramento Bee*, September 16, 1984, https://www.newspapers .com/image/622547948/.

127 *many critics interpreted Sharlene's words* Anne Taylor Fleming, "New Miss America Is 'Morally Smug,'" *Florida Today*, September 23, 1984, https://www.newspapers .com/image/125072770/.

127 *450 journalists swarmed Convention Hall* Elizabeth Kastor, "Putting On a Happy Face," *Washington Post*, September 12, 1984, https://www.washingtonpost.com/ar chive/lifestyle/1984/09/12/putting-on-a-happy-face/0e7fbd6e-de36-4b48-b2d0 -576292918190/.

127 *"unforeseen events"* Ibid.

127 *contestants found themselves quizzed* Maddox, "Miss America Pageant's Influence," 37–39.

127 *pleaded "no contest" to a shoplifting charge* United Press International, "Miss Ohio Busted; Arrested for Shoplifting in 1982," *Philadelphia Daily News*, September 11, 1984, https://www.newspapers.com/image/184725872/.

127 *Within a day of Miss Ohio's* Bruce McCabe, "In Atlantic City: Pageantry and Durability," *Boston Globe*, September 14, 1984, https://www.newspapers.com/image /437572381.

127 *"that's how great she is"* Elizabeth Kastor, "Pageant's Penthouse Plague," *Washington Post*, September 13, 1984, https://www.washingtonpost.com/archive/lifestyle /1984/09/13/pageants-penthouse-plague/911fdb14-fd2d-4c41-a94c-25d150372 991/.

128 *State directors started policing evening gowns* Maddox, "Miss America Pageant's Influence," 38–40.

128 *Miss Texas found herself the focus* Ibid., 37–38.

128 *B. Don had put out a press release* Associated Press, "'Sexist' Remark on Miss Texas Defended," *Austin American-Statesman*, September 8, 1984, https://www.newspa pers.com/image/363548084/.

128 *Many were convinced* Maddox, "Miss America Pageant's Influence," 40.

128 *"To then show their hands"* Ibid., 38.

128 *Debra Deitering* Maddox, the former Miss Iowa Ibid., 55–63.

128 *"I don't think I would do it"* Ibid., 41, 51, 64–65, 67–68.

129 *beginning at the age of six* Carla Hall, "America's New Miss . . . and the Near Misses," *Washington Post*, September 16, 1985, https://www.washingtonpost.com /archive/lifestyle/1985/09/16/americas-new-miss-and-the-near-misses/de8c1854 -5acf-4321-b856-e1f8554b95d1/.

129 *"virtual profession"* Stephen Chapman, "Miss America Rides a Rancorous Wave into the Future," *Chicago Tribune*, September 19, 1986, https://www.chicago tribune.com/news/ct-xpm-1986-09-19-8603100273-story.html.

129 *diet, exercise, rigorous interview prep* Hall, "America's New Miss."

129 *"I guess you could say I sacrificed"* United Press International, "Miss America Pursued Dream of Title," *St. Louis Post-Dispatch*, September 16, 1985, https://www .newspapers.com/image/140964650/.

129 *"The only thing I did was put Firm Grip"* "Susan Shares Secret of Swimsuit Helper," *Jackson Clarion-Ledger* (MS), September 18, 1985, https://www.newspapers.com /image/181700531/.

129 *Susan's body-mass index* Linda Massarella, "The Skinny on 'Sickly' Miss Americas," *New York Post*, March 22, 2000, https://nypost.com/2000/03/22/the-skinny-on -sickly-miss-americas/.

129 *"Pageants Hurt All Women"* Nikki Finke, "The Great Pretender: Always an Outsider, She Bluffed Her Way Inside a Beauty Pageant; That's When Things Got Ugly," *Los Angeles Times*, June 16, 1988, https://www.latimes.com/archives/la-xpm -1988-06-16-vw-6760-story.html.

129–130 *went on to become a legal scholar* Joe Patrice, "The Law Dean Who Became an Undercover Beauty Queen," *Above the Law*, May 16, 2016, https://abovethelaw .com/2016/05/the-law-dean-who-became-an-undercover-beauty-queen/.

130 *"To be the icon"* Finke, "The Great Pretender."

130 *"I was this title"* Billy Watkins, "Miss America's Sobering Truth," *Jackson Clarion-Ledger* (MS), October 14, 2000, https://www.newspapers.com/image/18416 7189/.

130 *finally made her Off-Broadway debut* Williams, *You Have No Idea*, 152.

130 *the critics were* meh D. J. R. Bruckner, "Stage: 'One-Man Band,' at South Street Theater," *New York Times*, June 26, 1985, https://www.nytimes.com/1985/06/26 /theater/stage-one-man-band-at-south-street-theater.html.

130 *"She looks sensational, too. . . ."* Michael Kuchwara, Associated Press, "'One Man Band' in Tedious New Musical," *Asbury Park Press*, June 24, 1985, https://www .newspapers.com/image/145193025/.

130 *She recorded a single* Williams, *You Have No Idea*, 157.

131 *"I can be some type of a role model"* 1996 Soul Train Music Awards, WGN America, March 29, 1996, https://youtu.be/t5gcj85ItDU.

CHAPTER SEVEN

137 *Gretchen Carlson had unexpectedly resigned* Amy Kuperinsky, "Gretchen Carlson Steps Down as Miss America Chairwoman a Year After Critics Called for Her Resignation," *Newark Star-Ledger*, June 5, 2019, https://www.nj.com/entertainment /2019/06/gretchen-carlson-steps-down-as-miss-america-chairwoman-a-year-after -critics-called-for-her-resignation.html.

138 *the pageant's contract with the state* Lauren Carroll, "Miss America Not Returning to Boardwalk Hall," *Press of Atlantic City*, April 11, 2019, https://pressofat lanticcity.com/missamerica/miss-america-not-returning-to-boardwalk-hall/article _dd722f6d-a544-5d4b-9e02-2afe748b6e68.html.

141 *Jogging took root in the late 1960s* Shelly McKenzie, *Getting Physical: The Rise of Fitness Culture in America* (Lawrence, Kansas: University Press of Kansas, 2013), 110.

141 *a younger generation embraced it* Ibid., 119.

142 *"The frame"* Richard Corliss, "Coming On Strong: The New Ideal of Beauty," *Time*, August 30, 1982, http://content.time.com/time/subscriber/printout/0,8816, 921278,00.html.

142 *the 1977 documentary* Pumping Iron McKenzie, *Getting Physical*, 160.

142 *"the powerful neck and shoulders"* Corliss, "Coming On Strong."

142 *Nautilus's newfangled weight-lifting machines* Charles Leerhsen, "The New Flex Appeal," *Newsweek*, May 6, 1985, Nexis.

142 *machines were too bulky and expensive* McKenzie, *Getting Physical*, 148.

143 *"cornball looks"* Stephanie Mansfield, "Tennessee Cashes In," *Washington Post*, September 15, 1986, https://www.washingtonpost.com/archive/lifestyle/1986/09/15/ten nessee-cashes-in/ef363445-a4f6-491e-bb12-cf19d7c59086/.

143 *lifting weights can lift moods* Brett R. Gordon, Cillian P. McDowell, Mats Hallgren, et al., "Association of Efficacy of Resistance Exercise Training with Depressive Symptoms: Meta-analysis and Meta-regression Analysis of Randomized Clinical Trials," *JAMA Psychiatry*, June 2018, https://jamanetwork.com/journals/jamapsy chiatry/article-abstract/2680311; Gretchen Reynolds, "Weight Training May Help to Ease or Prevent Depression," *New York Times*, June 6, 2018, https://www.ny times.com/2018/06/06/well/weight-training-may-help-to-ease-or-prevent-depres sion.html.

143 *the Zen-like power* Melissa Pandika, "Lifting Heavy Weights Is My Favorite Way to Help Manage My Anxiety," *Self*, November 16, 2018, https://www.self.com/story /weight-lifting-anxiety-management.

148 *"She acted like she knew"* Anne Groer, "Pageant Loss Painful, Liberating for Pesce," *Orlando Sentinel*, September 15, 1986, https://www.newspapers.com/image/229 626557.

148 *Miss Ohio demanded an audit* Charlotte Porter, "Ex-Rivals Rally to Cash's Defense," *Shreveport Times*, September 17, 1986, https://www.newspapers.com/image/2171 38401/.

148 *Miss Florida got booked on* Larry King Bob Morris, *Orlando Sentinel*, September 19, 1986, https://www.newspapers.com/image/229495965/.

149 *"That's a really good question"* Miss America 2016, ABC, September 13, 2015, https://youtu.be/8qNUs0Ut-rA. ·

CHAPTER EIGHT

159 *On their college campuses* "Total fall enrollment in degree-granting institutions, by level and control of institution, attendance status, and sex of student: Selected years, 1970 through 2010," *Digest of Education Statistics* (National Center for Education Statistics), Table 205, https://nces.ed.gov/programs/digest/d11/tables/dt 11_205.asp.

160 *"I want to be famous"* Jennifer L. Stevenson, "What's Driving Miss America," *St. Petersburg Times*, April 18, 1993, https://www.newspapers.com/image/324006020/.

161 *"Elbow, elbow, wrist, wrist"* Molly Gordy, "Broadway Cares to Laugh," *Newsday*, December 3, 1992, Nexis.

161 *"I can adhere to any school board's needs"* Ron Word, "Miss America Angry after

School Bars AIDS, Condom References," *Tallahassee Democrat*, June 3, 1993, https://www.newspapers.com/image/247166100/.

161 *writers across the country were hailing her moxie* Leanza Cornett interview by Harry Smith, *CBS Morning News*, CBS, June 4, 1993, Nexis.

161 *"Being Miss America certainly isn't about condoms"* Jennifer L. Stevenson, "Of Chastity, Womanhood, and Miss Americas Past and Present," *St. Petersburg Times*, May 2, 1993, https://www.newspapers.com/image/323961812/.

161 *a mesmerizing, hip-quivering Tahitian dance Miss America 1988*, NBC, September 19, 1987, https://youtu.be/MoyMJ57hNeI.

162 *"Death is a part of life"* Daniel LeDuc, "She Sleeps, She Wakes as Miss America," *Philadelphia Inquirer*, September 21, 1987, https://www.newspapers.com/image/169904078/.

162 *one reporter challenged Gretchen Carlson* Gretchen Carlson, *Getting Real* (New York: Viking Penguin, 2015), 1–2

162 *She fielded questions on hot topics* Joyce A. Venezia, "Miss America Begins First Leg of Journey Cross-Country," *Vineland Daily Journal* (NJ), September 21, 1987, https://www.newspapers.com/image/280811682/.

162 *"I have gone up to AIDS patients"* Ibid.

162 *"Stepford Wives"* Leonard Horn frequently made this comparison to the 1972 novel and 1975 film *The Stepford Wives*, about a suburb populated by interchangeably perfect housewives who turn out to be robots. Frank Ahrens, "The Master of Miss America," *Washington Post*, September 13, 1996, https://www.washingtonpost.com/archive/lifestyle/1996/09/13/the-master-of-miss-america/88dbc9c6-892d-44ff-9976-511171255558/.

163 *He just asked them questions* Venezia, "New Miss America Says"; Goldman, *Hype and Glory*, 290.

163 *"Oh, lunchtime"* Miss America 1989, NBC, September 10, 1988, https://youtu.be/TNnyELBuTPc.

163 *he instituted a flurry of rule changes* Nathan Cobb, "Next They'll Call Her Ms. America," *Boston Globe*, August 4, 1993, https://www.newspapers.com/image/440689737.

163 *opening the door to bikinis* Jacque Hillman, "Is Two Better Than One? For the First Time Since 1947, Miss America Contestants Can Wear Two Pieces," *Jackson Sun* (TN), July 24, 1997, https://www.newspapers.com/image/282252516/; Leonard Horn, "Two-Piece Swimsuits: It's HER Choice, Not Ours, Not Yours," *Morristown Daily Record* (NJ), July 30, 1997, https://www.newspapers.com/image/255648641/.

165 *her family contributed a six-figure gift* Kevin Simpson and Carol Kreck, "Beauty Queen: I Survived Incest—Marilyn Van Derbur Atler Reveals Childhood Horror," *Denver Post*, May 9, 1991, Nexis.

165 *"Beauty Queen: I Survived Incest"* Ibid.

165 *"Miss America Triumphs Over Shame"* Marilyn Van Derbur Atler, "The Darkest Secret," *People*, June 10, 1991, https://people.com/archive/cover-story-the-darkest-secret-vol-35-no-22/.

166–167 *her Hawaii Pacific University grade-point average* Valerie Helmbreck, "Meet the New Miss America," *Wilmington News-Journal*, September 16, 1991, https://www.newspapers.com/image/158635040/.

167 *"It got one"* Joel Achenbach, "The Ugly Truth: Beauty Reigns," *Washington Post*, September 16, 1991, https://www.washingtonpost.com/archive/lifestyle/1991/09/16/the-ugly-truth-beauty-reigns/a913eae4-d736-402c-a054-89c7ceac1e19/.

167 *"the other contestants promenaded"* Karen Heller, "A Turn for the Hotter," *Philadelphia Inquirer*, September 16, 1991, https://www.newspapers.com/image/175247565/.

167 *Carolyn crushed it in her interview* Leonard Horn said at the time: "The American public did not see this interview and she did extremely well." Jodi Duckett, "Beauty, Brains or Both: Despite Criticism, Pageants Remain Big Winners," *Allentown Morning Call*, November 24, 1991, https://www.newspapers.com/image/284010058/.

167 *"I don't know if you remember me . . ."* Karen S. Schneider, "Off-Again Romance," *People*, October 7, 1991, https://people.com/archive/off-again-romance-vol-36-no-13/.

167 *Donald and Marla broke up* Ibid.

168 *she blamed herself* Karen S. Schneider, "Breaking Away," *People*, October 14, 1991, https://people.com/archive/cover-story-breaking-away-vol-36-no-14/.

168 *she got the police involved* Ibid.

169 *"The problem was me"* Schneider, "Breaking Away."

169 *"Old Ex-Beau Troubles"* Stu Glauberman, "Miss America: Old Ex-Beau Troubles," *Honolulu Advertiser*, September 17, 1991, https://www.newspapers.com/image/266860674/.

169 *"stormy relationship"* Harold Morse, "Sapp Spat Reports Called Cheap Shot," *Honolulu Star-Bulletin*, September 18, 1991, https://www.newspapers.com/image/273673833/.

169 *her "troubled past"* "Troubled Past Haunts Newest Miss America," *Fort Myers News-Press* (FL), September 18, 1991, https://www.newspapers.com/image/216685881/.

169 *"the Miss America pageant may have gotten"* "There She Is, the Latest Gossip Topic," *Salem Statesman Journal* (OR), September 19, 1991, https://www.newspapers.com/image/198414193/.

169 *"Bikinis are very popular"* Valerie Helmbreck, "More Miss-takes?: Some Think Our New Miss America Might Have a Less Than Ideal Past," *Wilmington News Journal*, September 18, 1991, https://www.newspapers.com/image/158642312/.

169 *"sensationalism"* "Readers Disagree over Miss America Story," *Honolulu Advertiser*, September 20, 1991, https://www.newspapers.com/image/266862636/.

169 *Roseanne Barr, La Toya Jackson, or Suzanne Somers* Karen Heller, "Dirty Little Secrets, Courtesy of the Stars," *Philadelphia Inquirer*, October 6, 1991, https://www.newspapers.com/image/174936399/; "Playing the Abuse Gig," *Palm Beach Post*, October 3, 1991, https://www.newspapers.com/image/132184865/.

169 *Miss America's story could help other women* Susan Baer, "Women Increasingly Ready to Speak Out About Abuse, Family Violence," *Baltimore Sun*, September 21, 1991, https://www.newspapers.com/image/375929870/.

170 *"taking charge of her life"* Stu Glauberman, "Women's Groups, Lawmakers, Call Sapp Revelations Positive," *Honolulu Advertiser*, September 21, 1991, https://www.newspapers.com/image/266862948/.

170 *"A BATTERED MISS AMERICA"* Schneider, "Breaking Away."

170 *"we are today friends"* Glauberman, "Miss America: Old Ex-Beau Troubles."

172 *she had style mavens cheering* Genevieve Buck, "Pageant Comes Out a Winner with Stylish, Articulate Queen," *Chicago Tribune*, September 23, 1993, https://www.newspapers.com/image/241527812/.

172 *they traveled to Shawntel's introductory press conference* "Federal File: Enlisting Miss America," *Education Week*, September 27, 1995, https://www.edweek.org/education/federal-file-enlisting-miss-america/1995/09.

172 *"You probably brought more attention"* "New Miss America Plugs School to Work," *New York Beacon*, October 4, 1995, Nexis.

172 *She and her talk-show partner* Frank Rich, "There She Is," *New York Times*, September 20, 1995, https://www.nytimes.com/1995/09/20/opinion/journal-there-she-is.html.

173 *"I support Shawntel Smith"* Darlene Superville, "Miss America and the Senator: No Quarrel, They Say," October 11, 1995, *APNews.com*, https://apnews.com/article/24ffd626ddeef8f8715c233a48ad484d.

173 *Would the* Los Angeles Times *have bothered* Andrew D. Blechman, "Miss America Speaks Out for Education," *Los Angeles Times*, October 24, 1995, https://www.newspapers.com/image/157204357/.

174 *"As we struggle to alter our own body shape"* Shelli Yoder, "Pursuing a Crown of Perfection," *The Spire*, Fall 2002, 23–25, https://ir.vanderbilt.edu/bitstream/handle/1803/2157/spire_fall02_18-29.pdf.

174 *When she tried pageants again* Kate Shindle, *Being Miss America: Behind the Rhinestone Curtain* (Austin: University of Texas Press, 2014). 100–101.

174 *she held forth on the symbolic power* Ibid., 6.

177 *its ratings spike the following year* Deborah Starr Seibel, "Why Miss America Can't Get a Date: Eighty-Three-Year-Old Pageant Seeks Extreme Makeover," *Broadcasting & Cable*, January 3, 2005, https://www.nexttv.com/news/why-miss-america-cant-get-date-73467.

178 *The inevitable post-game whispers* "Miss Virginia Says Loss Was Unfair," *Newport News Daily Press*, May 5, 1995, https://www.newspapers.com/image/236371461/.

179 *Social psychologists and management consultants argue* Three books helped me understand these dynamics: John Neffinger and Matthew Kohut, *Compelling People: The Hidden Qualities That Make Us Influential* (New York: Hudson Street Press, 2013); Olivia Fox Cabane, *The Charisma Myth: How Anyone Can Master the Art and Science of Personal Magnetism* (New York: Portfolio/Penguin, 2013); and the aforementioned Amy Cuddy, *Presence: Bringing Your Boldest Self to Your Biggest Challenges* (New York: Back Bay Books/Little, Brown and Company, 2015).

180 *"She will be a Miss America"* "Crowning Achievement," *Boston Globe*, September 20, 1994, https://www.newspapers.com/image/440576775/.

180 *"Person of the Week"* Peter Jennings, *ABC World News Tonight*, ABC, September 23, 1994, Nexis.

180 *the medical community flipped out* Sandra Evans, "Miss America's Hearing Loss Story Disputed: Deafness Not Linked to Shot, Doctor Says," *Washington Post*, September 23, 1994, https://www.washingtonpost.com/archive/politics/1994/09/23/miss-americas-hearing-loss-story-disputed/af58a558-9f7e-4211-a859-4e77e92b79bb/.

180 *the pertussis vaccine had nothing to do* Daphne Gray, *Yes, You Can, Heather!* (Grand Rapids, MI: Zondervan Publishing House, 1995), 33–51.

180 *it was a bacterial infection* Evans, "Miss America's Hearing Loss Story Disputed."

180 *she favored hearing aids* Mark Bowden, "When Speaking Out Spurs Debate: Among the Deaf, Miss America Spotlights Controversy," *Philadelphia Inquirer*, September 24, 1994, https://www.newspapers.com/image/169524255/.

181 *protest the hiring of yet another* Nick Anderson, "Gallaudet Marks 'Deaf President Now,'" *Washington Post*, February 7, 2013, https://www.washingtonpost.com/local/education/gallaudet-marks-deaf-president-now/2013/02/07/17666740-6fdc-11e2-8b8d-e0b59a1b8e2a_story.html.

182 *"I practice what I preach"* Shindle, *Being Miss America*, 105–106.

183 *"I have lived my life to be ready"* Frank Ahrens, "America Calls on Miss Kansas for

Pageant Title," *Washington Post*, September 15, 1996, https://www.washingtonpost
.com/archive/politics/1996/09/15/america-calls-on-miss-kansas-for-pageant-title
/d805ab98-bac0-4829-9f8e-d38014beb138/.

184 *"She talks the talk"* Chris Burbach, "Newly Engaged Pair Upstaged During Mall
Trip," *Omaha World-Herald*, December 11, 1997, Nexis.

184 *his ex-wife filing an affidavit* C. David Kotok, "Judge Grants Divorce to Rep. Christensen," *Omaha World-Herald*, June 27, 1996, Nexis.

184 *"A man announcing that his betrothed"* Rainbow Rowell, "Christensen Said Too
Much," *Omaha World-Herald*, December 19, 1997, Nexis.

186 *Carolyn hosted a surprise birthday* Ben Wood, "Wood Craft: Miss America Sur-
prises Nuu," *Honolulu Advertiser*, January 19, 1992, https://www.newspapers.com
/image/264864593/.

CHAPTER NINE

189 *the organization announced there would be no more* Lauren Carroll, "Miss America Changes Competition Format Once Again," *Press of Atlantic City*, October 29,
2019, https://pressofatlanticcity.com/missamerica/miss-america-changes-competi
tion-format-once-again/article_d0ee803f-89bd-5c1f-bb4c-bbc4efa63b8f.html.

189 *"what you would wear to give a TED Talk"* Ibid.

190 *A Miss Virginia typically covered* Camille Schrier interview by Adam Martin, *Fit
Pharmacist*, August 12, 2019, https://thefitpharmacist.com/episode-73-miss-virginia
-brings-in-pharmacy-to-mind-your-meds-with-camille-schrier-miss-va-2019.

191 *she was reading two newspapers* Douglas R. Sease, *Wall Street Journal*, "Training to
Become Miss America," *Des Moines Register*, August 5, 1978, https://www.news
papers.com/image/128465403/.

192 *"This could be a million-dollar deal"* Ibid.

192 *"That's why I entered"* Ibid.

192 *"Maybe I worked too hard"* Emma Edwards, "Miss Georgia's Work Backfired at Pageant,"
Atlanta Constitution, September 12, 1978, https://www.newspapers.com/image/39
8645250/.

192 *some New York state pageant sherpa* Williams, *You Have No Idea*, 28.

193 *word began to get around* Jeff Chu, "The Pageant King of Alabama," *New York Times
Magazine*, July 18, 2014, https://www.nytimes.com/2014/07/20/magazine/the-pag
eant-king-of-alabama.html.

194 *Nina was Miss America* Miss America 2014, ABC, September 15, 2013, https://
youtu.be/OToP2THpuUw.

195 *Debbie Mosley became the top-rated anchorwoman* Karen Barr, "Interview: Deborah Brewer," *Raising Arizona Kids*, March 1, 1990, https://www.raisingarizonakids
.com/1990/03/deborah-brewer-1990-interview/.

195 *Shivali Kadam* Ellen Spitaleri, "Shivali Kadam Wins Miss Oregon Pageant," *Portland Tribune*, June 30, 2019, https://pamplinmedia.com/pt/11-features/432464
-341733-shivali-kadam-wins-miss-oregon-pageant.

196 *the first black woman* Associated Press, "New Miss Alabama Takes 'a Very Complex
Job,'" *Selma Times-Journal*, June 16, 1986, https://www.newspapers.com/image
/570044702/; Ken Roberts, "Alabama Student to Compete in Miss America Pageant," *Tuscaloosa News*, December 18, 2019, https://www.tuscaloosanews.com
/news/20191218/alabama-student-to-compete-in-miss-america-pageant.

196 *she collapsed to the ground* Chandler Foreman interview, CBS-DFW, July 5, 2019,
https://youtu.be/kJ48oXA5548.

196 *highlighted over the summer* "Scientist Who Won Miss Virginia with Experiment as Talent Vows to Bring Chemistry to Miss America Stage," *Inside Edition*, July 5, 2019, https://www.insideedition.com/scientist-who-won-miss-virginia-experiment-talent-vows-bring-chemistry-miss-america-stage-54209.

196 *the* Daily Mail Danielle Zoellner, "Stunning BIOCHEMIST Wins the Miss Virginia Pageant After Wowing Judges by Doing a Fun Science Experiment as Her Talent—as She Vows to Keep 'Breaking' Beauty Queen 'Stereotypes,'" DailyMail.com, July 3, 2019, https://www.dailymail.co.uk/femail/article-7209455/Biochemist-performed-science-experiment-talent-WINS-Miss-Virginia.html.

196 Kelly Clarkson Show "Jessica Alba Kelsea Ballerini, and Miss Virginia Explode a Nitrogen Cloud," *The Kelly Clarkson Show*, September 17, 2019, https://youtu.be/1Y0j3W-ET5c.

197 *"As someone who is breaking the boundaries"* Gabby Birenbaum, "Richmond Woman Performs Science Experiment Onstage, Wins Miss Virginia 2019," June 24, 2019, https://richmond.com/news/virginia/richmond-woman-performs-science-experiment-onstage-wins-miss-virginia-2019/article_e13f0473-1aa8-5c68-b11e-7ab8aac85c25.html.

197 *Camille herself, captured in Disney princess mode* Camille Schrier, *Fit Like a Queen*, fit-like-a-queen.tumblr.com, retrieved from Wayback Machine Internet Archive, https://web.archive.org/web/20130618172404/http://fit-like-a-queen.tumblr.com/.

198 *the public-facing Camille* Essence Cosmetics, retrieved from Wayback Machine, https://web.archive.org/web/20150520042443/http://essence.brewery.ws/stylist/camille-schrier/.

198 *"I am thrilled to finally announce"* Camille Schrier, Instagram, January 31, 2015, https://www.instagram.com/p/yiwN-RB59E/.

198 *the professional-caliber makeup sessions* Camille Schrier, Instagram, March 8, 2015, https://www.instagram.com/p/z-mWPfh5y9/.

198 *her photo highlighted* Big10Tens, http://michigan549.rssing.com/chan-16678883/latest.php.

198 *"You were like a celebrity"* Comment, "What I learned in Engineering School is . . . ," fit-like-a-queen.tumblr.com, retrieved from Wayback Machine Internet Archive, https://web.archive.org/web/20150920090423/http://www.fitlikeaqueen.com/2014/10/what-i-learned-in-engineering-school-is.html#comment-form.

198 *she was struggling socially* Schrier interview, *Fit Pharmacist*.

198 *"I am succeeding here"* Camille Schrier, "What I learned in Engineering School is . . . ," *UM Engineering*, October 17, 2014, https://umengineering.tumblr.com/post/100244965570/the-admirable-difficult-bittersweet-realization.

199 *"PLEASE seek help"* "The Pressure of Perfection: My Story," fit-like-a-queen.tumblr.com, retrieved from Wayback Machine Internet Archive, https://web.archive.org/web/20160220104231/http://www.fitlikeaqueen.com/.

CHAPTER TEN

202 *"the first reality TV"* James Hibbard, "Makeover for Miss America; Recast as Multipart Reality Show, Probably for Cable," *Television Week*, February 21, 2005, Nexis.

202 *Despite the trepidation* Sam Haskell, *Promises I Made My Mother* (New York: Ballantine, 2009), 131–132.

202 *"Your sequins are burning my retinas"* Miss America: Reality Check, TLC, 2008, https://youtu.be/WmXvGqlvBz8.

203 *"Miss America will be a new type"* Ibid.

203 *"It's for strippers"* Heather Svokos, "Pageant Contestants Given Dose of Reality," *Fort Worth Star-Telegram*, January 4, 2008, https://www.newspapers.com/image/65 1822594/.

204 *the new archetype in girl culture* Peggy Orenstein, "What's Wrong with Cinderella," *New York Times*, December 24, 2006, https://www.nytimes.com/2006/12/24/maga zine/24princess.t.html.

205 *Whiteman headed to a business meeting* Deford, *There She Is*, 193; Osborne, *Miss America, The Dream Lives On*, 106.

205 *On the Boardwalk* Don Rayno, *Paul Whiteman, Pioneer in American Music, 1930–1967, Volume 2* (Lanham, MD: Scarecrow Press, 2009), 291–292.

206 *twenty-one-year-old Evelyn Ay* Donald Kirkley, "Look and Listen," *Baltimore Sun*, June 2, 1954, https://www.newspapers.com/image/374847903/.

206 *Pops also had a side gig* Rayno, *Paul Whiteman*, 267.

206 *the local gas company executive* "Wathen to Head Shore Pageant," *Philadelphia Inquirer*, December 6, 1953, https://www.newspapers.com/image/177693204/; "Hugh Wathen; Rite Thursday," *Hackensack Record*, December 17, 1963, https://www .newspapers.com/image/491625538/.

206 *2.3 percent of households* James L. Baughman, *Same Time, Same Station: Creating American Television, 1948–1961* (Baltimore: Johns Hopkins University Press, 2007), 31–32, 43–46, 51–53.

206 *the coaxial cable* Ibid., 5–6, 88.

206 *the youngest, smallest and hungriest* Ibid., 253.

206 *offering $5,000 to air* Osborne, *Miss America, The Dream Lives On*, 106.

206 *ABC backed away* Ibid.; Riverol, *Live from Atlantic City*, 49.

206 *It would be a cinch* Rayno, *Paul Whiteman*, 292.

206 *His crew was already in town* "Miss America Contest to Be On Television," *Central New Jersey Home News*, May 9, 1954, https://www.newspapers.com/image/31 5422929/.

206 *a leading manufacturer of television sets* Rayno, *Paul Whiteman*, 261.

207 *ABC was a half-tolerated guest* Riverol, *Live from Atlantic City*, 50.

207 *her identity revealed to the audience* BeBe Shopp interview, "A Grand Dame: The Story of Minnesota's First Miss America," Zandolee Media, https://vimeo .com/277112642.

207 *"I hope Daddy knows"* Riverol, *Live from Atlantic City*, 55; Deford, *There She Is*, 194; Cynthia Lowry, Associated Press, *Greenville News* (SC), September 19, 1954, https://www.newspapers.com/image/191623753.

207 *Her beloved father had died* "Beauty Queen Father Dies," *San Francisco Examiner*, July 16, 1954, https://www.newspapers.com/image/458175185/.

207 *it sounded rather cold* Allen Rich, "Listening Post and TV Review," *Valley Times* (North Hollywood, CA), September 14, 1954, https://www.newspapers.com/image /580328566/.

207 *"There have been few"* Paul Cotton, "On Television," *Des Moines Register*, September 14, 1954, https://www.newspapers.com/image/127846710/.

208 *"Something no script writer could have foreseen"* Rich, "Listening Post and TV Review."

208 *39 percent of the national audience* Deford, *There She Is*, 193.

208 *Al Marks, who extracted $25,000* Ibid., 194.

208 *the show had moved to CBS* Ibid.

208 *Miss America beat the game* Ibid., 195.

208 *Nielsen ranked the pageant* Ibid., 196.

209 *Leonard Horn had left* John Curran, Associated Press, "Head of Beauty Pageant Is Hanging Up His Tiara," *Bridgewater Courier-News*, July 14, 1998, https://www .newspapers.com/image/223577646/.

209 *Kate Shindle's highly successful reign* David E. Wilson, Geoff Mulvihill, and Jennifer Weiner, "Miss America's Father Connected to Pageant," *Philadelphia Inquirer*, September 16, 1997, https://www.newspapers.com/image/178018933/.

210 *the pageant was the most watched program* Deborah Hastings, "NBC, Miss America Pageant Win Ratings for Week," *Albuquerque Journal*, September 13, 1990, https:// www.newspapers.com/image/158570721/.

210 *Miss America drew 12.3 million* Associated Press, "Miss America Helps ABC End NBC's Streak," *Orlando Sentinel*, September 17, 1997, https://www.newspapers .com/image/235529257/.

210 *the pageant lost 2 million households* John Curran, "Miss America Pageant TV Ratings Less Than Crowning Achievement," *Morristown Daily Record* (NJ), September 23, 1998, https://www.newspapers.com/image/256091086/.

210 *a business executive* Alfred Lubrano, "Ex-MADD Official to Head Miss America," *Philadelphia Inquirer*, September 9, 1998, https://www.newspapers.com/image/17 8596879/.

210 *fifty-odd women had poured hearts* John Curran, Associated Press, "Miss America Preview: Personal Peeks," *South Florida Sun-Sentinel*, September 16, 1999, https://www.newspapers.com/image/238947984/.

211 *women who'd been divorced* John Curran, Associated Press, "Miss America Board Votes to Open Pageant to Divorcees, Women Who Had Abortions," *Miami Herald*, September 14, 1999, https://www.newspapers.com/image/618851478/.

211 *State pageant organizers headed to court* Ibid.

211 *"Miss America has a long history"* John Curran, Associated Press, "Spotlight on New Rules," *Philadelphia Daily News*, September 15, 1999, https://www.newspapers .com/image/184772394/.

211 *The old prohibitions would stand* Peter Genovese and Jennifer Del Medico, "Ugly Reaction Makes Pageant Backpedal," *Newark Star-Ledger*, September 15, 1999, Nexis.

211 *they fired Rob Beck* John Curran, Associated Press, "There He Goes: Pageant CEO Gets the Boot," *Lancaster Intelligencer Journal* (PA), September 28, 1999, https:// www.newspapers.com/image/566775082/.

211 *the ratings had stayed flat* Tom Bierbaum, "'Miss America' Stumbles," *Variety*, September 20, 1999, https://variety.com/1999/tv/news/miss-america-stumbles-111 7755802/.

211 *ebb and flow* Jacqueline L. Urgo, "Miss America Finds a CEO Down by the Boardwalk," *Philadelphia Inquirer*, March 1, 2000, https://www.newspapers.com /image/167885774/.

211 *He sent her out on a media charm offensive* Michael Klein, "Miss America Made a Believer of Him," *Philadelphia Inquirer*, July 23, 2000, https://www.newspapers .com/image/179744239/.

212 *it was a watercooler phenom* Mike Conklin, "Can This Pageant Be Saved?" *Chicago Tribune*, October 27, 2000, https://www.newspapers.com/image/169690521/.

212 *the Atlantic City community* Amy S. Rosenberg, "Miss America Warns A.C. It May Leave," *Philadelphia Inquirer*, December 19, 2001, https://www.newspapers.com /image/179168548/.

212 *his own board rebuffed him* Amy S. Rosenberg, "The Show Will Go On in A.C., for Now," *Philadelphia Inquirer*, December 28, 2001, https://www.newspapers.com/image/179135764.

212 *the exodus of the last high-end sponsors* Shindle, *Being Miss America*, 155; Judy DeHaven, Newhouse News Service, "Miss America Stumbles on the Runway," *Detroit Free Press*, March 29, 2002, https://www.newspapers.com/image/361366145.

212 *"get the hell out"* Steven V. Cronin, "States Say Renneisen Fired First Shot," *Press of Atlantic City*, February 14, 2002, https://pressofatlanticcity.newsbank.com/doc/news/0F1B2A938DDC2D40.

213 *fifty-one women voted* Hank Stuever, "Miss America the Beautiful: In Turbulent Times, the Pageant Gently Evokes the Good Ol' Days," *Washington Post*, September 22, 2001, https://www.washingtonpost.com/archive/lifestyle/2001/09/22/miss-america-the-beautiful/e908f025-725f-413a-8264-84d312f86e27/.

213 *a more stripped-down and sentimental pageant* Ibid.

213 *the ratings even bounced up* David Bauder, Associated Press, "Two TV Specials Draw Huge Audiences," *Binghamton Press and Sun-Bulletin* (NY), September 28, 2001, https://www.newspapers.com/image/258295207/.

213 *she was bumped* John Lehmann, "Miss America Trumped: Donald Fave Bumps Her as Macy's Parade Star," *New York Post*, October 26, 2001, https://nypost.com/2001/10/26/miss-america-trumped-donald-fave-bumps-her-as-macys-parade-star/.

214 *the pageant wasn't getting Katie booked* John Curran, "Miss America's Parents Complain about Treatment," *Camden Courier-Post*, February 13, 2002, https://www.newspapers.com/image/184217136/.

214 *four state pageant executives* Ibid.; Shindle, *Being Miss America*.

214 *"the rebellion of the beauty queens"* Alex Kuczynski, "State Pageants at War with Miss America Organization," *New York Times*, February 16, 2002, https://www.nytimes.com/2002/02/16/us/state-pageants-at-war-with-miss-america-organization.html.

214 *"Miss America's Whine List"* John Curran, Associated Press, "Beauty Pageant Answers Critics," *Hackensack Record*, February 17, 2002, https://www.newspapers.com/image/499461588/.

214 *she realized she had no choice* Ibid.

214 *"Miss America vs. Parents"* Bill Hutchinson, "Miss America vs. Parents," *New York Daily News*, February 15, 2002, https://www.newspapers.com/image/408264979/.

214 *two weeks after that awkward press conference* Rose Ciotta, Kaitlin Gurney, and Harold Brubaker, "Pageant Officials Caught by Surprise," *Philadelphia Inquirer*, March 3, 2002, https://www.newspapers.com/image/199617729/.

215 *"attempt to defame my character"* "Miss North Carolina Resigns Title," *Raleigh News and Observer*, July 24, 2002, https://www.newspapers.com/image/656524585/.

216 *reinstated her as Miss North Carolina* Estes Thompson, Associated Press, "Judge Says Woman Should Keep Miss North Carolina Crown," *Asheville Citizen-Times* (NC), September 5, 2002, https://www.newspapers.com/image/200070959/.

216 two *Miss North Carolinas* Dan Robrish, Associated Press, "Two Beauty Queens, One Crown, Add Up to a Nasty Court Fight," *Greenville News* (SC), September 7, 2002, https://www.newspapers.com/image/194178931/.

216 *"Beauty Queen Cat Fight"* Aly Sujo, "Beauty Queen Cat Fight May End Today," *New York Post*, September 12, 2002, https://nypost.com/2002/09/12/beauty-queen-cat-fight-may-end-today/.

216 *"Miss-mosh at the Pageant"* "Still a Miss-mosh at Pageant," *New York Daily News*, September 11, 2002, https://www.newspapers.com/image/408470701/.

216 *"The fur is flying in North Carolina"* Greta Van Susteren, *On the Record*, Fox News Channel, September 9, 2002, Nexis.

216 *"It's awkward"* Katie Harman, interview by David Bloom, *Saturday Today*, NBC, September 7, 2002, Nexis.

217 *She joined them for rehearsals* "Uncover Story," *New York Daily News*, September 10, 2002, https://www.newspapers.com/image/408467119/.

217 *"The fact of the nude photos"* Jeffrey Gettleman, "One Miss North Carolina Pleads Her Case," *New York Times*, September 11, 2002, https://www.nytimes .com/2002/09/11/us/one-miss-north-carolina-pleads-her-case.html.

217 *a federal judge refused to restore her* Jeffrey Gettleman, "A Miss North Carolina Loses Her Court Bid," *New York Times*, September 13, 2002, https://www.nytimes .com/2002/09/13/us/a-miss-north-carolina-loses-her-court-bid.html.

218 *a runway-model frame* John Curran, "Medical School on Hold for New Miss America," *Hackensack Record*, September 20, 2004, https://www.newspapers.com /image/499923077/.

218 *when she wed her girlfriend* Maria Pasquini, "Former Miss America Winner Deidre Downs Marries Girlfriend in Romantic Southern Wedding," *People*, April 15, 2018, https://people.com/tv/former-miss-america-winner-deidre-downs-gunn-marries -abbott-jones/.

218 *fewer than 10 million watched* Seibel, "Why Miss America Can't Get a Date."

218 *A month later, ABC announced* Michael Klein and Gail Shister, "ABC Drops Miss America Pageant," *Philadelphia Inquirer*, October 21, 2004, https://www.newspa pers.com/image/200863006/.

218 *No other network stepped forward* Seibel, "Why Miss America Can't Get a Date."

218 *The Apprentice, topped the ratings* David Bauder, Associated Press, "How NBC Trumped Its Rivals," *Tampa Bay Times*, April 23, 2004, https://www.newspapers .com/image/329294276/.

218 *"I'd like to do whatever I can"* John Curran, Associated Press, "Donald Trump Court-ing Miss America Pageant," *Bridgewater Courier-News* (NJ), March 12, 2005, https://www.newspapers.com/image/220036078/.

219 *for years, they mostly saw one another* Shindle, *Being Miss America*, 178–179.

219 *email made it that much easier* Ibid., 177.

219 *the Miss Americas started emailing one another* Seibel, "Why Miss America Can't Get a Date."

219 *still trying to make the broadcast work* John Curran, Associated Press, "Miss Amer-ica Viewers Tune Out Talent Contest," *Morristown Daily Record* (NJ), February 7, 2004, https://www.newspapers.com/image/256033452/.

219 *This was intolerable* Seibel, "Why Miss America Can't Get a Date."

219 *"We want to do more"* Shindle, *Being Miss America*, 180.

220 *they were joined by two other* Ibid., 178–180.

220 *The board responded coolly* Ibid.

220 *"They're not used to hearing a lot"* Seibel, "Why Miss America Can't Get a Date."

220 *The board agreed* Ibid.; Shindle, *Being Miss America*, 181.

220 *both parties were galvanized* John Curran, Associated Press, "Last Beauty Standing? Miss America Pageant to Televise 2 Routines," *Camden Courier-Post*, August 13, 2004, https://www.newspapers.com/image/184242639/.

220 *Lauren Nelson looked more like a high school America's Most Wanted*, April 2007, excerpted on YouTube, https://youtu.be/_Kc-KHpobKw.

220 *"You didn't come to have sex" America's Most Wanted*, April 2007, excerpt in transcript, *Today*, NBC, April 26, 2007, Nexis.

221 To Catch a Predator "Miss America Goes Undercover in Predator Sting," *Today*, NBC, April 27, 2007, https://www.today.com/news/miss-america-goes-undercover -predator-sting-1C9011082.

221 *as few as 3 million viewers* Ryan Underwood and Brad Schmitt, "Miss America Show Takes Top Star in CMT Crown," *Nashville Tennessean*, January 25, 2006, https://www.newspapers.com/image/277504239/.

221 *the pageant had finally left* Kathleen Hennessey, Associated Press, "Miss America Pageant Moves to Las Vegas," *Reno Gazette-Journal*, January 15, 2006, https:// www.newspapers.com/image/149617848/.

222 *a company selling an acupuncture magnet* Phil Galewitz, "Miss America Plugs Local Firm," *Palm Beach Post*, February 14, 2009, https://www.newspapers.com /image/206650560/.

222 *the first Miss America crowned* Jennifer Berry, *Good Morning America*, ABC, January 23, 2006, Nexis.

222 *Tucker Carlson asked* Jennifer Berry, interview, *Tucker Carlson*, MSNBC, January 23, 2006, Nexis.

222 *days-long public deliberations* Dan Mangan, "Miss USA 'Fire'Storm—Trump Threat to Dethrone Party Princess," *New York Post*, December 15, 2006, https://nypost .com/2006/12/15/miss-usa-firestorm-trump-threat-to-dethrone-party-princess/.

222 *He did not* "Trump Decides Not to Fire Miss USA Tara Conner," FoxNews.com, December 19, 2006, https://www.foxnews.com/story/trump-decides-not-to-fire-miss -usa-tara-conner.

222 *"So, I didn't really keep up" Showbiz Tonight*, CNN, January 11, 2007, Nexis.

222 *"As long as there are people"* Caressa Cameron interview by Neil Cavuto, *Your World with Neil Cavuto*, Fox News Channel, April 22, 2010, Nexis.

224 *Miss America 2004 Amazing Race*, CBS, Season 15 cast, https://www.cbs.com /shows/amazing_race/cast/season/15/.

224 *"Please say it again" Miss America 2004*, ABC, September 20, 2003, https://youtu .be/y_YHf3Aos_E.

CHAPTER ELEVEN

227 *she had published a memoir* Shindle, *Being Miss America*.

228 *she made her entrance singing Miss America 2016*, ABC, September 13, 2015, https://youtu.be/XrwF5FxGEOQ.

229 *"I want it to look different"* John-John Williams IV, "For Christian Siriano, dressing celebs like Taylor Swift is the new normal," *Baltimore Sun*, September 23, 2015, https://www.baltimoresun.com/features/fashion-style/bs-hs-christian-siriano -20150923-story.html.

229 *"I want to apologize" Miss America 2016*.

229 *Sam had met Vanessa* Haskell, *Promises I Made My Mother*, 127.

230 *He had approached her gently* Brian Edwards, *I Might Have Been Queen (And Other Things I Didn't Mention Before)* (Bloomington, IN: Archway Publishing, 2019), Chapters 19–21.

230 Will they apologize to Vanessa Williams? Both sides deny that any behind-the-scenes dispute occurred. "Miss America Pageant Meltdown Over Vanessa Williams

Apology," TMZ.com, September 11, 2015, https://www.tmz.com/2015/09/11/vane
ssa-williams-miss-america-officials-nude-pictures-apology/; "TMZ Live: Miss America & Vanessa Williams: Who's Going to Apologize?" TMZ.com, September 11, 2015,
https://www.tmz.com/2015/09/11/tmz-live-miss-america-vanessa-williams-new
-york-fashion-week-rihanna-chris-brown-royalty/.

230 *a rare uptick in the ratings* Amy Kuperinsky, "The 2016 Miss America Pageant
Holds Its Own Against Football Game," *Newark Star-Ledger*, September 14, 2015,
https://www.nj.com/entertainment/2015/09/miss_america_2016_ratings.html.

230 *a new three-year contract* Lacey Rose, "ABC, Dick Clark Prods. Extend 'Miss
America' Pact Through 2018," *Hollywood Reporter*, November 23, 2015, https://
www.hollywoodreporter.com/news/abc-dick-clark-prods-extend-miss-america-pact
-2018-843129.

230 *"Your leadership, your integrity"* Miss America 2016.

230 *The finances, for one thing* Dan Wascoe Jr., "Miss America's First Loyalty Is to
Pageant Sponsors," *Minneapolis Star-Tribune*, September 26, 1988, https://www
.newspapers.com/image/191540808/.

230 *when Phyllis was just another former Miss America* "50 Girls Compete for Miss
Mississippi," *Jackson Clarion-Ledger* (MS), July 14, 1974, https://www.newspapers
.com/image/183340531.

230 *Sam was an Ole Miss sophomore* Sam Haskell, email to friends, May 24, 2020.
While Haskell recalls their meeting as happening at the 1975 pageant, news arti-
cles from the time indicate that George hosted the 1974 pageant and that her job
with CBS Sports would have kept her from hosting the 1975 pageant.

231 *Five years later* Haskell, *Promises I Made My Mother*, xvii–xviii, 10, 20–22, 41–48, 68.

231 *disarming clients like Ray Romano* Ibid., ix–xiv, 95–99.

231 *he nailed down the deal* Ibid., 119–121.

231 *there were agents* Ibid., 189.

231 *he was the one to dissuade them* Ibid., 122–125.

231 *"He will be good as gold"* Ibid., 124.

231 *Sam eventually landed* Ibid., 181–190.

231 *he cashed out his ownership stakes* Laura M. Holson, "3 Longtime Executives Resign from William Morris Agency," *New York Times*, December 18, 2004, https://
www.nytimes.com/2004/12/18/business/3-longtime-executives-resign-from
-william-morris-agency.html.

231 *Would he please join the board?* Haskell, *Promises I Made My Mother*, 127.

231 *Sam was working his magic* Ibid., 127–129.

231 *A grateful board* Ibid., 128.

232 *"The girls get it"* Ibid., 128–132.

232 *Billy's Buckeye Group* The Buckeye Group, Inc. vs. Miss America Organization
(1:2014-cv-04214), New Jersey District Court, deposition of Samuel Haskell;
deposition of William Goldberg.

232 *"We needed to change the perception"* Buckeye, deposition of Samuel Haskell.

232 *he signed Amway for $750,000* Ibid.

232 *with 6.6 million viewers* Scott Collins, "Miss America Ratings Rebound," *Los Angeles Times*, January 18, 2011, https://www.latimes.com/entertainment/la-xpm-2011
-jan-18-la-et-quick-20110118-story.html.

232 *"the sky was the limit"* Buckeye, deposition of Samuel Haskell.

232 *"I didn't look at us as a brand"* Ibid.

233 *an unpaid board chairmanship* Ibid.

233 *7.1 million viewers tuned in* Lynette Rice, "Miss America Pageant Draws Best Audience since 2004," *Entertainment Weekly*, January 13, 2013, https://ew.com/article/2013/01/13/miss-america-pageant-draws-best-audience-since-2004/.

233 *by the time they had to negotiate Buckeye*, deposition of Sharon Pearce.

233 *Miss America tickled the news cycle* Amy Kuperinsky, "Miss Kansas Interview: Theresa Vail Is More Than Just Her Tattoos," *Newark Star Ledger*, September 13, 2013, https://www.nj.com/entertainment/2013/09/miss_america_tattoos_theresa_vail_miss_kansas_interview.html.

233 *the first out lesbian* Monica Hesse, "What's a Nice Lesbian Like You Doing at Miss America? Erin O'Flaherty's Historic Quest," *Washington Post*, September 9, 2016, https://www.washingtonpost.com/lifestyle/style/whats-a-nice-lesbian-like-you-doing-at-miss-america-erin-oflahertys-historic-quest/2016/09/09/5ebdeea2-769e-11e6-be4f-3f42f2e5a49e_story.html.

233 *a small but nasty social-media backlash* Maura Judkis, "Miss America Nina Davuluri Fights Post-Pageant Racism with a Beauty Queen's Poise," *Washington Post*, September 22, 2013, https://www.washingtonpost.com/lifestyle/style/miss-america-fights-post-pageant-racism-with-a-beauty-queens-poise/2013/09/22/a90590ac-22f8-11e3-966c-9c4293c47ebe_story.html.

233 *"Our Miss America is one of you"* Alex Williams, "Beauty Pageants Draw Social Media Critics," *New York Times*, September 20, 2013, https://www.nytimes.com/2013/09/22/fashion/beauty-pageants-draw-social-media-critics.html.

233 *social-justice warriors and millennial media* Ryan Broderick, "A Lot of People Are Very Upset That an Indian-American Woman Won the Miss America Pageant," *BuzzFeed*, September 16, 2013, https://www.buzzfeednews.com/article/ryanhatesthis/a-lot-of-people-are-very-upset-that-an-indian-american-woman.

233 *and Jezebel* Laura Beck, "Racists Are Being Hella Racist Because Miss America Isn't White," Jezebel, September 16, 2013, https://jezebel.com/im-actually-annoyed-miss-new-york-won-because-not-2-day-1326369668.

233 *"that's why my platform is so timely"* "Miss America Nina Davuluri Opens Up About Racist Remarks," *extratv*, September 17, 2013, https://youtu.be/EX7oi_BzLUM.

233 *the state offered financial incentives* Erin O'Neill, "It's Official! Miss America's Coming Home to Atlantic City," *Newark Star-Ledger*, February 14, 2013, https://www.nj.com/news/2013/02/miss_america_atlantic_city.html; Nicholas Huba, "Guess How Much Money N.J. Has Given Miss America since 2013," *Press of Atlantic City*, January 5, 2018, https://pressofatlanticcity.com/missamerica/guess-how-much-money-n-j-has-given-miss-america-since-2013/article_8b5db22b-bf49-5c9d-87f1-d0efb0b6adfe.amp.html.

234 *"I didn't want to set myself up"* Gretchen Carlson, *Getting Real* (New York: Viking Penguin, 2015), 81–82.

234 *her mother had just read a news story* Ibid., 76.

234 *They wanted contestants from top schools* Ibid.

234 *Gretchen had been a violin prodigy* Ibid., 46.

234 *he spoke of his plans* Daniel LeDuc, "Miss America Seeks New Image," *Philadelphia Inquirer*, September 27, 1987, https://www.newspapers.com/image/169825570/.

234 *Gretchen was already looking past* Carlson, *Getting Real*, 82–84.

234 *This lonely regimen resonated* Ibid., 61, 63, 84.

235 *"I believed in pushing myself beyond my limits"* Ibid., 53.

235 *"This wasn't luck"* Allen Short, "New Standard: Miss America Not Typical Bathing Beauty, but the Judges Loved Her Talented Ways," *Minneapolis Star-Tribune*, September 12, 1988, https://www.newspapers.com/image/191147811/.

235 *she lost the weight* Ibid.

235 *the seamstress who told her* Carlson, *Getting Real*, 85.

235 *the coach who told her* Ibid., 78.

235 *the news director who scoffed* Ibid., 5.

235 *"I'm the Miss America"* Ibid., 1–2.

235 *The woman later said* Belinda Luscombe, "Gretchen Carlson's Next Fight," *Time*, October 21, 2016, https://time.com/4540095/gretchen-carlsons-next-fight/.

236 *playing violin with regional orchestras* Carlson, *Getting Real*, 125, 128, 132, 133.

236 *she would remember the Nobel laureate* Ibid., 132; Irvin Molotsky, "Furor Among Laureates Is Stuff of Peace Prizes," *New York Times*, December 9, 1988, https://www.nytimes.com/1988/12/09/us/furor-among-laureates-is-stuff-of-peace-prizes.html.

236 *"a five-foot-three"* Carlson, *Getting Real*, 132.

236 *airhead, bimbo, beauty queen* Ibid., 130.

236 *prying media left her jaded* Ibid., 122.

236 *"I could never wake up"* Ibid., 129.

236 *she met Bill Farley* Ibid., 134–136. In her book, Gretchen only identified him as Bill, a corporate executive who was one of the celebrity judges from the pageant, but that matches Farley's description, who was also publicly identified in media accounts at the time as her escort to the 1989 Bush inaugural.

236 *The company was a pageant sponsor* "These Fruits Are Made for Walking," *Ad Day*, August 31, 1988, Nexis.

236 *a barely averted scandal* Lynn Van Matre, "Healthy Ego," *Chicago Tribune*, June 28, 1989, https://www.chicagotribune.com/news/ct-xpm-1989-06-28-8902130083-story.html.

236 *they showed up together* Stephanie Mansfield, "Fetes and Lines in Texas Time," *Washington Post*, January 20, 1989, https://www.washingtonpost.com/archive/lifestyle/1989/01/20/fetes-and-lines-in-texas-time/fe752a0f-1ab0-45a1-9d87-d4c8435f3ac9/.

236 *Her pageant chaperone once apprehended* Carlson, *Getting Real*, 135.

236 *"It was a great release"* Ibid., 136.

236 *"uncooperative, unfriendly behavior"* Valerie Helmbreck, "Uneasy Gretchen Carlson Relaxes as '89 Reign Winds Down," *Wilmington News Journal*, September 10, 1989, https://www.newspapers.com/image/155191987/.

237 *"A Beauty of a Mistake"* DePaulo, "Miss America—Was Last Year's Voting Suspect?"

237 *the all-important test of X factors* Ibid.

237 *"there were very many women"* Ibid.

237 *The pageant later tweaked Leonard's new system* Joyce A. Venezia, Associated Press, "Miss Missouri Named 1990 Miss America," September 17, 1989, Nexis.

237 *"Real bright. Chunky"* Goldman, *Hype and Glory*, 191.

237 *"Miss Piggy"* Ibid.

238 *"This kind of degrading talk"* Carlson, *Getting Real*, 3–4.

238 Super Bloopers and Practical Jokes Ibid., 118–119.

238 *the clip became part of the reel* Ibid., 147.

238 *she abandoned the law-school path* Ibid., 140.

238 *the guys from Infinity flipped out* This account is based on filings in *The Buckeye Group, Inc. vs. Miss America Organization.*

239 *"And lost money" Buckeye*, deposition of Ike Franco.

239 *"I was ready to be friends again" Buckeye*, deposition of Samuel Haskell.

240 *"Get Up Offa That Thing" Miss America 2013*, ABC, January 12, 2013.

240 *the tabloids gawked over paparazzi photos* "Miss America Mallory Hagan Stomaching Life After the Pageant," TMZ.com, February 13, 2013, https://www.tmz.com /2013/02/13/miss-america-mallory-hagan-bikini-body-photo/; Jennifer Pearson, "Miss America and Miss Hawaii Get Back in Bikinis . . . But This Time They're Off the Strict Pageant Diet," DailyMail.com, March 12, 2013, https://www .dailymail.co.uk/tvshowbiz/article-2292136/Miss-America-Miss-Hawaii-battle -best-bikini-body-Maui.html.

240 *"I'm real!"* Mallory Hagan interview by Jane Velez-Mitchell and Tamar Braxton, *Anderson Live*, syndicated talk show, Warner Bros. Domestic Television Distribution, March 14, 2013, http://www.allthingsandersoncooper.com/2013/03/anderson -live-thursday-march-2013.html.

240–241 *the cataclysmic story* Yashar Ali, "The Miss America Emails: How the Pageant's CEO Really Talks About the Winners," HuffPost.com, December 21, 2017, https:// www.huffpost.com/entry/miss-america-ceo-emails_n_5a3bd266e4b025f99e1 53fdb.

241 *Brent started working for Sam* M. Scott Morris, "Area Residents Have Roles In Today's 'Miss America' Pageant," *Northeast Mississippi Daily Journal*, January 12, 2013, https://www.djournal.com/news/area-residents-have-roles-in-today-s-miss-am erica-pageant-pageant/article_95e8aeaf-557b-5cdc-9d30-45bf84eedc95.html.

241 *he had been given the title* Barry Burleson, "Adams Director of Development for Miss America," *South Reporter* (Holly Springs, MS), September 11, 2014, http:// archive.southreporter.com/wk37/index.html.

241 *Brent joined the Haskell family* Mary Lane Haskell, Facebook, December 23, 2012, https://www.facebook.com/marylane.haskell/posts/10151147324716573; Brent Adams, Instagram, May 28, 2013, https://www.instagram.com/p/Z4QgsxqhSP/.

241 *"Good to see the fam"* Mallory Hagan, Instagram, @itsmalloryhagan, October 16, 2013, https://www.instagram.com/p/fh16V0HafM/.

241 *Brent would later share* Ali, "The Miss America Emails."

242 *she eventually found herself thwarted* Ibid.

243 *"There are a lot of successful people"* Venezia, "New Miss America Says."

244 *Sam had consolidated power Buckeye*, deposition of Art McMaster.

244 *"arrangements between friends"* Jennifer Bogdan, "Miss America's Finances Fluctuate, Records Show," *Press of Atlantic City*, February 8, 2014, https://pressofat lanticcity.com/news/breaking/miss-americas-finances-fluctuate-records-show/arti cle_3c8ab438-913a-11e3-9c28-001a4bcf887a.html.

244 *"borderline fraudulent"* Shindle, *Being Miss America*, 196–198, 211.

244 *"And then you'd be good and better"* Gabriel Sherman, "The Revenge of Roger's Angels: How Fox News Women Took Down the Most Powerful, and Predatory, Man in Media," *New York*, September 5, 2015, https://nymag.com/intelligencer/2016/09 /how-fox-news-women-took-down-roger-ailes.html.

245 *She sued Roger for sexual harassment* Paul Farhi, "Ex–Fox News Host Gretchen Carlson Sues Network Head Roger Ailes for Sexual Harassment," *Washington Post*, July 6, 2016, https://www.washingtonpost.com/lifestyle/style/ex-fox-news-host-gretchen

-carlson-sues-network-head-roger-ailes-for-sexual-harassment/2016/07/06/80b8e
f28-438d-11e6-88d0-6adee48be8bc_story.html.

245 *more than a dozen women* Paul Farhi, "Roger Ailes Resigns as CEO of Fox News;
Rupert Murdoch Will Be Acting CEO," *Washington Post*, July 21, 2016, https://
www.washingtonpost.com/lifestyle/style/roger-ailes-resigns-as-ceo-of-fox-news
-rupert-murdoch-will-be-acting-ceo/2016/07/21/816c1dc4-4f80-11e6-a422-83ab
49ed5e6a_story.html.

245 *Gretchen had both an epic $20 million* Paul Farhi, "$20 Million Settlement and a
Host's Abrupt Exit Add to Fox's Summer of Discontent," *Washington Post*, September 6, 2016, https://www.washingtonpost.com/lifestyle/style/former-fox-host-gretch
en-carlson-settles-sexual-harassment-lawsuit-against-roger-ailes-for-20-million
/2016/09/06/f1718310-7434-11e6-be4f-3f42f2e5a49e_story.html.

247 *it also arranged for Miss Americas* Michael O'Connell, "Miss America Partners
with Dick Clark Productions," *Hollywood Reporter*, September 8, 2014, https://
www.hollywoodreporter.com/news/miss-america-partners-dick-clark-produc
tions-731044.

249 *a generation of pageant women* Shindle, *Being Miss America*, 128–130.

251 *Fox News's sexual harassment scandals* Steven Perlberg, "Who Is Yashar?" *BuzzFeed*,
October 25, 2017, https://www.buzzfeednews.com/article/stevenperlberg/who-is-yashar.

251 *the Miss America emails* Ali, "The Miss America Emails."

251 *"join me in a collective effort"* Gretchen Carlson, Twitter, @gretchencarlson, December 21, 2017, https://twitter.com/GretchenCarlson/status/944032157017759744,
https://twitter.com/GretchenCarlson/status/944032449390088192, https://twitter
.com/GretchenCarlson/status/944032502661791744; Yashar Ali, Twitter, @yashar,
December 21, 2017, https://twitter.com/yashar/status/944031271574962177.

252 *Leonard Horn and the mayor of Atlantic City* Yashar Ali, "CEO Suspended After 49
Former Miss Americas Call On Organization's Leaders to Resign," *HuffPost*, December 22, 2017, https://www.huffpost.com/entry/miss-america-leadership-resign
_n_5a3d3fdce4b025f99e16eca8.

252 *"I was under stress"* Maeve McDermott, "Miss America CEO Sam Haskell Suspended over Offensive Emails," *USA Today*, December 22, 2017, https://www
.usatoday.com/story/life/people/2017/12/22/former-miss-america-mallory-hagan
-slams-disgraced-ceo-sam-haskell-following-email-scandal/976037001/.

252 *"In this #MeToo cultural revolution"* Statement captured in screengrab, Yashar
Ali, Twitter, @yashar, December 23, 2017, https://twitter.com/yashar/status/944
630273785974784.

252 *Sam resigned, and Lynn resigned* Yashar Ali, "Miss America CEO and Board Chair
Resign Under Pressure Amid Scandal," *HuffPost*, December 23, 2017, https://
www.huffpost.com/entry/exclusive-president-of-miss-america-organization-re
signs-amid-email-scandal_n_5a3e8dbce4b0b0e5a7a27c6e.

252 *They demanded the resignation* Kate Shindle, Twitter, @kateshindle, December 23,
2017, https://twitter.com/kateshindle/status/944692916479545344.

252 *Mallory threw herself into the holiday* Mallory Hagan interview by Paula Faris and
Dan Harris, *Good Morning America*, ABC, December 26, 2017, https://www.good
morningamerica.com/news/story/miss-america-mallory-hagan-hopes-scandal-sig
nals-reinvention-51993012.

253 *"stood by and allowed these people"* Mallory Hagan, Facebook Live video, December 27, 2017, https://www.facebook.com/MHHagan/videos/10213134931340406.

253 *she was online again* Mallory Hagan, Facebook Live video, December 28, 2017, https://www.facebook.com/MHHagan/videos/10213141312179923.

253 *An* entirely new board *should select* Wayne Parry, Associated Press, "Ex–Miss Americas Asked to Help Find New Leaders," APNews.com, December 28, 2017, https://apnews.com/article/f2a30d6bb2a649b9ae781238fd512ebe; Wayne Parry, Associated Press, "Ridiculed Former Miss America Calls Board Offer 'Laughable,'" AP News.com, December 28, 2017, https://apnews.com/article/b7bca9dc7deb437cb4 5e1f981aa99626.

253 *an entire board could not resign* Nicole Bitette, "Here's What Would Happen if Every Miss America Board Member Resigns," *New York Daily News*, December 28, 2017, https://www.nydailynews.com/entertainment/happen-america-board-member -resigns-article-1.3724380.

253 *Kate Shindle was also* Daniel Victor, "Gretchen Carlson, Miss America 1989, Is Picked to Lead Pageant," *New York Times*, January 1, 2018, https://www.nytimes .com/2018/01/01/business/gretchen-carlson-miss-america.html.

255 *"We will no longer judge our candidates"* Carlson interview by Amy Robach, *Good Morning America*.

255 *"Please stay tuned"* Ibid.

255–256 *Sam's old antagonist* Interviews with board members; also detailed in *Jennifer Vaden Barth, et al, vs. The Miss America Organization, et al*, ATL-C-95-18 (New Jersey Superior Court, Atlantic County).

257 *"We'll also be revamping our evening gown"* Ibid.

257 *they pushed talking points on her* Amy Argetsinger, "'No Miss America Should Be Humiliated,' Before Giving Up Crown, Cara Mund Blasts Pageant Leadership," *Washington Post*, August 17, 2018, https://www.washingtonpost.com/news /arts-and-entertainment/wp/2018/08/17/no-miss-america-should-be-humiliated -before-giving-up-crown-cara-mund-blasts-pageant-leadership/.

259 *the official agenda was now complete Jennifer Vaden Barth, et al, vs. The Miss America Organization, et al.*

259 *"The misperception is that we have"* Amy Argetsinger, "It's Not Just About Bikinis: Inside the Battle for the Future of Miss America," *Washington Post*, July 25, 2018, https://www.washingtonpost.com/lifestyle/style/its-not-just-about-bikinis-in side-the-battle-for-the-future-of-miss-america/2018/07/25/0f1796c6-8ea9-11e8 -b769-e3fff17f0689_story.html.

260 *Gretchen clapped back in a Facebook post* Gretchen Carlson, "A Statement from the Miss America Organization Board of Trustees," posted in Facebook's MAO Fan Forum, June 27, 2018, https://www.facebook.com/groups/596839997142436 /permalink/984247151735050/.

260 *she deployed a loophole that allowed her* Valerie Bauerlein, "Miss America Organization Split by #MeToo Era Swimsuit Decision," *Wall Street Journal*, July 8, 2018, https://www.wsj.com/articles/miss-america-organization-split-by-metoo-era-swim suit-decision-1531047601.

260 *the names of thirty fellow former Miss Americas* Lauren Carroll, "Split Developing in Miss America Organization Over New Leadership," *Press of Atlantic City*, July 8, 2018, https://pressofatlanticcity.com/missamerica/split-developing-in-miss-amer ica-organization-over-new-leadership/article_66843ce8-51e4-5cb0-bec8-af7a 62faba4d.html.

260 *"She wanted to be the face"* Heather Whitestone and Suzette Charles interview

by Megyn Kelly, *Today*, NBC, August 20, 2018, https://www.today.com/video/for
mer-miss-america-winners-speak-out-amid-controversy-surrounding-the-pageant
-s-leaders-1302530627867.

260 *"keep the Miss America pageant"* Gracen, "The Battle for Miss America."

261 *Gretchen still did not resign* Erin Serpico, "Miss America Organization Announces
Several Changes to Board of Trustees," *Press of Atlantic City*, August 28, 2018,
https://pressofatlanticcity.com/missamerica/miss-america-organization-announces
-several-changes-to-board-of-trustees/article_36af90ae-8bc6-58d2-b39a-ab9c7c5
e6301.html.

261 *Gretchen's team yanked the licenses* Wayne Parry, Associated Press, "Miss America
Terminates Agreements with N.J., N.Y., and Fla.," *Philadelphia Inquirer*, December 5, 2018, https://www.inquirer.com/news/new-jersey/miss-america-terminates
-agreements-with-nj-ny-fl-20181205.html.

261 *spearheaded by ousted board member* Interviews with board members; also detailed
in *Jennifer Vaden Barth, et al, vs. The Miss America Organization, et al.*

261 *It dragged on for a few months* Lauren Carroll, "Lawsuit Against Miss America
Organization Dismissed," *Press of Atlantic City*, March 6, 2019, https://pressofat
lanticcity.com/missamerica/lawsuit-against-miss-america-organization-dismissed
/article_1dd5726d-1802-5288-9753-889a1addf5fe.html.

261 *the following spring, there was little celebrating* Kuperinsky, "Gretchen Carlson
Steps Down."

CHAPTER TWELVE

262 *Mallory, now the Democratic nominee* Twitter thread exchange between John H.
Merrill and Mallory Hagan, October 29, 2018, https://twitter.com/haganstrategies
/status/1057102226819301378.

262–263 *Alabama announced it had cleared out* Tim Lockette, "Purge of Voter Rolls Cre-
ates Stir in Alabama Congressional Race," *Anniston Star* (AL), October 22, 2018,
https://www.annistonstar.com/news/election2018/purge-of-voter-rolls-creates
-stir-in-alabama-congressional-race/article_77bf2e46-d652-11e8-934f-bbbb
7e2c4628.html.

263 This *is a born politician* Ellen McCarthy, "The Political Playbook for 2018: Get
Angry, Then Get Elected," *Washington Post*, February 19, 2018, https://www.wash
ingtonpost.com/lifestyle/style/the-political-playbook-for-2018-get-angry-then-get
-elected/2018/02/16/d29df57e-1265-11e8-9065-e55346f6de81_story.html.

264 *"To prepare great women for the world"* Jessica Bennett, "Goodbye, Swimsuit Competition. Hello, 'Miss America 2.0,'" *New York Times*, June 5, 2018, https://www
.nytimes.com/2018/06/05/business/miss-america-bans-swimsuits-metoo.html.

264 *"many of them actually believed the old canard"* United Press International, "Ex–
Miss A Loses: 'My Beauty Fatal at Polls,'" *New York Daily News*, August 6, 1951,
https://www.newspapers.com/image/450337013/.

264 *"Sure, I'd like a woman as vice president"* "Miss America of 1980 Attacks Ferraro on
TV," *New York Times*, September 15, 1984, https://www.nytimes.com/1984/09/15
/us/no-headline-166803.html.

264 *Heather Whitestone, who campaigned for Bob Dole* Heather Whitestone, Republican Convention Evening Session, C-SPAN, August 14, 1996, https://www.c-span
.org/video/?74343-1/republican-convention-evening-session&start=7475.

264 *sponsors snubbed her* Dworkin, *Miss America, 1945*, 167–180.

264 *"Inwardly, I felt a rage"* Ibid., 189.

264 *She transformed her reign* Ibid., 190–202.

265 *an attempt to draft* "Names and Faces," *Battle Creek Enquirer*, April 12, 1994, https://www.newspapers.com/image/204561819/.

265 *talk of Phyllis George* Liz Smith, "A Good Year for the Brits," *Variety*, January 31, 2007, https://variety.com/2007/voices/columns/a-good-year-for-the-brits-1117958442/.

265 *Cara Mund told reporters* Sara M. Moniuszko, "Miss America 2018 Cara Mund on Wanting to Run for Office and Winning the Crown," *USA Today*, September 12, 2017, https://www.usatoday.com/story/life/entertainthis/2017/09/12/miss-america -2018-cara-mund-wanting-run-office-and-winning-crown/657475001/.

265 *"and beauty queens are uniquely prepared"* Hilary Levey Friedman, "Here She Comes, Miss (Elected) America," Slate.com, June 26, 2012, https://slate.com/hu man-interest/2012/06/miss-america-and-politics-why-are-so-many-beauty-queens -running-for-office.html.

266 *He was* my son *Miss America 2003*, ABC, September 21, 2002, https://youtu.be /_BCxsPqmMos.

267 *her favored cause: sexual abstinence?* "Miss America Told to Zip It on Chastity Talk," *Washington Times*, October 9, 2002, https://www.washingtontimes.com/news/2002 /oct/9/20021009-092059-8028r/.

267 *"I will not be bullied"* Ibid.

267 *She had spent her college years* Shindle, *Being Miss America*, 164–165.

267 *she made it clear to Miss America* Ibid., 165–166.

267 *Erika had savvily outflanked them* Ibid., 168.

267 *a seat in New York mayor John Lindsay's cabinet* Susan Berman, "Bess Myerson Is One Tough Customer," *New York*, November 14, 1977, https://nymag.com/news /politics/49908/; Enid Nemy and William McDonald, "Bess Myerson, New Yorker of Beauty, Wit, Service and Scandal, Dies at 90," *New York Times*, January 5, 2015, https://www.nytimes.com/2015/01/06/nyregion/bess-myerson-miss-america-and -new-york-official-tarnished-in-scandal-dies.html.

268 *"I have 35 years of public service"* Ibid.

269 *Mallory was also about forty pounds heavier* Ron Maxey, "Former Miss America Applauds Swimsuit Decision," *Commercial Appeal*, June 6, 2018, https://www .commercialappeal.com/story/news/2018/06/05/mallory-hagan-memphian-and -miss-america-2013-tuesday-applauded-decision-pageant-leadership-drop -swim/673647002/.

270 *"a blanket over our family"* Clyde Haberman, "Reflecting on a Dream, and Pre- paring to Move On," *New York Times*, November 3, 2013, https://www.nytimes .com/2013/11/04/nyregion/mallory-hagan-talks-about-living-in-new-york-and -being-miss-america.html.

273 *"Be mad at our own"* Brian Lyman and Melissa Brown, "Alabama Democratic Party Sat on Cash as Election Day Approached," *Montgomery Advertiser*, November 14, 2018, https://www.montgomeryadvertiser.com/story/news/politics/elections/2018/11/09 /alabama-democratic-party-sat-cash-election-day-approached-democratic-party-crit icism-reed-worley/1942847002/.

274 *Teenage girls won six-figure science prizes* This story appeared on a back page of the *Washington Post*: Debbie Truong, "This Northern Va. Student Won the $250,000 Prize in a Top Science Competition," *Washington Post*, March 13, 2019, https:// www.washingtonpost.com/local/education/this-northern-va-student-won-the

-250000-prize-in-a-top-science-competition/2019/03/13/859d6330-45a0-11e9 -90f0-0ccfeec87a61_story.html.

CHAPTER THIRTEEN

279 *one of her flaming batons escaped her grip* Miss America 1963, CBS, September 8, 1962, https://youtu.be/fZ22q9Jip0o.

279 *the pageant quickly banned onstage combustibles* Ann-Marie Bivans, *Miss America: In Pursuit of the Crown* (New York: MasterMedia Limited, 1991), 78.

280 *he cut down a pool cue* Marjorie Whitmyer, "Firefighter Continues Baton Shop," *South Bend Tribune*, April 8, 1984, https://www.newspapers.com/image/517789 368/.

280 *a callback to the rifle-spinning* World Baton Twirling Federation website, https://www.wbtf.org/About/History.

280 *high-stepping majorettes* "History of Majorettes," June 16, 2019, http://majorettes .ca/history-majorettes-part-3/.

280 *so many girls were twirling* World Baton Twirling Federation website.

280 *"inextricably mixed up with vaudeville"* Inez Robb, "Spectacle as a Folly," *Kansas City Star*, August 31, 1949, https://www.newspapers.com/image/650779395/.

280 *in which baton twirling was not mentioned* Michael Arkush, "Good Looks and Baton Twirling Are Not Enough to Capture the Tiara in Today's Beauty Pageants," *Los Angeles Times*, April 13, 1989, https://www.latimes.com/archives/la-xpm-1989-04 -13-vw-1711-story.html.

292 *I paid $75 to stream a video* Miss America Top 15 interviews, December 2019, JC Productions, https://watch.jcproductions.tv/maprelims/item1.html.

EPILOGUE

296 *Camille started her reign with a spot* "Here she is, Miss America 2020: Biochemist Camille Schrier of Virginia," *Today*, NBC, December 20, 2019, https://www .today.com/video/here-she-is-miss-america-2020-biochemist-camille-schrier-of -virginia-75427397949.

296 *Camille held a bouquet of roses* The 2020 Rose Parade, KTLA-5, https://youtu.be /JGMLEsR-Hb4.

296–297 *Only 3.6 million viewers had tuned in* Will Thorne, "TV Ratings: Miss America Drops 16%, NBC Wins Quiet Thursday," *Variety*, December 20, 2019, https://vari ety.com/2019/tv/news/tv-ratings-miss-america-2020-nbc-1203449866/.

297 *"Regina Hopper is no longer with the organization"* Mark Melhorn, "Miss America President and CEO Regina Hopper No Longer with Organization," *Press of Atlantic City*, January 28, 2020.

297 *There would be no Miss America pageant* Molly Bilinski, "Miss America Postponed Due to COVID-19 Pandemic," *Press of Atlantic City*, May 8, 2020, https://presso fatlanticcity.com/news/local/miss-america-postponed-due-to-covid-19-pandemic /article_dd1c462e-14fb-57db-a66d-57be112bc026.html.

298 *Phyllis George died* Amy Argetsinger, "Phyllis George, Miss America Who Became a Trailblazing Sportscaster, Dies at 70," *Washington Post*, May 17, 2020, https:// www.washingtonpost.com/local/obituaries/phyllis-george-miss-america-who-be came-a-trailblazing-sportscaster-dies-at-70/2020/05/17/49527f66-9845-11ea -ac72-3841fcc9b35f_story.html.

298 *Leanza Cornett died* Amy Argetsinger, "Leanza Cornett, Miss America Who Was

Crusading AIDS Activist, Dies at 49," *Washington Post*, October 29, 2020, https://www.washingtonpost.com/local/obituaries/leanza-cornett-miss-america-who-was-crusading-aids-activist-dies-at-49/2020/10/29/c464165c-198b-11eb-befb-8864259bd2d8_story.html.

298 *"You move from space to space"* Ibid.

INDEX

ABOUT THE AUTHOR

AMY ARGETSINGER is an editor for the *Washington Post*'s Style section. A staff writer since 1995, she covered a variety of news beats and went on to write the "Reliable Source" column for eight years. She lives in Washington, D.C., with her husband and daughter. You can follow her on Twitter @AmyArgetsinger.